The Canal War:
Four-Power Conflict in the Middle East

Center for International Studies,
Massachusetts Institute of Technology

Studies in Communism, Revisionism, and Revolution
(formerly Studies in International Communism)
William E. Griffith, general editor

1. Albania and the Sino-Soviet Rift
William E. Griffith (1963)

2. Communism in North Vietnam
P. J. Honey (1964)

3. The Sino-Soviet Rift
William E. Griffith (1964)

4. Communism in Europe, Vol. 1
William E. Griffith, ed. (1964)

5. Nationalism and Communism
in Chile
Ernst Halperin (1965)

6. Communism in Europe, Vol. 2
William E. Griffith, ed. (1966)

7. Viet Cong: The Organization
and Techniques of the National
Liberation Front of South
Vietnam
Douglas Pike (1966)

8. Sino-Soviet Relations,
1964–1965
William E. Griffith (1967)

9. The French Communist Party
and the Crisis of International
Communism
François Fejtö (1967)

10. The New Rumania: From
People's Democracy to
Socialist Republic
Stephen Fischer-Galati (1967)

11. Economic Development in
Communist Rumania
John Michael Montias (1967)

12. Cuba: Castroism and
Communism, 1959–1966
Andrés Suárez (1967)

13. Unity in Diversity: Italian
Communism and the
Communist World
Donald L. M. Blackmer (1967)

14. Winter in Prague: Documents
on Czechoslovak Communism
in Crisis
Robin Alison Remington, ed.
(1969)

15. The Angolan Revolution, Vol. 1:
The Anatomy of an Explosion
(1950–1962)
John A. Marcum (1969)

16. Radical Politics in West Bengal
Marcus F. Franda (1971)

17. The Warsaw Pact: Case Studies in
Communist Conflict Resolution
Robin Alison Remington (1971)

18. The Transformation of
Communist Ideology: The
Yugoslav Case, 1945–1953
A. Ross Johnson (1972)

19. Radical Politics in South Asia
Paul R. Brass and Marcus F.
Franda, eds. (1973)

20. The Canal War: Four-Power
Conflict in the Middle East
Lawrence L. Whetten (1974)

The Canal War:
Four-Power Conflict in the Middle East

Lawrence L. Whetten

The MIT Press
Cambridge, Massachusetts, and London, England

This book was set in Linotype Baskerville,
printed on R&E Book,
and bound in G.S.B. S/535/16
by The Colonial Press Inc.
in the United States of America

Library of Congress Cataloging in Publication Data

Whetten, Lawrence L
  The canal war

  (Studies in communism, revisionism, and revolution 20)
  Bibliography: p. 507
  1. Jewish-Arab relations—1967–1973. 2. Near East—Politics. I. Title.
DS119.7.W47   327.5694′017′4927   74–11424
ISBN 0–262–23069–0

To My Wife

Contents

Preface   ix

1   The Middle East: A New Arena for Great-Power
Adversary Relations   1

2   Russian Attempts to Penetrate the Middle East   14

3   The June War and Initial Efforts to Secure an Accord:
June 1967–October 1968   39

4   The Problem of Parity and the Two-Power Talks:
October 1968–December 1969   67

5   Strategic Warfare and Renewed Diplomatic Initiatives:
January–July 1970   89

6   Cease-Fire and Diplomatic Nadir:
August 1970–March 1971   123

7   The Quest for a Partial Settlement:
February–July 1971   162

8   Interim Maneuvering on the Road to War:
August 1971–August 1972   196

9   The October War and Its Aftermath:
August 1972–January 1974   233

10   On the Roles of Great and Small Powers in
Regional Confrontations   301

Appendix 1
Eastern European Reactions to the June War:
A Case Study in Soviet Foreign-Policy
Compartmentalization   363

Appendix 2
The Mediterranean Military Confrontation:
Has Parity Been Achieved?   389

Appendix 3
U.N. Security Council Resolution 242 and
Document S/10070   444

Notes   474

Bibliography   507

Index   515

Preface

My intention in preparing this book is to examine a case study of political and military interactions among four states (Israel, Egypt, the United States, and the Soviet Union) over a limited period of time (June 1967 to January 1974) and on a fairly selected set of variables (the military conduct of the limited Canal War during this period and the political negotiations for its settlement). Instead of bringing behavioral and quantitative analyses to bear on this case study, I have confined myself to a more traditional approach, identifying a series of simple progressions and asking a few questions about the historic perspective of these four actors' aims and their relevance to the contemporary confrontation along the Suez Canal. But by reconstructing the military and political developments during this time span and relating them to the announced or perceived policy aims of all four states, I have attempted to identify the impact of the changing military balance or imbalance on efforts to negotiate a political solution to the Arab-Israeli confrontation.

David Morison's formulation of the present state of the art in Middle East studies seems an appropriate point of departure. "Herein lies the particular contradiction of the present phase of strategic studies on the Middle East: on the one hand it has never been so clearly recognized how limited is the scope for action by the great powers in the area, and on the other there has never been such a proliferation of forecast, suggestion, and advice about what they might, could, or ought to do." [1]* The Canal War provides abundant evidence of the astuteness of this observation.

A secondary purpose of the book is to examine Morison's proposition and the general framework of great-power relations

* Notes will be found at the back of the book.

within a regional context. The Middle East provides a unique environment for such a case study because of the lack of precedents and the degree of pioneering thus imposed on the policies of both great powers in this "virgin" territory. This "newness" attribute affords a different framework for the examination of adversary relations from the more conventional European and Asian Cold War testing grounds. Indeed, a working hypothesis for the project is that great-power relations in the Arab-Israeli confrontation are an accurate barometer of the adversaries' perceptions of and intentions toward each other; an index of the swing toward Cold War or détente.

Excellent studies have been written on the twenty-year great-power confrontation in the Middle East; and most methodological approaches have been explored. From this author's viewpoint, it appears most rewarding to place emphasis on the Soviet involvement. Soviet policies generally appeared to both the United States and local contestants to be assertive and/or provocative, while American actions seemed to be reactive and defensive. It has become widely believed that the Soviet Union has been, over the past two decades, the pacesetter for adversary relations in the Middle East. Thus, one of the underlying purposes of this project is to examine the veracity of this assumption over time and to determine the impact that Soviet policy, whether assertive or reactive, has had on the nature of the détente process at the regional level.

The key question in this approach can only be answered inconclusively, namely, through what means has Soviet political influence been extended into the Middle East, how durable and decisive is it, and how can it be accurately measured? One general implication of this study is that Soviet policy in the Canal War tends to support the school of Kremlinologists who argue that the underlying motives in Moscow's developing overseas strategy have been military factors and political balances, and who attribute the Soviet pursuit of its imperial will to apprehension about American deterrence and influence. A contending school holds that Soviet behavior is molded by the attractiveness of its economic system for developing countries and that constraints result mainly from indigenous politics and Soviet resource limitations. This study does not suggest that global strategy dominates all other facets of Soviet foreign policy. It does indicate that Moscow has attempted to compartmentalize its foreign policy by isolating and preventing regional problems and substantive issues from infecting or disrupting problems in related areas. Further, the study suggests that Moscow's emphasis on broad strategy during the Canal War at the expense of meeting the needs of its sponsored state has become the primary constraint on Soviet influence in the Middle East.

Several methodological limitations on the study must be mentioned. On contemporary subjects, such as the Canal War, almost no classified government documentation is available for consultation. For the political reconstruction, only declaratory policy and personal interviews could be used, with the accepted handicap that such statements are often intended for specific audiences or specific effects rather than for the general record. These difficulties will hopefully be partially offset by a systematic ordering of data.

Military aspects of the study also present problems. Weapons and equipment specifications are generally known, but employment under combat conditions, the only time it really counts, is often subject to heated controversy. Likewise, probable tactics and most-preferred strategies can be surmised with confidence, but the exact variation of a scenario that will occur cannot usually be accurately predicted. Finally, training proficiency, leadership, morale, and general discipline are even less tangible in peacetime and more difficult to quantify or measure. Consequently, intuitive insight and judgment must frequently be employed in assessing the interaction between politics and strategy in contemporary policy.

I am deeply indebted to several of my colleagues for advice and encouragement, especially Willard Beling, Michael Johnson, Edwin Gillis, and Richard Heuer. But I am also the beneficiary of the many excellent works already published in fields related to the present study of the Canal War. I would, finally, like to acknowledge my gratitude to the editors of *World Today* for permitting the use of material previously published in their journal.

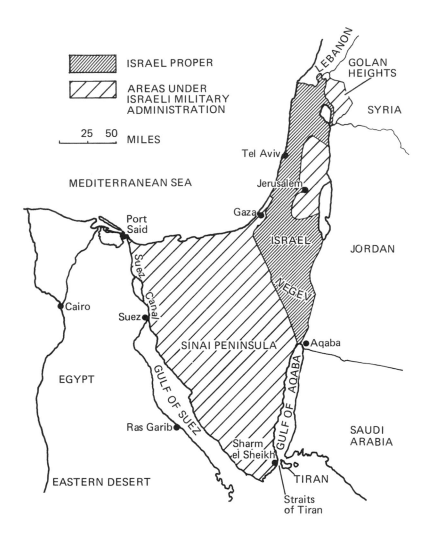

ISRAEL PROPER

AREAS UNDER
ISRAELI MILITARY
ADMINISTRATION

25   50   MILES

MEDITERRANEAN SEA

LEBANON

GOLAN
HEIGHTS

SYRIA

Tel Aviv

Jerusalem

Gaza

ISRAEL

JORDAN

NEGEV

Port
Said

Suez Canal

Cairo

Suez

SINAI PENINSULA

Aqaba

EGYPT

GULF OF SUEZ

GULF OF AQABA

SAUDI
ARABIA

Ras Garib

Sharm
el Sheikh

TIRAN

EASTERN DESERT

Straits
of Tiran

Cease-fire positions, June 1967

1
The Middle East: A New Arena for Great-Power Adversary Relations

An examination of the war conducted by Israel and Egypt along the Suez Canal can be expected to provide important insights into contemporary international relations for several reasons. The pressure-cooker atmosphere of the Cold War tended to refine outstanding East-West issues down to the basic elements of fundamental issues. This has not, however, been true of the Canal War, despite the higher level of tension and bloodshed. The issues involved have proven far more complex and more susceptible to varying interpretations, which indicates the intensity of the interrelated problems. The Canal War is a graphic demonstration both of the continuing injustices inflicted by small powers on one another and of the continuing responsibilities of the great powers in perpetuating these injustices. It has all the characteristics of a genuine crisis in human affairs.

Indeed, the Arab-Israeli conflict has been called a human tragedy—the struggle of right against right, in which evil is brought about not by evil men, but by good, honorable men who cannot make the right decision.[1] The tragedy has been compounded because the external powers have had no clear, precise interests, only ambiguous aspirations focused largely on each other rather than on any inherited legacies and assumed responsibilities for assisting in resolving the local injustices. Indeed, only if the rights of one local contestant could be asserted overwhelmingly against those of the other could the situation prove detrimental to both great powers and thus crystallize their interests. All four actors in the Canal War are keenly aware of the dimensions of their dilemma and have tried urgently to seek a peaceful settlement.

It is pointless to argue which nationalist movement has the

better claim to the Palestinian real estate. If irredentist claims
2,000 years old are to be honored, then the entire world will have
to be reordered; yet, if opposing demands for self-determination
are accepted, the Middle East could be splintered even further.
It is, perhaps, more relevant to see the situation within the framework of European intolerance. Antisemitism bred Zionism,
which in turn fed Pan-Arabism. The appeal of Zionism before
Hitler was limited; and it is probably reasonable to assert that,
without the holocaust and the subsequent European rejection of
those who survived, Zionism would not have come to seem such
an immediate necessity as it did after World War II. But the
creation of a refuge for Jews certainly in no way justified the
creation of Arab refugees.

The resolution of contending rights in the Middle East will
not be found in the equitable division of territory and allocation
of resources. A durable solution can only rest on reconciliation.
The compelling task for the Arabs is to modernize their decayed
societies; the compelling task for the Jews is to pluralize and
demilitarize their society—a society with an officially acclaimed
stature as having the greatest firepower per citizen in history. But
antagonisms have been so virulent that these urgent responsibilities have been superseded by the more stringent demands for
personal security on the part of all the participants in the regional conflict.

Essentially, then, the Arab-Israeli conflict is a contest between
two emergent mass nationalist movements for the same real estate; it is a political succession crisis in the post-British Mandate
of Palestine. Since the signing of the famous Balfour Agreement
in 1915, numerous solutions for securing an accommodation between Arabs and Jews have been proffered, deliberated, and attempted. The bargaining positions of both sides eventually cal-
cified into an impasse, however, and the Arabs seemed finally to
fall back on the contention that they could outwait the Israelis—
that isolation would eventually cause the Jewish state to disappear: "We waited two hundred years for the Crusader state to
disappear and finally, just through patience, it did disappear,

leaving nothing behind but a very few attractive ruins." To date, however, the policy of isolation has generally backfired, since it has intensified the "siege mentality" that increasingly obscures the Israeli perception of Arab determination. Israelis repeatedly express the conviction that in time the Arabs will "get used to our presence; they will see that Israel is a very nice country and will be reconciled to its existence." In this political deadlock, both sides have relied on intensified military pressure to assert the persuasiveness of their respective solutions.

From the wider historical perspective, the Israelis have viewed their relations with the Arab world in terms of three major issues: the right of Israel to exist as a Jewish political entity; the status of the Arab population within its borders and the claims of the Palestinian refugees; and the appropriate borders to be maintained with its neighbors. Early Zionist immigrants perceived their new homeland in an ideological framework. Ben Gurion has explained the aim of this pioneer spirit: "Long before I took office as prime minister, my goal was the creation of a model society which could become, in the language of the Biblical prophets, a light unto the nations." [2] The same ideal was also expressed by his controversial defense minister Pinhas Lavon. "I believe," Lavon wrote, "that the state of Israel requires additional dimensions, not in technology and not in numbers. . . . It is clear [that this dimension] cannot be expressed in the economic field. . . . If there is no serious about-turn . . . we shall be a completely normal society without a special attraction. We shall then be, in the last analysis, another Levantine country." [3]

Mass immigration, industrialization, and social striation have, however, gradually diluted the influence of the European-born Jews—who presently form only 25 percent of all Israeli Jews, but who still dominate the political apparatus. Thus, three-fourths of the Jewish population know little of European social and political ideals and have immigrated largely because of Jewish patriotism rather than necessity, retaining their oriental values and traditions. These differing backgrounds are largely responsible for the endless debates over national priorities: between practicality and ideology, between a physically secure, modernized, secularized society and an elitist "chosen society." [4]

The persistence of these differences has left Israel unable to resolve its most serious domestic and international problem: the rights and status of the Arabs living within its borders. The overwhelming public sentiment is that Israel must remain an undiluted Jewish state. As a result, Arabs are denied any effective voice in national policy and cannot identify with the society in which they live. As one longtime foreign resident of Israel has observed, "The Arabs are kept in a condition of weightlessness, belonging neither here nor there, victims of the Israelis' own feelings of insecurity and confusion and their inadequate understanding of the human situation." [5] Israel's continued disregard for the interests of its political minorities is considered by all Arabs as a sign of disdain and contempt for her neighbors. In the past one hundred years, there have been repeated instances when a social minority has felt victimized and has solicited sympathy from kinsmen abroad, resulting in tensions and wars; Israel's present civil-rights policies underscore this point.

"Ghettoization" of the Palestinians in the Arab countries, on the other hand, has been largely responsible for their rising national consciousness. In their insulated environment, the Palestinians have developed many of the characteristic complexes and attitudes of a minority: they marry among themselves more frequently than with others; they choose their friends from among their fellow countrymen more often than from Syrians or Egyptians; and their vocational objectives are to attain a middle-class status rather than that of a peasant or common worker. Furthermore, isolation and oppression of the refugees has bred a camaraderie and group identity that did not exist before 1948. Israel's present "open bridges" policy, designed specifically to maintain communications with the Arabs through the Palestinians, is a step forward, but it remains only a partial solution, leaving the grievances of both parties outstanding.

What then should be the political borders of a Jewish state with an "insoluble" minority problem? Foreign Minister Eban pointed to the dilemma in his statement on the second anniversary of the June War that "all Israeli government leaders are unanimous that peace must not give us another million Arabs." [6] But how was this to be achieved without further massive Arab evacuations or substantial Israeli withdrawals? Until 1974 Israel refused to issue a formal statement of its minimal territorial requirements. Several private schemes were offered by various leaders for the incorporation of specific features of the "new territories" necessary for defensive borders, for example, the Allon Plan for the West Bank and the Dayan proposal for the Israelization of strategically secure borders. The border issue was the chief source of debate in the 1969 general election that resulted in a sharp swing toward national conservatism, especially at the municipal level. The compromise that was developed within the ruling Labor Alignment party and that has since governed Israeli policy on the issue is that defendable borders are vital to national interest, but that their precise location is an important bargaining counter and, therefore, no action should be taken that might jeopardize the use of this tool. Accordingly, Israel has refrained from incorporating all the "new territories," but has officially announced that it will never withdraw behind the 1967 borders.[7]

From the Arab perspective, the goals of ejecting foreign domination and blocking Jewish immigration have been the immediate motives behind the drive for Pan-Arab unity that has emerged in the twentieth century. When World War II resulted in irresistible pressure for Jewish immigration to Palestine, as well as the continuation of foreign rule in the Middle East, Arab nationalism was expressed in increasingly violent forms, culminating in the first Arab-Israeli war in 1948. The Arab defeat, resulting from a lack of unity, became the driving force that made Nasser and Nasserism the dominant power in Arab politics for the next twenty years. Nasserism soon became identified as an attempt to organize antimonarchical forces throughout the Arab world under Egyptian leadership and patronage.

Nasser's image and Nasserism emerged seriously discredited from the third and most decisive Arab defeat by Israeli arms in

1967; yet Arab unity preserved a tattered facade. Nasser was still the most influential man in the Arab world, and he attempted to cut his losses by accepting a truce with his archfoe, King Faisal of Saudi Arabia, and conveying the impression that he would entertain a genuine détente with other Arab monarchs. To reinforce his beleaguered position, Nasser largely suspended his interference in the internal politics of other Arab states and launched a successful campaign to regain Soviet confidence. It became clear that he was the only Arab leader who could conceivably control the issues of war and peace in the Middle East. Yet his death in September 1970 has not reduced the central position that Egypt plays in the search for a political settlement.

During the Canal War the Arabs have been seeking a restitution of personal and national honor through the recovery of lost territory. They insist that international justice demands that the aggressor forfeit his unjust gains before the Israeli demands can be considered. King Hussein gave a clear impression of the moderate Arab viewpoint when he told the National Press Club in Washington on 10 April 1969: "On our part, we are prepared to offer the following as a basis for a just and lasting peace . . .

1. the end of belligerency;
2. respect and acknowledgment of the sovereignty, territorial integrity, and political independence of all states in this area;
3. recognition of the rights of all to live in peace within secure and recognized boundaries, free from threats or acts of war;
4. guarantees for all of freedom of navigation through the Gulf of Aqaba and the Suez Canal;
5. guarantees of the territorial inviolability of all states in the Middle East through whatever measures necessary including the establishment of demilitarized zones; and
6. acceptance of a just settlement of the refugee problem." [8]

From the Arab viewpoint, territorial inviolability is meant to include the pre-June 1967 borders.

While the Arabs claimed to be the victimized party, the Israeli position was that of a victorious power, determined both to extract a heavy price from its opponents for disrupting the peace and to insist upon their acceptance of more durable conditions for future relations and regional stability. The United States and the Soviet Union generally endorsed the latter proposition but rejected, for different reasons, the appropriateness of the former. At the outset, there was a sufficient commonality of interests for the two great powers to agree, in November 1967, to sponsor jointly United Nations Security Council Resolution 242, which called for both the withdrawal of Israeli forces and negotiations between the belligerents. Their mutual efforts for the next five years were directed toward securing compliance with the resolution's provisions. The failure of these endeavors was due largely to the acceptance by both great powers of the reasonableness of the grievances of their respective clients and to their differing views about the most appropriate means for rectifying these complaints: the Soviet Union was publicly committed to guaranteeing Arab military parity with Israel, and the United States had announced its intention to insure Israeli superiority. The two smaller states viewed a political settlement as contingent on a favorable outcome of the continuing military contest, and the great powers were explicitly tied to this priority by their own prescriptions for inducing regional negotiations.

The Canal War was fought because of opposing viewpoints about how security should ultimately be preserved. The great powers share responsibility for the Canal War; but they also share credit for attempting to seek an equitable political settlement that could serve as an interim measure toward a final reconciliation. This study does not deal with the injustices of the Arab-Israeli conflict nor in the nature of the required reconciliation. It deals only with the attempts of the four major actors in this phase of the conflict to reach a solution for the most immediate and dangerous aspect of the overall dispute: a cessation of the fighting and an adjustment of political differences.

This study will also examine great-power adversary relations within a regional context. Since the Canal War became a major focal point of the Arab-Israeli conflict, which has, in turn, held the center stage in Middle Eastern affairs, the study will concen-

trate on the Soviet involvement in the Canal War in an attempt
to gain insight into Soviet policy in a crisis situation and into
any transformations that may be taking place in Moscow's attitude toward the broader spectrum of international relations and
the contemporary détente process. In light of the international furor over the Vietnam War, the
Canal War did not command as much global attention as would
normally be expected. There were many reasons for the different
levels of world concern for the two areas, but certainly the fact
that both great powers allegedly had greater national interests
in the Middle East, coupled with their lack of historic grounding
in regional problems, served to introduce ambiguities for the
world public. The Canal War became a unique theater for the
great-power adversary relationship. It is an important case study
with direct application to the broader context of traditional
studies of East-West relations because it provides the best example of the adaptability of Soviet foreign policy to a new arena of
influence competition. Indeed, unlike its European or Far Eastern
policy, Moscow's Middle Eastern policy and specifically its military and political policies toward developments during the Canal
War have provided what is probably the strongest example of
the virtuosity and mistakes in Soviet diplomacy since the 1920s
and 1930s.

There are several characteristics of the Middle East's gradual
transition to modernity that raise uncertainties about great-power
interests and relations in the region. Contemporary alignments
are a reflection of the fundamental change in the status of the
Middle East in world politics: it is no longer the nexus between
Europe and Asia that was once almost universally regarded as a
"vital strategic interest." Relations with both Europe and the Soviet Union have become more complex, but remain vulnerable
to the vagaries of nationalist sentiment. (In the past thirty years,
every Middle Eastern and Mediterranean nation has ridden the
emotions of nationalism through at least one violent revolution,
civil war, or foreign intervention.) Finally, allegiances in the

Middle East oscillate rather frequently; and in some countries civil unrest is now regarded as endemic.

The extension of Soviet influence into the Middle East has been erratic and has failed to provide consistent guidelines for assessing subsequent Soviet aims and tactics in the Third World. In 1955 and 1956 Moscow became the beleagued victim of its own ambition. Invited into the Arab world, the Soviets proved unprepared to grasp their opportunity fully. They lacked the political, military, and ideological equipment necessary to assess the implications of fluid situations accurately and to exert effective control over changing circumstances for their own benefit. They regarded the retrenchment of the colonial powers and the developing power vacuum as vindications of communist ideological prophecies, and they indiscriminately underwrote those nationalist movements that promised to provide opposition to Western "imperialism" with impressive military and economic aid.

But the Soviets' overambitious offensive resulted in a series of diplomatic reversals. Ten years after their initial entry into the region, only Nasser remained of the original Soviet-sponsored cast of anti-imperialist personalities. All the others had either been deposed by their own people or had broken with Moscow because of disenchantment with grandiose Soviet schemes for world liberation, overly extravagant economic projects, or intrigues in local political circles. Ghana, Guinea, and Mali were no longer stalwart Soviet props in the Third World. Indonesia had "fallen back" into a pro-Western orientation, and the local Communist party had been decimated. Even in Cuba, Soviet influence was minimal: Castro claimed primacy over Latin American communist movements. And in the Middle East, Soviet fortunes had been subjected to repeated vicissitudes. Ironically, these political changes have frequently forced Moscow into attempts to preserve its local influence through support of cliques of ultraconservative military strongmen, rather than radical revolutionary leaders.

These failures resulted from several conceptual oversights.

First, it is now recognized that Moscow's indiscriminate commitment to all "national liberation movements" was the result of an overreliance on the Leninist dictum that lumped all former colonial peoples into the same category of "oppressed" peoples ready to embrace a "higher" social form. Such an oversimplification minimized the desire within these new states for an authentic national identification. Moscow had failed to perceive that, although in the more settled societies the Left tends to be less nationalistic than the Right, in the postcolonial societies the "revolutionary Left" is usually more nationalistic than the local propertied classes with their broader international perspectives.

Second, the Soviets lacked the capability to influence crises abroad through the injection of adequate material aid or military forces. Moscow could only verbally protest the 1958 landing of United States forces in Lebanon and the British paratroop landings in Jordan. In 1960 and 1964 Soviet maneuvers in the Congo nearly succeeded; but, in the end, Moscow was unable to maintain sufficient physical support for its local candidates. The American naval quarantine of Cuba was the classic example of the limits of Moscow's conventional strategic capabilities.

A third difficulty resulted from a seeming inability to adjust Soviet standards for economic and military aid to Afro-Asian requirements and absorption capabilities. The initial overconfidence and subsequent poor performance of the Arab armed forces in the June 1967 War clearly illustrates this problem.

A final reason for the setbacks sustained by Soviet diplomacy before the June War was the failure of the Soviets to distinguish between their commitments to international revolutionary forces and their responsibilities to legitimate governments. This classic dichotomy in Soviet foreign policy nurtured deep suspicions among friendly Arab governments without increasing the prospects of local radical movements for seizing power. Indeed, Moscow's indecisive policy toward Arab radical groups proved to be one of its most serious handicaps.

Before the outbreak of hostilities in 1967, Moscow had already demonstrated an awareness of the limitations of its policies and had initiated a study of its reversals in the hope of devising possible remedial actions. Soviet diplomacy began to demonstrate increasing responsibility and circumspection at this time. The Kremlin no longer seized upon every international incident and domestic crisis as an opportunity to promote revolution or propagandize the faults of its adversaries. Indeed, Soviet discussions of revolution began to place greater stress on thorough preparation than on execution, using arguments that ultimately preclude rather than foster radical action. The present leadership has predicated the penetration of Soviet influence into the Middle East upon the precept that Moscow is a peaceloving nation, dedicated to the concepts of coexistence and mutual respect among sovereign states. Moscow's growing prudence was demonstrated by Kosygin's personal diplomacy during the 1965 Indo-Pakistani conflict, clearly indicating Moscow's high priority on maintaining stability among its southern neighbors. Furthermore, Moscow adopted more stringent foreign aid policies. Total funds were reduced, rigorous criteria were applied to project-feasibility studies, and closer controls were exercised over project development. Despite the earlier diplomatic reversals, by the late 1960s Moscow had substantially enhanced its ability to challenge Western hegemony in the Middle East.

The initial factor eroding the Western military position was the loss of control over the intensity of regional conflicts. After the Egyptian-Czechoslovak arms agreement of 1955, the United States, Britain, and France could no longer "enforce" their 1950 Tripartite Agreement to restrict the arms race between Israel and the Arab states. Subsequent Soviet arms supplies have provided the Arabs with the qualitatively best military equipment that has been delivered outside the Warsaw Pact, including that supplied to the Asian communist countries. The arms buildup on both sides finally reached such a high level that external intervention would require a force of considerable size and sophistication. This has added a new dimension to the specter of great-power involvement in local hostilities.

A further erosion occurred when the Soviet Union successfully established a permanent military presence south of the Dardanelles. The very existence of a viable Soviet overseas strategy fundamentally alters the power balance and potential political alignments in the Middle East. If adroitly handled, these new conditions could challenge the role of the American Sixth Fleet as a protector of NATO's southern flank, and demonstrate to nonaligned nations the limits of the American role in the Middle East. By emphasizing the alleged erosion of American maneuverability, and by providing tangible evidence of Soviet support for proxy forces, Moscow has been able to make significant inroads into Arab politics, including powerful leverage against pro-Western regimes. This alteration of the power balance has underscored new political realities: the Soviets' minimum demands for recognition of their regional role must now be accepted by other interested powers.

But while the Soviets may have successfully compromised the West's freedom of action in the Middle East, it is questionable to what extent they have been able to translate their achievements into positive political influence that can be asserted to alter regional developments decisively in their favor. Both of the superpowers now share many of the same constraints, and neither has sufficient advantages inherent in its political or military posture to manipulate these constraints to its adversary's detriment. Indeed, both powers have accrued significant liabilities that may now hamper the exercise of effective influence in the Middle East.

This case study of the four-power interactions[9] during the Canal War will analyze the military postures and political objectives of the four during the various attempts to resolve the conflict. For convenience I have divided the period into seven rounds of negotiation, with the last "round" being the preparations for and aftermath of the October 1973 War, which has seemingly brought an end to the confrontation along the Canal. Moscow's position in the conflict and its reactions to the various developments provide one of the best examples of the transformation that Soviet foreign policy is currently undergoing. The study will also provide insight into problems related to influence competition and great-power–small-power relations, as well as into Soviet techniques for securing recognition as a regional power to be reckoned with.

In order to analyze the durability of the Soviet position, it will be necessary to examine Moscow's attempts to overcome the three principal constraints on its political posture during the Canal War:

1. its military inferiority in the region compared to its great-power adversary;
2. the military imbalance between Arabs and Israelis; and
3. the adverse reactions of its allies to this aspect of its overseas strategy.

The degree of its success in offsetting these constraints is an important measure of the viability of Moscow's political authority in the Middle East.

The examination of these constraining factors will be preceded by a survey of historic Soviet interests in the Middle East and a discussion of the impact that these minimal traditional ties have had on the development of Moscow's present political stance.

Two separate but related case studies have been prepared as appendixes: one dealing with the Soviet military buildup and the other with the reaction of the Warsaw Pact nations to Moscow's post-June War Middle Eastern policy.

2

Russian Attempts to Penetrate the Middle East

Since the Soviet Union has set the pace in converting the Middle East into an arena of Soviet-American influence competition, it is appropriate to examine the historic perspective of Moscow's efforts to employ political cooperation with the governments in this region as a means of establishing a reliable basis for exercising political influence. The Soviet Union's recent astonishing feat of gaining general recognition from all interested parties of its parity for responsibility for Middle Eastern stability has a long historical background of trial and error, experimentation and reversal. The degree of Soviet success has triggered an inevitable question: Was it due to Western default, or was it, perhaps, the product of a diabolical Grand Design? This controversy lies beyond the scope of the present study. Instead, this chapter will attempt to analyze the fundamental components of Soviet international behavior by comparing Soviet and Tsarist aims and policies in the Middle East to determine whether the recent success has been due to a more dynamic pursuit of traditional Russian objectives or to the adoption of totally new objectives and methods for their implementation.

Penetration via Turkey

Tsarist Russia pursued a fairly clear policy toward the main Middle Eastern states, but this did not preclude periods of relative disinterest or distraction because of commitments in other regions. In general, Tsarist policy was predicated upon a broad acceptance of the existing world order and of such relatively constant factors as geographic location, strategic vulnerability, and economic viability.

Russian political interest in the Middle East dates back several centuries. After the decline of Byzantium, Moscow claimed protectorship rights over the Orthodox Church in the Levant. The assertion of these prerogatives was a contributing factor to several of the wars between Russia and Turkey. More vital issues involved the security of the Black Sea, assured access through the Dardanelles to the Mediterranean, and hegemony over the Balkans both as an end in itself and as a safeguard for the first two objectives. The importance of these strategic waters to Russian security was demonstrated during the Crimean War, when an enemy operating through the Turkish Straits inflicted decisive damage; and again in the Russian Civil War, when hostile forces operating from the Black Sea occupied vast regions of southern Russia. These waters also have an obvious commercial value; the elimination of hostile threats in this region was vital to the sustained industrial development of southern Russia. In 1913 the Tsar's minister of the navy summed up the traditional Russian position as follows: "The Straits in the hands of another state would mean the complete control of the economic development of southern Russia by a foreign power and the transfer to that state of the hegemony of the Balkans and the key for an aggressive advance into Asia Minor." [1]

Turkey, of course, viewed these ambitions as infringements of its own sovereign territorial rights in the Balkans and the Middle East. Thirteen major wars and continual border clashes marred relations between the two countries during the seventeenth and eighteenth centuries and produced a tradition of distrust. During periods when common external threats were mutually recognized, however, both states were able to reconcile their differences and collaborate on security arrangements. For example, during the Napoleonic era Russia and Turkey signed their first mutual defense agreement. A second mutual defense pact in 1833 provided, among other things, for the withdrawal of fourteen thousand Russian troops and twenty-five warships stationed at Constantinople to protect the Porte against Arab insurrectionists. Both countries agreed in 1840 to the Treaty of London, which closed the Straits to all warships. Tsarist advances toward the

Middle East and the responding series of anti-Russian coalitions produced the "Eastern Question" that preoccupied European diplomacy for nearly a hundred years. In World War I, Turkey held a pivotal position in the security alignment of the Central Powers. Accordingly, the Western Allies agreed to a secret Constantinople Agreement defining Russian claims in this region: if the Allies were victorious, Russia was to receive Constantinople, the western shore of the Bosporus, plus defensive islands in the Aegean and the eastern territories of Anatolia.

In the turmoil of the postwar era, revolutionary Turkey and Russia became the renegades of European politics. Moscow was the sole quarter open to Ataturk in his rebellion against the Western Allies. Lenin supplied arms for three divisions and other assistance, and in return Turkey gave its support for a redefinition of the rules governing passage of the Straits, presently embodied in the 1936 Montreux Convention.[2] A 1921 Soviet-Turkish Treaty of Neutrality and Nonaggression formed the framework for Turkish security arrangements until 1939, when Ankara joined a collective defense system that stretched from the Danube to the Indus River.

After World War II, Stalin demanded Turkish Thrace and the western shore of the Bosporus, plus the Dodecanese Islands which serve as chokepoints to the Straits, as a reward for Russia's vast wartime contribution. He also claimed the Italian possessions of Libya and Eritrea at the entrance to the Red Sea. In view of the communist civil war in Greece and the Soviet occupation of northern Iran, Turkey abandoned its preference for neutrality and became committed to yet another anti-Russian coalition, NATO, which still provides the backbone of its security arrangements. The lid was firmly clamped on Soviet aspirations by a joint American-Turkish communiqué on 22 April 1950 that marked the formal American assumption of the security responsibilities toward Turkey that Great Britain had relinquished in 1947. The communiqué "finally and conclusively" rejected Soviet demands for joint control of the Turkish straits.

Thus, it was the resolution of the Western powers, primarily Britain, Austria, and later the United States, that prevented Russian domination of the collapsing Ottoman Empire or the extension of its political influence on a permanent basis south of the Dardanelles.

Russia's Second Avenue South

A second axis for Russian penetration into the Middle East has been through Persia, aiming at the Persian Gulf and positions that flank either the Arab lands to the west or the Indian subcontinent to the east. A strong Persia was regarded by Britain as vital to the security of India; but the Caspian region became the victim of larger European diplomatic compromises that weakened London's resolve to defend Persia's territorial integrity. Between the Treaty of Gulistan (1813) and the Treaty of Turkmanchai (1828), virtually all of Transcaucasia was ceded to Russia by Persia. From its stronghold in Azerbaijan south of the Caucasian passes and its domination of the Caspian, Russia was able to reduce northern Persia to the status of a veiled protectorate and to annex piecemeal the khanates in Central Asia. By midcentury Russian authority over northern Persia was generally accepted. From 1879 until World War I, the only effective military force in the northern half of the country was the Persian Cossack Brigade, officered by Russian personnel. This force exercised de facto administrative authority as far as Isfahan, the rough demarcation line with the British, who controlled the Gulf.[3]

After the 1917 Revolution, the new Bolshevik regime promptly renounced all claims against Persia. However, as the Red Army advanced to the former Tsarist boundaries, it supported the establishment of the Soviet Republic of Gilan (May 1920) at Resht, which claimed nearly all of Russia's former sphere in northern Persia. International intervention then supported a successful coup d'etat by Riza Khan, who managed to secure general diplomatic recognition, the dismissal of the Persian Cossack Brigade, and a Treaty of Friendship with the Soviet Union, contingent upon the withdrawal of Red Army troops in the fall of 1921.

During World War II, Soviet troops again occupied northern Iran, including the capital. Utilizing these forces, Moscow created an autonomous state in southern Azerbaijan, with a capital at Tabriz, and further south proclaimed an independent republic of Kurdistan. Moscow agreed to withdraw its troops after obtaining a concession for oil development from the Shah. The Soviet republics fell as soon as the Soviet troops withdrew, and the Iranian legislature refused to ratify the oil accord.

Thus, while Soviet pressure against Turkey has stemmed largely from strategic factors, its claims against Iran have had slightly more substance: it exercised de facto administration, however brigand, over northern Persia for more of the last century than did the native rulers. The fact that the Russians had enjoyed little public support did not enter Soviet calculations.

The Quest for Warmer Waters
There is also a long history of Russian interest in the Mediterranean and the Arab lands. During the late eighteenth and early nineteenth centuries, Tsarist Russia made three determined efforts to outflank Turkey and establish itself as a Mediterranean power. In 1770 the Russian Baltic Fleet, in cooperation with the British navy, entered the Mediterranean for the first time in strength and defeated the Turkish Fleet off Izmir; but it failed to force the Straits. For the next four years the Russian Fleet dominated the eastern Mediterranean. Using Cyprus as a base, the Russians occupied Beirut for several years, held Latakia, Jaffa, Gaza, and Alexandria for shorter periods, and patrolled the entire coastline to the Straits. The success of this operation was due mainly to their access to British bases and logistics facilities, a dependence the Russians attempted to correct during their second thrust into the region in 1798, when Corfu was conquered and converted into a naval base. From there, an unsuccessful operation was mounted against British-held Malta. In 1806 a third Russian naval expedition was dispatched to the Mediterranean, and several Dalmatian ports, including Dubrovnik, were captured. After the collapse of Napoleon, however, Britain reasserted

its mastery of the Mediterranean. The Russian navy was denied its bases and was thereafter, and until recently, incapable of conducting independent operations in these waters.

Egypt's strategic location, proximity to the Black Sea, importance to the British and the Turks, and intrinsic commercial value made it a key factor in Russian strategy. To undermine the Turkish Sultan and cultivate local support, Russia provided military advisors, arms, and even volunteers to rebellious Arabs. By 1786 the Mamelukes, a powerful Egyptian Guards formation, were one-fourth Russian, and the Russian consul was defending the independent-minded beys against the Sultan, stating that they were under the protection of the Russian Empress.[4]

In other activities reminiscent of the current Soviet interest in Egypt, the Russians distributed gifts and decorations, maintained spiritual contacts through missions and schools, provided medical aid, afforded technical training in Russia for local students, and extended technical assistance in mining operations and scientific explorations. Furthermore, trade relations were systematically expanded. At the beginning of the nineteenth century, Russia had become the second most important market for Egyptian products, mainly cotton.

Whenever the Egyptians supported the Porte against Russia, however, they suffered severe losses. In roughly one hundred years, from 1770 to 1878, the Russian navy successfully engaged Arab contingents of the Turkish navy in seven encounters that cost Egypt alone over eleven thousand sailors. During the last major Russo-Turkish War (1877–1878), an Egyptian army of over thirty thousand was defeated by the Russians in Bulgaria. Massacres of captured ship crews were not uncommon, attacks on enemy warships at anchor were frequently recorded, and the sacking of hostile ports (notably Beirut) was a recurring abuse.[5] Thus, the initial stages of Russian-Arab relations were marred by hostility and bitterness. Indeed, in the two hundred years preceding World War I, Arab arms were more frequently and more severely defeated by Russia than by any other European power.

As Turkey weakened during the nineteenth century and as

French and British interests in the Middle East and Africa correspondingly expanded, Russia entertained second thoughts about the value of encouraging Arab insurrections against Constantinople. When the rebellious Egyptian beys under Mohammed Ali marched against Constantinople in 1833, Russian warships and troops were dispatched to aid the Porte. In the face of a stern Russian warning, the victorious Egyptian army withdrew and Egypt's bid for independence failed.

The changing environment was prophetically illuminated by Russian Foreign Minister Giers when he stated that "the proclaimed principle of Egypt for the Egyptians is a utopia. Egypt, because of its geographical location at the junction of three continents, holds a position of such political importance that its independence is impossible. It would be too weak to defend itself. It would become a battlefield for European rivalries." [6]

Russia's anxiety about access to the Mediterranean and Egypt's strategic importance had both increased by the turn of the century, at which time France held Morocco, Turkey possessed the Straits, and Britain controlled Gibraltar and Egypt: all Mediterranean routes were thus dominated by powerful rivals. Accordingly, Tsar Nicholas II paid a state visit to England in 1896 to promote a bargain with the British: London could exercise uncontested control of the Suez Canal if it would recognize Russia's claim to the Dardanelles. Britain did not accept the principle of Russian entry into the Mediterranean, however, until the pressure of World War I forced a capitulation to Saint Petersburg's terms. If Russia had remained in the war, the Constantinople Agreement would have assured Russian access to the Mediterranean and the Arab lands.

Communist Ideological Approaches

The Soviet Union has frequently sought to cultivate radical Middle Eastern political movements as instruments of its foreign policy. In the Middle East, two categories of political movements have been the most consistent objectives of Soviet policy: Arab socialist or "progressive" governments and Arab Communist par-

ties. Soviet policy toward these two forms of regional revolutionary grouping has been subject to the basic contradiction that can
usually be found in Moscow's relations with bourgeois regimes
and local radical movements: the attempt to protect Soviet state
interests while simultaneously advancing its international communist commitments. In light of Moscow's powerful new military, political, and economic interests in the region, it is appropriate to examine the extent to which Moscow estimates that
these interests can be protected through its support of either or
both of these radical groupings. In the event of conflict between
the two, what preference has Moscow established for the advancement of its interests? When is it feasible to envision the advancement of Arab socialist, local communist, and Soviet national objectives simultaneously? And when the aspirations of these three
political entities are not compatible, to what extent does the resulting pursuit of contradictory aims impose natural barriers to
Soviet political influence on both the less powerful, nonruling,
radical factions and the foreign patron state?

In pursuing this line of inquiry, several aspects of Soviet-Arab
relations will be lightly surveyed:
1. the degree of Soviet involvement in local communist activities;
2. Moscow's tolerance level for local revolutionary demands;
3. the identity of interests between the Soviet Union and its
   client states;
4. tactics and practices that are likely to be the preferred means
   for containing local opposition, controlling client states' policies, and advancing Soviet strategic aims; and
5. the role of Arab politics in Soviet regional designs.

There are more Muslims in Soviet Asia than in any Arab country. This was initially regarded by the Bolsheviks as an asset that
could be used as a natural lever for penetrating the Middle East.
The blueprint laid down by the 1920 Comintern-organized "Baku
Congress of Toilers in the East," which governed communist
tactics until the mid-1950s, called for collaboration of local Communist parties with selected bourgeois patriots in the struggle
for national independence. This course was influenced by several

factors: strategic security requirements along the Soviet Union's
southern borders; the need to "buy time" in areas of less vital interest to Moscow until the struggles in Europe and the Far East
were resolved; and the Leninist view that the chief value of colonial peoples to the communist world revolution was the aggregate pressure they could bring to bear on the imperialist powers.[7]
   This Comintern policy was largely unsuccessful for several reasons. Communist ideology remained alien to the Middle Eastern
mentality. Nationalism and religion were more compelling motives in Arab political behavior than the promotion of international communism. Small, local Communist parties were unable
at that time to establish firm foundations for a mass movement
in any Middle Eastern state, and their activities as a regional
group never compared with those of the European parties. Second, Moscow remained during this period fully committed to "socialism in one country." Indeed, throughout the period, Soviet
policy toward the Arabs was noteworthy for its studied disinterest. Higher priorities and more immediate dangers were heavily
taxing Soviet resources and energies.
   Stalin's preference for Soviet strategic interests over Comintern
obligations resulted in the demoralization of local party cadres,
factionalism, the decline of proselytizing activities, and isolation
in national politics. Coupled with the firm suppression of revolutionary activities by local authorities, the lack of external support
and leadership made it impossible for local Communist parties
to make original contributions to national development or to
"creative" Marxism.[8]
   By the mid-1950s, however, the Kremlin had become aware that
its traditional distrust of national bourgeois forces was now
counterproductive and that new opportunities existed in the
Third World for exerting influence at Western expense. Newly
independent states were recognized as a distinct force in world
politics. While requisite policy changes may have been decided
upon as early as 1952, by 1955 the new orientation was clearly
established. The Bandung Conference, at which Moscow accred-
ited itself as a major source of military and economic aid and as

a friend of oppressed peoples, created a détente atmosphere within the Third World.

The reassessment of Soviet policy probably stemmed from several developments:

1. The cohesion of the newly established containment barriers —NATO, the Baghdad Pact, and the Balkan Pact—limited Soviet diplomatic opportunities in contiguous countries.

2. The decolonization process provided a highly fluid environment susceptible to outside pressures.

3. Moscow's gradual economic recovery from the war and its attainment of a degree of industrial stability afforded a limited economic cushion for investment abroad.

4. The achievement of nuclear-power status had earned substantial psychological profits among the developing countries that could be compounded by demonstrations of benevolence.

5. Political developments in the Arab East underscored the dysfunctional effect of the traditional Marxist line and need for a new definition of Soviet strategic and state interests.

6. Fundamental differences in foreign policy had emerged within the West, especially between the American penchant for a universalist approach to world problems and the French and British preference for sphere-of-interest concepts (the Suez crisis of 1956 graphically demonstrated the dichotomy between idealism and pragmatism that divided the Western alliance).

7. Nasserism had by this time become recognized as the main anticolonial force in the region.

Moscow thus combined dangers and new opportunities as the grounds for new policies. It legitimized these policy revisions toward the nations in what Khrushchev called a vast "zone of peace" at its twentieth Party Congress and in a preliminary statement by the Foreign Ministry in *Pravda*.[9] These statements cataloged Moscow's anxieties about the formation of military alliances along its southern borders, especially since they might be linked with NATO and SEATO and seriously restrain Moscow's freedom of movement. Moscow committed itself to countering military consolidation on its southern flank by extending military and economic aid to Arab countries, thus, hopefully, expanding their range of options and reducing inducements for joining hostile alliances.

Wanted: A New Approach to the Third World

While the Kremlin recognized the need for greater flexibility, it was slow to devise a comprehensive conceptual framework to govern its relations with the Third World. Not until after Castro's seizure of power in Cuba, and General Kassem's apparently genuine espousal of correct socialist tenets in Iraq, both in 1959, was the Kremlin compelled to devise a formula that would justify close association with such potentially communist regimes. Moscow then improvised the concept of "national democracy," which received official endorsement at the 1960 World Communist Conference. This approach sanctioned communist cooperation with peasants and the petite bourgeoisie in progressing from colonial dependency toward noncapitalist development without moving first through the stage of capitalist revolution. Through united-front tactics, the communists and "progressive forces" were to defend political and economic independence; a rigorous struggle was to be waged against "imperialism"; the state sector of the economy was to be steadily expanded; and dictatorial and despotic methods of government were to be firmly rejected. As these steps were implemented, Moscow could justify extending material aid and moral support to assist such reforms.[10]

As it turned out, however, the concept had only marginal utility. Castro denied that Cuba fell into the category of "national democracy," and proclaimed that his country had reached the status of a "people's socialist republic" two years before Moscow accepted this progression. In the Arab countries, where the concept was considered especially feasible, all "progressive" governments quickly developed into one-party regimes that vigorously suppressed local communist activities. Indeed, Moscow was forced to espouse a policy of assimilation between socialists and communists as the price for continued influence in Algeria and Egypt, countries where it had become heavily committed. "National democracy" provided the ideological justification for massive aid, but it failed either to insure adequate control over the policies of client states, or to guarantee the interests of Moscow's traditional allies, the local Communist parties.[11] What should be the appropriate relationship with noncapitalist, anti-imperialist, friendly, but anticommunist governments? In other words, how could the transition from the nationalist to the socialist phase of local revolutions be encouraged or directed when local leaders persisted in their own views as to the "laws of history"?

From 1962 to 1964, the term "revolutionary democracy" received increasing currency as the conceptual vehicle for incorporating these countries into the Soviet sphere. Mali, Ghana, Guinea, and Congo (Brazzaville) were soon added to the list of candidates. But the dissimilarities in the social and economic levels of these countries reaffirmed that the most important aspect of this new classification of leftists was the intensity of their anti-imperialist sentiments. Nonetheless, Moscow apparently expected that countries willing to increase gradually the ratio of public to privately owned property, and to accept Soviet technical and managerial guidance, would inevitably evolve toward the Soviet model of economic and social progress. The principal domestic reform the Soviets envisioned was a broadening of the local political base so that the ruling one-party system could be at the same time more representative and more selective.

In socially underdeveloped countries, where class conflicts were not pronounced and the industrial proletariat was nonexistent, such innovations were both devoid of classical theoretical underpinnings and irrelevant to local conditions.[12] Hence, "revolutionary democracy" also failed. The attachment of Soviet aid and prestige to single personalities, whose subsequent fall jeopardized the whole investment, revealed the bankruptcy of this latest concept of social progress. The Soviets also chronically miscalculated the authority of local elites and the strength of nationalism among the newly independent peoples. In addition, competition with China often forced Moscow to adopt a more radical ideological stand than was compatible with its strategic interest.

Finally, the persistence of the Arab-Israeli dispute and the prospect of continuing regional instability made any gains in the Middle East temporary at best. In the councils of the Kremlin, the argument was eventually broached that a more methodical policy, based on realistic long-term interests, would yield greater political profits over the long haul than tactical maneuvering for immediate gains.[13]

One consequence of Moscow's conceptual innovations was that it was forced to maintain two separate policies: one dealing with radical opposition movements, and another with friendly governments whose continued tenure was desirable. Moscow could no longer indulge in the duplicity of its traditional diplomacy by publicly dissociating itself from local Communist party revolutionary activities while privately continuing to support them. With unfriendly governments, the interests of local radical movements and Moscow could still potentially coincide, as in the Congo, and local revolutionary operations could still be assisted in the traditional manner. But in countries that afforded the opportunity of advancing its global interests, Moscow was often forced to sacrifice radical demands to Soviet expediency. In consequence, the future of Arab communism and of Soviet influence among the Arab socialists now hangs in the balance.

Hurdling the Containment Barriers

While the initial Soviet overtures to the Third World were accompanied by lavish ideological trappings, the extension of military, economic, and technical aid and the expansion of commerce indicated that Moscow was now also prepared to resume the traditional Russian interests in the Middle East. To carry out this policy, it first attempted to secure the neutrality of its southern neighbors. When these endeavors boomeranged and stimulated the erection of "containment" barriers, the Soviet Union outflanked them by adopting an activist policy toward the Arabs. Khrushchev's historic arms transaction in 1955 and his new ideological offensive marked the beginning of this phase of Soviet policy.[14]

When the crisis developed over the nationalization of the Suez Canal, Moscow assumed the role of Egypt's protector. The Soviets attended the 1956 London Conference on the Canal and for the first time played an important part in international deliberations on Mediterranean affairs. During discussions in Britain just before the Suez War, Prime Minister Anthony Eden told Bulganin and Khrushchev that the United Kingdom was prepared to use force, if necessary, to restore tranquility in the Middle East. The Soviet leaders replied with a similar warning that the Soviet Union, as a great power interested in the maintenance of peace, could not stand aside from this question (the threat of Western intervention). In short, Moscow used the crisis to legitimize its status as a great power by seeking Western recognition of its standing as an authority in the Middle East.

When the crisis erupted into hostilities, the Soviet Union acted with extreme circumspection. When it threatened to launch strategic strikes against England, the danger was not taken seriously; and Moscow offered to send "volunteers" only after a cease-fire had been arranged. While such caution demonstrated to the West the limits of Soviet support for its regional clients, the Soviet Union did make some advances in terms of influencing local leaders. The prestige of the Soviets was enhanced throughout the Third World when they championed the cause of victimized Egypt and agreed to resupply it with even greater quantities of arms.

Revisionist historians have recently provided a new interpretation of events leading to the Suez War that cast new light on the nature of Soviet involvement:

1. The Egyptian-U.S.S.R. arms deal was a reaction to British-American machinations during the Baghdad Pact episode and not to Dulles's abortive Aswan Dam scheme.

2. The Soviet arms transaction was substantially for political, rather than purely military reasons.

3. Egypt had submitted requests for arms to both the United States and the Soviet Union and strongly preferred U.S. aid.

4. Nasser's pan-Arab policy, promulgated before the Aswan

Dam project, forced him to search for an external ally, preferably one antagonistic to those of his Arab rivals who favored the West.
5. U.S. policy at that time favored rapprochement with Nasser on his terms (e.g., ousting the British, etc.), but it proved ill-conceived and has contributed to national misperceptions since then by all parties.[15]

As the Soviet image unexpectedly rose as a result of these confusing and fluid circumstances, the opportunities multiplied to score against the "imperialists." Yet a degree of uncertainty still remained for Moscow about the precise dimensions of its new posture. Soviet behavior during the 1957 Syrian crisis may be viewed as an attempt to probe the interested parties' evaluation of Soviet stature. The Turkish-Syrian confrontation developed over reports that the Soviets were planning to construct a major base at Latakia, south of the vital Turkish port of Iskenderun. Both sides deployed military forces, and the Egyptians and Soviets partially mobilized in support of the Syrians. The firmness of Western warnings, the clear indications of Turkey's determination to defend its interests, and the unity of the alliance structures illustrated a degree of Western solidarity that Moscow could not shake. The crisis ended abruptly when Khrushchev announced publicly that "there will be no war with Turkey." [16]

Nevertheless, Moscow apparently estimated that it had made important gains during the crisis. The negative aspect of enhanced Western unity was offset by the Soviet Union's improved image as a regional arbitrator, protector of Syria, and defender of peace. In fact, Moscow had initiated no measures to preserve stability; rather, it had sought to keep regional tensions high.

The 1958 Lebanese crisis marked a high point in Soviet challenges to rival great powers in the Middle East during this period, and was noteworthy for Moscow's return to the circumspection it had exercised during the Suez War. Moscow's inability to counter American and British intervention effectively provided a harsh display of the restricted nature of Soviet influence in the region. Moscow itself undoubtedly concluded that its authority had been undermined. Thereafter, it maintained an active role in Middle Eastern affairs (for example, in the 1959 Kirkuk riots), but refrained for nearly ten years from confrontations that could result in foreign interventions and further illustrations of Soviet limitations. Nonetheless, its position had been partially consolidated. Although it did almost nothing during the crisis, Moscow had weakened the Western alliance by successfully pressuring Jordan not to join the Baghdad Pact and by influencing Iraq to abrogate its commitments to Western security.

A New Look in Moscow's Middle Eastern Policy

The outcome of the Middle Eastern crises of the late 1950s stimulated a reappraisal of Soviet strategy. The Soviet Union had scored inroads into the domestic politics of selected countries, but their durability and utility were questionable. Syria's political upheavals and its temporary union with Egypt were setbacks to Soviet prestige, while the Iraqi coup offered new opportunities. The Soviet intrusion into the Middle East was welcomed by some and openly encouraged by others, but the Western-sponsored alliance and its own lack of adequate military capacity for effective intervention significantly limited the level of the influence Moscow could exert. The activist policy had not advanced the ultimate Soviet aims of assuring access through the Turkish and Iranian corridors into the Middle East or of gaining general recognition of its authority in regional matters.

Besides these political difficulties, the union of Syria and Egypt in February 1958 had ideological implications that quickly pointed the direction for Soviet policy in the late 1950s and early 1960s. Nasser had been reluctant to accept union with Syria for a variety of domestic and foreign-policy reasons; but he finally yielded, although with the proviso that the experiment could only succeed if the local communist threat in Syria was eliminated. Accordingly, he resumed full-scale prosecution of communists—a trend that soon dominated Arab politics and raised serious obstacles to the advancement of broader Soviet aims.

Such a severe affront to the Soviet Union, as the leader of the communist world, resulted in criticism of earlier assumptions about the correct values and guidelines for advancing Soviet state interests with the Arabs. Moscow's immediate counter to Nasser's effective destruction of the Syrian communists' power base was to mount a "stop Nasserism" campaign. Iraq's General Kassem refused to accept Egyptian supremacy in the Arab world, thereby offering Moscow a natural fulcrum. To consolidate his junta regime, Kassem relied heavily on local communist support, which prompted Nasser to broaden his anticommunism to include the entire Pan-Arab movement. In March 1959 Iraqi communists were instrumental in helping Kassem suppress a Nasserist uprising in Mosul. Invigorated by their new official favor, local communists, against Soviet directives, attempted in July 1959 to seize power in Kirkuk. Kassem reacted forcefully against his former allies and eliminated the Iraqi Communist party as a political factor.[17] The Iraqi action marked the end of organized communist influence at the national level in the Arab world— with the exception of the Sudan—and denied the Soviet Union the further use of local Communist party organizations as instruments of its foreign policy.

This reversal accelerated the nascent policy reappraisal in the Kremlin. Even before Khrushchev's political demise, a new look in Soviet Middle Eastern policy had begun to emerge. Moscow had decided to adopt a more systematic diplomacy toward both neighbors and client states. In place of missile rattling and the sponsorship of local subversive activities against Turkey and Iran, Moscow now sought recognition for its friendship. Instead of actively engaging in Arab infighting, such as pitting Kassem against Nasser, the Kremlin sought to bind the "progressive" Arab governments into a loose regional entity capable of coordinated policy. After the Chinese challenge had been overcome, Moscow modified the ideological trappings formerly required to justify its patronage of noncommunist states. In theory, the shift of emphasis in these areas provided a sounder basis for Soviet policy.

The fundamental issue at stake was whether there was sufficient common interest, despite the supremacy of Nasserism over

Arab communism, between Cairo and Moscow to restore the primacy of Egypt in Soviet Middle Eastern policy and the priority of state interests in relations between the two countries. The Kremlin concluded that the gravest threat from Nasser was not his persecution of communists but his Pan-Arab ambitions. A tacit understanding emerged between 1961 and 1963 that provided the rough outlines of a modus vivendi. The Soviet Union downgraded even further the role of local Communist parties and consistently advocated their assimilation into the dominant Arab Socialist parties (meeting Nasser's terms for rapprochement), and agreed to support Egypt in roughly inverse proportion to Nasser's success in unifying the Arab world.[18] The breakup of the Arab Federation in 1961 and Ben Bella's subsequent demise were indications that Arab unity was not imminent. Finally, when Egypt, and to a lesser extent Syria, Iraq, and Algeria, introduced socialist domestic reforms, Moscow's confidence in Nasser was substantially restored. Indeed, during Khrushchev's May 1964 visit to Egypt he called her a socialist state.

The new look became more visible after Khrushchev's departure. In their first year of power, the new Soviet leaders invited an unprecedented number of foreign dignitaries to Moscow. No less than ten leading representatives of Afro-Asian states, including the heads of all the Asian CENTO states, were Soviet guests. Brezhnev or Kosygin responded by visiting Egypt four times between 1965 and 1968. Between 1968 and 1972, Kosygin also visited India four times, as well as Iran, Pakistan, and Afghanistan. In addition, there have been visits by numerous lower-ranking governmental delegations. Agreements were negotiated on a variety of topics: the suspension of polemics; scientific and technical cooperation; exchanges of students, tourists, and cultural groups; economic aid and improved trade conditions; and pledges of mutual respect and friendship. Collectively, these accords were designed to demonstrate Moscow's intention to establish broader contacts on all levels of official activity with its neighbors to the south.

This revised policy has produced steady and significant results.

Turkey has accepted a $210 million credit for industrial development in exchange for agricultural products. State visits by Soviet President Podgorny, Foreign Minister Gromyko, and Premier Kosygin, and reciprocal visits by their Turkish counterparts have reduced the former atmosphere of mutual suspicion.[19] Soviet support in the 1964 Cyprus crisis seems to have convinced Ankara that Moscow had legitimate interests in the Mediterranean and was prepared to choose sides in order to protect them. Moscow reminded Ankara that, as in Ataturk's time, the Soviet Union alone had provided Turkey with support when vital interests were endangered.[20] In return, Ankara has adopted a nonprovocative policy toward the U.S.S.R., as demonstrated by its present interpretation of the Montreux Convention governing passage of the Straits. At the same time, Ankara renegotiated its treaty commitments with the United States, resulting in sharp restrictions on the freedom of American forces in Turkey and seriously straining relations between the two allies. Later, in response to Soviet complaints,[21] Ankara directed the suspension of all U.S. intelligence-collection flights launched from Turkish bases, reflecting Ankara's determination to control strictly its commitments to the West.

This is probably as near to formal neutrality as Moscow can expect Turkey to move, in light of Ankara's continuing preference for Western aid and protection. (The $210 million Soviet credit extended over fifteen years compares poorly with the approximately $350 million annual public and private investment in Turkey by the West; the United States alone has provided a total of $2 billion in economic aid.) Moscow's drive for improved relations has nonetheless significantly counteracted what was thought to be a profound Turkish animosity in a remarkably short time.

In Iran, Moscow curtailed the subversive activities of the local Communist party and extended impressive commercial aid to demonstrate the sincerity of its desire for improved relations. Teheran reciprocated by announcing in 1962 that it would not allow nuclear missiles on its soil. From this point, the reconciliation has steadily moved forward. By 1965 the Shah had visited all Warsaw Pact countries, and communist markets soon became important outlets for Iranian trade. In that same year the Soviet Union extended a $290 million loan for economic assistance, which represented 44 percent of total Soviet aid to noncommunist countries in 1965. In 1966 Moscow recognized Iranian dissatisfaction with American military-aid policies and granted a $100 million loan for the purchase of Soviet equipment. The loan was to be repaid in Iranian natural gas over a twelve-year period.[22] In early 1970 the Iranian Gas Trunk Line (1,300 kilometers long with a capacity of 10 trillion cubic meters per year) began delivering natural gas to the U.S.S.R. The line cost nearly $700 million, and was built with pipe from a $230 million Soviet-donated steel mill at Isfahan.[23] This is the largest single transaction between the two countries. It has enabled the U.S.S.R. to import $66 million of relatively cheap Iranian gas annually, while exporting Soviet gas to Western Europe for hard currency or producer goods. Iran's trade with the Soviet Union represents only about one-eighth of its total volume, but the nature of its prime export commodity—natural gas—is a powerful incentive to preserve friendly political relations. Indeed, Soviet-Iranian ties have become stronger than at any other time in recent history.[24]

The warming of Moscow's relations with Turkey and Iran has relieved the sense of a threat from the north in both countries. Their former priority on close adherence to collective security arrangements has received progressively less attention, allowing each to concentrate on other regional problems—namely, Greece and the Persian Gulf for Turkey and Iran, respectively. The accommodation, however, has specific limits. Both countries realize that they are increasingly vulnerable to Soviet military pressure: Turkey can now be attacked by Soviet missiles from every quarter, and Iran is increasingly exposed to Soviet warships in the Persian Gulf. Furthermore, both countries are aware of the dangers inherent in excessive dependence upon a great power, and both are studiously avoiding commitments that would eventually trap them in political positions similar to that of Finland or

Afghanistan.[25] Moreover, both are growing stronger politically and economically, and this, too, makes Soviet encroachments increasingly difficult.

Soviet access into the Middle East was placed on a more durable basis by the Turkish and Iranian policies of accommodation. The immediate result was a systematic naval buildup in the Mediterranean, accompanied by new, large-scale economic and military aid to Syria, Algeria, and Egypt. During his 1966 visit to Cairo, Premier Kosygin attempted to coordinate Soviet efforts and Arab needs still further by advancing concrete proposals to erect a more substantial basis for Soviet commitments. He called on the Arabs to remedy their internal weaknesses, suspend their debilitating infighting, and coordinate common actions for the isolation of Israel and curtailment of "imperialist" influence. While arguing that time favored the Arabs, Kosygin advised against rash action that would endanger internal improvements and afford opportunities for "imperialist" manipulations.[26]

The first and only fruit of Kosygin's bidding was a rough resolution of the differences between Syria and Egypt on their foreign-policy priorities. They agreed on 4 November 1966 to restore diplomatic relations, severed since 1961, and concluded a mutual defense pact. The latter accord was the factor that was to precipitate the 1967 confrontation with Israel.

The Consistency of Russian and Soviet Diplomacy

In this review of Russian and Soviet Middle Eastern policy, several consistent policy objectives have appeared. Tsarist Russia's aims in the Mediterranean and Middle East stemmed largely from classical sphere-of-influence motives. In the more contemporary sense, Moscow viewed the region as an arena of active influence competition and sought assured access to it mainly because other great powers enjoyed this privilege. During the last fifty years of Tsardom, Great Britain gradually assumed the status of Russia's arch antagonist, mainly because of Britain's successful efforts to deny Russia access to this and other regions of great-power competition. Saint Petersburg began to see its stature as a global power in terms of the credibility of its challenge to England's containment policy. Only a quirk of history forced the two powers—the only states at the time that confronted each other in Europe, the Middle East, South Asia, and the Far East— into alliance during World War I.

During the first 35 years of Soviet history, Moscow had little or no interest in the Arab world. When it did devote some attention to that area in 1954–55, it was for the minimal aim of countering and reducing Western influence, rather than for establishing a credible power base for itself. Soviet arms were provided to give the Arabs new options, not to intensify the regional conflict. Exacerbation of Arab-Israeli hostilities would have been counterproductive at a time when Moscow had no military presence to act as a deterrent or to defend its interests and those of its client. Indeed, Moscow made efforts to convince the West of its moderation and limited goals.[27] But, inevitably, Soviet arms were used in a variety of regional conflicts, and this suggested that duplicity was intentional and a permanent characteristic of Soviet diplomacy. More accurately, it revealed the aspects of gullibility, naiveté, and irresponsibility that marked Soviet policy in the mid-1950s.

By the early 1960s Moscow's minimal aims of eroding Western influence had largely been achieved, though this was probably due less to Soviet design than to Western default. The emerging vacuum and the potential opportunities for successful influence competition were prime motives in compelling the reappraisal of Soviet Middle Eastern policy during this period.

The major result of this reassessment was the decision to seek for the first time a viable basis for positive Soviet influence. The vehicle was to be the formation of a bloc of progressive Arab states closely associated with the Socialist Commonwealth. Soviet aims had progressed beyond the use of arms, economic aid, and neutralist sentiments to reduce Western interests. But the key problem with the upgraded goals was how to insure the reliability of the bonds between the progressive Arabs and Moscow. Movement by both sides toward firmer common ground would be required. On its part, Moscow accepted the necessity of these new commitments. Between 1966 and 1967 it moved much closer to the bellicose and extreme Syrian regime and even extended support to the Palestinians. Finally, it abandoned its earlier presumption that the dispute with Israel unnecessarily distracted Arab attention from the higher-priority aim of countering imperialism. The Soviet Union adopted a new approach, hoping that deliberate escalation in Arab-Israeli tensions would proportionally increase the Arabs' psychological, military, and political dependence on Moscow. The fabricated Soviet reports of Israeli troop deployments along the Syrian border in April 1967 were a deliberate incremental use of tension to promote these aims.

There is no evidence that Moscow wanted armed conflict or the defeat of its sponsored states. All three key Soviet leaders (Brezhnev, Kosygin, and Podgorny) were on vacation at the time, and the frantic Soviet efforts to gain a cease-fire indicate that Moscow was completely surprised. (Indeed, there is no evidence that the Soviets directly sanctioned any of the subsequent outbreaks of Arab-Israeli hostilities.) The Soviets had probably calculated that U.S. restraints on Israel and their own influence in Cairo would prevent a serious deterioration. In fact, they must have realized that a sharp conflict would be counterproductive, for the modest size of the Soviet military buildup and the nonexistence of Soviet protection would then be exposed. Under such circumstances, what value would close ties with the Socialist Commonwealth have for the Arabs?

In the decade 1955–1964, the Soviets pursued aims in the Middle East that were roughly similar to those of Tsarist Russia: they sought regional access because they felt that this was due a great power (as manifested by the presence of its rivals) and they then sought to use this arena to expand the overall scope of their challenge to their adversaries. It was a period of maturation, and of the identification of competing, and sometimes conflicting, interests. In the period 1965–1967, the Soviets elevated their sights to a goal Saint Petersburg had not sought: the establishment of a viable base for durable political influence in the Middle East.

However, they found their advances countered by the lack of such comprehensive linkages as existed between Eastern Europe and the Soviet Union. The Arabs were either too backward or too bourgeois to accept Soviet socialism, and the Soviet army could not impose the Kremlin's writ. Moscow's overextension during the June War introduced new limitations to these unattained aims. Regardless of their value, Moscow was not prepared to risk a great-power confrontation for their achievement. The shock of this revelation of an upper limit on Soviet commitments was ameliorated, however, by the understanding that the continuing consolidation of Moscow's minimum objectives could hereafter proceed with less danger of great-power interference, for the United States now also viewed the consolidation of great-power influence as essential for durable regional stability.

With this brief description, several preliminary and iconoclastic assumptions about the Soviet entry into the Middle East can be offered as the premises upon which the reconstruction of the Canal War can be erected. First, it is not true that the June War was critical for Soviet penetration of the Middle East, although it certainly helped. Second, it is also not accurate to assert that Soviet military aid itself perpetuated the Canal War, although it has obviously exacerbated tensions. Third, it is also a misperception to allege that the subsequent commitment of Soviet combat forces for the defense of a nonsocialist state was the most audacious and malign Soviet act since the false report about Israeli troop mobilization along the Syrian border in 1967 and without parallel since the attack on South Korea and the Cuban missile gambit, although it did escalate the arms race. Fourth, it is far too simplistic to charge that without Soviet influence and meddling the Arabs and the Israelis would have made peace long ago—for the Canal War is a symptom and a consequence of much deeper cultural antagonisms. Finally, it is pointless to claim that, without Soviet arms deliveries, regional limitations could have been established. The fact is that with or without great-power military aid, neither sponsored state has been able or can now inflict a mortal wound on the other. Arms diplomacy has been used by both great powers from the outset mainly for political purposes, and their competition has stemmed from and been perpetuated by misperceptions of military strength—Israel and the United States measure the balance in aggregate numbers of Arab weapons systems and Egypt and the Soviet Union estimate the threat in terms of Israel's infrastructure, technological proficiency, and close reliance on the United States.[28] Moscow's immediate goal after the June War was to restore its credibility through increased arms deliveries to the defeated Arabs.

3

The June War and Initial Efforts to Secure an Accord: June 1967–October 1968

John C. Campbell has observed that "The Six-Day War was remarkable in the manner of its origin, the rapidity of its operations, and the one-sidedness of its outcome." [1] The war was one of the most decisive military operations in modern history; yet the victors failed to secure the fruits of their triumph. There are few parallels in history where hostilities were so conclusively settled militarily and yet remained politically so indecisive. For five years after the initial cease-fire, the Egyptians and Israelis conducted a prolongation of the June War along the Suez Canal. Indeed, the extension took on many characteristics distinguishing it from the original conflagration: it became largely an Egyptian-Israeli war, with the other Arab states making less significant military contributions; both sides were far more heavily armed; and the Soviet Union became actively engaged in the defense of Egypt.

The circumstances surrounding the collapse of the Arab armed forces during the June War are well known. After the Arab defeats in 1948 and 1956, Soviet succor had appeared to be the only means for restitution. Soviet policy during this period was to furnish sufficient military aid for the Arabs to gain and maintain a posture of parity with Israel. The reasoning was that only from a position of military equality could Israel be deterred or stalemated and then forced through political pressure to negotiate a settlement favorable to the Arabs. Soviet estimations that the Arabs had reached that level of military proficiency led to the mounting political pressures that forced the Israeli attack. Nevertheless, the June War, in which Soviet arms were the most heavily committed, proved the most disastrous of the three conflicts for the Arab nations. Egypt alone lost nearly two-thirds of its 500 combat aircraft in the first three hours. Two Egyptian armored divisions, five tank brigades, and as many as twelve armored artillery regiments were routed in sixty hours, losing 800 of their 1,000 deployed tanks and leaving the Expeditionary Force in Yemen as the only organized fighting unit at Egypt's disposal.

The June War and the Backdrop for Political Tensions

Soviet-Arab reasoning behind the reopening of their diplomatic offensive in early 1967 was apparently based on the thesis that the United States was so heavily involved in Southeast Asia that it could not devote concentrated attention to a Middle Eastern crisis and would not participate actively in an anti-Arab coalition. France, Israel's chief arms source at that time, had already provided indications that it was interested in cultivating Arab favor by a more balanced Middle Eastern policy. If forced to take sides, both France and Britain might very well choose to protect their broader interests among the Arabs rather than their sentimental ties with Israel, thus splitting the Western position. If successful, this maneuver could reverse the 1956 situation, in which the United States had sided against Britain and France, who had supported Israel, and had actively sponsored Arab demands for restitution. Now there was a possibility of the two Western powers withholding support for Israel and forcing the United States into the position of being Israel's sole source of external assistance. Moreover, even if these calculations failed, it was assumed that the Soviet naval presence in the Mediterranean—numbering as high as 45 vessels—would effectively deter U.S. overreaction, thus providing a degree of assurance that the increased tensions would not deteriorate into a major conflict.

With this degree of support from the Soviets, Nasser surmised that he had a sufficient margin of safety to promote a military confrontation with Israel as an instrument for securing a favorable political settlement. His prestige could not withstand further recriminations from the Syrians for his failure to honor Cairo's mutual defense pact with Damascus while the latter was facing increasing Israeli reprisals for its advocacy of terrorist raids. Also, a successful political/military confrontation with Israel might counter the damage done to Nasser's image by his disastrous Yemen undertaking. (After five years and enormous expenditures, Egypt's largest expeditionary campaign in over 150 years had failed to defeat the Saudi-supported Royalist tribesmen.) Finally, Nasser saw the numerical superiority of the combined Arab forces as an effective deterrent against Israeli aggression. To be credible, however, the deterrent would require full Jordanian participation. When King Hussein signed a mutual defense pact with Nasser in May, the Arab position was consolidated.

With these considerations in mind, the Soviets warned the Syrians in April of an alleged impending Israeli attack.[2] These allegations struck responsive notes in Damascus since nearly one-fourth of its MIG-21 inventory had just been shot down by the Israeli Air Force in a single aerial engagement. Syria's clamor for assistance was the catalyst for the Arabs' combined efforts against Israel, but the decisive turning points occurred in the Sinai. First, Egypt deployed the bulk of its armed forces outside Yemen to the Israeli border. Since the 1964 Arab summit conference on possible military responses to counter the Israeli diversion of the Jordan River waters, Cairo had resisted Syrian demands that it commit its regular forces against Israel; it could not support two fronts and had instead agreed to irregular military activities by the fedayeen. The Egyptian buildup in the Sinai in early May, therefore, was a significant departure from its previously known policy position.[3]

The second important development was the demand for and withdrawal of the United Nations peacekeeping force along the Egyptian-Israeli border. Such precipitous action eliminated any restraints against either side and also blunted Syrian charges that Nasser was hiding behind a U.N. screen. This was the first time in over a decade that the Egyptian and Israeli armies faced each other in anger, each convinced of its military and moral superiority, yet neither genuinely expecting an outbreak of hostilities. Therefore, the crucial juncture was Nasser's move on 22 May to close the Straits of Tiran and Washington's failure to respond decisively. A blockade of international waters is regarded by conventional standards of international law as an act of belligerency, and Israel declared it an act of war against its vital national interests. As the price for Israeli withdrawal from Sinai and Gaza in February 1957, President Eisenhower and Secretary of State Dulles had provided firm assurances that the United States would regard any interference in the Straits as a violation of international law and would support Israeli interests in such an eventuality. In May 1967, however, President Johnson told Foreign Minister Eban that the United States was prepared only to sponsor an international conference of maritime powers to discuss joint action. When Eban replied that Israel could not wait weeks or months for international support, however favorable it might be, Johnson responded that the United States could not undertake unilateral action at that time unless the Soviets intervened.

Thus, by the end of May the Moscow-Cairo initiative had proven highly satisfactory. The Arabs were in the strongest political bargaining position against Israel that they had ever enjoyed. They had established a combined military command, eliminated the United Nations as a deterrent, splintered Western opposition, and gained a vital bargaining counter in the hoped-for political negotiations by securing control of the Straits. Finally, U.S. inaction and seeming indifference was interpreted by the Arabs as an indication that they would be allowed to deal with Israel without external interference. At the beginning of June, it appeared as though the Soviet-Arab strategy would succeed in altering the decade-long status quo in the Arabs' favor.

The unknown factor in the equation remained Israel's reactions and the proficiency of its armed forces. Former Defense Minister Shamseddin Badran, in testimony during his trial for plotting against Nasser in August 1967, stated that Nasser had been warned by the Americans on 3 June of the Israeli attack that would come two days later. The High Command was split over the decision to strike first or await an Israeli attack. Former Deputy Supreme Commander Abd-al-Hakim Amer and President

Nasser decided the issue in favor of restraint on the grounds of the adverse international reaction that would follow Arab aggression and the possibility of U.S. intervention with the Sixth Fleet.

Indeed, there was adequate warning. The former commander of the air forces in the Sinai, Major General Abd-al-Hamid Daghidy, stated in a letter to the Beirut magazine *Al Hawadess* on 29 June 1973 that four separate warnings of an impending attack were flashed to the Egyptian forces on 4–5 June: one from President Nasser two days before; one from an intelligence officer in El Arish; an army report of preliminary skirmishes; and a radar report of Israeli aircraft launchings. Allegedly, none of these reports reached Daghidy. Enciphering codes were being changed on the morning of the attack. According to Daghidy, he was the only senior officer at his post when the Israelis struck.

From the Soviet perspective, the amount of warning and the subsequent deliberation at the national level on the question of the impending Israeli attack merely underscored the lack of military proficiency of, and the dereliction of duty by, many senior Egyptian officers. Former Air Force Commander Mohammed Sidky Mahmoud had participated in these deliberations and had then conducted an inspection of the forward air bases; yet he apparently did not direct any precautionary measures in either aircraft dispersals or routine flying operations. Thus, Soviet embarrassment over the debacle that their plans had created posed more of a problem for them than the mere loss of equipment and arms. The Soviets had not accurately assessed the military competence of the officers with whom they had had the most frequent contact. Subsequent charges in *Pravda* that the entire Egyptian officer corps was corrupted by bourgeois elements, and consequent demands for thorough purges, reflected Moscow's serious disenchantment with the Arab hierarchy and the threat it had posed to Soviet prestige.

The Soviets correctly estimated that direct involvement in the hostilities under these circumstances could only compound the disaster. Yet they knew that their failure to rescue their Arab clients during this hour of direst need would create bitter resentments which could seriously erode their stature as a great power. They accurately concluded that such a blow to their world standing could be avoided only by escalating their military assistance to create a situation in which the Arabs could first successfully deter Israel and then gain a sufficient degree of military parity to force a favorable settlement. Yet the military aspect was only a single factor, and probably the most facile one, in the complex problem of a political settlement. Indeed, the nonmilitary aspects of the dispute were probably as profound, deep-seated, and diverse as in any contemporary international crisis, and both great powers took prompt but limited action to initiate a political accord.

When hostilities erupted on 5 June 1967, each great power immediately notified the other of its intention not to intervene and to seek an early termination of the conflict. The Soviet Union sponsored a draft resolution before the United Nations Security Council demanding Israeli acceptance of a cease-fire and the withdrawal of its armed forces to the 5 June lines. On 7 June, however, Moscow dropped its insistence on the withdrawal clause and supported an American-sponsored draft that simply called for an immediate cease-fire. Israel ignored the joint great-power demand and turned its forces against Syria. On 9 June Moscow convened a hasty summit conference of socialist leaders which issued a communiqué threatening decisive action if Israel did not immediately accept the proposed cease-fire. Premier Kosygin then notified President Johnson of the Warsaw Pact's decision to take firm action if necessary. President Johnson countered by ordering the Sixth Fleet closer to the Syrian coast to intervene if necessary on Israel's behalf, but he apparently also warned Israel of the Soviet threat. (General Bar Lev later confirmed that American pressure had been the determining factor in halting Israeli forces before they could attack Damascus.)[4] Thus, the first indications of the nature and scope of Soviet interest in the crisis and its settlement were revealed even during the war, namely that the vital centers and existing regimes of its sponsored states must remain immune from Israeli attack. This remained the fundamental Soviet position throughout the Canal War.

The American position had been made clear by the pledge of four presidents to insure both the continuing existence and the territorial boundaries of the state of Israel, and to work toward preserving all existing Middle Eastern borders.[5] The United States was prepared to sponsor the peaceful adjustment of frontiers but would use its influence to restrain states from forcefully altering existing lines. The United States had also repeatedly attempted to contain the potential level of conflict by securing international agreement on arms supplies. While the United States placed the highest priority on Israel's survival, it has also traditionally tended to view regional stability in the broad context of a territorial status quo and arms limitations.

Initial Positions and Diplomatic Maneuvers
When the Security Council was convened on 5 June, the Israeli representative referred to the lessons of 1956–1957 and stated the objectives that his country was prepared to pursue:

To permit the momentum gained by Israel's Army, in cutting through the formidable Egyptian buildup, to take its full course;

To prevent the adoption of any resolution calling for the withdrawal of forces prior to the establishment of peace, meaning that the Israeli forces would remain on the cease-fire lines until replaced by agreed boundaries;

To oppose any resurrection of the collapsed armistice regime and insist on the erection of a new structure of complete and lasting peace;

To cooperate closely with the United States to avoid the reactivation of that fatal Soviet-American vice whose closing jaws cracked in 1956 the position of America's friends and enabled its opponents to regroup and to recuperate their strength.[6]

The Arab states, conversely, sought immediate and total withdrawal of Israeli forces and a return to the pre-June lines, condemnation of Israel as an aggressor, and full compensation to the Arab states for all war damages.

The positions of both great powers were amplified at the Glassboro, New Jersey, summit conference in late June and at the U.N. General Assembly Emergency Special Session, which opened on 19 June. When it became apparent that the U.N. Security Council would not adopt several Soviet-sponsored resolutions condemning Israeli aggression, the U.S.S.R. demanded, on 13 June, the convocation of this Special Session in order to "liquidate the consequences of Israeli aggression." Kosygin issued a harsh attack, comparing Israeli "atrocities" to the heinous crimes committed by Hitler and charging that Israel had been aided in these crimes by certain imperialist circles. Kosygin demanded that the General Assembly condemn Israel for aggression and insist upon both troop withdrawals from occupied territory and the payment of war reparations. If the Assembly failed, he warned, other aggressors would follow the Israeli example.

Abba Eban replied by charging the Soviet Union with a major share of responsibility for the conflict. Moscow's policy had spread war fever among the Arabs, escalated the arms race, and blocked efforts to resolve the crisis. He condemned the U.S.S.R. for falsely alleging that Israel was massing troops along the Syrian border and for twice refusing to endorse a reciprocal inspection by the United Nations Observer Team of the Syrian-Israeli frontier. (Prime Minister Levi Eshkol had actually invited the Soviet ambassador to make a personal inspection; he declined.) Eban then called for direct talks with the Arabs.[7] When the Special Session adjourned on 21 July, it was apparent from two separate draft resolutions submitted by the Soviets that they were prepared to ask the Arabs to extend recognition to Israel as the price for withdrawal. The Soviet ambassador to the United Nations, Jacob Malik, attended an urgent summit meeting on 14–15 July of Egypt, Iraq, Syria, Algeria, and the Sudan to present the Soviet proposal. Algeria and Syria demanded unconditional withdrawal and refused to consider the question of recognition while Israel occupied territory. (The Algerian ambassador to the United Nations maintained this position during a reportedly stormy session with Soviet Foreign Minister Gromyko on 20 July, and Presi-

dent Houari Boumédienne proved the most intransigent of the
Arab leaders during his state visit to Moscow.)

When stymied by Arab intransigence, Soviet diplomacy became noticeably more frantic. Apparently, Moscow had concluded that the restoration of its prestige throughout the Middle
East depended in large part on its ability to aid the Arabs in recovering politically from their military defeat. With the Glassboro Summit Conference already scheduled, the Soviets wanted
some spectacular demonstration of great-power solidarity that
would lend credence to their claim of being a regional power and,
at the same time, convince the Arabs of their willingness and
ability to deal firmly with the United States at Israel's expense.
Soviet Ambassador Anatoly Dobrynin met with Secretary of State
Dean Rusk to break the deadlock at the Special Session. He
agreed to drop the condemnation of Israel and demands for compensation, but insisted upon Israeli withdrawal. Because of radical Arab resistance, he could offer in return only a noncommital
understanding about the cessation of hostilities. These terms were
unacceptable but sufficiently attractive to warrant further bargaining with Soviet Foreign Minister Andrei Gromyko in New
York.

The American position during the Special Session was that the
Arabs must provide assurance for Israeli security and concrete
evidence of their desire to live at peace with Israel. Without at
least acceptance of Israel's right to exist, which the Soviets had
never questioned, the United States could not recommend the
withdrawal of Israeli forces to less advantageous borders.[8] The
general position of the United States was sufficiently close to that
of the Soviet Union that the two powers could sponsor a joint
resolution calling for recognition in exchange for withdrawal.
The Soviet-American draft resolution read:

The General Assembly . . .

1. Declares that peace and final solutions of this problem can
be achieved within the framework of the Charter of the United
Nations.

2. Affirms the principles under the Charter of:
A. Withdrawal without delay by the parties to the conflict of their forces from territories occupied by them, in keeping with the inadmissibility of conquest of territory by war.
B. Acknowledgment without delay, by all member states of the United Nations in the area, that each enjoys the right to maintain an independent national state of its own and to live in peace and security; and renunciation of all claims and acts inconsistent therewith.
3. Requests the Security Council to continue examining the situation in the Middle East with a sense of urgency, working directly with the parties and utilizing a United Nations presence to achieve an appropriate and just solution of all aspects of the problem, in particular bringing to an end the long-deferred problem of the refugees and guaranteeing freedom of transit through international waterways.[9]

To Israel's profound relief, the draft resolution was not submitted because of a lack of endorsement by all Arab states.

The historic Glassboro summit conference between Johnson and Kosygin also proved barren on substantive issues. This was the first meeting between the leaders and consisted of two long sessions on 23 and 25 June 1967. While major outstanding differences between the two countries were discussed, the main focus was on the Middle Eastern crisis. Johnson commented later to a press conference on the meeting's results, "We reached no new agreements [about peace], but I think we understood each other better." Procedurally, it was agreed "to keep in good communication in the future." He also cited points of earlier accord that were apparently reaffirmed at Glassboro: the need for a prompt and durable cease-fire, the right of every state to live in peace, and the withdrawal of troops under proper circumstances.[10]

By the time the cease-fire was implemented and the negotiations began to define the outline of an armistice or settlement, the rough parameters of the two great powers' respective interests were already evident. The common ground established for the purpose of jointly sponsoring the U.N. Security Council's request for a cease-fire was gradually expanded to include the terms for a more durable armistice. The initial efforts at settlement under U.N. auspices proved futile, but the Soviets did succeed in convincing Nasser that the joint Soviet-American proposal should be presented to the meeting of Arab foreign ministers on 1–4 August and at the larger Arab summit meeting on 29 August in Khartoum.

The Khartoum Conference was one of the most important Arab gatherings in recent years. Its purpose was to chart a common course for the next phase of the confrontation with Israel, and it deliberated on two basic options: a political settlement along the broad lines of the Soviet-American proposal or shared responsibility for the continued struggle. The majority of the delegates placed little credence in the immediate utility of the joint proposal, regarding it as a statement of general intent and a false front to mask the inability of either power to counteract Israel's aggression or to act decisively to end the fighting. It was generally concluded that neither power had sufficient authority to compel Israeli acceptance of the terms of the proposal and that, therefore, the Arabs would have to rely on their combined efforts to restore the balance. Accordingly, the Conference viewed a political settlement only as an ultimate goal and called for "no peace, no recognition, and no negotiations" until the Arab states had returned to a "position of strength"—the slogan of the more defiant Arab states. The Conference also adopted a resolution establishing a fund to provide Egypt and Jordan $378 million quarterly ($154 million from Kuwait, $140 million from Saudi Arabia, and $84 million from Libya) as aid for the restitution of their armed forces and as compensation for the loss of revenues from the Suez Canal and the West Bank. (Syria had boycotted the Conference and therefore was not entitled to compensation for its loss of the Golan Heights.) To provide these funds, the Conference agreed that each individual country could use its own discretion in lifting the oil embargo against Western states that had been imposed because of Egyptian charges of "imperialist" collusion with Israel during the June War.[11]

The Conference was by no means unanimous. Syria had refused to participate, and, just five days before it opened, Tunisian

President Habib Bourguiba had publicly urged the Arab states to abandon their "dead-end policy of belligerency." He explained his stand by noting that "the State of Israel has been recognized by both the United States and the Soviet Union . . . its existence is challenged only by Arab countries. . . . In these circumstances, it is useless to continue ignoring reality and to claim to wipe Israel off the map. In so doing, one drives himself into near-total isolation." [12] Despite the lack of consensus, the intransigent "no concessions" position was approved by the Conference and governed the policies of most Arab states for the next three years.

When the issue was returned to the United Nations during the regular session of the General Assembly in September, Secretary-General U Thant rebuffed the Israeli insistence on direct dealings with the Arabs. He claimed that negotiations without third-party involvement were not feasible under the existing circumstances and called for a mandate to appoint a U.N. mediator to assist in a settlement. Israeli Foreign Minister Abba Eban replied that Israel would not return to the political and juridical anarchy or to the strategic vulnerability from which it had emerged. He noted that, apart from the cease-fire agreement, Israel had no valid contractual agreements with its neighbors, and he called for the creation of a durable edifice of peace, based on treaties directly negotiated among the contracting parties.[13]

Israeli Prime Minister Levi Eshkol increased the pressure for direct negotiations when he told the Knesset that Israel planned to consolidate its position in the occupied areas until the negotiation of a permanent peace with the Arabs:

The area that was under Jordanian occupation [the West Bank] and the Gaza region, which the Egyptians ruled, were held by them not by right but by force, as the result of military aggression and occupation. This occupation was recognized, it is true, in the armistice agreement [of 1949], but these agreements have been nullified by military provocation and aggression on their part. Moreover, it was agreed between the parties in 1949 that the armistice lines had been determined only by military considerations and did not have the character of frontiers. . . . For these rea-

sons, there is ample justification . . . for Israel's attitude that the
aim should now be to determine agreed-upon and secure boundaries within the framework of peace treaties.[14]

He later expanded the Israeli goal to include directly negotiated
peace treaties that explicitly acknowledge Israel's right to exist
within mutually agreed borders, acceptance that Jerusalem will
never again be divided (East Jerusalem had been incorporated
into the Jewish sector in July), free passage through the Tiran
Straits and the Canal, and the establishment of various forms of
regional cooperation to include a solution to the problem of the
Palestinian refugees and a common market.

On the Arab side, some movement had been registered. In his
first interview after the war, President Nasser told Sir Dingle
Foot, a Labor member of the British Parliament, that he was prepared to start talks with Israel under U.N. chairmanship *before*
a withdrawal of Israeli forces from Sinai. He was also ready to
accept the end of the belligerency with Israel, but he stated that
there could be no final settlement as long as Israel occupied
Egyptian territory. Furthermore, he linked free passage through
the Canal with a solution to the refugee problem.[15] These points
were later amplified by an official Egyptian government spokesman, Mohammed H. el-Zayyat, who stated that Cairo had accepted Israel's right to exist since the signing of the Egyptian-
Israeli armistice in 1949, but added that this did not endorse recognition of Israel (raising the distinction, frequently cited since
then by Arab leaders, between acceptance of the de facto existence of a state and the establishment of diplomatic relations with
it). He also claimed that Egypt was prepared to accept Israel's
use of the Tiran Straits pending a verdict on its status by an international court, but that passage through the Canal required a
state of "normalcy" and the complete solution of the refugee
problem.[16]

In summing up the Arab position, Nasser told the Egyptian
National Assembly on 23 November that the Khartoum Conference's acceptance of the need for a political settlement, within the

framework of the "no concessions" policy until a position of strength had been achieved, had justified the risks that it imparted. He stated that this element of realism had already yielded important returns in terms of world opinion and U.N. support. (He was referring to the adoption the previous day of U.N. Security Council Resolution 242.) However, he complained that unless Egypt received more support from Washington it could achieve little else.[17] Nasser's association of great-power influence with further progress toward a political settlement accurately prophesied the inability of the local powers to reach an understanding on even the next step toward accord.

The Evolution of Resolution 242
When hostilities were again resumed on 21 October, with the sinking of the Israeli destroyer *Eilat* and the shelling three days later of the oil refinery at Port Suez, the U.N. Security Council adopted a resolution urgently calling upon both sides to observe the cease-fire. The possibility of resumed fighting was viewed with growing alarm, and the great powers again sought a proper framework for a joint diplomatic initiative. The permanent members of the Security Council were unable to reach agreement among themselves, however, and they urged the other ten members to try drafting an acceptable resolution. But they too were split, with Denmark and Canada insisting that the central aim must be to establish secure and recognized boundaries within the context of a durable peace settlement. The Third World representatives placed a higher priority on a combination of withdrawal of occupation forces and termination of hostilities. On 3 November the ten admitted their failure to reach agreement.

Moscow sent First Deputy Foreign Minister Kusnetsov to help break the deadlock. He reported to Secretary Rusk that the Arab states were now prepared to accept the Soviet-American formula that they had rejected in July. But the United States now felt that a more comprehensive effort was required to produce a durable settlement and launched its own initiative. As a start, wide-ranging discussions were held with Egyptian Foreign Minister Riad and King Hussein, who were in New York at the time. Hussein agreed to support an American formulation, but Riad maintained an ambiguous stand. While tentatively endorsing the U.S. proposal, he energetically prodded India into presenting a draft reflecting the position of the majority of the Security Council members—the Third World representatives.

On 7 November the American and Indian draft resolutions were submitted to the Council, and an impasse promptly developed. Latin American delegations, the Soviet Union, and Great Britain subsequently offered independent drafts to bridge the gaps between the initial entries. Britain accepted the U.S. draft almost verbatim, and introduced only minor changes to accommodate Israel. Israel had insisted that five guiding principles must be included in any workable resolution:

1. The central objective is the establishment of a just and a lasting peace between Israel and the Arab states.
2. The withdrawal of Israeli forces from the cease-fire lines will take place only after secure and recognized boundaries have been agreed upon within the terms of a peace treaty.
3. Peace must be the outcome of an agreement between the parties, achieved through free negotiations and not by outside imposition.
4. Freedom of navigation must be guaranteed through all the international waterways in the area without limitations or reservations.
5. The United Nations special representative should be authorized to render good offices to the parties and not to act as a mediator presenting them with proposals of his own.[18]

The British also included a clause concerning the "inadmissibility of the acquisition of territory by war" for the Arabs' sake, but to insure Israeli support they placed it in the preamble rather than in the operative paragraphs. To meet Israeli demands, Britain included in the operative section the proviso that the U.N. special representative was "to promote agreement between the parties concerned," and that the peace settlement "must be acceptable to them." The draft resolution, however, omitted the provision in the U.S. draft calling for an arms embargo, which had been included, surprisingly, in the Soviet draft in an almost identical wording.

Ambassador Goldberg presented the American interpretation of the operative provisions:

> To seek withdrawal without secure and recognized boundaries, for example, would be just as fruitless as to seek secure and recognized boundaries without withdrawal. Historically, there have never been secure and recognized boundaries in the area. . . . An agreement on that point is essential to a just and lasting peace, just as withdrawal is. Such boundaries cannot be determined by force. They cannot be imposed from the outside. For history shows that imposed boundaries are not secure and secure boundaries must be mutually worked out and recognized as part of the peacemaking process.[19]

The Arabs were still insisting upon a comprehensive and definitive statement on withdrawal. To gain acceptance of this point, Kusnetsov surprised the delegations by stressing that the Soviet Union recognized the right of every state in the Middle East to national and independent existence as inalienable. However, when it became apparent that the Council was lining up behind the British draft, Kusnetsov was forced to seek an adjournment. At the next session, he introduced a new draft resolution, a repeat of the July draft and a clear bid for time. During the interval, the Soviets pressed the United States for agreement on the phrase "withdrawal of Israel forces from *all the* territories." Premier Kosygin actually addressed personal notes to President Johnson asking for endorsement. When this wording was rejected, Kosygin offered "from the territories occupied," but was again turned down.

Finally, after nearly six weeks of involved debate, the Security Council unanimously adopted the British proposal that emphasized "the inadmissibility of the acquisition of territory by war and the need to work for a just and lasting peace in which every state in the area can live in security." The resolution called for a settlement based upon the following principles:

1. the withdrawal of Israeli armed forces from occupied territories;
2. the termination of all states of belligerency and the acknowledgment of the sovereignty, integrity, and right to peace and security of every state in the area;
3. freedom of navigation through international waterways in the area;
4. a just settlement of the refugee problem; and
5. guarantees of territorial integrity, including the establishment of demilitarized zones.

The resolution also called for the appointment of a special representative "to assist efforts to achieve a peaceful and accepted settlement."

Resolution 242 (reprinted below in appendix 3) is quite rightly regarded as an important sign of the degree of common interest that had emerged between the two great powers. They had agreed to endorse the basic demands of both smaller powers, that is, negotiations and withdrawal, and had authorized appointment of a mediator to help establish a timetable for their implementation. Thus, the resolution seemed to open the way for an eventual solution of the deadlock between "no negotiations without withdrawal" on the one side and "no withdrawal without negotiations" on the other. But the task of the U.N. special representative, Ambassador Gunnar V. Jarring of Sweden, proved to be far more complex and arduous than the great powers had at first envisioned.

The Jarring Mission

When Jarring first met with Abba Eban on 27 December, Eban underlined the limitations of the mediator's role and strongly stressed Israel's continued insistence on direct negotiations. Then he proposed several suggested agenda items for formal talks with Egypt: the negotiation of durable peace treaties; the determination of territorial boundaries, security arrangements, and practical methods for ensuring free navigation of the waterways; and the termination of economic boycotts. Israeli proposals for discussions with Jordan included the above items plus a solution to the refugee problem and access to sites of religious significance. Both Arab governments subsequently refused to accept these recommendations while Israeli forces occupied Arab territory.[20]

In view of these conflicting positions, Jarring sought to obtain from the parties assurances that they would implement the provisions of Resolution 242. On 19 February 1968 Israel replied that it would respond affirmatively to the provisions, but interjected the interpretation that they were principles recommended for inclusion in a peace settlement and that they were integrally linked and interdependent. Thus, from the Israeli standpoint, 242 was merely a framework for agreement, and the elaboration of this framework and its terms would require direct consultations with Arab governments. Subsequently, Eban expressed the view that Israel was prepared to engage in indirect talks through Jarring's "good offices" if there was reasonable assurance that they would lead to a later stage of direct negotiations and accord.

Egypt replied to Jarring's query that it was prepared to implement 242 in its entirety and to fulfill its obligations under it, but cited reservations about the qualified tone of Israel's response. Egypt was prepared to accept indirect talks if Israel would state unequivocally that it would implement 242.

Thus armed, Jarring prepared a report to the secretary-general which stated that: the parties involved accepted 242 and were prepared to devise arrangements under Jarring's auspices for the implementation of the resolution; they were willing to work toward a final settlement; and they would accept invitations to meet with Jarring in Nicosia to begin consultations.[21] However, when the draft report was submitted to Egyptian Foreign Minister Riad on 7 March, he expressed disappointment that Jarring had not been able to gain a satisfactory explanation from Israel of its qualifications to the implementation of the resolution. Indeed, he cited recent statements by Israeli leaders that Israel would never withdraw to the 1967 border as evidence of its expansionist objectives. Riad insisted that the terms of 242 required a complete withdrawal from Arab territory and that the United

Arab Republic could only participate in talks on the grounds that the other party intended to implement the resolution fully. On its part, Israel agreed to the draft report without reservations and declined to elaborate on its terms for fulfilling 242.

In light of Israel's ambivalent position, the Arabs sought to downgrade the level of the talks without refusing participation. Jordan amended Jarring's draft report to transfer the site of the talks from Nicosia to New York. Israel then objected that this change of venue would convey the impression that Jarring would only be holding meetings with the respective parties rather than mediating between them. Moreover, the idea of holding the talks in New York carried the implication that they would be conducted at the permanent-representative level and within the scope of normal U.N. activities, rather than at the national level for extraordinary purposes. Talks in a European city, therefore, would be acceptable. Egypt then submitted another addendum to the Jarring report, calling for a specific timetable for implementing the resolution. It had informally proposed several schedules to Jarring but asked in the addendum that he devise his own time sequence for implementation.

Jarring was thus confronted with a situation of only partial agreement on the first two aspects of his report and no endorsement of the last and most immediately relevant aspect, the means of initiating the talks and their format. In consultation with the secretary-general, it was agreed not to issue formal invitations to the respective parties or to make any further attempts to reach an understanding on a proposed site, but rather to begin informal discussions in New York at the ambassadorial level. The deadlock over the issues to be discussed, however, destined this approach to failure. Neither party had any incentive to commit its bargaining position further because of the seeming intransigence of its opponent.

Encouraged as much by the continuing relative lull in military activities as by the repeated claims by both sides of their intentions to seek a political settlement, Jarring gained permission to open a second round of direct talks on 16 August 1968 in the various capitals. This time he adopted a new technique of requesting written replies to formal questions submitted to the respective governments. It was hoped that written replies would eliminate the difficulties of interpretation that had arisen in prior verbal exchanges, reduce misunderstandings, and amplify the positions of the various parties. In this regard, Jarring was successful; he was able to clarify points of difference and to demonstrate the distance between the two sides, but he was unable to bring the parties nearer to agreement on any outstanding issue. Egypt and Israel merely expanded the statements of their earlier positions without promoting any modifications that could foster accommodation. The secretary-general was compelled to conclude that conditions did not exist for convening a productive series of talks between the belligerents, and Jarring returned to his post in Moscow.[22]

Further arguments were presented by both sides in addresses to the annual U.N. General Assembly. Foreign Minister Eban declared on 8 October Israel's readiness to accept 242 as the *basis* for the establishment of a just peace and for preliminary exchanges of views through Ambassador Jarring. He also outlined nine principles on which Israel was prepared to negotiate:

1. full commitment by all parties to the ending of the Middle Eastern conflict and to peaceful relations;
2. establishment of secure and recognized boundaries;
3. redeployment of troops to agreed-upon lines and a nonaggression pact;
4. freedom of movement in the Middle East, especially between Jordan and Israel;
5. a joint Egyptian-Israeli declaration that the Suez Canal and Tiran Straits are international waterways;
6. a conference of Israel, the Arab states, and other interested governments and agencies to develop a five-year plan to solve the refugee problem;
7. multilateral administration of holy places;
8. specific contractual engagements by the Arab states guaranteeing Israel's right to sovereignty and integrity; and

9. common work on some of the resources of the Middle East in order to build a community of states.[23]

Egyptian Foreign Minister Riad replied on 10 October by accusing Israel of demanding "the surrender of the Arab people to its will," of engaging in "racist colonialism" in its policies toward Arabs under its rule, and of unilaterally denouncing previous agreements with Arab states, leading to suspicion about the value of further negotiations. He rejected Eban's nine-point plan and demanded unequivocal Israeli acceptance of 242.[24] Riad later stated that Egypt was prepared to agree to Israeli use of the Canal and the Tiran Straits if Israel would carry out the provisions of 242, thus providing the first public indication that Cairo might accept reopening of the Canal in exchange for an Israeli withdrawal from the Sinai.

Military Developments

In reconstructing the military developments that paralleled these political events, the scale of the Arab military defeat and the required reequipment task should not be underestimated. The Soviet Union clearly recognized that its sponsored Arab states were on the verge of utter collapse, and the promptness and efficiency of its resupply operation must be regarded as one of the most decisive great-power acts since World War II. Israeli sources claim that within several weeks over 200 crated tactical aircraft were airlifted to Arab capitals. Throughout the summer an average of two to three merchant ships per week arrived in Egyptian ports carrying replacement arms, and, by October, 80 percent of the Egyptian losses had been replaced.

The effectiveness of this operation was the principal reason why Israel was denied the political fruits of its military victory. Since the large-scale Soviet airlift operation began before the cease-fire, many Arab observers concluded that it had deterred Israel from pursuing its campaign further into the Arab heartlands. ("Without the Soviet arms which were received before the June defeat, Moshe Dayan would perhaps be living here in Cairo," Nasser later asserted.)[25] Moreover, the operation also provided tangible evidence that a military option was still open for the Arab governments, and thus provided a basis for the defiant, "no concessions" stand taken at Khartoum in September. General Dayan acknowledged that he expected the "telephone to ring" at any time during the summer of 1967, conveying the Arabs' surrender terms, but he only heard the alert alarms. The resolute Arab position at Khartoum convinced him that more energetic measures would be required to consolidate Israel's political gains. He then abandoned his policy of restraint and returned to a strategy of reprisals. On military grounds, this choice was difficult. Israel's borders had been shortened by one-third and were more defendable; but they also decreased the maneuvering area that had been provided by the former borders and thus increased the ease with which the Israeli reprisals could be deterred. The new borders, except for the Golan Heights, were as defendable for the Arabs as for the Israelis. The Canal was an effective antitank moat that denied the Israeli Defense Force (I.D.F.) the opportunity to engage and neutralize the Arab armed forces in the manner of the June blitzkrieg. To inflict the same amount of destruction as in 1967 would now require a general war of attrition. When the fighting resumed in August 1967, the I.D.F. was forced to expand its former, relatively inexpensive but effective, strategy of limited reprisals to a more costly program of heavier attacks.

The Arab aim in resuming the fighting was to restore national honor through regaining lost territory. Israeli aims were twofold: to force the Arabs, mainly the Egyptians, to respect the cease-fire, and to deny them any military leverage in a political settlement by breaking up plans and preparations to reconquer the lost territories. The first year of the renewed hostilities was marked by sporadic Egyptian artillery shellings across the Canal and occasional guerrilla raids, followed by heavy I.D.F. retaliation against military targets.

This minimal effort was restrained because Egypt needed time. Morale was low and the army was being purged, retrained, and reequipped under close Soviet supervision (the deputy supreme commander, Field Marshal Abd-al-Hakim Amer, and an estimated 500 other officers were dismissed).[26] Arms deliveries had proceeded far ahead of the broken army's absorption capabilities, and much of this new equipment was of later model than that lost in Sinai, requiring new skills and proficiencies. Yet demands for intensified military pressure were being made by other Arab countries with contingents on the "front line" and by the various Palestinian groups. While none of these units contributed much militarily to the Arab cause, Cairo could not ignore the belligerency of their demands.

As Egyptian shellings gradually intensified, the I.D.F. sought to minimize its force expenditures and maximize the impact of its reprisals by shifting, in September 1967, from military to economic targets. The port facilities and refineries at Suez were destroyed, and Ismailia and other Canal towns were evacuated under heavy bombardment (by October, 60 percent of the civilian population on the west bank had been evacuated). However, the attacks did not have the desired effect and in some instances were counterproductive. For example, in retaliation for the 21 October sinking of the destroyer *Eilat*, the I.D.F. attacked Egyptian missile-equipped motor boats in their home ports. Eight Soviet warships, which had been stationed in Port Said and Alexandria apparently until only several days before, returned on 27 October and thereafter maintained a constant vigil, thereby deterring the I.D.F. from further reprisals against these key facilities.[27]

A general standoff developed, with both sides consolidating their respective positions and seeking new options. In September 1968, though, the level of conflict on the Canal started to increase, reaching a climax in October. In a single night, a massive Egyptian artillery barrage killed 15 I.D.F. soldiers and demonstrated to Israel that the Arabs had amassed a greater superiority in men and equipment on the west bank of the Canal than the I.D.F. had estimated. Only two I.D.F. brigades of 10,000 men held the 110-mile east bank of the Canal and its land approaches. Their tactics were to rely on mobility to repel hostile forays and they had, therefore, constructed no effective cover against heavy shelling. The

Israelis responded on 1 November, not by a frontal assault but by a sweeping attack deep inside Egypt. A helicopter-borne commando raid at Nad Hamadi in Upper Egypt demonstrated to Cairo and Moscow that the reconstituted Egyptian armed forces were still not capable of defending important facilities in the country's interior.

The shock had the desired effect of contributing to civil disturbances, and the Egyptians relaxed their pressure on the Canal. The I.D.F. immediately dug into hardened bunkers and fortified the positions now known as the Bar Lev Line. As in the Battle of Britain, had the attackers maintained their pressure on the primary targets, the scales might have been tipped in their favor; that is, the defenders might have been forced to withdraw beyond artillery range, giving the Egyptians a moral victory. The fortifications could not have been completed as rapidly as they were under barrages on the scale of those in October; but when they were resumed in March 1969 the Line had been completed barely two weeks before.[28]

General Characteristics of the First Round
Thus ended the initial phase of the international efforts to promote a political settlement. Several observations can be made about the substance of these endeavors and the reasons for their failure. First, the great powers demonstrated a realistic sense of adjustment in supporting a document that embraced the principal grievances of both sides. Consistent with their common position taken during the Special Session of the General Assembly, they expanded their efforts to promote an acceptable settlement. Nonetheless, their common ground was shallow. While the United States appeared anxious to secure a political accord for its own value and as an instrument for reducing regional tensions, the Soviet Union was more skeptical about the prospects for purposeful negotiations in light of the existing military imbalance along the Canal. Accordingly, Moscow pursued a dual course: restoring Arab military parity while exploring the terms for eventual negotiations. Moscow was careful, however, to take pre-

cautions lest its multiple approach appear as sinister or cynical to the United States.

Second, the ambiguity of Resolution 242 was both its failing and its virtue. Incorporating withdrawal and other provisions for a peace treaty without specifying the format for negotiations or their timing allowed both sides to apply differing interpretations of both the substance and the relevance of the resolution. Israel regarded 242 as a statement of principles within the framework of which the parties might negotiate peace. Specifically, Israel considered that the withdrawal clause would apply only to an extent to be determined by a final settlement among the parties involved on secure and recognized borders. Egypt, conversely, viewed the resolution as a plan for settlement, requiring only mutual approval and a timetable for implementation. It interpreted the withdrawal clause to mean withdrawal from all Arab territory taken during the June War, and cited the preamble of the resolution, disavowing territorial acquisition through conquest, as evidence of the sponsor's intent.

At the same time, the statement of principles rather than provisions had the advantage of allowing all parties ample room for maneuver once favorable circumstances for negotiations arose. The framework of the negotiations and a final accord, therefore, imparted no prescribed constraints or limitations other than those imposed by the interested parties themselves. Thus, the Security Council members were not acting as outside powers attempting to impose terms for a settlement; rather, they were expressing a consensus on the principles that would most likely garner a durable peace.

These differing views on substantive matters were reflected in the attitudes of Egypt and Israel toward the Jarring mission and the utility of the United Nations, which in part impaired the effectiveness of the special representative. Israel saw the ambassador as a mere communicator and a conveyor of general ideas rather than official correspondence. He was certainly not to act as a mediator with a capacity to generate his own diplomatic initiatives. His task, according to the Israelis, was to bring the warring parties together, regardless of the immediate tactics required to achieve this end; the interjection of his own analyses, views, and recommendations would be regarded as an unwarranted interference and, like any other external influence, would be held as detrimental to the negotiating process. Jarring was aware that the effectiveness of his endeavors depended in large part on not offending Israeli sensitivity about U.N. involvement and, accordingly, exercised circumspection in defining the limits of his undertaking.

The Arabs, on the contrary, viewed 242 as an operational program and a great-power mandate to commence bargaining. They were therefore prepared to afford Jarring far broader latitude in fulfilling his charge. Furthermore, because of their reluctance to negotiate directly with Israel until the contents of a settlement became clear, the Arabs were anxious to let Jarring become as closely involved in the talks as possible. The Arabs saw him as more than a mere postal clerk and hoped that he would undertake a wider mandate on his own initiative. Indeed, in the last Egyptian addendum to his draft report, Jarring was encouraged to assert his role by actually formulating and submitting his own implementation plan. Finally, Moscow's dualist policy reinforced Arab confidence in the United Nation's ability to provide important services: the presence of their powerful sponsor in the Security Council led to self-assurance that the exertion of American influence in a manner detrimental to Arab interests could be counterbalanced or neutralized. As a result, the Arabs tended to invest more attention in the Jarring mission than did Israel.

Partly because of their greater expectations from Jarring, the Arabs demonstrated more flexibility in their suggested bargaining position than did Israel. It is true that Israel did modify its stand on direct negotiations to include preliminary indirect talks, but this was an expediency that did not alter its basic positions. Also, Israel did expand its proposed agenda to include economic and humanitarian issues as incentives for negotiations, but these did not weigh heavily in light of the stand taken on the key political obstacles. On the other hand, the Egyptians and Jordanians agreed to accept the principles of 242 as treaty provisions and to implement them fully. To have actually done so, however, would have been in direct violation of Khartoum Conference resolutions and would have exposed the involved Arab leaders to changes of "capitulation," such as were heard two years later when Nasser only accepted the U.S. cease-fire proposal and thereby precipitated the Jordanian Civil War.

Adjustments of this scale could not be suitably exploited by those seeking a settlement, however, because of the high value that both sides attached to military strength as a key to political bargaining power. Israel remained confident that its vast technological superiority at that time and its overall military proficiency, as demonstrated by heavy reprisals and humiliating raids, would eventually convince the Arabs of their perpetual military inferiority and the futility of holding out for favorable settlement terms.

The Arabs regarded this attitude as a manifestation of exaggerated confidence and arrogance resulting from a "capitulation complex." Determined not to surrender, the Arabs accepted the arduous, time-consuming task of gaining military parity. This undertaking was relatively more difficult in Egypt than in Jordan or Syria, mainly because of the scale of the defeat and the scope of the resulting purges. As a consequence of these developments, the officer corps remained demoralized, and the process of reorganization became protracted. The Soviet Union had kept its agreement to replace lost equipment, but the ability of the Egyptian forces to absorb new deliveries remained low. Not until October 1968 was Egypt able to mount even a limited artillery offensive, and this effort quickly collapsed when Israel countered with spectacular commando raids.

Thus, during the opening phase of the Jarring mission, Egypt was in a relatively prostrate strategic position that did not augur well for a favorable outcome in the proposed negotiations. While good intentions undoubtedly existed in both the Israeli and Egyptian governments, the military disparity provided little incentive for either side to alter its political bargaining position or its policies intended to support this position. The initial effort of the great powers and other interested parties to secure a settlement thus proved abortive because of the lack both of common ground on political issues among the belligerents and of sufficient military power by either side to induce a change in the opponent's position.

4
The Problem of Parity and the Two-Power Talks: October 1968–December 1969

The initial phase of the international endeavors to promote a political settlement in the Middle East collapsed in October 1968, in the wake of Egypt's abortive attempt to resurrect its military option with the resumption of heavy artillery barrages. The opening of the second phase six months later coincided with the unilateral Egyptian abrogation of the cease-fire and declaration of a war of attrition. During the interval between the two phases, Egypt redoubled its efforts to reorganize its armed forces in order to assure a higher degree of proficiency and credibility to reinforce its political options. At the same time, the United States was holding a presidential election and undergoing a change of government, and, during the transition period, little initiative could be expected either from the lame-duck administration or from the new arrivals.

The Soviet Initiative
The evolution of the Soviet position during this period can be traced most conveniently from Nasser's visit to Moscow in July 1968. The final communiqué revealed that the leaders had had a "frank exchange of opinions," which usually means, in Soviet diplomatic terms, that existing views have remained unchanged.[1] Mohammed Hassanein Heikal, who accompanied Nasser on the visit, stated that the reason for the unexpected two-day prolongation of the trip was the persisting differences. The Soviets did not want a "hot confrontation" with the United States in the Middle East and were skeptical about the outcome of a resumption of heavy fighting. According to Heikal, the Soviets attempted to induce a more moderate Arab stand, claiming that continued firm-

ness was only indulging in "daydreams." At the same time, the
Soviets granted little satisfaction to Nasser's comprehensive list
of requests, and apparently both sides were disappointed in the
results of the consultations.[2]

With the suspension of the Jarring enterprise and the lack of
progress during the fall session of the General Assembly, Moscow
decided to restart deliberations by its own formal initiative. It
tempered the new campaign with an important lead editorial in
Pravda on 3 December stating: "The Soviet Union is deeply convinced that, despite all difficulties, the Middle Eastern crisis can
and must be settled by political means. This is in the interest of
all nations. The U.S.S.R. . . . will not permit a new, dangerous
flareup in that area." Soviet Foreign Minister Gromyko then
paid a surprise visit to Cairo on 22–23 December and, according
to the semiofficial newspaper *Al Ahram,* conveyed an important
message addressed to President Nasser.[3] The subsequent joint
communiqué expressed total Soviet support for Egypt's just
struggle and applauded Cairo's "disposition to cooperate completely" with Jarring's undertaking.[4] The general tone implied
conciliation rather than hostility. On balance, it appears that
Gromyko had presented a draft of Moscow's first comprehensive
plan for a peace settlement.

In a formal note to the United States on 30 December, the
Soviet Union outlined its plan. According to a leading Beirut
newspaper that published the text "verbatim," the plan envisioned the full implementation of 242 according to a prescribed
timetable, beginning with formal confirmation by the belligerent
states that they intended to carry out the provisions of the resolution. This would have been followed with proclamations by all
belligerents that they were prepared to reach a peaceful settlement and by Israel that it was prepared to withdraw from the
occupied Arab territories before a fixed date. Negotiations or
"contacts" among the belligerents would then be used to reach
an agreement on secure and recognized borders, freedom of navigation in international waterways, a just solution of the refugee

problem, and the territorial integrity and political independence of each state. Following an initial, partial Israeli withdrawal, Egypt would begin to clear the Suez Canal. At a later date to be agreed upon, Israel would complete its withdrawal to the pre-June 1967 borders, and Arab military and political control would be reestablished over the occupied territories. At the same time, U.N. forces might return to the Sinai Peninsula and the situation of May 1967 might be restored. (On 6 July 1968 an Egyptian spokesman had stated Cairo's concurrence with this provision, which was viewed as a reversal of the position on the presence of U.N. forces on Arab territory that had been maintained since May 1967.) The Security Council would guarantee freedom of passage through the Tiran Straits and the Gulf of Aqaba. Agreed-upon borders would be guaranteed by the four big powers and might include demilitarized zones between Israel and its neighbors. Documents containing this agreement would be deposited with the United Nations on the day that Israel commenced the withdrawal of its troops.[5]

The United States replied on 15 January 1969 with a twelve-point counterproposal:

1. Cessation of Arab terrorism is of primary importance if peaceful solutions are to be found.

2. The U.S. government is of the opinion that Israel has accepted U.N. Security Council Resolution 242 and the United States recommends that the belligerents seek to clarify their interpretations of that resolution.

3. Israeli withdrawal from the occupied territories must be part of a general solution.

4. The 1949 armistice lines do not constitute definite political frontiers and can be modified by agreement; nor does Resolution 242 imply that "secure and recognized boundaries" must conform to the frontiers of pre-June 1967.

5. The resolution does not state that Israeli troops must be withdrawn from the "occupied territories" but from "the territories occupied during the conflict."

6. The U.S. government believes that there must be agreement on all aspects of the problem of carrying out 242 before any actual measure is taken to carry out the full resolution.
7. The U.S. government interprets the Soviet note to mean that the Israeli troops will be withdrawn before the agreements entered into by the Arab states become binding.
8. The U.S. government is prepared to discuss with the Soviet Union the problems of a settlement between Israel and the Arab states.
9. Peace can only be realized through an agreement between the parties concerned and cannot be imposed by the United States and the Soviet Union.
10. All precautions must be taken to insure free passage through the Tiran Straits, including, if necessary, the stationing of U.N. troops at Sharm el Sheikh.
11. The U.S. government can only with difficulty be convinced that a partial demilitarization of the Sinai will be sufficient to guarantee peace.
12. An agreement on the level of armaments and their limitation in the Middle East is essential to the establishment of peace.[6]

As diplomatic movement between the great powers became apparent, their sponsored states sought reassurance, and their reactions to the two sets of proposals were predictable. The Israeli ambassador to the United Nations, Yosef Tekoah, labelled the Soviet Plan a "Middle East Munich," while *Al Ahram* charged that the American response showed "absolute partiality" in favor of Israel.

Nasser then restated the hard line before the Egyptian National Assembly on 20 January: "We will never negotiate with an enemy that occupies our territory. The enemy will not withdraw unless we force him back militarily." He argued further that the Palestinians have the right to reject Resolution 242 since it is aimed at eliminating the consequences of the Israeli aggression, but not at solving the Palestinian problem—the solution to which cannot be a mere charitable gesture. On the same day, Nasser sent a congratulatory letter to President Nixon on the occasion of his inauguration in which he solicited a more balanced American position in the Middle East.[7]

The Two-Power Talks

Based on this exchange of notes, the Soviet Union agreed to the American suggestion that the individual points be further discussed through the medium of two-power talks. On 3 April 1969 the two powers began their historic deliberations on possible solutions for the Middle Eastern crisis. According to Secretary Rogers, the dialogue was opened on the assumption that both great powers had a direct responsibility for promoting a settlement and that a protraction of the conflict would serve the interests of no nation. Specifically, the purpose of the talks was "to determine whether we can achieve parallel views which would encourage the parties to work out a stable and equitable solution." [8] To broaden the perspective, Britain and France were brought into the discussions at appropriate intervals in meetings that eventually became regularized as four-big-power talks.

The limitations on the scope of the talks were readily acknowledged. Rogers opined that nations not directly involved could not make a durable peace for the peoples and governments engaged in the conflict. The great powers could provide a catalyst, they could stimulate and encourage the parties to talk, and they could help define a realistic framework for agreement. But an accord between the external powers could not be a substitute for an agreement among the parties themselves.

Secretary Rogers records that substantial progress was made during the first eight months of deliberations. Both sides rejected Israel's contention that the proper function of the great powers was merely to bring the parties together without suggesting any specific proposals. In fact, the great powers examined the entire spectrum of the controversy and did establish sufficient common ground to present specific proposals for individual portions of a comprehensive settlement, for example, an Egyptian-Israeli accord. Finally, enough forward movement was made for the great powers to consider the mechanics of Arab-Israeli negotiations and the implementation of each component of the settlement.[9] Implicit in Washington's acceptance of Moscow as coresponsible for a durable settlement was a realization that each power had important but not vital interests in the region and that the influence of each was limited largely to issues and did not extend to political structures. Opening the talks also inferred a mutual agreement that it was in the interest of both nations to seize the issue of the June War to demonstrate their credibility and responsibility in a perennially turbulent region. Most important, each power seemed convinced of its opponent's sincerity in promoting a negotiable settlement, and this allowed them both to increase cautiously their stakes in a political solution. Finally, the talks registered American acceptance of Soviet claims of military parity in the region and acknowledgment that cooperation would be preferable to confrontation with this strategic equal.

From these inferences, several deductions can be made regarding the implicit nature of the great-power talks and the related issues that emerged. First, at the outset it was probably generally understood that a great-power confrontation would be unlikely while the discussions continued. Second, both powers probably accepted the proposition that, because of their implied interests in a political settlement, they would have to act quickly, and possibly jointly, to restore a cease-fire in the event of a major outbreak of hostilities. Third, both probably recognized that unilateral intervention, except for the most urgent requirements, would most likely be counterproductive to the motives for holding the two-power talks. Both still reserved the right to act independently, however, to prevent the annihilation of vital urban centers, such as Tel Aviv or Cairo, if the other side refused to apply joint pressure. It is doubtful that an explicit agreement on these points was made. But, regardless of the degree of formality, the other interested governments probably also reached the above conclusions about the nature of the talks, and they are thus relevant to subsequent proceedings and most likely influenced the policies of the sponsored states.

Note, Counternote, and Military Escalation
As progress was made in the verbal and informal contacts in
Washington, the United States formulated "some concrete ideas,"
dealing mainly with a proposed compromise on the format of
a settlement, and these were transmitted on 26 May in a formal
note to the Soviet Union. The American proposals underscored
a concern that the settlement be embodied in a contractual agreement between the Arabs and the Israelis. In the American view,
this recommendation could serve as a satisfactory compromise
between Israel's demands for a peace treaty and the Arabs' reluctance to undertake a formal treaty. Arab endorsement of a contractual "engagement," to use Eban's term, would be matched
with the requirement that Israel withdraw to agreed-upon borders
"that did not reflect the weight of conquest." This formula would
allow room for minor adjustments but would deny Israel major
territorial gains. The note pointed out, however, that the great
powers had refrained from drawing specific boundary lines, leaving this task to the next stage of Arab-Israeli negotiations.[10]

Foreign Minister Gromyko discussed these ideas between 10
and 13 June in Cairo before preparing the Soviet response. The
Soviet note of 17 June restated an insistence upon establishing a
timetable for Israeli withdrawal from *all* Arab territory; it made
no provisions for direct Arab-Israeli talks on any subject; in a
reversion from the previous informally agreed position, it considered a package settlement rather than individual accords; it
called for a formal declaration ending belligerency only at the
completion of the Israeli pullback; it insisted upon the return of
Sharm el Sheikh to Egyptian sovereignty, though placed under
U.N. control; it called for demilitarized zones on both sides of
the frontiers; and it demanded a full restoration of the political
rights of the Palestinian refugees, instead of leaving the issue of
repatriation or compensation from Israel to individual choice as
recommended in the U.S. note.[11]

The Soviet note represented a reversion to earlier hard-line
positions and even introduced new claims, thereby nullifying the
major results of the previous three months of two-power talks.

Indeed, Heikal reports that during Gromyko's visit the utility of the talks was seriously questioned by both the Soviets and Egyptians. It was agreed that participation should be continued, but with the stipulation that no deviations would be made by the Soviets without prior consultations.[12]

This resurrection of former positions and the creation of probably the most inflexible stand to date was probably the result of the favorable Arab progress in the "war of attrition" along the Canal (see below). Under these circumstances, there was no inclination toward compromise in Cairo, and assurances of a military solution were frequently heard. Once again, Moscow interpreted the evidence as favoring the Arab side and agreed to conditions that would obviously frustrate for the time being further diplomatic demarches. Growing Soviet indifference toward a political settlement was confirmed during the 9–17 July visit to Moscow by U.S. Assistant Secretary of State Joseph Sisco, whose mission was to attempt to resolve the deadlock.[13]

The Israeli escalation of the conflict on 20 July initiated a new, seemingly decisive phase. Sensing this, Nasser announced to the opening session of the Arab Socialist Union party congress on 23 July 1969 that Egypt had embarked on the stage of liberation of occupied territories. He warned, however, that the Arabs must be prepared for a long battle to exhaust the enemy.[14]

August and September were the crucial months. It was uncertain whether the Arabs could absorb the Israeli air attacks and still retain adequate staying power to prevent a deterioration along the front and at a later date restore the momentum of the summer offensive. The outcome had not been decided by September, when the leaders of Egypt, Syria, Jordan, and Iraq met in Cairo to coordinate measures to save the situation. At the same time, Dayan announced his new plan for a "limited offensive" to accelerate the pressure along the west bank of the Canal.

The first indication that the military position of the Arabs had deteriorated to a point where they might reconsider their political bargaining position came in September, in Gromyko's address before the 1969 session of the United Nations General Assembly.

He reiterated the standard Soviet demands for an Israeli withdrawal, but omitted the more onerous terms of the 17 June Soviet
note, such as the provision for declaring a termination of hostilities only after the withdrawal of Israeli forces was completed.
Instead, his main thrust was against the relatively insignificant
American call for a regional arms limitation agreement. (The
consistent Soviet position has been that, while the sources of
tensions persist, the imposition of arms controls is an artificial
solution to a still explosive situation; they therefore do not regard the American stand as realistic.) Finally, Gromyko renewed
Moscow's pledge to work for peace in the Middle East.[15]

The 28 October Rogers Peace Plan

The breakthrough apparently came sometime in late September
or early October, when Foreign Minister Riad informed the State
Department that Egypt was prepared to reconsider the format for
opening talks and suggested acceptance by both sides of the
Rhodes formula for indirect talks (the device, which had proven
successful during the 1949 negotiations, provided only for separate discussions between Jarring and each side, with no commitment for direct talks at any stage of the negotiations).[16] Assistant
Secretary of State Sisco and Soviet Ambassador Dobrynin then
met repeatedly to prepare a brief to guide Jarring in the hoped-
for negotiations for an Egyptian-Israeli agreement. This brief
was completed on 28 October, and the United States then unilaterally undertook in November and December to draft a second brief relating to Jordan. The two briefs were then transmitted to Britain, France, Israel, Egypt, and Jordan.

This "joint initiative," known as the 28 October Rogers peace
proposal, was stymied almost immediately. Israel publicly leaked
its refusal to accept any procedural arrangement other than direct
talks. This disclosure forced Riad to deny publicly that he had
accepted the Rhodes formula. The proposals were locked in a
downward spiral; with the failure of the United States to deliver
an Israeli endorsement, Cairo and Moscow had greater latitude
in rejecting the proposals.

The aim of the Sisco-Dobrynin consultations on the drafting of an Egyptian-Israeli brief was to combine key elements of previous Soviet and American peace proposals and, according to the note, to present a detailed elaboration of the necessary and fundamental aspects of a Middle Eastern settlement. Although it participated in the drafting, the Soviet Union subsequently refrained from cosponsoring the brief or from being closely identified with it. Thus, the unofficial text of the note contained many principles that the Soviets had already sponsored or endorsed, including the following:

1. A timetable would be established for the withdrawal of Israeli troops three months after the signing of the accord.

2. The instruments of agreement would become effective as soon as it was deposited with the United Nations.

3. Both governments would agree to and then officially define their mutual borders.

4. The future of the Gaza Strip would be the subject of discussions between Israel, Egypt, and Jordan.

5. Refugees should have the right to either repatriation according to an agreed annual quota or resettlement outside Israel with compensation.

6. Freedom of navigation through the Suez Canal should be guaranteed.

7. The Tiran Straits and the Gulf of Aqaba should be declared international waterways and open to shipping of all countries at all times.

8. The discussion of the above principles should be conducted under the aegis of Ambassador Jarring on the basis of the Rhodes formula.[17]

From the American point of view, the note incorporated new provisions on several key points: a timetable for withdrawal; the repatriation of refugees; and the Rhodes formula for negotiations. The Americans were encouraged by the Arab and Soviet acceptance of the Rhodes formula and saw in it a sufficient degree of ambiguity to satisfy both Israeli insistence upon direct negotiation and Arab demands for only indirect talks.

The Israeli-Jordanian brief also contained several significant departures from earlier recommendations. The preamble called for the conclusion of a final, reciprocally binding accord between Israel and Jordan that would be negotiated under Jarring according to the Rhodes formula and that should reflect the following recommendations:

1. The procedures and timetable for the withdrawal of Israeli forces from substantially all of the West Bank would be determined by the two parties.

2. Each country would accept the state of peace between them and prohibit acts of violence from its territory against the other.

3. The two governments would agree upon a permanent frontier "approximating" the pre-June 1967 line, but allowing for mutually acceptable alterations.

4. The two governments would jointly settle the problem of ultimate control over Jerusalem, recognizing that it should be unified with both governments sharing in the civic and economic responsibilities of the city.

5. Jordan and Israel, in conjunction with Egypt, would determine the final disposition of the Gaza Strip.

6. The two governments would negotiate appropriate security arrangements for the West Bank, including the delineation of demilitarized zones.

7. Jordan would affirm that the Tiran Straits and Gulf of Aqaba are international waterways and open to Israeli shipping.

8. Ambassador Jarring would establish an international commission to determine the choice of each refugee on returning to Israel, but Israel and Jordan would determine jointly the total number of refugees involved (giving Israel a partial veto over the figure to be readmitted).

9. The two governments would enter into a formal agreement recognizing each other's sovereignty, territorial integrity, political independence, and right to live in peace.

10. The signed accord would be deposited with the United Nations and any breaches of its provisions would entitle the other signatory to suspend its obligations.

11. The signed document would be endorsed by the four big powers, who would undertake to assist the parties in upholding its provisions.

12. The accord would come into effect only with a simultaneous agreement between Israel and Egypt.[18]

Reactions to the Rogers Plan

The two briefs were the most definitive proposals yet offered by any power, and the response of each party was a categorical rejection. Nasser told the opening session of the National Assembly on 6 November that in light of this latest peace bid the United States was the "number one enemy of the Arabs" and that they now had no other choice but to continue the war against Israel. Foreign Minister Riad followed with an address on 8 November to the Arab League Joint Defense Council in Cairo in which he rejected the American brief and accused the United States of being an accomplice of Israeli aggression. Despite point twelve of the Israeli-Jordanian brief and point six of the 15 January 1969 U.S. note, both of which prohibited endorsement until an accord was signed between Israel and Egypt, Riad charged that the submission of separate proposals was designed to split the Arab world.[19]

The bitterness of these attacks reflected in part the rapidly deteriorating conditions in the battle for the west bank (see below). The prospects for conducting favorable negotiations from their current inferior posture seemed to the Egyptians to be almost nonexistent. In desperation, Nasser appealed to the Arab world and the Soviet Union for massive, immediate aid. (On 9 December Minister of Defense Fawzi and Vice President Sadat made an urgent visit to Moscow to report on conditions along the collapsing front and to explore alternative military options. The Soviets apparently remained noncommittal.)

On 20 December an Arab Summit Conference was convened in Rabat to hear Cairo's plan for total war. Several choices were presented to the delegates for possible combined efforts, ranging in price from $70 million to $250 million in hard currency, mainly for the purchase of Western electronic equipment of a type that the Soviets had been reluctant to furnish. Observers claimed that this was the most forthright Arab meeting to date and that, for the first time, comprehensive action plans were deliberated. It also proved to be the least successful. Traditional animosities and residual fears of Nasser's ambitions were too strong. Other Arab leaders refused to pay for strengthening his army. The meeting ended in a shambles, without even the facade of unity or the customary communiqué, and Nasser was forced to rely even more on Moscow.

The Soviet Union apparently delayed transmitting its reply to the American note of 28 October until the reports from Rabat revealed the degree of Nasser's dependence and the extent of Soviet latitude. On 23 December Moscow formally responded, rejecting the Egyptian-Israeli brief with a point-by-point criticism that covered in part its reaction to the Israeli-Jordanian brief, which had not yet been published. Specifically, the Soviets sought:

1. a precise, predetermined timetable on the withdrawal of Israeli troops within two months;

2. an adjusted concept of peace, to which the United States had apparently already agreed in principle, whereby a de facto or effective cessation of the state of war would take place when the Israeli forces started to withdraw and a de jure or legal termination of hostilities would come into effect when the withdrawal was completed;

3. Egyptian sovereignty over all the Sinai Peninsula, including Sharm el Sheikh;

4. the return of the Gaza Strip to its pre-1967 status, that is to Egyptian authority, even though the legal claims to this territory are still held by a nonexistent Palestinian entity;

5. demilitarized zones to be extended on both sides of the Egyptian-Israeli border;

6. Israel to fulfill uncompromisingly all previous resolutions on the repatriation of refugees, which would mean an unlimited return;

7. passage through the Canal to conform with the 1888 Constantinople Convention, which granted Egypt the right to prohibit transit to any state with which it is at war;

8. passage through the Tiran Straits to comply also with the relevant principles of international law (implying that test cases of the international character of the Straits would likely have to be periodically presented to the International Court of Justice); and

9. rejection of the Rhodes formula on the grounds that "once an understanding is reached on the principal aspects of the settlement, it should be possible to find a proper forum acceptable to both sides."

The Soviets concluded that agreement on the substance of a future settlement would have to be achieved by the four big powers before there could be further discussion of the procedures for bringing the two sides together.[20]

The Soviet note was labelled by State Department spokesman Robert McCloskey as a negative and retrogressive deterioration in the Soviet position that was apparently designed to introduce a pause in the two-power talks. However, there was sufficient leeway in the wording to indicate that Moscow wanted only a temporary suspension and not a total cessation of the dialogue. The Soviet amplification on an adjusted peace was a timely contribution; but its adoption of the maximalist Arab position on sovereignty, borders, and territorial waters raised sizeable substantive obstacles, and its rejection of the Rhodes formula left no hope for an early commencement of negotiations.

The sharpest denunciation of the American peace endeavors, however, came from Israel. After a key policy speech by Secretary Rogers on 9 December, in which he outlined the rationale behind the note, the Israeli cabinet met in emergency session and later issued a statement accusing the United States of attempting to dictate Middle Eastern peace terms. Abba Eban then held a press conference on 16 December in which he asked the "outsiders" to confine themselves to promoting direct negotiations rather than indulging in conjecture about the character of a final settlement.

Next, the United States submitted a minor modification of its Israeli-Jordanian brief to the four big powers, calling for more liberal adjustments of the borders. Again, Israel held an emergency cabinet meeting and subsequently released an official communiqué: "The cabinet rejects these American proposals, in that they prejudice the chances of establishing peace and disregard the essential need to determine and secure agreed borders through the signing of peace treaties by direct negotiations." Finally, Mrs. Meir explained before the Knesset on 29 December the content of her reply to the American note. She claimed that there had been a serious erosion of the American position. "Each of the U.S. proposals concerning boundaries and the return of refugees is a threat to Israel's security. Both, if enforced, would gravely endanger Israel's very existence." In sum, she complained that the American proposals failed to impose on the Arab states the duty to recognize explicitly the sovereignty of Israel. They did not urge the need to delineate secure, recognized, and agreed boundaries by free negotiations between the parties. They did not impose on the Arab states the duty to take concrete action to end terrorist activities from their territories. "We have the right," stated Mrs. Meir, "to demand that U.S. policy should not be conducted at the expense of our vital interests." She concluded by insisting once more that the great powers were obliged only to bring the warring parties together, not to impose independent solutions.[21]

This was the strongest pronouncement by the Israeli government since the June War and reflected the view, widely held among Israeli circles, that the United States was becoming cornered by Soviet meddling, the intractability of Cairo, and its own growing impatience about a settlement. Israeli reactions were largely a response to genuine fears that the United States might again impose a "solution" that it would later fail to honor (as had happened with the 1957 agreement), and that the United States was apt to place such a high priority on preserving the Soviet dialogue, for the sake of larger issues, that Israeli interests might be jeopardized. Accordingly, it was felt that something dramatic was needed to increase the Americans' latitude in dealing with the

Soviets and to reduce the intransigence of the Arabs. However, the cause for the breakdown in diplomatic efforts was more fundamental and could not be rectified merely by spectacular raids, such as the theft of Egyptian radar from Ras Ghareb. The chief reason for the temporary termination of political endeavors was the success of Israel's 1969 campaign against the Canal zone, which resulted in the almost total collapse of Egyptian air defenses.

Military Developments

A review of the military events during this period suggests that by the spring of 1969 the Egyptians were less apprehensive about the damage that could be inflicted by Israeli commando raids; they were felt to be psychologically infuriating but militarily insignificant. A National Defense Council headed by Nasser was formed on 29 January 1969 to provide a broader base for the prosecution of the war. Accordingly, it directed a return to frontal attacks across the Canal. On 1 April Nasser announced a unilateral abrogation of the cease-fire and the opening of a war of attrition under a strategy of "preventive defensive operations." The new strategy was supported by heavy shelling of the Bar Lev Line throughout the spring and summer. The I.D.F. brigades repulsed several Canal crossings, but the constant Egyptian pressure was having an obvious effect—the casualty rate had reached 70 per month by July (from June 1967 to April 1969 there had been a total of 70 soldiers killed and 188 wounded), and resupply efforts for the forward units were becoming increasingly hazardous.[22] On 7 July U Thant announced that "open warfare has been resumed." Most important, Egypt felt that at last it had succeeded in forcing the I.D.F. to fight a style of war in which they could employ their preponderant numbers of men and matériel to greatest advantage. Only in this manner could the Egyptians hope to offset the gap in military technology between them and the Israelis and demonstrate that they could achieve a posture of strength from which they could negotiate a favorable political settlement.

Casualties have always been a major policy consideration in Israel. During the summer it was anticipated that current trends would lead to an annual combat death rate of approximately 300. This is only .012 percent of the total Jewish population of Israel and 0.4 percent of Israel's armed forces. Numerically, Israel could absorb such losses, but it was questionable whether it could do so psychologically. For example, Moshe Dayan has testified that the deaths of eighteen Israeli soldiers during the 11 October 1956 reprisal raid on Kalkiliah, Jordan, was considered excessive and clearly unacceptable by the cabinet. The casualties alone were a key reason for Israel's decision to accept the risks of a major escalation, and the result was the Suez War.[23] The same rationale seems to have governed Israeli policy in the Canal War; by May 1969, 284 I.D.F. soldiers had been killed and Israel began to consider corrective action.

To counter the impact of the adverse casualty trends in the dark days of 1969, Israel opened the next phase of the post-1967 conflict on 20 July with massive air attacks against Egyptian positions on the west bank, losing two aircraft but downing five Egyptian fighters in the initial assault. This was the first time air power had been directed against Egyptian artillery since the June War and marked the start of a major Israeli campaign. The I.D.F. sought to relieve pressure on the Bar Lev positions and to gain absolute freedom of action in the air over the Canal zone, thereby denying Egypt hope of opening a bridgehead on the Sinai. Accordingly, air defenses were attacked, including master radars, antiaircraft artillery (AAA), surface-to-air (SAM-2) missile batteries, and supporting facilities. These direct assaults were accompanied by audacious commando raids on the flanks and hinterland to demonstrate the continuing vulnerability of Egyptian defenses.

The new strategy was only partially successful. Commando raids had lost their impact on Egyptian policy, and the gun positions along the Canal were sufficiently well fortified to permit continued, though less systematic, harassment of the I.D.F. lines. In view of the continuing casualties, Dayan announced a new strategy of "limited offensive," whereby the I.D.F. would intensify its operations to whatever level would be required to force Cairo's observance of the cease-fire.[24] Dayan reasoned that time was on Israel's side, since the longer it maintained its present borders, the more difficult it would be to force a withdrawal without a genuine peace settlement. The new phase was underscored by a large-scale Israeli armored attack on fifteen Egyptian coastal positions, which inflicted substantial damage without arousing resistance even from nearby tank units.

In the three months following, the Israeli Air Force (I.A.F.) gained unchallenged air supremacy over the Canal and the approaches to the Nile Valley itself by destroying 24 SAM-2 batteries and 67 Soviet-made warplanes. The effectiveness of the Egyptian armed forces had dropped almost to the level of July 1967; and, as a result, Israeli casualty rates were dramatically reduced.

This climactic demonstration at the end of 1969 of Israeli military superiority over any combination of Arab forces was accompanied by a new hardening of Israel's diplomatic position. In view of the deadlocked political efforts to secure peace, Israel was dedicated, in Mrs. Meir's words, "to hit back with seven blows for each one she receives," [25] while the Arabs were determined to absorb any level of punitive retaliation short of general war and maintain a sufficient offensive level to prevent a total collapse of morale.

The battle of the west bank had been so extensive that some 500,000 civilians had been evacuated and so intensive that the morale of the Egyptian forces had reached a new low. The I.A.F. had gained absolute air supremacy and had destroyed Egyptian capacity to conduct even routine operations on the west bank. Nasser's summer offensive had been defeated, the effectiveness of his forward units had been neutralized, and the initiative had passed unquestionably to the I.D.F. As the degree of Egyptian paralysis became apparent, and as Israel consolidated its military authority over the west bank, Cairo's options were reduced: favorable negotiations were no longer feasible; only capitulation or the acceptance of more massive aid were possible. If it chose the latter, the next escalatory step would necessitate a new geographic and possibly a new conceptual dimension to the fighting, since nearly all of Egypt was now open to Israeli air attacks.

Characteristics of the Second Round

Thus, the vagaries of warfare dictated political policy to a greater extent in the second phase of the negotiating process than in the first. As the two sides approached military parity, that is, as the Egyptians reached a point where they could launch a sustained offensive and mount sufficient pressure to force Israeli escalation, the various political bargaining positions began to fluctuate according to the forecasted outcome of the Canal War. Each side estimated at some point that it could either inflict sufficient damage or absorb enough punishment to compel a change in the opponent's bargaining position. Yet the fine line of military stalemate, where negotiations are most likely to occur, was transgressed by both opponents as they mounted their respective offensives. As a result of the failure to reach a political settlement during the first phase, while Arab military proficiency was gradually being restored, the intensity of the war increased. Thus, with only limited operational restraints and minor political constraints, the attainment of military parity did not enhance the prospects for negotiations; indeed, it seriously jeopardized the entire process. If military power in these circumstances was to have a decisive influence on political policies, it would have to be applied either with more circumspection or on a much broader scale.

The Soviet bargaining position during the fluctuations of the war was consistent yet flexible. Moscow steadfastly sought throughout the second phase to probe and expand the area of agreement. The note of 23 December 1969 clarified and refined key points in the 30 December 1968 Soviet peace plan. Moscow's position had become more definitive on the issues of international waters, peacekeeping forces, and the timetable for the withdrawal of Israeli forces. The Soviets had concluded from the experience of the first phase that the main obstacle to a political settlement involved the implementation of the projected negotiations and agreements, rather than the substantive issues themselves. Accordingly, they incorporated into their first peace plan a programmed schedule for implementation rather than an outline of principles to which the parties had already agreed during the first phase.

Subsequently, Moscow gained Washington's acceptance of the concepts of phased, scheduled withdrawal, and of an adjustable peace. Finally, the Soviets consistently upheld Egyptian claims to sovereignty over all territory conquered during the June War; there had been no compromise on this central problem. Moscow's flexibility was demonstrated in its apparently intentional construction of bargaining counters in the area of international waterways that could be traded for concessions on higher-priority issues. Moreover, its shift from an insistence upon a comprehensive agreement to an allowance of individual agreements was a braking tactic designed to control the pace of the discussions. The complete abrogation of its acceptance of the procedural arrangements for conducting the negotiations was a more serious signal of its intention to suspend further deliberation of substantive matters until the military aspects of the settlement could be rectified. Nonetheless, while insisting on this holding action, Moscow skillfully provided enough elaboration of other matters to assure the United States and Israel that it did not want to abandon prospects for a political settlement.

At the same time, the United States can also be credited with imagination for accepting the merits of several Soviet recommendations as compared to its own and for a sustained determination to reach an agreement on the principles it felt to be fundamental. The desire for settlement sufficiently outweighed parochial intertests, yet the basic values were not jeopardized. As Secretary Rogers formally stated, "Our policy is to encourage the Arabs to accept a permanent peace based on a binding agreement and to urge the Israelis to withdraw from occupied territory when their territorial integrity is assured as envisaged by the Security Council resolution." [26] On specific provisions, he emphasized that, contrary to usual Anglo-Saxon customs in jurisprudence, the envisioned treaty should be as detailed as possible, but should also be "based on clear and stated intentions and willingness to bring about basic changes in the attitudes and conditions which are characteristic of the Middle East today." Furthermore, "a lasting peace must be sustained by a sense of security on both sides." Particular aspects of the suggested security arrangements, however, should, preferably, be worked out by the parties themselves. On the refugee problem, Rogers pointed out that lasting peace was not possible until this crucial issue was resolved. During the previous 20 years, the United States had contributed about $500 million for the logistic support and education of the Arab refugees, but this had not reduced the desire of the Palestinians to return to their homeland. Rogers therefore asserted that any settlement must take into account the legitimate expectations of the refugees and the concern of the governments in the area for a just settlement of this problem.

Rogers was more definitive on the issues of withdrawal and territorial boundaries.

The Security Council resolution endorses the principle of the nonacquisition of territory by war and calls for withdrawal of Israeli armed forces from territories occupied in the 1967 war. We support this part of the resolution, including the withdrawal, just as we do its other elements. The boundaries from which the 1967 war began were established in the 1949 armistice agreements and have defined the areas of national jurisdiction in the Middle East for 20 years. Those boundaries were armistice lines, not final political borders. The rights, claims, and positions of the parties in an ultimate peaceful settlement were reserved by the armistice agreements. The Security Council resolution neither endorses nor precludes these armistice lines as definitive political boundaries. However, it calls for withdrawal from occupied territories, the nonacquisition of territory by war, and the establishment of secure and recognized boundaries. . . . We believe that, while recognized political boundaries must be established and agreed upon by the parties, any changes in the pre-existing lines should not reflect the weight of conquest and should be confined to insubstantial alterations required for mutual security. We do not support expansionism. We believe troops must be withdrawn as the resolution provides . . . [The envisioned agreement] would require withdrawal of Israeli armed forces from U.A.R. territory to the international border between Israel (or the Mandate of Palestine) and Egypt, which has been in existence for over a half century.

On the territorial aspects of the status of Jerusalem, Rogers stated, "We have made clear repeatedly in the past $2\frac{1}{2}$ years that we cannot accept unilateral actions by any party to decide the final status of the city. We believe its status can be determined only through the agreement of the parties concerned, which in practical terms means primarily the governments of Israel and Jordan." Rogers concluded his definitive statements with the assertion that, "We believe that this approach is *balanced* and fair."

But Israel viewed the American position as catastrophic. Eban countered, "Israel will oppose with all its strength every effort to fix restrictive conditions prior to negotiations directly with the Arabs." [27] Direct negotiations had become a strait jacket for Tel Aviv from which it would not move. Israel was winning the war and thus had no incentive to alter its policy. Indeed, it was sufficiently confident that it undertook to lecture its patron in disrespectful terms and levy demands that were incongruent with Washington's stated principles and interests. Had Israel not been winning the war, it is safe to conclude that relations with the United States would have deteriorated substantively over differences about settlement terms. But, while the I.D.F. was scoring such remarkable successes, Washington did not feel compelled to increase pressure against Israel, and Israel saw no need to formulate a bargaining position without the prospect of favorable negotiating conditions. Neither government foresaw the consequences of its determination to maintain a dominant military posture as the prerequisite for successful negotiations, a condition that the Soviets and Arabs would not accept.

5
Strategic Warfare and Renewed Diplomatic Initiatives: January–July 1970

The defeat of the reconstituted Egyptian forces on the west bank of the Suez Canal strengthened Israel's confidence that military success was imminent and doomed the second phase of the efforts to secure a political settlement. Cairo's military and political situation had reached a new nadir. By the time Minister of Defense Fawzi and Vice President Sadat made their urgent visit to Moscow in early December to report on the military situation, Egypt had lost over one-third of its first-line combat aircraft and all of its SAM defenses in the Canal zone, while inflicting only minimal damage on the I.A.F.

Thus, Jon Kimche observed at the time, "Israel has never been stronger, and more dominant. She cannot be forced to act against her own interests, not by Americans nor by Russians, not by Egyptians nor by Fatah. . . . [But] she cannot achieve a Middle East peace and real independence with a weak Egypt and a weak Palestine on her borders." [1] Given this posture of dominance, Israel could either lower its price for a settlement with the assurance that it had won the Canal War and retained military superiority or it could escalate military pressure and insist that the Arabs acknowledge this fact publicly by accepting Israel's unyielding political terms. Israel decided not to show any leniency and to intensify the military pressure against Cairo.

Israeli Offensive
In January 1970 Israel adopted a new policy of strategic warfare and launched a series of air attacks against military targets in the heart of Egypt. The I.A.F. employed its newly acquired American F-4 Phantom fighter-bombers carrying their maximum 15,000-lb ordnance loads on missions 80–100 miles inside Egypt. At first the

strategic raids were confined to targets on the periphery of the Nile Valley, but by 25 January Defense Minister Moshe Dayan announced publicly that the purpose of the deep raids was to relieve pressure on the Canal, to prevent Egyptian preparations for a renewed offensive, and to convince the Egyptian public that its leadership was unable to protect them; in short, to topple Nasser, who, in Dayan's view, was dedicated to preparations for another war. All Egypt is our field of battle, he asserted. There will be no limits on military objectives within Egypt until Cairo respects the cease-fire.[2] Mrs. Meir stated the reason more pointedly in a private interview: "We're not bombing the interior to force him to make peace. We go into the interior in order to make it well known to him and the people of Egypt that either it's quiet on both sides or there's bombing on both sides. . . . People say to us, how do you expect Nasser to negotiate peace with you? He's humiliated and frustrated! Of course he's being humiliated. But then we have to ask ourselves—so what? Are we supposed to sit on the Canal and take the shellings?" (When asked whether a successor to Nasser would be easier to negotiate with, she replied, "He couldn't be worse.")[3]

The January 1970 Israeli offensive had grave consequences for the various peace initiatives and led to serious misunderstandings among all interested parties about the political motives of both friends and opponents. Instead of capitulating, Nasser requested on 22 January an urgent meeting with the Soviet leaders and departed the same day for Moscow. During four days of hard bargaining, he acknowledged that his defenses were completely inadequate and that the Soviet equipment was no match for the electronic measures employed by the Israelis with their new American weapons. He further revealed his lack of confidence in Soviet arms by arguing that Israeli attacks could most effectively be deterred by reciprocal raids against Israeli urban centers, and he requested improved long-range aircraft—at least as an interim measure until Egyptian air defenses could be modernized. The Soviets rejected both the logic and the request, but they agreed to aid in the defense of civilian and economic targets and to provide the necessary assistance within 30 days,[4] indicating the outside limits of the Soviet commitment.

Soviet Political Counteroffensive

The Soviets were apparently aware of the implications of introducing a major new increment into the Canal War and confined their commitment to the protection of civilian and economic targets while seeking tacit American cooperation to impose some form of limitation on the expanding conflict. However, the impasse over the 28 October proposals now stymied movement on any Soviet bid for conciliation. Despite the rejection of the Rogers proposals, the United States continued to view these suggestions as the soundest approach to a political settlement and to insist that a solution needed only firmer pressure to dislodge Soviet recalcitrance.

When the 16 January session of the four-big-power talks proved barren, the State Department warned that there was no point in further two-power talks unless Moscow adopted a more flexible stand. Dobrynin promptly replied directly to Assistant Secretary Sisco in unmistakable terms: the continuing Israeli aggression and their latest escalation were the reasons for the failure of the peace talks. A deadlock ensued and the two powers could agree neither on the reason for the stalemate nor on ways around it.[5]

On 31 January the Soviet Union underscored the urgency it attached to the situation by the unusual procedure of sending President Nixon his first personal note from Premier Kosygin. The note was short and nonbellicose, but firm and focused squarely on the reasons, from the Soviet viewpoint, for the increasing tensions in the Middle East. Israel was attacking Egypt at will; the entire country seemed defenseless against Israeli attacks. If the West could not restrain Israel, the Soviet Union would have no alternative but to supply new arms to Egypt.[6]

A wide-ranging campaign was launched against Israeli strategic bombing following the Kosygin note. On 4 February *Izvestia* published the first of several sharp denunciations of Israel and the United States, warning that they were approaching the brink of a major war. The Soviets asked French President Pompidou to reiterate their viewpoint during his visit to the United States. Nasser made a major policy statement in Cairo on 2 February in which he insisted that "the United States bears the largest responsibility for the escalation in our area." Later that month he gave a lengthy discourse to a senior American journalist, acknowledging that the F-4 was a serious offensive threat for which there was no equivalent counter in the Egyptian inventory. Moreover, Nasser complained, the F-4 was being used aggressively at a time when Israel already enjoyed air supremacy and a vastly superior electronic-warfare capability.[7] Finally, Secretary Rogers was warned during his African tour in February by the pro-Western Tunisian prime minister that the sale of the F-4 was a provocation against all Arab peoples.

What were the motives behind this campaign? There was probably a genuine apprehension about American indifference toward Moscow's avowed commitment that the Arabs would not be allowed to negotiate from an inferior position. The United States appeared to be challenging this policy outright by guaranteeing Israeli supremacy. Furthermore, Moscow probably calculated that the arms escalation manifested by the sale of F-4s and electronic-warfare equipment would inevitably require shipments of new Soviet equipment and that, if this equipment was again mishandled by inexperienced Arab troops, the Soviet image in the Middle East would be further compromised. Moscow may also have wanted to appease moderate Arab opinion by demonstrating that it was both supporting Cairo *and* working for peace. An additional factor may have been that Egyptian morale clearly needed an injection similar to that supplied to the South Vietnamese by the American bombing of North Vietnam. Finally, the campaign coincided with an Israeli request for an additional 24 F-4s and 80 A-4s, and an effort to block this sale was an understandable Soviet concern. In sum, Moscow probably saw sizeable risks in a major escalation of the arms race.

However, in view of Moscow's rejection of the Rogers proposals and its seeming intransigence toward a political settlement, the

White House took the position that Kosygin's threat was hollow and aimed merely at calming the Arab furor over effectiveness of the F-4s. Accordingly, Nixon replied on 4 February to the Soviet note by denying responsibility for the escalation in the Canal War and asking that both powers strive for a restoration of the cease-fire. He also pledged American willingness to discuss an arms limitation agreement in the region. In the event the Soviets rejected this offer, Nixon warned that the United States would have to supply Israel adequately. Finally, he reaffirmed American confidence in the terms of the 28 October proposals.[8]

A decisive event in determining the course of Soviet policy was probably the Israeli attack on the Abu Zabal factory, on Cairo's outskirts, on 12 February. Two F-4s inflicted nearly 200 casualties in their first direct raid on a civilian target. Moscow may have concluded that this attack was an intentional flaunting of its request for restraint and discretion, and a direct, audacious challenge to its commitment to maintain Arab military parity. After Abu Zabal, subsequent decisions seem to have related only to how much and what type of active Soviet participation in Egyptian defense was required. TASS reported that the Soviet Union would provide the Arabs "with necessary support" to strengthen their defenses against Israeli attacks, strongly implying that a decision had been made to furnish SAM-3s.[9]

Meanwhile, in his State of the World Message, President Nixon struck a harsh tone by warning the Soviet Union against seeking a special position in the Middle East or exploiting the conflict for its own advantage. He again pledged American determination to supply Israel with enough arms to maintain the military balance and once more pegged the American peace aims firmly to the 28 October proposals. (Secretary Rogers later remarked in a press conference that the American proposals had been useful and were "about all we can do at this point." He asserted that more time was needed for others to think through the American position, which was sound.)[10]

But the October peace plans received a setback at the four-big-power talks on 19 February. In the wake of the Abu Zabal raid and the seeming unwillingness of the United States to restrain Israel's deep penetration raids, the Soviet Union struck an uncompromising stand. It would not endorse an American proposal for a standstill cease-fire that did not condemn aggression. Furthermore, it insisted that Israel must agree to the principle of withdrawal before a cease-fire would be relevant. Finally, the Soviet representative, Jacob Malik, again rejected the American call for a regional arms limitation accord and implied that this call was hypocritical, since the United States was supplying Israel with the major offensive weapons that had created an imbalance, while the Soviet Union was furnishing only defensive weapons. The Soviets were apparently firmly convinced after Abu Zabal and the rigidity of the American position at the 19 February session that they must rely on their own resources to achieve their aim of Arab parity with Israel.

Soviet Arms Buildup
Although the new Soviet aid program for Egypt was clearly in full swing by March, its dimensions remained obscure. Airlift traffic to Egypt increased four times above normal, and between 12 and 16 March ten Soviet merchant ships arrived in Alexandria and off-loaded at night, which is usually a sign of arms deliveries. Yet the State Department concluded that no additional threat was posed against Israel and on 23 March turned down for the time being Israel's aircraft request, granting instead $100 million in economic aid. The United States pledged to maintain the military balance and reiterated the request for cooperation that had been made in Nixon's reply to the Kosygin note. Most important, Washington cited its "no aircraft now" decision as a sign of restraint that other nations should follow. The aims of the two powers were becoming increasingly divergent: the Soviet Union was insisting that military parity was a prerequisite to negotiation and the United States was maintaining that political reconciliation was a precondition for military de-escalation.

In April Assistant Secretary of State Joseph Sisco made the first of several fact-finding tours of the Middle East to test reactions to the idea of renewing the political talks. He found Nasser more bellicose than ever, confident that the new Soviet aid would redress the military scene. Nasser later explained to the 23 July 1970 session of the Arab Socialist Union party congress that he had been fully satisfied with his January talks in Moscow. As a result, "the situation and time are in favor of the Arabs. We have a feeling of steadfastness and are optimistic." The Israelis were equally determined to continue the policy of maintaining maximum pressure against Egypt, including attacks throughout the country. The most significant change in American policy resulting from the tour was a modified attitude toward the Palestinian factions. At his 23 December press conference, Secretary Rogers still held to the standard American-Israeli position: "We have no intentions of dealing with the Palestinian groups." Sisco, on the other hand, concluded after his visit that a more active interest in the Palestinian political movements was now warranted, not to legitimize their terrorism, but to exercise eventually more effective curbs.[11]

Nasser's rejection of Sisco's overtures and his confidence in a favorable military outcome was based on Soviet acceptance of partial responsibility for the defense of the Nile Valley. During the first four months of 1970, the I.A.F. had flown 3,300 sorties and dropped 8,000 tons of ordnance on Egyptian territory.[12] According to Dayan, four-fifths of Egypt's total air defense capability had been destroyed and by March the Soviets had begun replacing these loses with SAM-3 missiles: "This is the first stage of the Sovietization of the Egyptian military disposition. The Russians are building air infrastructures on the ground which will permit Soviet crews to pilot Soviet planes. . . . I do not expect this to occur." [13] Moreover, he stated, Israel would try to prevent the new Soviet missiles from being placed in vital areas of Egypt. Yet by 13 April there was irrefutable evidence that Soviet pilots had assumed responsibility for the air defense of the Nile Valley, and Soviet crews were reportedly manning some of the 20 advanced SAM batteries in point defenses for critical targets. The deep penetration raids were suspended on that date. To demonstate that this new additive would release Egyptian pilots for offensive operations, Egypt staged on 18 April its largest, best executed air assault since the June War against the Bar Lev Line. Egyptian artillery activity was also systematically increased and, by the month's end, Israeli battle deaths reached 27, the highest monthly toll since July 1969.

Soviet actions had drastically altered the nature and scope of the war. In a comprehensive review of the military situation on 4 May, General Dayan confirmed that the Soviet Union had taken over defensive responsibility for the entire Nile Valley, including Upper Egypt. "I shouldn't and I don't wish to engage in prophecy, but in what the Russians are doing today there is an element of throwing down the gauntlet, of saying: We Russians are not only defending Cairo, we are not only relieving Egyptian forces of the job of defense so that they may be free to attack Israeli forces all along the Canal, but we are also involved in this Egyptian war against Israel. This threat, this throwing down of the gauntlet, is no less significant than the actual fighting, the personnel and equipment themselves. . . . [By this action] the Soviets have revived Egyptian spirits . . . [to the point] that Nasser has called, 'taking the battle initiative back into our hands.' " Nasser admitted, Dayan stated, that the deep raids had wrested the military initiative from him and forced his army to disperse into a scattered defensive posture. But since the Soviets have now assumed this role, "I would prefer to wait and see what we can and ought to do." [14]

Clearly, the Soviet Union had expanded its initial commitment to provide point defenses (SAM and AAA weapons systems) for key urban centers to a broader commitment to oversee aerial defense for the general area of the Egyptian heartland. Moreover, it was much faster and more effective to provide Soviet tactical aircraft rather than an entire air-defense ground environment as a deterrent against Israeli strategic attacks.

At that time this appeared to be the limit of the intended Soviet involvement. Its intervention was intended to force the conflict back into the Canal zone proper, and Egyptian confidence was indeed soaring. In Nasser's words, "Brothers, in the past

15 days [or since 13 April], a change has taken place. Our armed forces have regained the initiative with bold military operations in the air and on land. Our determination to liberate our territory is the primary legitimate right of any nation which values its dignity." [15]

This new confidence was conveyed on the battlefield. On 14 May the Egyptians sank an Israeli trawler, and during the night frogmen penetrated into the harbor of Eilat and sank an Israeli vessel. The artillery barrages had a renewed gusto, reminiscent of the previous year, and the Egyptian air force conducted several successful sorties against Sinai positions. Finally, on 30 May Egypt conducted its first successful commando raid against the east bank, wiping out an Israeli armored platoon (13 killed, 4 wounded, and 2 captured).

The I.D.F. responded vigorously. In one week, 526 sorties were reportedly flown over the Canal, and an Egyptian destroyer and missile patrol boat were sunk. At the same time, prolonged raids were conducted against fedayeen bases in Lebanon and heavy reprisals were inflicted against Syria. As a result of the renewed aerial engagements, I.D.F. shootdowns by June totalled 101 Egyptian and 23 Syrian aircraft, at the cost of 20 planes, with an air-to-air kill ratio of 20 to 1.

Israel clearly inflicted more damage than it received, but normal cost-effectiveness standards do not apply to the Arab-Israeli conflict. Over-confidence is a common malady among Arabs. A minor Egyptian Canal crossing was now psychologically plausible, though militarily still irrational. An acknowledged presence on the Sinai, even if followed by a withdrawal, would be hailed as a major victory and would be worth whatever penalty the Israelis inflicted. In light of such uncertainties, Dayan's chief task was to keep Nasser off-balance, denying him the physical capacity to gamble on marginal options. At the same time, however, preemptive strikes and spectacular raids[16] were becoming increasingly risky because of the unknown reactions of the Soviet pilots. The precise limits of Soviet responses became the outer limits of Israeli counteractions to deter Nasser. Israel attempted to establish mutually respected sanctuaries by warning that if the Soviets ventured beyond the Nile Valley into the Canal zone they would be subject to attack.[17] Thus, by the spring of 1970 the Israelis considered the degree of Soviet participation as the heart of the matter in the Canal War.[18]

So did the Egyptians. On 20 May Nasser told German interviewers that Soviet pilots were flying "armed missions and could indeed confront Israeli fighters. . . . We are always receiving new equipment," he said, "today we are stronger than we were two, than six, months ago." [19]

Nasser's terms for political settlement rose with his soaring confidence in the possibility of successful military operations. He set forth his maximum demands to James Reston; ultimate peace would require: the total withdrawal of Israeli troops from occupied Arab territories, including Jerusalem; a solution of the refugee question on the basis of individual choice; and the creation of a nonfanatical, multireligious Israeli state in Palestine. The Arab governments would guarantee to this state both recognition and freedom of navigation through the Canal and the Tiran Straits. Given an equitable solution of the refugee problem, there would be no need for demilitarized zones or policing actions, since local states would be fully capable of meeting their own security needs.[20]

Yet Nasser also seemed prepared to accept substantially lower aims as the basis for negotiations. In his 1970 May Day speech, Nasser stressed that the resolution of the military aspects of the confrontation was a prerequisite for exploring a political settlement, and he added that this was now being achieved. Speaking at the Abu Zabal factory, Nasser viewed a military solution in terms of a rectification of the "arms balance." He referred to the often-stated basis for the American "no aircraft now" decision as a formula for "arms balance" that was predicated upon maintaining Israeli superiority. In other words, Nixon's pledge to maintain the present Israeli arms level, which everyone agreed was overwhelmingly superior, represented not a policy of preserving military parity, but rather one of subjecting the Arabs to continued inferiority. He praised the Soviet Union for offsetting this inferiority and for "helping Egypt to prevent Israel from raiding Egyptian towns, factories, schools, and economic targets with American Phantoms. . . . The U.S.S.R.'s serious crime, alleged by the West, is that it is helping to safeguard our skies against the American-made Phantoms' raids." Nasser then addressed two specific pleas personally to President Nixon. First, he called on Nixon to order Israeli withdrawal and, if this was not within his power, to refrain from furnishing additional arms to Israel. In Nasser's view Washington bore the primary responsibility for the outcome of the Canal War, since the latest American weapons were being employed "strategically," and this clearly imbalanced the military contest. "I address all this to President Nixon as the central actor," Nasser concluded, "and if he does not respond we can only assume that the United States is determined to support Israel's intentions to dictate to us its terms of surrender." [21]

The Soviet arms buildup and the engagement of Soviet pilots in operation missions, however, remained the dominant concern for the time being in Washington. President Nixon became convinced that a firm gesture toward Israel was required. In late April the U.S. ambassador to Moscow, Jacob Beam, officially voiced American concern over the active Soviet involvement in Egyptian defenses and requested an explanation. On 6 May the State Department revealed that Moscow claimed its pilots were only serving in an advisory capacity, a claim that was countered officially by the American, British, and Israeli governments. The State Department announced that, because of this unsatisfactory explanation, it would now reconsider the Israeli request for additional aircraft. Accordingly, in a personal note to Mrs. Meir, Nixon promised to supply sufficient aircraft replacements to insure Israeli air superiority, a direct counter to Nasser's explicit request. He balanced this grant, for the first time, with advice to exercise restraint in attacking strategic targets. This was over one month after Israel's voluntary suspension of deep penetraton raids and, therefore, had little effect on Israeli policy and none on the Soviets'.[22]

The effect of Nixon's neglect of the Soviet policy position was apparent in Soviet Ambassador Malik's bellicose address to the U.N. Security Council on 13 May. To the astonishment of seasoned observers, he delivered the most scathing denunciation of American Middle Eastern policy since the height of the Cold War. U.S. Ambassador Yost replied that Moscow was the real culprit, and the two-power talks appeared about to be relegated to history books. TASS followed on 21 May with the assertion that the Soviet provision of purely defensive weapons was the first step toward halting Israeli aggression. At the same time, Kosygin sent personal notes to the leaders of Turkey and Iran which reiterated Moscow's assertion that it sought the speediest achievement of a political settlement in the Middle East by rendering aid to the victims of Israeli aggression and by preventing Israel from imposing "from a position of strength" a solution that would recognize the aggressor's right to keep Arab territory.[23]

The Second Rogers Plan

At a press conference during the May NATO Ministerial Meeting, Secretary Rogers amplified American concern by stating that the United States would take very seriously any further Soviet involvement. Rogers defended the sale of aircraft to Israel, and he implied that the policy would be continued unless the Soviet Union agreed to cooperate in a de-escalation, because Israel had unquestionably associated the employment of its attack aircraft with the continued prosecution of Nasser's war of attrition. (This was an unfortunate association; it reinforced Arab charges that the F-4 was used primarily to counter Arab aims and that Israel was dependent upon the United States for the pursuit of its ambitions.) This represented, however, a "bottoming out" of the cul-de-sac in which the United States found itself during the spring of 1970. While maintaining an unwavering stand on the military issue, Washington now sought to restart its political initiative along the lines set forth in a study ordered by Nixon in the wake of the direct Soviet involvement and subsequently known as the Second Rogers Peace Plan.

In assessing the sincerity of Nasser's May Day appeal, American planners reportedly drew several inferences from the speech. First, Nasser obviously attached high priority to the suspension of the offensive attacks against his country. He seemed to equate this prospect with some form of military stand-down rather than with a military showdown, if it could lead eventually to an acceptable settlement. Furthermore, his statement seemed to indicate that no definitive ceiling had been placed on the level or exact nature of Soviet participation, as implied in the phrase that American intransigence would force Egypt to "adopt an attitude on which it will not go back." Nasser's tone also suggested a growing interest in de-escalating the war and in reducing his rapidly increasing dependence upon Moscow; yet, at the same time, the note of confidence in the possibility of a military solution resounded sharply.

Secretary Rogers was asked at a press conference in June why the United States had reopened its peace bid at that time. He enumerated several reasons:

1. The deteriorating military situation in the Canal War was becoming critical.

2. Nasser's May Day speech was interpreted as an appeal.

3. Nasser's statement on 14 June on a New York television program that he might consider a cease-fire in six months or less opened the possibility of a military stand-down.

4. Mrs. Meir's acceptance in principle of 242 and, presumably, its implications, and statements made in Washington by Foreign Minister Eban that Israel would make surprising concessions once talks began indicated a cautious flexibility on the Israeli side.[24] While the indicators seemed valid, the preliminary soundings had proven inconclusive or negative.

Washington's renewed efforts had received an important stimulant when a breakthrough had occurred in the Israeli stand. In the wake of the successful Soviet-Egyptian deterrence of Israel over the Nile Valley, Mrs. Meir publicly accepted in principle on 26 May both Resolution 242 and the Rhodes formula for negotiations.[25] This represented the most lenient Israeli gesture yet toward a negotiated settlement and was seen as the price for a formal American pledge to furnish additional F-4 aircraft. Armed with this Israeli concession, the United States hoped to establish a dialogue in response to Nasser's personal May Day appeal to Nixon. The United States then sought to provide Israel a positive signal of its intentions by agreeing to supply more F-4s; this action was, however, viewed by Egypt as a negative reply to Nasser's appeal verging on a personal affront. Accordingly, Cairo did not react favorably to the American bid.

But, despite Arab indifference, the American peace initiative moved forward. Preliminary U.S. overtures in May had tested current reactions to the 28 October proposals or slight variations thereof; but Soviet-Arab hostility finally forced the United States to abandon these guidelines. Accordingly, Washington lowered its focus to basic procedural matters. On 19 June the United States transmitted its new peace proposals to Israel, Jordan, Egypt, and the four big powers. No effort was made, as had been done in the preceding year, to secure a joint Soviet-American accord, though Dobrynin was apparently provided advance information about American intentions. The new proposal called for a cease-fire of limited duration, the reactivation of the Jarring mission, and acceptance by the belligerent parties of Resolution 242 as a point of departure, with specific procedural arrangements for the negotiations to be left to the discretion of Jarring and the bargaining parties (it being understood that the Rhodes formula or a slight modification had already been informally accepted by both sides). Following a British suggestion, the revised Rogers peace plan sought only for written endorsements by the three key belligerent parties—Egypt, Jordan, and Israel—of their willingness to participate in talks along these lines. If written concurrence could be obtained, the United States would then sponsor a limited cease-fire and pass the initiative for opening and conducting the talks to Jarring and the U.N. secretary-general without further formal guidance or recommendations.[26]

Initial Reactions to the Rogers Plan

Once again the prosecution of the war affected Nasser's outlook. The unmistakable demonstration of Soviet power in the Nile Valley and the gradual movement of Soviet air defenses toward the Canal were clear indications of Moscow's determined support of Nasser, and public confidence within Egypt rose dramatically. Reflecting this escalating confidence, Nasser reverted to a tough stand in his policy statement at Benghazi, Libya, on 25 June. He delivered a "Holy War" speech, demanding that Israel withdraw or accept the consequences. He also informally rejected the latest American peace initiative. Although it must be taken into consideration that Nasser was speaking to a "militant and revolutionary" foreign audience, it did appear that the question of the timing for a cease-fire and negotiations was, in fact, receding from its prior central role in his plans. At any rate, it was in this militant frame of mind, rather than that of the May Day speech, that Nasser proceeded to Moscow for consultations on the next phase of the confrontation.[27]

On 29 June Mrs. Meir also publicly took exception to the new plan, stating that in the present military situation the Egyptians were likely to exploit a cease-fire to Israel's disadvantage. She agreed, however, to postpone a final decision while awaiting Nasser's formal response, or an elaboration of his Benghazi stand. Movement forward now rested with the great powers.

On 29 June Nasser and a large delegation departed for Moscow, where a marked change of emphasis from the militancy of his Benghazi address was noted in several public statements. In Libya he had stated, "We are preparing for a big battle against Israel." In Moscow he pledged his people to "a peace based upon justice." The Soviets had apparently set a strong conciliatory theme for the talks and pressed for Egyptian compliance. President Podgorny restated Moscow's desire for a settlement based on Resolution 242 "with due account for the legitimate rights and interests of all peoples in the area," including Israel. The Soviet Union favored a political settlement to be approached through a further strengthening of the economic and defensive potential of the Arab states, and Podgorny stressed the correctness of the Soviet policy and the importance of Arab compliance.[28] Moscow had no intention of repeating the mistakes it had made in 1967, when it lost control of Arab policy after providing an initial prod.

Little is known of the position Moscow took during the talks on the tactics to be followed in advancing the political settlement. However, at the 24 June meeting of the four big powers, the last before Nasser arrived in Moscow, the Soviets had set forth a proposal that they regarded as being more flexible than the Israeli formula of cease-fire, negotiations, and peace, and that was later described by Secretary Rogers as a "step forward." Rather than a formal peace treaty ending the state of belligerency, they called for an indefinite extension of a cease-fire into a "formalized state of peace," similar to the arrangement that existed between the Soviet Union and Japan. The "state of peace" could be mutually proclaimed after the initial stages of an Israeli withdrawal. The scheme had the advantage of being more binding than a cease-fire, implying a heavier penalty for its violation.[29]

A more detailed presentation of Soviet strategy in the confrontation was presented by a leading Soviet analyst of Middle Eastern affairs, I. Belyaev, in the semiofficial professional journal *International Affairs*. Belyaev argued that "to be realistic in this situation, it must be acknowledged that the happiness of one people cannot be built on the misfortune of another," and that the final settlement of the Palestine problem "should in no way prejudice the civil and religious rights of the non-Jewish nationalities." In pursuing their objectives, it is reasonable for the Arabs "to reject all attempts to compel them to negotiate a settlement from positions of strength." As an immediate solution Belyaev proposed that a schedule be established for the withdrawal of Israeli forces at a rate commensurate with the pace of negotiation for a peace accord. When a final accord was deposited with the United Nations, the Israeli troops would be simultaneously moved behind the 1967 borders. The 1967 borders would then be demilitarized and appropriately patrolled on both the Arab and Israeli sides. To establish such a schedule, it was suggested that

Jarring be commissioned with greater authority. The final accord would include a mutual agreement among all parties "to respect and recognize one another's sovereignty, territorial integrity, inviolability, and political independence and their mutual right to live in peace and within secure boundaries, free from the threat or use of force." [30] Such terms were substantially more moderate than those advanced during the second phase and reflected a degree of conciliation that had been absent for nearly a year.

The joint communiqué issued on 17 July, after Nasser's unprecedented 19-day stay in the Soviet Union, did not reveal that an important juncture had been reached. The central theme of the communiqué was that "the two sides believe that the sooner the peaceloving forces compel Israel to give up her policy [of dealing] from positions of strength in relations to the Arab peoples . . . the sooner will a just and lasting peace be ensured in that area." [31]

Immediately upon the delegation's return, however, top Egyptian dignitaries traveled to other key Arab capitals to explain the consequences of the prolonged negotiations, and on 22 July the first concrete evidence emerged of what had transpired in Moscow: Egypt accepted without qualification the revised American peace plan. In explaining his actions before the 23 July session of the Arab Socialist Union party congress, Nasser implied that there was an element of subterfuge in his choice. The most important and immediate requirement was to halt the sale of additional American weapons to Israel. "We must be prepared to confront all types of arms the United States gives Israel. At the same time, we must try with all our strength and all the pressure of the Arab nation to check the flow of modern war equipment into Israel from the United States. . . . We must check this alarming flow of equipment." Nasser stated that there was nothing new in the American proposal; indeed, it was no more than a procedural recommendation. There could be nothing new in the American position, he insisted, until it took a definitive stand on supplying Israel with modern weapons. On the other side, he argued polemically, Egypt was in a stronger position than at the time of the earlier peace initiatives. "We built up our armed forces because we sensed there could be no peace unless the enemy and those behind him felt that we had reached a degree of strength that would enable us to liberate the territories. . . . the enemy only understands the language of force." Nasser viewed his acceptance of the peace bid as "a final opportunity." [32]

If agreement to the American peace bid was the price required to block the further modernization of the I.D.F., then Nasser felt compelled to accept the uncertainties related to a cease-fire and negotiations. His preference was probably based on an assessment of the progress of the Canal War, which had by then reached new and unprecedented proportions, with Soviet missile crews having downed their first F-4s in the renewed battle for the west bank.

In a press conference on 12 August, one of Nasser's closest advisors, Minister of National Guidance Heikal, elaborated on these arguments. He concluded that there were three reasons behind the American initiative: the failure of the Israeli offensive against the Nile Valley; the reinforcement of the Egyptian army ("taking into account the last crossing operation undertaken by Egyptian forces, the efficiency of the artillery, and the huge amelioration of the air defense efficiency, the Israelis were convinced of the process of rebuilding the Egyptian army"), and the increased Soviet aid. "All these," Heikal stated, "were positive pressures . . . that really pushed the American government to present this initiative." He pointed out that Cairo welcomed the American approach because it established for the first time a direct connection between the June 1967 cease-fire resolution and 242, a link that Israel had steadfastly refused to accept. Since Israel acknowledged only the cease-fire resolution but insisted upon its own formula for entering into negotiations, Egypt viewed the American bid as exploratory in nature rather than as a conclusive proposal. Finally, Heikal reaffirmed that Egypt would not meet directly with the Israelis while they occupied Egyptian territory.[33]

Nasser had made major concessions in meeting the Soviets' demands for a more flexible political position. He had formally abandoned the Khartoum formula of no recognition, no negotiations, and no peace with Israel, and had accepted a limited cease-fire and negotiations without a prior Israeli pledge to withdraw and before an Israeli commitment to negotiations had been guaranteed. To put this action in perspective, it must be realized that such a decisive move jeopardized Egyptian subsidies from the conservative Arab governments and had a potential to split the Arab world, thereby reducing Nasser's bargaining strength. Finally, it might also have served as a catalyst for the warring fedayeen factions, coalescing them into a viable opposition to Nasser's objectives. (Indeed, 40 Egyptian officers were cashiered for opposing the peace bid.) Despite the weight of these constraints, Nasser apparently placed Egyptian security ahead of his obligations to the Arab world and agreed to the Soviets' conditions for their further participation in Egyptian defenses.

Soviet Missile Movements

In May Egypt had begun the reconstruction of missile sites in the Canal zone to provide relief for its battered forward positions and to reduce casualty rates. At that time the activity appeared to have little Soviet participation. Similar operations during the previous summer and fall had been disastrously defeated by the I.D.F., and, when the Egyptians renewed their effort in May, they could once more provide only light and ineffectual resistance to the predictable Israeli suppression attacks. The endeavor made little progress, forcing Moscow to assert closer supervision and to introduce its own integral batteries to provide staying power for the overall operation.

The Soviet-Egyptian strategy was predictable. A demonstration of Arab military parity would first require an effective deterrence against Israel's strategic options. Then the fighting would have to be returned to the tactical level. The most realistic means of engaging the I.D.F. tactically would be to resume large-scale cross-Canal hostilities. This strategy, however, necessitated the provision of adequate air protection against I.A.F. attacks. The only other option was commando raids, which could hardly influence the parity issue and would probably prove to be counterproductive because of I.D.F. reprisals.

But the Egyptians were unable to reestablish even the basic prerequisites for effective air defense, and the Soviets were forced to assume the responsibility. On 1 June the first reports were published that the SAM defenses were being inched toward the Canal zone. When it became known that the Soviets were manning some of the batteries, it was feared that Moscow would not risk a setback and would provide adequate air cover for the construction of the sites. However, the Soviet fighters did not appear over the Canal zone; Moscow adopted a more deliberate, less provocative approach, establishing a systematic logistics base and adequate ground support facilities with each echelon advance.

Devastating attacks by the I.A.F., approaching the scale of the American raids in Southeast Asia, blunted but did not halt the gradual buildup.[34] The I.A.F. had recognized before that the outcome hanged precariously on the balance of Soviet participation and, accordingly, repeatedly tested Soviet intentions. On 23 June a helicopter commando raid was conducted against Bir Araida, 50 miles inland from the Red Sea and 50 miles south of Cairo, on the doorstep of the Soviet-commanded base at Beni Suef. Soviet fighters did not react to these provocations, but they did react to the follow-up penetrations by Israeli aircraft. With each probe, the I.A.F. undoubtedly measured the Soviets' reaction times and crew proficiencies, and estimated the limits of Moscow's intentions. At the same time, the continued probes provided a suitable justification for the Soviets to expand systematically the perimeters of their defensive responsibilties. By the end of June the Soviet Union commanded three main operating bases north of Cairo and three in Upper Egypt, and combat patrols were reportedly being flown by Soviet aircraft on either flank of the Canal zone, well forward from the Nile Valley.

Whether the Soviet Union had originally intended to extend its commitments beyond the Nile Valley or felt itself compelled to do so because of Egyptian incompetence and Israeli arrogance, by the end of June it was clear that Moscow was committed to the defense of the entire Canal front. The direct aerial approaches to the Nile from the Sinai along the Ismailia-Cairo axis were protected by ground defenses, and the flanks by interceptor aircraft. Yet it was still uncertain whether Moscow intended to expand its defensive system directly to the Canal and both north and south along its west bank.

When the I.A.F. suspended attacks on the Nile Valley in mid-April, it concentrated the full weight of its air strikes on the Canal front. Under optimum conditions, the Israelis pounded the Egyptian gun positions and logistics systems daily, with devastating impact. In a press report specifically released by Egyptian censors, Egypt for the first time informally acknowledged its casualties: in June alone 1,500 casualties were reported along the Canal, and morale had again plummeted.

The Soviets graphically changed this situation by successfully engaging the I.A.F. and contesting Israel's superiority over the west bank. On the nights of 29 and 30 June, the Soviets moved forward twelve batteries of improved SAM-2s and two or three SAM-3 batteries, along with supporting AAA guns. Before they were spotted on the morning of 30 June, they were able to ambush a flight of Israeli F-4s. What probably happened was that the batteries were located in semifinished, camouflaged sites, did not activate their radar until the aircraft were overhead and unaware of their presence, and then fired in multiple salvos when the aircraft were in a stern position. Two F4s were destroyed at a cost of $8 million and four crewmen.

In the next few days the SAM defenses were consolidated in a belt 17-miles deep along the Ismailia-Cairo road and within 20 miles of the Canal. On 6 July the I.D.F. chief of staff, Lieutenant General Chaim Bar Lev, held a rare press conference, at which he revealed that the second battle for the Canal's west bank had opened on 1 July. The initial shootdowns had apparently been by the improved SAM-2, which reportedly has a faster computer for its radar and better flight characteristics for lower-altitude maneuvers. Since 1 July, he stated, at least two Soviet-manned SAM-3 batteries had fired on Israeli aircraft, but had scored no hits. Five of the twelve SAM-2 batteries had been destroyed by direct hits and two had been rendered inoperative by indirect hits, at the cost of one additional F-4. General Bar Lev acknowledged that most of the destroyed sites were again operational after only short periods. He also revealed that the SAM crews were employing a new tactic of "ripple" firing, where an entire battery of six missiles was launched in a short, integrated time sequence, making evasive maneuver more difficult. (In North Vietnam SAM-2s were usually fired as single shots or dual salvos, and the attrition rate against American aircraft was only 1:1,000 or 1 kill per 1,000 launches. Egyptian crews had fired hundreds of missiles, with no hits on combat aircraft and at the cost of the bulk of the Egyptian missile batteries.) General Bar Lev concluded that the balance had shifted seriously but not irrevocably against the Israelis.[35]

In July a total of seven Israeli aircraft were downed in the battle for the west bank. Even accrediting the first two losses to surprise, the subsequent kills represent an extremely high attrition rate for the results they produced. Destroyed missile sites became operational nearly overnight, or else alternative locations were utilized. The use of ripple-fire tactics and a seemingly inexhaustible supply of launchers, radar sets, and support facilities clearly indicated that the Soviets had invested heavily in a logistics train that would guarantee a successful operation. The crew composition of the batteries became a matter of wide speculation: How many batteries had integral Soviet crews, and what percentage of the remainder were Soviet? Such exercises were less important than the fact that the Soviets had chosen to lay their prestige on the line. The Kremlin had concluded that Soviet arms and equipment would not be disgraced again. The gauntlet, to use Dayan's words, had been thrown down. The second battle of the Canal's west bank had become, literally overnight, a Soviet-Israeli confrontation, with Egypt providing little more than real estate and muscle. As the commander of the Israeli Air Force, Mordechai Hod, has stated, the new threat was a "Russian fist covered by an Egyptian glove."[36]

New Attitudes Toward the Rogers Plan

Mrs. Meir's initial rejection of the revised Rogers Plan on 29
June was thus based not on substantive or procedural questions,
but on suspicions of Soviet intentions and the fear that Egyptians
would use the cease-fire as a military reprieve.[37] Supervision of
the cease-fire became the dominant issue in the Israeli attitude
toward negotiation. Washington, on the other hand, felt that the
bargaining process itself would have a tranquilizing and stabilizing effect. Accordingly, the United States placed a high priority
on simply getting the talks started. The Soviets and Arabs, for
their part, were more concerned with the substantive quality of
the talks, and sought prior commitments on as wide a range of
issues as possible.

Israeli reservations about the cease-fire forced the United States
to consider appropriate means for enforcement. Foreign intervention was unappealing and fraught with political risks. The State
Department preferred some form of great-power assurances, coupled with reciprocal surveillance by local forces. Thus, the implementation of the cease-fire assumed a much larger perspective
than the United States had originally envisioned. However, the
Arabs and Soviets were reluctant to digress from seeking consideration of the outstanding substantive issues in order to resolve what seemed to them to be merely a procedural problem
that would become meaningless if the deliberations could get
underway and register reasonable progress.

In view of this reticence and the mounting evidence that the
Soviets had expanded their commitments beyond the defense of
the Nile Valley, President Nixon took a new tough stand on 1
July. He warned that the present Soviet-Israeli battle for the west
bank could lead to a great-power conflict. He stated bluntly that
American interests in the Middle East were of far greater importance than those in Southeast Asia and that the United States
would not allow the security of Israel to be endangered.[38] Henry
Kissinger privately described the situation as "terribly dangerous" and asserted the White House's determination to "expel" the
Soviets from the Canal.

Washington followed up this hardening attitude with pressure on all three parties. The Soviet presence and the conditions placed on the supply of additional aircraft were used to bring leverage against the other parties. The United States implied to Israel that, in view of the strong Soviet presence, it would be reluctant to furnish additional aircraft until a cease-fire and subsequent talks had tested the parameters of a political settlement. To the Soviets and Egyptians, Washington inferred that it would have to commit additional F-4s in light of the Soviet presence unless the cease-fire was accepted and talks begun. In the long run the United States had to borrow from both arguments to develop its final position. A new aircraft formula was released on 12 July whereby the United States would replace only combat losses. This resulted from a fear that the American peace bid would appear as a complete capitulation in the face of the Soviet presence on the Canal unless a formal adjustment was made to the "no aircraft now" policy.

The use of the aircraft issue as a counter to Soviet involvement in Egyptian defenses, however, demonstrated how inextricably dependent the local contestants had become upon the external powers. The options of the sponsored states were being gradually constricted, but at the same time the level of the conflict was being raised to a contest of wills between the great powers, where appeasement, capitulation, and compromise carried greater consequences. Arms diplomacy had reached an importance heretofore unattained. For the first time both great powers could apply decisive pressure through the threat of suspended deliveries. Conversely, great-power intervention would from now on have to include some factor greater than the sum of the quality and quantity of weapons supplied to the rival's sponsored state, and the prospects of a major confrontation were thus enhanced.

On the substantive bargaining issues, Assistant Secretary Sisco stated in a "Meet the Press" interview on 12 July that there were still important differences between the great powers. While they had reached agreement on certain key aspects of the disputes (the termination of hostilities, Israel's right to exist, and freedom of

navigation), there remained serious obstacles, such as the definition of territorial boundaries and the disposition of the refugees.
He revealed a significant shift in the American interpretation of
Resolution 242: it did not explicitly require the withdrawal from
all occupied territory, and the precise boundaries were to be the
subject of negotiations. This view was contrary to the strong position taken seven months before by Secretary Rogers, namely,
that the preamble determined the interpretation of the subsequent provisions when it stated: "Emphasizing the inadmissibility
of the acquisition of territory by war and the need to work for
a just and lasting peace in which every state in the area can live
in security. . . ." This "no conquest" clause, according to Rogers,
explicitly affirmed that the 1967 boundaries must be respected
and reestablished. Upon further questioning, Sisco implied that
there was little latitude for maneuver on this point until the belligerent parties themselves began negotiations and established
bargaining priorities—a partial qualification. Nonetheless, Sisco
indicated that the United States had moved back to its early position that the borders should not reflect the weight of conquest.

On the refugee problem, Sisco revealed an additional change
in the American stand. A durable peace must include the just
rights and claims of the Palestinians, and their interests must be
represented in the negotiations. He stated that the United States
was now prepared to negotiate with the Palestinians. This was
a new advantage for American negotiators, but it was difficult to
exploit since it was highly unwelcome in both Israel and Egypt.
A change of this scale, however, reflected Washington's growing
anxiety that the parochial interests of the belligerents were endangering larger global affairs. In this vein, Sisco asserted that
the Soviet Union had been deriving extensive unilateral advantage from the present turmoil and that further gains could best
be reduced by launching the political talks. He concluded pessimistically, "If the political initiative of the United States is rejected . . . the options that are open to the parties in the area
as well as to the major powers will be slowly narrowed. If this
opportunity is lost, what we can look forward to, unfortunately,

is a continuation of the violence and counterviolence and at an escalated level." [39]

When no formal responses were forthcoming, Nixon held another press conference on 21 July, at which he again referred to this subject. "The U.S. position is to maintain peace in the area. We felt that it was important to maintain a military balance of power so that no state in the area would be encouraged to launch an offensive against another state or be driven to launching a preemptive strike because of the fear of an offensive or buildup." [40] In light of the 12 July announcement that the United States would supply replacement aircraft and electronic countermeasures (ECM) equipment to use against the Soviet SAMs, Nixon's reiteration of a definition for a "proper military balance" carried the implication that Washington still equated "proper balance" with Israeli superiority, a formulation that afforded distinct dangers in the new situation along the Canal. In response, one Soviet diplomat commented, "Doesn't he realize that our commitment to Egyptian defense is every bit as firm as the American commitment to Israeli security?"

Although it was unknown at that time, the deadlock had been partially broken earlier in Moscow. After Nasser's unconditional acceptance of the peace bid on 22 July, Dobrynin quickly endorsed Egypt's move on 23 July. No formal Soviet acceptance was necessary since the U.S.S.R. was not a party to the negotiations. On 27 July Jordan also accepted without qualification. Syria did not formally commit itself—it had denounced Resolution 242 and had not been addressed in the peace plan—but President Atassi stated publicly on 24 July that Egypt and Syria shared an identity of views on the subject.

On the negative side, the ten most important Palestinian organizations and Iraq rejected the plan, pledging themselves to a military solution. The opposition of these groups was aimed as much against Nasser's stature as it was against a peaceful settlement. On 31 July Yasser Arafat led massive demonstrations in Amman against the peace bid, successfully indicating that the center of gravity among the Palestinians was shifting toward extremism. After popular demonstrations in Baghdad on 29 July against Arab acceptance of the peace bid and for the formation of a separatist faction with Syria for the prosecution of the war, a high-level Iraqi delegation was urgently invited to Moscow.[41] It was told that the Kremlin intended to do everything possible to see the peace initiative advanced. Under the threat of a suspension in Soviet aid, Iraq carefully muted its opposition. Nonetheless, Jordanian acceptance of the peace proposal was the precipitating factor in the September civil war that nearly toppled Hussein and threatened to jeopardize the favorable attitude of the moderate Arabs toward the political talks.

After the Soviets had delivered the Arabs' acceptance, Dobrynin presented, on 23 July, Moscow's "final compromise" position for a substantive settlement. The latest proposal provided for a detailed negotiated accord between Israel and the Arabs that would be signed *before* the Israeli withdrawal. The package would include the provisions of the Belyaev scheme and would be guaranteed by both great powers; but it would not include a plan for refugee rehabilitation. It is not clear whether Nasser had explicitly agreed to this latest Soviet compromise or it was offered by the Soviets without his knowledge. If he had endorsed the proposals, then this marked an important concession and indicated a new flexibility in the Egyptian position.

Pressure was now on the Israelis from all sides. Nasser had explained to the Palestinians that he had accepted the Second Rogers Plan to prevent the Israelis from charging that the Arab governments were not in favor of peace and thereby increasing their demands for more American weapons. If Israel now held out against the peace bid, however, it could expect a much less sympathetic response to its arms requests. In a hawkish statement before the Knesset on 23 July, Foreign Minister Eban rejected the Soviet peace protestations as merely a plan to maintain tensions in the region and to gain a foothold in Africa. He reiterated Israel's acceptance of 242 and the Rhodes formula, but implied that Israel's hesitation to accept the American peace bid was due to apprehensions about Soviet designs in the region.

In a dramatic speech before the Knesset later on 23 July, Eban officially rejected the American bid and announced an Israeli counteroffer based on five points:

1. There would be an effective cease-fire and preliminary talks about a peace settlement.
2. All subjects would be negotiable.
3. Territorial boundaries would remain an open issue.
4. An international conference would be convened to deal with the refugees.
5. The Israeli-Jordanian border would eventually be communal and open, with guaranteed access to the Mediterranean.

On the same day Nixon sent Mrs. Meir a second personal note in which he attempted both to ease Israeli fears and to offer incentives relative to Israeli security. He reportedly pledged that the United States would not press for *any* Israeli withdrawal until after a contractual settlement had been signed. The United States would also not demand a large return of Palestinians and would continue to seek an understanding on arms limitations. Nixon also suggested that some form of military relationship and possibly a formal political alignment could be arranged after a peace treaty had been signed. (This was followed on 22 August by Senator Fulbright's proposal for a formal bilateral American-Israeli mutual defense treaty.) Furthermore, the cease-fire would not become effective until Israel was satisfied that it could be enforced. Moreover, Nixon pledged that the United States would not withdraw from the region and would maintain a balance against Soviet military pressure in the Middle East. Large-scale economic assistance and additional weapons were also promised; and finally, assurances were extended of active support for peace-keeping operations in the demilitarized zones. (The possibility of American troops in the Middle East was clearly registered with the arrival on 16 July of Lieutenant General James V. Edmundson, U.S. Strike Command, to survey possible contingency use of American personnel.)[42]

These terms represented the strongest presidential commitment ever offered by Washington to Tel Aviv and exceeded by far the assurances extended by Eisenhower in 1957. Although Congress was strongly pro-Israeli, Nixon's private commitments bordered on the limits of congressional tolerance for the unchallenged exercise of executive authority. Beyond these terms Nixon could not prudently venture.

When the Israelis still held out, Nixon called yet another press conference on 30 July at which he made a further strong plea. "Some concern has been expressed by Israeli government officials that, if they agree to a cease-fire, they run the risk of having a military buildup occurring during the cease-fire. We and others have attempted to assure them that that would not be the case." [43] He restated firm American guarantees of Israeli security (commitments provided by four previous presidents) and pointed to a statement of intent by 71 senators endorsing this support. He asserted that these assurances should alleviate Israeli apprehensions.

But the Israeli cabinet remained split into three distinct factions: one, led by Deputy Prime Minister Allon and Foreign Minister Eban, demanded an unconditional acceptance of the American bid; another, centered around Prime Minister Meir and Defense Minister Dayan, argued for qualified acceptance; and a third, formed by the right-wing Gahal ministers, called for outright rejection. Differences were so deep that domestic politics became heavily involved. The six Gahal ministers threatened to resign, destroying the National Coalition.

The Soviets were becoming increasingly uneasy as the situation developed. Israeli intransigence or American indecisiveness might allow the entire movement toward a political settlement to bog down and deny Moscow important gains. Dobrynin was called home on 29 July, and *Pravda* printed a long statement praising Nasser's personal courage for accepting the American peace bid despite the dissidence of other Arab elements. Moscow acted promptly and actively to silence opposition in Algeria, Syria, and Iraq, and Palestinian obstructionism was denounced.[44] A vigorous attempt was made to deliver the Arabs to the bargaining table through coercion and an extraordinary flexibility in formulating a common negotiating stand. (Nonetheless, not all of the Arab governments responded favorably; and a formal split in the Arab camp was registered on 5 August by the convening of a ministerial meeting of the Arab League in Libya composed of only five "progressive" governments, minus Iraq, Algeria, and the Palestinians. But the gathering demonstrated that the moderate faction had effectively isolated the extremists on the settlement issue, signalling an important gain for Soviet diplomacy.)

Moscow's increasing pressure on the Arabs to get the talks underway was probably motivated by several factors:

1. The military balance was gradually improving, allowing the Arabs to bargain from a position of parity, without the risk of a major offensive or confrontation.

2. Arab military proficiency was still marginal, and the Soviets needed time to improve their defenses before rash actions or frustrations provoked a major challenge that could damage Soviet prestige.

3. Further military augmentation and its eventual utilization would require a consolidation of the Soviet political authority in Cairo, also demanding time and an element of stability.

4. The latest Jordanian crisis had jolted Hussein to the extent that he was compelled to announce publicly that he would not abdicate—a Palestinian takeover east of the Jordan River would raise major new uncertainties in a region where previous Soviet estimates had seldom proved accurate.

5. The outer limits of the Sovietization of the Arab defenses were probably not defined, but the danger of repeating the American slide into a Vietnam was apparent.

6. A cessation of the fighting at that point, even if accompanied by prolonged or inconclusive negotiations, would allow the Soviets to claim that their commitment to the Arab cause, demonstrated by their active defense of Egypt, was the decisive factor in stabilizing the region—not the American diplomatic initiative.

Pressure was building up inside Israel for some movement toward negotiations, one sign of which was the "Goldmann affair," when the leader of the World Jewish Congress offered to

mediate with Nasser. Accordingly, Mrs. Meir decided on 31 July
to sacrifice her National Coalition government by accepting the
American proposal and the resignations of her conservative ministers. Israel agreed to negotiate without prior conditions under
the auspices of Ambassador Jarring within the framework of the
Resolution 242, with the aim of reaching a binding contractual
peace agreement. Israel based its acceptance of the cease-fire,
however, on the provision that it be honored on all fronts on a
basis of reciprocity and that it govern the terrorists. (Cairo had
previously declared that its acceptance had no bearing on Palestinian decisions or actions.) This loophole was left open for the
protection of Israeli interests in both the cease-fire and the negotiations.

In explaining her decision to the Knesset on 4 August, Mrs.
Meir said it was strongly influenced by the declared policy on the
Middle East of various American leaders. She stated ambigu-
ously Israel's minimum bargaining position: "Israel has the right
to secure and defensible borders; she will not return to the frontiers of 4 June 1967, which lay the State open to the temptations
of aggression and which, on various fronts, lend the aggressor
decisive advantages." A contractual agreement would have to be
signed before Israeli forces would withdraw to negotiated borders. She implied that final Israeli signing of such a document
would hinge upon face-to-face negotiations with the Arabs, even
if this was preceded by a stage of indirect talks.[45]

Mrs. Meir accompanied the Israeli acceptance with a strong
reply to Nixon's 23 July note, which she subsequently discussed
on an American television program. She acknowledged that this
was the first time the Israeli government had ever referred to a
withdrawal of Israeli forces and reiterated that her acceptance
of this concept had been strongly influenced by the American
guarantees. She would, however, "never utter the word again" because that was what the Arabs wanted to hear. Mrs. Meir disavowed charges that Israel had sought to negotiate from a position of power, but acknowledged that she had offered to negotiate
secretly with Nasser after the destruction of Egyptian air defenses

and in the wake of the first wave of deep penetration air raids. After Nasser's refusal, she saw the first indication of sincerity about a cease-fire in his 23 July speech. On specific negotiating items, she advanced a new hard formulation. Rather than the quota system for repatriation of refugees, Mrs. Meir advanced an even more stringent formula: only those who had formerly possessed property would be considered for reentry (the bulk of this category had either resettled permanently or died). Finally, she conditioned Israeli acceptance upon the procedural arrangement that Ambassador Jarring receive his instructions and guidance directly from the U.N. secretary-general rather than from the four big powers (a counter to the only partial Egyptian qualification that Jarring must receive his guidance from the four big powers and a reservation intended to dispel the impression that Israel had accepted all of Cairo's conditions).

In accordance with Nixon's assurance that the cease-fire would not go into effect until Israel was satisfied that it would be honored, the United States proposed that Egypt and Israel endorse in writing explicit provisions governing the cease-fire. The agreement provided that, effective 2200 hours G.M.T. on 7 August 1970 for a 90-day period, both sides would refrain from changing the military status quo within zones extending 50 kilometers on either side of the Canal. Construction of new sites and installations was prohibited, but maintenance of existing facilities was allowed. To verify compliance with these provisions, each side would rely on national resources, including reconnaissance aircraft operating up to 10 kilometers of the cease-fire line, and could avail themselves of United Nations machinery to report suspected violations.[46] (The use of Soviet and American surveillance apparatus was understood but not explicitly written into the agreement, lest minor infringements impugn the effectiveness of great-power reconnaissance capabilities.)

Characteristics of the Third Round
Again the vicissitudes on war had directly influenced the prospects for a political settlement. Israel's launching of a strategic

offensive in January 1970 was accompanied by both a hardening of its terms for political discussions and its most concerted campaign yet to bolster American determination. Israel's endeavors, however, were only partially successful. Egypt's complete inability to defend itself effectively and the failure of the Arab world to provide adequate aid forced Cairo to decide between seeking immediate relief from Moscow or capitulating to the Israeli terms for a settlement. The introduction of Soviet tactical aircraft defeated the I.A.F. strategic offensive by deterring deep penetration air attacks.

The nadir in political discussions during this period and the increasing Israeli pressure against the exposed Arab units east of the Nile Valley required the extension of Soviet air defenses up to the Canal banks. This inevitably led to a Soviet-Israeli contest for control of the air space over the west bank. Once again the Soviets defeated Israeli aims, this time by directly engaging I.A.F. aircraft.

Moscow's ever increasing responsibility created suspicion and anxiety in the United States. Yet, more than any other factor, the escalation in Soviet commitments induced a bargaining climate: it deterred the I.A.F., thereby creating an artificial impression of Arab military parity that demanded Israel's respect, and it created sufficient anxiety in Washington to rekindle American interest in negotiations. Significantly, it was the Soviet military posture in Egypt rather than its diplomatic argumentation that finally convinced the United States to abandon its cherished but abortive October 1969 peace formulations and to opt for the most simple suggestions possible in order to get some form of talks underway.

Soviet policy choices at this juncture seemed to reflect renewed confidence in Cairo's bargaining position, not only because of its strengthened military posture but also because of the paucity of alternative power fulcrums in the Middle East. Despite the marginal military value of the Egyptians' limited operations after mid-April, they had also an important political consequence in that they had helped to refurbish Nasser's image as the central figure in the Arab world. While he was becoming increasingly dependent upon Soviet participation for success in his campaign for the restoration of national honor, Moscow was correspondingly bound to Nasser as the only Arab leader whose stature was sufficient to balance eventually the combined American-Israeli superiority. The Arab summit conference at Rabat in December 1969 had demonstrated to the Soviets the utter chaos in the Arab world and the hopelessness of seeking alternative alignments. Conversely, the Egyptian military operations in May indicated that Nasser possessed the only military instrument capable of advancing Soviet designs and controlling the options of war and peace. The extent of Moscow's single-mindedness in accepting these hard realities, as manifested by its decision to engage actively in Egypt's defense, significantly strengthened Nasser's hand against his most intractable opponents—the numerous fedayeen factions that opposed his plans for a settlement. (Nasser had told a session of the Egyptian National Assembly on 24 March that a "peaceful settlement as we understand it" may soon be possible. "But," he added, "there is no hope of a political settlement until we reach a stage of military strength sufficient, if necessary, to secure our rights by means other than political.")[47]

Thus the Soviets gained significantly more than the other parties during the third phase of the political confrontation. They had established a powerful base for continuing influence in Egyptian policy and had convinced the Americans and the Israelis of the necessity of accepting talks, largely on Soviet terms. At the same time, however, the failure of the talks to materialize was due in large part to the degree of Israeli frustration over the dimensions of the Soviet buildup. It must be concluded, then, that the Second Rogers Peace Plan was in reality a Soviet product and its failure was largely Israel's responsibility.

6

Cease-Fire and Diplomatic Nadir:
August 1970–March 1971

The 1970 battle for the Canal's west bank was short but intensive. The full impact of the Soviet-Israeli confrontation was registered by Mrs. Meir in mid-July: "Today, I mean literally today, Israel is facing a struggle more critical than we have ever had to face before." When the confrontation opened after the 30 June shootdown of two F-4s, the I.A.F. struck heavily at the complex of twelve SAM-2s and two or three SAM-3s located just within the cease-fire zone in the area bounded by the Ismailia-Cairo road, running from the center of the Canal, and the Suez City-Cairo road in the south. Because of the system's relative simplicity and its localization in the southern sector along the most readily accessible supply routes, the missile complex could only be regarded as a demonstration of Soviet capabilities and intentions to relieve pressure on Egyptian units in the forward area. Moscow had increased its commitment from the active air defense of the Nile Valley to a deterrent posture for the aid of the ground forces by accepting partial responsibility for forward air defense. It had not yet accepted responsibility for the defense of the west bank. It was this demonstrated Soviet intention to deter attacks on Egyptian forces that the I.A.F. challenged.

In destroying eight batteries, the I.A.F. lost at least five F-4s and two A-4s, and the batteries were operational within such short periods that their loss had only a marginal impact on the total defense. As a result of this costly and unrewarding experience, the I.A.F. shifted the weight of its attacks to the Egyptian front lines. Flying under the effective engagement altitudes of the SAMs and beyond the ranges of the supporting AAA guns, Israeli aircraft inflicted heavy punishment on Egyptian artillery positions, cutting their own battle deaths in July to one-seventh those of the previous month. By the beginning of the cease-fire on 7 August, I.D.F. casualties numbered 642 killed and 2,333 wounded since the June War, with 330 deaths along the Canal. But during the 1970 spring offensive alone Egypt had suffered an estimated 10,000 casualties, many of them technicians who would be extremely difficult to replace.

At this point Israel's military options were limited. An all-out preemptive attack across the Canal would require complete mobilization, and even then might not succeed because of limited amphibious craft and inadequate bridging equipment. Even if a bridgehead could be established against the 60,000 Egyptian defenders, the Soviets were apt to intervene with air support and possibly with hastily organized ground units mustered from Soviet advisors and Egyptian equipment. The most that could possibly be achieved by a bridgehead would be to provoke American intervention, an unlikely gamble at best. (Former experience with the fidelity of American commitments made such gambles seem highly risky to most Israelis.) Denied plausible options, most Israelis were prepared to dig in militarily and let Hawk missiles face the SAM-3s and patrolling Mirage IIIs pace patrolling MIG-21s. As the minister of transportation, a member of the conservative Gahal party, said, "If I have to face the Red Star of Russia instead of Egypt's two stars, then I prefer not to play." [1]

As the forecast darkened in the first weeks of July, Israeli cabinet ministers leaked the contents of the American peace bid to the press, hoping to prepare public opinion for the possibility of a full deliberation of the Second Rogers Plan. Many commentators reacted negatively, however, and public references were made to "another Munich" and "an American capitulation." The first reaction was that Israel would have to defend itself by *all* means available, read in Israel as meaning weapons of mass destruction. Before this attitude reached serious proportions, U.S. Senator Stuart Symington, a former secretary of the air force and generally respected for his candor in military matters, held a press conference on 13 July and charged that Israel was developing nuclear weapons for its existing delivery vehicles

(Jericho missiles and F-4 aircraft). A lively press debate ensued. American analysts concluded that if Israel did not already have a nuclear capability the last wire could be inserted on short notice. In other words, the project was nine-months pregnant. On 19 July an Israeli government spokesman stated that reports of Israeli possession of nuclear weapons had been exaggerated, but he did not deny the presence of a limited capability. He reiterated, however, his government's pledge not to be the first to use nuclear weapons in a regional conflict. A State Department official then made a similar pronouncement, thus closing the debate.[2]

The Symington revelation and the subsequent public discussion indicated to Israel both the American assessment that the use of nuclear weapons could in no way improve its situation along the Canal and the outright American rejection of the use of such drastic measures in a larger context. The upper limits on Israeli reprisals had been firmly established, yet the episode indicated the degree of frustration that was becoming apparent in Tel Aviv. (The implications of the nuclear debate were immediately perceived in Cairo. Nasser told the July A.S.U. congress that he would seek Soviet nuclear protection if threatened by Israeli nuclear blackmail.)

Military Moves and Countermoves
By the end of the month international pressures had significantly reduced Israel's military and political options. The Soviets had demonstrated their ability and determination to strengthen Egyptian defenses and to move SAM batteries at will inside Egypt, despite energetic Israeli counterattacks. (Eban later admitted that Israel had to accept the cease-fire because the advance of the missiles to the Canal was inevitable.) After the Arab acceptance of the Rogers Plan in July, further Israeli intransigence would have been counterproductive. Furthermore, British and French endorsement of the American plan denied Israel further leverage in the West and signalled that world opinion had shifted against its hard line. Finally, the hardening of the American position had

relieved many Israeli anxieties; and a growing number of Israeli leaders were concluding that lower bargaining aims and a compromise solution were the price of peace and that this price was likely to be inflated with time. Accordingly, on 31 July Mrs. Meir accepted the Rogers Plan and the way was opened for a 90-day cease-fire, commencing on 7 August. At that time, however, Soviet-manned missiles were already being redeployed within the cease-fire zone. On 2 August five SAM batteries were moved within 30 kilometers of the Canal, the line beyond which these weapons could theoretically inhibit the freedom of action of Israeli aircraft in repulsing an Egyptian bridgehead on the Sinai. Just prior to the cease-fire deadline, 12–15 batteries were noted in movement within the Canal zone or in the proximity of the cease-fire zone. The optimism over the cease-fire was thus short-lived.

The continued intensive military activities along the west bank were a direct consequence of Israel's audacious actions against the Soviet Union. The heavy losses inflicted on the Egyptians had apparently been intended both to relieve frustration arising from the inability of the I.A.F. to defeat the new missile complex and to demonstrate continuing Israeli superiority over the Egyptian lines, but this unrelenting pressure led to a new phase of the Soviet-Israeli contest. On 25 July the first aerial contact was reported between Soviet and Israeli aircraft, when Soviet MIG-21Js apparently engaged two A-4s on a bombing run. The Israelis jettisoned their ordnance and withdrew. The Israelis then intentionally baited the Soviet air force on 30 July by feinting an attack on the Nile Valley and ambushing the scrambled interceptors.[3] Israeli Phantoms flew a high-altitude penetration profile toward Cairo, while Mirage fighters remained at low altitude beneath radar surveillence and ambushed the Soviet MIG-21Js as they climbed to intercept the F-4s. (MIG aircraft have poor cockpit visibility by Western standards and, accordingly, are relatively more vulnerable to suprise when they are not under positive radar control.) Four MIGs were immediately downed and the rest fled in the confusion of low-level interception tactics.

The deliberate provocation of a great power on this scale had serious international overtones. The baiting was timed to coincide with Tel Aviv's acceptance of the peace bid, which apparently diluted adverse American reactions. The implications were, however, not overlooked: the Israelis were attempting to gain an important psychological advantage before entering the negotiations. By "evening the score" for the lost F-4s, Israel certainly demonstrated to the Arabs that the Soviets were not invincible and that Tel Aviv was prepared to assume the consequences for directly engaging Soviet troops in the event that the talks were inconclusive. (This was the first firm evidence at that time of Soviet combat casualties in the Canal War; Soviet losses among ground crews could only be presumed. As Mrs. Meir stated in New York on 25 October, "[We know there are Soviets in Egypt] because we shot down four of their pilots." [4] Sadat later admitted that six Soviets had been killed in the missile battle.) The incident was thus a clear signal to the Arabs that Israel was determined to bargain from a "position of strength," despite the Soviet participation in Egyptian defenses. Indeed, it must have been viewed by the Soviets as the most flagrant disdain yet shown for their repeated requests that Washington restrain Israeli use of American arms.

On the other hand, Moscow had made a serious gamble when it placed so much of its military prestige on the line. It probably estimated that Israel would be reluctant to engage a great power and that a Soviet presence in the Canal zone would deter Israel from expanding hostilities, as it had in the Nile Valley. Once its prestige was committed on such a scale, however, it could not accept a situation that risked a compromise or defeat of Soviet arms by Israel. Any jeopardy to Soviet military proficiency would seriously damage Moscow's image abroad. General Herzog, a semi-official spokesman for the I.D.F., observed that the successful challenge of a Soviet-constructed air defense system equal or superior to that of the Warsaw Pact could have a serious impact on the European confrontation. (He also speculated that the rapid pace of the deliveries indicated that much of the equipment was either in place or programmed for the defense of the Pact and the Soviet Union.)[5] Moreover, a tarnished Soviet military image would undermine the confidence and bargaining position of the Arabs at the Jarring talks and would also impair Soviet authority in the two-power and four-big-power talks.

While the Soviets viewed the stakes in the heightening confrontation as the value of their political prestige, Israel saw the clash in terms of its national security. Both sides, accordingly, were forced to place a high priority on the demonstration of their respective military prowess before any political settlement could be sincerely negotiated. When Israel refused to exercise restraint in bombing the interior, Moscow felt compelled to accept a large responsibility for the defense of the Nile Valley; when Israel was not deterred by a Soviet presence in the Canal zone, Moscow systematically expanded that presence to induce greater prudence. At the expense of creating an international image of perfidious and irresponsible behavior by its cease-fire violations, Moscow decided that it would be necessary to erect a deterrent force along the Canal which would more nearly approximate a military stalemate than at any time since May 1967. On its side, Israel increased its demands for modern American weapons with each escalatory move.

The seriousness of the "MIG-baiting" for Moscow was registered by the departure for Cairo of the commander-in-chief of the Soviet Air Forces, Air Marshal Pavel S. Kutakhov, within hours of the clash. During the ensuing investigation, Soviet pilots carefully avoided further contact with Israeli aircraft. On 2 August, however, the first forward movement of SAM defenses was reported, indicating that the Soviets had decided to strengthen their ground environment, rather than their air component, as the appropriate countermeasure against further Israeli attacks. Accordingly, a virtually impregnable air defense wall was constructed along the entire length of the west bank.

Moscow apparently felt compelled to justify its decision in a series of press articles and public statements. On 16 August *Izvestia* made the first reference to the violations of the 7 August cease-fire, but couched its denial of complicity in the context that Soviet aid to Egypt was the first step toward establishing the proper atmosphere for a settlement. Soviet efforts were equalizing the military balance and ending Israel's reliance on negotiating from a position of strength. On 18 August *Izvestia* carried a categorical denial of Israeli charges, and *Krasnaya Zvezda* stated on 9 September that "the Egyptian side has the full right to carry out a redeployment of missiles already in the Suez Canal zone." And *Izvestia* stated on 10 September that the redeployments were necessary for the security of installations and personnel in the event of a resumption of hostilities.

The most definitive argument correlating the MIG losses with the expanded Soviet commitment, however, was made by Brezhnev in a rare public policy statement on 28 August at Alma Ata: "Opportunities now exist for approaching the settlement of the Middle Eastern conflict from the positions of realism and responsibility. What is needed now is not new provocations and subterfuges designed to circumvent or violate the cease-fire, but honest observance of the agreement reached [Resolution 242] and real steps in favor of peace." [6] While most Western observers viewed this as hypocrisy reminiscent of the Cuban missile crisis, it was more likely a signal that the Soviet defenses were nearing completion and that the west bank defensive posture had been satisfactorily consolidated. It was specifically directed at Israel for its audacious "MIG-baiting" tactics. Brezhnev followed the above statement with the comment that "those who have been trying in recent years to impose their will from a position of strength on Arab countries now have a new opportunity to reconsider their adventuristic policy." Moscow clearly laid responsibility for the escalations in the Canal War, especially since January 1970, mainly on Israel and secondarily on the United States.

The Soviet Cease-Fire Violations and Their Immediate Consequences

By 12 August the Israeli cabinet had deliberated on the validity of the intelligence data and the seriousness of the infringements. It was then decided to complain formally to the U.N. secretary-general. On 13 August Defense Minister Dayan reported to the Knesset that at least six SAM launchers had been moved and called on the United States, "which has a heavy responsibility as guarantor of the cease-fire," to insist upon the withdrawal of the missiles. Foreign Minister Eban later charged that the Soviet-Egyptian activities in the cease-fire zone amounted to mockery. The basic credence of these governments, he stated, must be questioned: "What are signed commitments worth?"

Seeming American ambivalence toward the initial cease-fire violations led to Israeli charges that the United States did not have the facts and that its reluctance in obtaining them was detrimental to vital Israeli interests.[7] Charges of American incompetence are more easily discounted than those of reticence. In anticipation of the forthcoming cease-fire, the United States launched a reconnaissance satellite on 22 July into the unusual orbit of 60° inclination. The satellite covered the Canal daily at 0430 and 1930 hours, optimum times for daylight and infrared photography. The low-definition photography was probably transmitted immediately by television to receiving stations, but the high-resolution photography (discriminating between objects one or two feet in dimension) could only be recovered at the end of the mission. No additional launches were made on this trajectory during the satellite's mission, indicating that it functioned satisfactorily. Thus, adequate coverage of the missile buildup was probably available for the two-week period before 7 August.[8]

Strategic reconnaissance SR-71 and U-2 aircraft were in place on 9 August and conducted high-altitude flights, taking high-resolution photographs more than 50 miles on either side of their flightpath. Furthermore, electronic intelligence data covering Soviet and Egyptian deployments were undoubtedly available both before and after the cease-fire. In sum, there appears to be little doubt that the United States had available the information to validate Israeli charges well before 1 September, and, if there had been a margin of doubt, the satellite could have been deorbited and replaced at the cost of only $1 million. But the satellite completed its mission on schedule and its data was processed upon recovery, providing detailed analyses by 3 September.

Belatedly, American Defense Secretary Laird commented on 16 August, "I think the important thing for us is to move forward toward negotiations and not debate what went on 12 hours before the cease-fire and 12 hours after." Mr. Eban responded at a press conference that Israel had irrefutable proof of Egyptian violations of the cease-fire, but that Mr. Laird did not have this evidence as yet. On the same day *Izvestia* voiced the first Soviet rebuttal to Israeli charges. Twelve days after the initial violation, the United States stated that it had evidence of Egyptian violations, but it was still not conclusive. By 20 August Cairo added to this bizarre exchange with charges that American intelligence flights over Israel were a violation of the cease-fire since they provided Israel with important military advantages. Two days later Egypt demanded that the United States halt its surveillance of the Canal zone. On the same day Israel issued another protest against the construction of new SAM sites in the cease-fire zone.

During this interval Israel deliberately delayed approval of an acceptable location for the talks and the designation of its representative. Finally, on 25 August the talks opened in New York with the respective U.N. ambassadors representing both sides. Israeli Ambassador Tekoah registered his government's complaint that the cease-fire had been repeatedly violated, jeopardizing the utility of the talks. Jarring responded that the cease-fire was beyond the scope of his terms of reference, which dealt specifically with the implementation of 242. Tekoah returned to Tel Aviv for consultations on the twenty-ninth, effectively suspending the opening round of the Jarring mediation of the American peace plan.

In a vain effort to allay Israeli fears and maintain interest in the talks, a White House advisor told a confidential press conference on 27 August that the United States was considering a plan for joint great-power peacekeeping operations under U.N. auspices in the Middle East. This was a remarkable somersault: the same officer had spoken on 2 July of "expelling" the Soviets from the

Canal. During the last three weeks in August it became more and more apparent that Washington's initiative had again been undermined and that it was groping for some means of restoring its momentum.

On 1 September American officials stated that they were finally satisfied with the evidence of Egyptian violations of the cease-fire standstill. By 5 September the authoritative Western military-research agency, the International Institute for Strategic Studies, London, reported that 45 SAM sites had been constructed within the Canal zone and that 30 of these had been armed since the cease-fire, giving Egypt a possible total of 270 launchers in the forward area. Moreover, the Egyptian aircraft inventory included 150 Soviet-piloted, MIG-21J interceptors. For its part, Israel claimed on 11 September that there were 90 missile sites in the standstill zone, as opposed to the questionable 12 on 7 August, and that the Soviets had moved their first SAM-3 battery into the zone.

The Soviets had also continued arms deliveries during the cease-fire; the ZSU-24, a four-barrelled, radar-controlled AAA gun mounted on a tracked vehicle and firing 4,000 rounds per minute, was introduced into the Egyptian inventory. (It had formerly been seen only in the Soviet Union and Poland and is regarded as the most lethal weapon the Soviets have against low-flying aircraft.) The SAM-4 GANEF, dual-mounted on a tracked vehicle, was also sighted in Egypt, its first appearance outside the Warsaw Pact. The mobility of this system augmented the versatility of Egyptian static defenses. Other arms being delivered included Soviet amphibious craft and 203-mm heavy guns.

The immediate course of action the United States should adopt remained a matter of controversy. Washington stressed the priority of opening negotiations over rectifying the violations, especially during the initial phase when the question involved only twelve SAM batteries. After three weeks, however, it had become apparent that the Soviets were not merely shuffling missiles from one site to another but were building an impregnable wall. Washington was then forced to side with the Israelis. During the initial three weeks, however, Israeli-American relations were probably more strained than at any time since 1957. Mrs. Meir commented on 3 September that her government had had a difficult argument with the United States over the facts of the cease-fire violations. Israel viewed the American attitude as a reflection on its integrity and an unjust reward for its explicit trust in American guarantees. The public acceptance by the United States of the cease-fire violations eased tensions with Israel but increased them substantially with the Soviet Union.

At this juncture Washington adopted a dual course of action: it urged Israel to continue the talks, and at the same time started probing Soviet intentions along the Canal and mounting pressure against Egypt to "rectify" the violations. In developing its charges, the United States stated that it had hard evidence from its own intelligence sources confirming that both "Egyptian-owned" SAM-2s and Soviet-operated SAM-3s had been moved into the cease-fire zone. This was a clear violation of both the spirit and the letter of the written cease-fire agreement. (As State Department spokesman Robert McCloskey said, "A standstill is a standstill.") "The immediate question now raised by these missile moves," according to one official source, "is whether Egypt, with Soviet support, is indeed attempting to achieve a decisive military advantage under cover of the cease-fire." [9] Answering the question, the source concluded, "All indications are that Egypt is not undertaking an offensive buildup on the west bank of the Suez Canal. . . . Israel still has overall military superiority." [10]

As an initial move the United States sent to Egypt on 3 September a formal protest of the violations of the standstill cease-fire. Cairo replied that it had not increased the absolute numbers but had merely dispersed missiles already within the zone for improved protection. It also countered with charges of Israeli violations by reinforcement of the Bar Lev fortifications and American infringements by shipments of new air-to-surface missiles to Israel in order to suppress Egyptian SAMs.[11] American officials replied that the cease-fire did not explicitly or implicitly pertain to the shipment of arms, although the United States had repeatedly stated a willingness to observe an arms limitation understanding.

Thus, there appeared little hope at that time of shifting attention from the military back to the political aspects of the confrontation. For Tel Aviv the issue had reached major proportions. Once again the Israeli cabinet was split on an appropriate course of action. Dayan, leading a small minority, sought a hard stand. He initially demanded that either the missiles be withdrawn or he be allowed to take appropriate action to neutralize the new threat. By early September, however, he realized that American indecisiveness at the outset of the violations made it unrealistic to expect a complete rollback to the 7 August posture. His minimum position then was that new options be sought which would nullify the effect of the violations and restore some form of mutual respect for a standstill. "If the United States is not in a position to restore the cease-fire," he said, "it must release us from our commitments. When one side deliberately violates an agreement and the other honors it, advantages will be gained that the latter side must be allowed to offset." It was not merely a question of holding the present cease-fire lines in the event of breakdown in the negotiations. Dayan hoped to be able to use Israel's remaining military advantages as leverage in a political solution. To underscore the urgency of the situation, he insisted that Israel suspend participation in the negotiations until a *rectification* of the cease-fire was satisfactorily resolved. Such a decision, of course, would flaunt American leadership in seeking a solution to the crisis. But in light of America's lack of resolution over the violations, it was a necessary price and could provide backbone in Washington's stand against the Soviets.[12]

A majority of the cabinet, however, agreed with Mrs. Meir that such a decision must await the outcome of her talks in the United States on 16–18 September. Dayan threatened to resign, and the crisis soon reached the proportions of May 1967. After losing one-fourth of her cabinet support in the Gahal walkout, Dayan's resignation would almost certainly number the government's days and leave the defense minister in a favorable position to form a new regime. (In an Israeli public opinion poll released at that time, Dayan was regarded as the most trusted leader by 87 percent of those polled and Mrs. Meir by only 74 percent.) The cabinet gradually shifted its support to Dayan's position, and Israel announced on 6 September that it was suspending further participation in the negotiations until such time as a rectification of the cease-fire had been achieved.

After the decision was made, Dayan reversed his field and acted to restore the momentum of the political talks. He apparently calculated that the decision itself would have the desired effect on both great powers, and he therefore began refocusing attention on the political talks by downgrading the impact of the Soviet intervention.

I do not think it is true that the Soviet Union stands shoulder to shoulder with the Egyptians in their fight with us. . . . I do not think there will be a basic change here. That is, I do not think they will leave, or that they will extract the finger which is stirring up and interfering in the war in one way or another. But I do not think they will jump into this war with both feet and both fists. . . . What exists in Egypt is a manifestation of Soviet military capability. If they wanted to put their full weight or even considerable weight behind the Egyptians, there would be much fiercer intervention.

Indeed, the factors that had constrained Soviet intervention in the past were still present and would continue to exist in the future: "They intervened as they did within a many-angled, many-sided framework of limitations." [13] Accepting these specific parameters that governed Soviet intervention, Dayan viewed "rectification" in terms of increased American weaponry. This was the condition for reentry into the talks with minimum loss of face.

The Israeli decision to withdraw from the negotiations apparently added some anxiety to the Soviet calculations but did not throw them off balance or out of sequence. Neither the announcement on 9 September that the United States would sell Israel eighteen additional F-4s as replacements, nor Mrs. Meir's threat over American television on 20 September of preemptive attacks against the new defenses dissuaded the Soviets from moving their first SAM-3s into the cease-fire zone around 11 September or from then consolidating the overall defensive network. Indeed, the Soviets apparently anticipated and discounted the impact of additional aircraft deliveries. Even two or more squadrons of F-4s were now irrelevant to the outcome of the larger game, and the possibility of a resumption of hostilities merely accelerated the consolidation program. The Soviet Union took the attitude that the charges of violations were much ado about nothing.[14] Soviet officials maintained privately that they had done their best to deliver the Arabs and that now the United States was faltering. The real test, they claimed, was the attitude of the belligerents toward 242, rather than the cease-fire. Progress on the substantive issues would be a more significant contribution to regional stability than the cease-fire. They argued that the "nonstart" of the talks could prolong the split between the hawks and doves in Israel and would further erode the government's authority, especially among the increasingly popular conservative parties, and thereby reduce its bargaining flexibility. Further, the situation was becoming critical in Jordan. If the country became paralyzed by a protracted civil war or if the Palestinians won, a principal protagonist of the cease-fire would be lost, and Nasser would probably not be able to fight off the Arab opposition single-handedly.

By mid-October the Arab-Soviet side was stressing the resumption of the talks. Egyptian Foreign Minister Riad informed the U.N. General Assembly that his country had completed its air defense network; he later told an Egyptian television audience that Egypt could not agree to a permanent cease-fire but, he implied, it might be willing to extend the present arrangement for another limited period. On 15 October *Pravda* published a comprehensive restatement of Soviet Middle Eastern policy in a manner normally reserved for major policy statements. The proposed solution closely paralleled the Belyaev scheme and included the Soviet Union's subsequent acceptance of substantial Israeli withdrawals *after* a contractual agreement was signed. Foreign Minister Gromyko conducted wide-ranging talks with Secretary Rogers and

President Nixon during his visit to the United Nations to promote acceptance of the Soviet proposal and to relieve anxieties about Soviet intentions. He argued that the entire issue of violations was having an unfortunate impact on the prospects of the negotiations and told the U.N. General Assembly on 21 October that the Soviet Union sought the prompt reactiviation of the Jarring mission without preconditions.[15]

But the U.S. Congress and the Nixon administration had become thoroughly aroused, despite the forthcoming national congressional elections. Sisco dismissed the latest Soviet peace proposal as "sour wine in old bottles." Massive arms shipments, amounting to nearly $500 million, were committed to Israel. The United States suspended participation in the working level, deputy ambassadorial echelon of the four-big-power talks. When the permanent representatives met on 13 October, the 46th session since April 1969, the United States maintained a hard "antiviolation" stand, demanding rectification of the breaches, while the Soviets called for reopening the talks under the existing conditions. The great-power impasse was clearly apparent to all parties.[16]

The United States was at this time also alarmed by the Soviet attitude in other East-West matters. The State Department publicly charged that the Soviets were building a submarine base at Cienfuegos, Cuba, a violation of the Soviet-American understanding on the withdrawal of Soviet offensive weapons from the western hemisphere. The Soviets had also sanctioned East German harassments along the Berlin access routes on 3–6 October, and Ambassador Abrasimov had introduced a proposal at the four-big-power Berlin talks that was similar to the 1959 demand for acceptance of West Berlin as a separate political entity—thus negating the months of previous deliberations aimed at reducing tensions in this area. At the same time, though, Moscow was apparently acting in good faith in the negotiations for the Soviet-West German Treaty and at the SALT talks. Furthermore, Moscow displayed apparently genuine alarm when two Syrian armored brigades with Soviet-supplied tanks invaded Jordan during the September civil war. Likewise, the Soviet Mediterranean Squadron was reportedly not reinforced during the crisis and maintained a discrete, nonprovocative posture at a time when American contingency forces were on full alert. Indeed, even Soviet propaganda followed a standard, predictable pattern during the crisis: warning against foreign intervention after the threat had subsided, and posing belatedly as a restraining influence by implying that, as a great power, the Soviet Union was prepared to act unilaterally (when, in fact, the opposite was true).

In light of this seemingly ambivalent Soviet attitude, Secretary Rogers ordered an intensive review of Soviet policy and the entire spectrum of East-West relations. The study was aimed at examining the reasons for the Soviet violations of the Canal zone cease-fire and determining whether the Soviet actions were a deliberate ruse, an opportunistic exploitation of the stated American preference to implement the talks, a move calculated to coincide with the favorable progress on the Soviet-West German and SALT negotiations, in which the United States had important interests, or whether they were motivated by yet other reasons.

Israeli-American arguments over the cease-fire also reflected fundamental policy differences that warranted examination. The Israelis viewed the cease-fire as the first test both of the credibility and impartiality of great-power guarantees and also of the veracity of Arab intentions to abide by any permanent settlement. If the cease-fire could not be supervised to the mutual satisfaction of all parties, then signed agreements would not be binding and could not be reliably enforced by the great powers. American arguments that the negotiations were likely to result in secure borders were regarded as irrelevant; if the United States could not honor its guarantees (as had happened in May 1967 during the dispute over passage through the Straits of Tiran), then Israel would have to rely on its own resources to protect its security interests. Israel viewed both the 1967 and 1970 violations as casus belli, but also, and more important, as tests of American intentions.

On the other hand, the United States maintained that, while it was possible to fight and talk at the same time, hostilities are generally not conducive to a successful negotiation process. After months of persistence, the State Department had finally given up its attempts to present mutually acceptable package solutions to both sides and, in compliance with Israeli demands, concentrated on bringing the parties together. To achieve this initial step toward a settlement, the United States had held that it was vital to cultivate an atmosphere of commonality of interests among the belligerents, and had therefore advocated the cessation of the conflict as a prerequisite for a favorable negotiating climate. If the talks broke down, Washington argued, then would be the time to discuss the credibility of great-power guarantees; to do so before would only prejudice the negotiations.

Developing Diplomatic Positions
An unexpected development occurred with the death of Nasser on 28 September. He had successfully restored his authority after the June War both at home and abroad. He was clearly the central figure in the Arab world and the only leader with sufficient stature to control issues of war and peace. Even in the controversial decision to accept the American cease-fire, he had effectively isolated or silenced his critics and had emerged in a stronger position than ever. Moreover, in his 18-year rule, Nasser had established strong personal respect and credibility in Moscow. Finally, his strong one-man rule had left his potential successors shrouded in mystery; few Arabs and outsiders had heard of Anwar el Sadat or knew anything of his personal opinions. Thus, when the cease-fire was nearly two-thirds expired and the talks suspended, an unknown figure entered the deliberations amid widespread speculation about persisting political turmoil in Cairo.

The transition proved to be remarkably smooth. Sadat's succession to Nasser's mantle was not challenged for nine months, and he quickly acted to dispel suggestions that Cairo would weaken its bargaining position because of domestic political rivalry. Sadat publicly stated upon accepting office that all the Arab territory must be returned; and, in a policy statement before the National

Assembly, he reaffirmed that there could be no partial surrender or partial withdrawal from Arab territory.[17] Thus, the bargaining positions remained roughly the same despite the change of leaders, and on 7 November Sadat agreed to an extension of the cease-fire for an additional 90 days. However, the long-term durability of his administration still remained to be tested, and it was not at all certain that Sadat would have the political stamina to make the hard choices about the resumption of fighting.

Israel entered the second cease-fire period with substantial handicaps. It wanted to preserve the cease-fire indefinitely if possible and was prepared to resume the peace talks. It was now clear that the Soviets had constructed a formidable bastion along the Canal with all the characteristics of permanency, and that the United States was unwilling or unable to restore the military situation to what it had been prior to the cease-fire. Failure to participate in the talks would soon be counterproductive, as world opinion concerning the onus for delaying peace shifted from the cease-fire violations issue to Israeli reticence. What price could it reasonably expect for resuming the talks and accepting the "unrectified" military situation?

On 18 November Eban went to Washington to explore these terms. He proposed four conditions: continued assurance of American military presence in the region and support if necessary for Israel; long-term financial aid and permission to buy the military equipment of its choice; assurance that the United States would not press its views on a territorial settlement; and guarantees that the United States would exercise its veto in the Security Council on any issue detrimental to Israeli interests. On the first matter, Washington reportedly reaffirmed the commitments, undertaken by Nixon in his July note to Mrs. Meir, concerning the permanency of the American military presence in the Mediterranean and the preservation of regional stability. Second, Nixon tried to accelerate disposition of the $300 million in credits and the $200 million grant that had been approved by Congress in December, but he could not provide long-term commitments and he refused to grant unrestrained purchasing powers. Third, the United States agreed that it was preferable to allow the parties concerned to work out the terms for a final settlement themselves and restated that its suggestions for a settlement were merely proposals, although it reserved the right to express its views if those efforts failed. Finally, the United States firmly refused to tie its Security Council veto power to Israeli interests in any future controversy.[18]

Israel's terms were high and reflected its concern about having to resume talks largely on Soviet conditions and without having secured redress for its grievances. They also registered continuing speculation in Israel about the ultimate value of the talks. It was widely feared that none of the Arab governments—Egypt, Syria, or Jordan—were strong enough to accept a compromise settlement and make it last.[19] Thus, it was not feasible to expect peace in the foreseeable future; only an improved armistice could be hoped for. If peace were possible, Israel could base its security on it, but without peace it could only rely on certain strategic advantages. In this situation it was generally felt that participating in the talks would only force Israel to make concessions that were detrimental to its national interests and that could not be reciprocated. These views were consistent with the growing conservative sentiments in Israel at that time.

Defense Minister Dayan advanced his own initiative for resuming the talks on 17 November before a meeting of the Labor party. He proposed that the Soviets offer some gesture, such as renewing the cease-fire a third time, as compensation for the violations. The two sides could then discuss a mutual thinning of military forces along the two sides of the Canal. Movement would include only heavy equipment—tanks and artillery—which would be withdrawn about 20 miles from both banks, but it need not include the new Egyptian air defenses. If successful, the Canal might be reopened and returned to normal operations. He viewed his proposal, however, as becoming a relatively permanent arrangement for the Canal zone, an obviously unappealing feature for the Arabs.[20] Dayan then made repeated public calls for an Israeli return to the talks, but the majority of the cabinet felt that the plan was unrealistic.

Instead, Mrs. Meir sent a note to President Nixon on 2 December asking for further clarification of the American position on the four conditions for Israeli resumption of the talks. The prompt American reply and additional amplifications on 18 December of essentially the unchanged U.S. stance apparently satisfied Israeli reservations, but the decision to reenter the talks was delayed until the end of the month.

At that time Mrs. Meir justified the cabinet's decision to resume participation in the Jarring mission by reference to the clarification of the American position on key issues, which she assessed in her own somewhat exaggerated terms:

The principle in American policy of preserving the balance of power in the Middle East, lest it be upset to Israel's disadvantage, has recently received strengthening and consolidation. . . . The efforts toward an agreed solution between the parties, to be brought about as a result of free negotiations between them, constitutes one of the principles of United States policy in all that concerns a solution to the Arab-Israeli conflict. . . . In accordance with this principle, we have grounds for assuming that the United States government will not be a party to the determination, by the Security Council, of solutions pertaining to territorial issues, the refugee problem, and other subjects, the solution to which is a matter for negotiation and agreement between the parties. Recently, we have been reinforced in our conviction that the United States administration is not of the opinion that we ought to enter negotiations, or conduct them, from a position of weakness. The United States holds that Israel is entitled to defensible borders, and does not accept the Arab demand that Israel should withdraw to the pre-June 5 demarcation lines. Furthermore, she does not accept the Arab plans on the refugee problem. We have been reinforced in our conviction that the basic principle is still in force, that the Israeli-Arab conflict must be ended by a contractual, binding peace agreement. Until such agreement is reached, not one Israeli soldier will be withdrawn from the administered territories. This attitude is in accord with, and reinforces, our position that, in the absence of peace, Israel is entitled to maintain the cease-fire lines on all fronts without withdrawal.[21]

In a seeming anticipation of the coming misunderstanding

about the Jarring mission, Mrs. Meir concluded, "We have reiterated, time and again, that we continue to oppose any change in Ambassador Jarring's terms of reference, in any form whatsover. . . . Ambassador Jarring's mission derives solely from the terms of reference laid down in the Security Council resolution of 22 November 1967. And, indeed, this principle was recently confirmed by Ambassador Jarring himself." Finally, she justified the initial decision to withdraw from the talks on the ground that, without this suspension of participation, Israel would not have obtained the military, economic, and political conditions which it deemed most vital.

During the interval of Israeli indecision, the Egyptian position had developed a new ambivalence. In an interview with the *New York Times,* Sadat outlined his revised terms:

1. Israel would have to give up "every inch" of Arab territory conquered during the June War.
2. After this withdrawal, Egypt would recognize its rights as an independent state and would welcome guarantees by the four big powers of all Middle Eastern borders.
3. Egypt was prepared to negotiate at once Israel's right of passage through the Canal and the Tiran Straits.
4. Israel's right of passage, however, would remain dependent upon a settlement of the refugee question.
5. Even if the above points could be settled on terms acceptable to the Arabs, Cairo would still not establish diplomatic relations with Tel Aviv.[22]

Moreover, a communiqué released at the end of Vice President Ali Sabri's visit to Moscow on 26 December stated that Cairo would not extend the cease-fire a third time unless Israel provided a timetable for the withdrawal of its troops from all occupied Arab territories.[23]

In January Foreign Minister Riad toured several Western capitals and elaborated on these views. He explained that the prospects for a settlement with Israel were extremely dim because Israel wanted not peace but a permanent cease-fire and because the United States had proven incapable of forcing a modification of this stand. Under these conditions, Riad held that the four big powers had the *duty to impose the settlement contained in 242* and to provide both Arabs and Israelis with peace guarantees. Without such drastic action, he stated, no accord would be possible. He added that even if a solution were found the Arabs would not establish diplomatic relations with Israel.[24] Diplomatic relations were thus not regarded as a condition for peace, a factor not publicly accepted by Mrs. Meir until March 1971.

In private, however, Riad revealed a willingness to consider important concessions:

1. Egypt recognized that more of the demilitarized zones along the reestablished 1967 borders would consist of Arab territory.
2. The U.N. peacekeeping forces should be, not observation teams, but actual combat troops capable of resisting aggression.
3. Gaza should be given self-determination to meet the wishes of its population.
4. A general arms limitation should be established for both Egypt and Israel.
5. Sharm el Sheikh should be manned by U.N. troops.
6. Egypt would be willing to sign a declaration limiting its application of Article 10 of the Constantinople Convention, which had granted it authority to restrict passage of the Canal if there was danger of war.[25]

Leaders of the four big powers expressed guarded interest in the changing climate in Cairo suggested by these ambivalent signals. They regarded them as indications that Sadat was consolidating his political position and was projecting renewed confidence that the Soviet military buildup had altered the balance in the Arab's favor. These leaders strongly urged Egypt to avail itself of the services of the Jarring mission, which was reactivated in January.

The Revival of the Jarring Mission

Ambassador Jarring's renewed efforts began with a visit to Tel Aviv on 8 January to test the prevailing attitudes. Mrs. Meir reportedly submitted a brief written statement outlining only one new proposal: Israel's willingness to accept its present boundary with Lebanon as the first settlement of all its frontiers. (This border is most critical to Israel since it had been generally accepted for 23 years and since the majority of the guerrilla attacks during the past three years had originated in Lebanon.) On the larger issue of agreed and secure borders, Israel reiterated its refusal to withdraw its troops until after a treaty had defined these lines—but it did agree to withdraw. Yet it avoided defining what it thought those lines should be.[26]

Egyptian Ambassador to the United Nations Mohammed el-Zayyat responded by presenting Jarring and then the U.N. Security Council with a list of minimum demands that did not deviate from Cairo's earlier hard-line stand, except for Egypt's first official acceptance of a peacekeeping force composed in part of the four big powers. It had become clear that Israel's demands for secure borders could be satisfied only with the added degree of stability that could be provided by outside powers. Accordingly, the main thrust of the Egyptian proposals in early 1970 was to employ great-power guarantees as reinforcements for an acceptable line; in Heikal's words, to protect Egypt from Israeli aggression as well as to provide Tel Aviv with adequate assurances. He stated further, "But more crucial for the long run, guarantees and security cannot be achieved by the use of military force. . . . I repeat: A state of peace in the Middle East cannot be achieved through Israeli military power." Only a just political settlement strengthened by four-big-power guarantees, "the maximum security that Israel could obtain," could survive.[27]

Yet both parties remained stalemated on central issues. Jarring, therefore, adopted a new approach for his mediation endeavors. Rather than soliciting from the interested parties position papers dealing with vague generalizations and principles, he formulated his own understanding of the substantive aspects of a possible agreement and submitted it to the three belligerents for endorsement.

I . . . feel that I should at this stage make clear my views on what I believe to be the necessary steps to be taken in order to achieve a peaceful and accepted settlement in accordance with the provisions and principles of Security Council Resolution 242/67, which the parties have agreed to carry out in all its parts. I have come to the conclusion that the only possibility to break the imminent deadlock arising from the differing views . . . as to the priority to be given to commitments and undertakings—which seems to me to be the real cause for the present immobility—is for me to seek from each side the parallel and simultaneous commitments which seem to be inevitable prerequisites of an eventual peace settlement between them.[28]

Jarring's initiative was submitted to both governments on 8 February. It called for a prior commitment by Israel to withdraw its forces behind the former Mandate lines on the understanding that satisfactory arrangements would be made for the establishment of demilitarized zones, practical security arrangements at Sharm el Sheikh, and freedom of navigation through the Canal and the Tiran Straits. Egypt was to give a prior commitment, simultaneously with the Israeli commitment, that it would enter into a peace agreement with Israel covering: the termination of all claims of states of belligerency, respect for each other's independence, respect for each other's right to live in peace within secure and recognized boundaries, responsibility to ensure that no act of belligerency against the other party would originate on its territory, and assurance of noninterference in each other's domestic affairs.

On 15 February Anwar Sadat held a detailed interview with Arnaud de Borchgrave of *Newsweek* magazine in which he revealed his willingness to extend major concessions. He called 242 an embryonic peace treaty and stated that his government's solemn commitment to fulfill the resolution revealed its intention to support a peace accord. This was the first indication by any Arab leader that he was willing to negate unilaterally the Khartoum formula for relations with Israel and accept a peace agreement embodying a political settlement. He called for secure borders. ("The party that needs secure borders is us, not Israel. . . . The Israelis have bombed our heartland, used napalm, with as many as 180 planes in 17 hours of raids in a single day . . .

dropping between half to one million dollars worth of bombs.") He also accepted self-determination for Gaza, and to test Israel's sincerity toward fulfilling 242 he broke new ground by proposing a partial withdrawal of military forces from the Canal and its prompt reopening.

On the same day Cairo replied to the Jarring initiative, accepting all provisos in their entirety. It also expanded its commitments to include assurance of freedom of navigation in the Canal in accordance with the 1888 Constantinople Convention, freedom of navigation in the Tiran Straits in accordance with principles of international law, acceptance of U.N. peacekeeping forces at Sharm el Sheikh, including contributions from the four big powers, and acceptance of demilitarized zones of equal distance on both sides of the former Mandate line. The note called for Israeli acceptance of the same obligations and responsibilities and for a settlement of the refugee problem in accordance with U.N. resolutions.

This was an important breakthrough in the deadlock. American authorities expressed "cautious optimism" and President Nixon called it encouraging.[29] But Israel reacted sharply in the opposite direction. It refused initially to accept Jarring's authority to formulate his own views or to act in the characteristic manner of a mediator, despite an explicit statement in January by Jarring that a more active outside role would be required if the parties themselves were not more cooperative. He was to confine himself to exchanging communications and views between the two sides. But as the scope of Sadat's concessions became apparent, Israel reluctantly accepted Jarring's standing as a third party with an independent viewpoint in the bargaining process.[30] Yet it qualified its acceptance of this demarche by refusing to comply with his formula of extending its prior commitments simultaneously with those from Egypt, a procedure intended to emphasize the equal status of both parties. Cairo bitterly complained that Israel intentionally sought to minimize the impact of both the new procedures and Egypt's concessions by delaying its reply for one week and then publishing it one week later, giving the impression that it was reacting to Egypt's proposals and not to Jarring's initiative.[31] In a preview of the Israeli stand, Eban stated on 17 February that Israel saw no reason to alter its policy of refusing to discuss future boundaries until Egypt declared itself ready to sign a peace treaty—a direct challenge to Egypt in view of Sadat's interview two days earlier, which Eban categorically dismissed. He stated Israel's refusal to withdraw from all occupied Sinai, meaning Sharm el Sheikh and its supporting corridor, and insisted that "peace was never achieved by indirect proceedings." The note of 26 February itself, contrary to Jarring's request for a simple endorsement of his wording rather than a counterproposal, deviated substantially from the original suggestion. This was due to the fundamentally different starting points for the two belligerents and to Israel's insistence upon direct negotiations. Accordingly, Israel remained adamant in its insistence that the provisions of 242 were only the basis for meaningful bargaining and not the outline of the principles to be negotiated.

Specifically, the Israeli note called for a peace agreement that would reciprocate Egyptian recognition of the rights of sovereignty and the formal cessation of hostilities. It added, however, important qualifications. "Israel will not withdraw to the pre-June 5, 1967, lines [meaning retention of Sharm el Sheikh]. . . . In the matter of the refugees and the claims of both parties in this connection, Israel is prepared to negotiate with the governments directly involved [concerning] the payment of compensation for abandoned land and property and participation in the planning of the rehabilitation of the refugees in the region." On the other hand, it called for an explicit Egyptian accord to guarantee free passage for Israeli ships and cargoes through the Suez Canal and for the termination of economic warfare in all its manifestations.[32]

Thus, the two parties remained as far apart as ever, and Sadat's dramatic break with the Khartoum formula had not generated a reciprocal concession of the same magnitude by Israel. Moreover, Jarring's procedural innovations, intended to maneuver around the direct versus indirect bargaining deadlock, also did not induce a favorable response from Tel Aviv. As a result Jarring tried still another device to elicit a more cooperative attitude from the belligerents. Between 5 and 14 March he submitted a list of fourteen general questions, expanding on the specific provisions contained in his requested prior commitments, and solicited formal replies. It was expected that developments in related areas during the interval might induce a more pliant stand. On the contrary, both Egypt and Israel assumed harder positions in their notes of 27 March and 2 April 1971, respectively. Egypt referred not to the pre-June 1967 lines as its conception of Israel's secure and recognized boundaries but to those outlined in U.N. General Assembly Resolution 181 of 29 November 1947. Furthermore, "In view of our past experience with Israel and her denunciation of four agreements signed by her with Arab states, we consider that the instrument to be signed by the United Arab Republic engaging her to carry out her obligations should be addressed to the Security Council," and Israel should do likewise (thus foreclosing any immediate prospects for direct negotiations of a peace treaty between the two parties). On the other hand, Israel reiterated its demand for direct negotiations based on the provisions of 242. Furthermore, it minimized the relevance of international forces and endeavors in providing security to borders with its neighbors; each contracting party, however, could explore whatever additional means it considered appropriate.[33]

These progressively harder stands signalled a new impasse and the growing indifference of the parties to Jarring's efforts. In one sense Israel won its challege to Jarring's authority: he suspended further attempts to engage actively in either mediation or even in his former indirect endeavors to bring about reconciliation. The weight of deliberations had shifted to more immediate and pressing matters, which could be more readily influenced by the great powers than by a U.N. representative, namely, the definition of borders, the cease-fire, territorial guarantees, and a partial agreement to reopen the Canal.

The Border Issue

The border issue had become the critical problem for Israel, as had guarantees for Egypt, and a partial settlement allowing reopening of the Canal was viewed by both as a potential avenue out of the impasse. Israel's firm refusal to withdraw to the pre-June 1967 line was regarded as a setback by the Americans and as a confirmation of Israeli expansionism by the Egyptians. Arab commentators frequently pointed to Israel's development plans as evidence supporting these charges. It had demolished buildings in East Jerusalem in order to construct 21,000 new dwellings for Jews, established 250 Jewish families in Hebron (on the West Bank of the Jordan River), created over 20 kibbutzim in the occupied territories, constructed a two-lane highway to Sharm el Shekih and five tourist hotels in that town, and had generally improved the infrastructure of the occupied territories, indicating an element of potential permanent residency in Israeli plans. These charges were difficult to counter (Mrs. Meir's reaction to a criticism of this policy was, "Why not: Jews have the right to live anywhere [in Palestine] they want").[34]

The generally adverse international reaction to the 26 February note convinced many Israeli leaders that Tel Aviv would for the first time have to establish more precise bargaining terms: the categorical refusal to withdraw, in place of a detailed statement as to what would be retained and why, had created a negative image. On the other hand, reports had circulated for some time throughout Israel that the government had already drawn up maps with maximum and minimum demands, and public opinion polls in March showed that 54.4 percent of the Israeli population opposed any withdrawal without a prior referendum—indicating the extent of the growing opposition to relinquishing any occupied lands.[35] Caught between these two forces, the government felt compelled, without the long-sought prior direct negotiations, a peace conference, or even a definition of peace, to outline its territorial ambitions.

The first public statement by any Israeli authority about gen-

eral border requirements was made by Mrs. Meir in a 13 March interview with *The Times* of London. She stated that:
  1. Israel must have Sharm el Sheikh and access to it, and the Sinai must be demilitarized.
  2. Egyptian troops, tanks, artillery, and missiles must never be allowed in the peninsula, because of the danger of Russians and missiles along Israel's southern border.
  3. Demilitarization should be supervised by both Israeli and Egyptian troops.
  4. The border around Eilat must be negotiated.
  5. Gaza could not be returned to Egypt; rather, Israel would assume responsibility for the refugees and Gaza could become a port for Jordan.
  6. Israel would retain the Golan Heights which dominate the Huleh valley.
  7. Jerusalem would remain united and part of Israel.
  8. The West Bank border must be negotiated, but never again would Jordanian troops be allowed within a few miles of the sea; they would not be permitted to cross the Jordan River. Israel would retain some force there and perhaps on the heights behind. She stated that she was opposed to the idea of retaining Judea and Samaria because of their 600,000 Arabs, and that she opposed the creation of a separate state on the West Bank because of its lack of viability. Jordan could have access through Israel to Gaza, Haifa, and the Islamic holy places.

The rationale supporting Mrs. Meir's tough demands had been released in an eight-page "Pink Paper" by the Israeli embassy in Washington two days earlier. The statement declared that Israel would neither withdraw from Sharm el Sheikh under the conditions suggested by the United States and Jarring nor accept the kind of international security arrangement they proposed. "Israel will resist all pressure, from whatever source, be it military or political, that aims at resurrecting Israel's past territorial vulnerability. . . . [Withdrawal would only be possible to boundaries] that were secure, and shall be rendered so by geography.

. . . [Again] Israel will not withdraw from and surrender a location such as Sharm el Sheikh to the protection of international agreements and guarantees that, by their very substance, cannot but be tenuous. After three wars and intermittent tension between them, Israel has the right to maintain with its own forces the security of Sharm el Sheikh, its only link with East Africa and Asia." It concluded that Israel would not yield, as it had in 1957, to international pressure to withdraw from the Sinai Peninsula and the Gaza Strip and to accept again that "mixed bag of international arrangements and assurances" that broke down a decade later.[36] Dayan elaborated further: "Ben Gurion is right when he says that an uncertain peace is preferable to a good war. . . . But how do we guarantee peace or at least prevent its rapid collapse in the special conditions of hatred and hostility which surround us. The Arabs have agreed to sign a peace accord with us not because they have come to terms with the existence of Israel but to induce Israeli withdrawal. We want security, not just peace documents, and would prefer that Israel hold sensible, effective lines for her defense, even if the Arabs refuse to regard them as permanent, rather than return to the 4 June borders." [37]

The publication of Mrs. Meir's statement on borders triggered two "no confidence" motions in the Knesset and a threat by the right-wing religious parties to withdraw from the cabinet, leaving the government dependent on a majority held by the four Arab deputies. Defending her stand, regarded as too generous by the opposition, she made only one amplification: she opposed stationing an international military force in the Sinai; only Israeli and Egyptian troops would supervise the demilitarization.[38] Mrs. Meir won the "no confidence" vote easily, but the distance between her first position on borders and Sadat's was viewed pessimistically by the other parties in the conflict.

Thus, another serious stalemate emerged between the United States and Israel over fundamental issues and principles. It was only partially resolved when Abba Eban proposed, during his 19 March visit to Washington, to revise the Israeli stand to include only "control" of Sharm el Sheikh and its dominance of the Tiran

Straits. This new formula led to detailed discussions by the
Americans and Israelis about the retention of sovereignty: how
it would be manifested and delegated or controlled; what uses of
the fortress would be envisioned and what facilities would be
required; whether an Israeli presence would be preferable to control; what mechanism could be improvised to allow the restoration of Egyptian sovereignty and a retention of de facto Israeli
administration over the area; whether four-big-power troops
should have observer, police, or soldier status and whether they
should patrol jointly or be confined to separate sectors; whether
there would be dangers to establishing such a precedent for other
disputed territories; and, finally, in the event of a dispute over
either sovereignty or administration, whether specific grievance
machinery should be incorporated into the licensing document.
Such complex problems were not to be easily solved, and six
months later they were still the subject of extensive debate.

The American reasoning was along the following lines: first,
Israel could not expect to gain the support of the United States,
much less that required from its Arab neighbors for a durable
peace, with such exorbitant demands. In other words, Tel Aviv's
emphasis upon geography at the expense of political realities
would deny it its terms for peaceful settlement—the former
would be self-defeating for the latter. Second, the sophisticated
weapons made available to Israel by the United States reduced
more than ever the requirement of territory for security purposes.
Third, there was no basis for Israeli assertions that any of the interested parties were proposing a restoration of Israel's former
vulnerability; indeed, efforts were being made through the provision of international guarantees to afford Tel Aviv maximum
security, whatever borders were finally accepted. Finally, it could
not be more wrong, according to Rogers and Sisco, to accuse the
United States of seeking a 1957-type solution. In 1957 the intent
was to return to an armistice agreement, but since 1967 the
United States has been striving for a peace settlement based on
"direct and reciprocal commitments of the parties." [39] The distance between these two positions marked a new deterioration

in relations between the two states, as evidenced by Rogers's decision to brief the entire Senate, in its first closed session on foreign policy since World War II, after Eban had conducted his own unprecedented closed chat with 40 concerned senators, some of whom subsequently charged that the United States was unduly pressuring Israel.[40] (See below for further details on the deterioration in American-Israeli relations.)

The Issue of Guarantees
After making important concessions, the Arab-Soviet side began stressing the issue of guarantees. Moscow tried to create an atmosphere of urgency in February 1971 by calling for an emergency session of the four-big-power talks and stepping up its propaganda campaign. But there were natural constraints on the Soviet efforts: they could not be too energetic or obvious since the Soviet presence was the chief obstacle, in the eyes of its opponents, to establishing four-big-power guarantees.[41] Yet from Cairo's viewpoint such guarantees had become a crucial matter, for it was felt that they would minimize the prospects of an Israeli attack. (Without guarantees that would allow a withdrawal, Israel could use its position at Sharm el Sheikh to blockade the Strait of Gubal and the Gulf of Suez, could conduct surprise air attacks with its longer-range aircraft with much less warning than could Egypt, and could again exploit its superiority in mobile warfare on the Sinai.) Moreover, an international force appeared to be the most feasible means of balancing and then curtailing the necessity for the Soviet military establishment in Egypt.

Serious signs of stress between Cairo and Moscow were first noted when President Podgorny told President Sadat during his January 1971 visit that Moscow could not support a resumption of the war of attrition in terms of either costs or potential risks. He asked for more time for diplomatic endeavors, but he balanced this restraint with a pledge to expand Soviet air defense responsibilities to the Upper Nile Valley, adding greater military pressure on Israel while providing more protection for Egypt. In view of these developments, Cairo took the lead, suggested at random

and separately by the other three parties, in organizing interest
in international guarantees, while Soviet attention remained
relatively subdued.

On 4 February the issue of guarantees was discussed preliminar-
ily in the four-big-power talks; after that it became the dominant
issue in this forum. But the main antagonists in the dispute remained Israel and the United States. This was illustrated when
Prime Minister Meir and Secretary Rogers issued definitive statements of their respective positions almost simultaneously. Mrs.
Meir rejected the American offer of guarantees, first seriously extended by Rogers on 23 December 1970, when she said, "We
cannot trust what Rogers offers, even if it is proposed in good
faith. . . . There must be certain things which a people must
stand up for, irrespective of the costs and risks. There must be a
deterrent border so that no Sadat can in five or ten years try
again. . . . Why should we serve as a guinea pig in a situation
where borders are not important? Why should we be the only
country in the world that is a protectorate in a framework peo-
pled by Russians, Americans, Yugoslavs, and Indians?" [42]

In a less emotional but equally serious vain, Chaim Herzog,
former chief of Israeli military intelligence and the semiofficial
spokesman for the I.D.F., justified Israel's distaste for guarantees
on historic grounds. He questioned the durability of a treaty with
any Arab government; in the 23 years since Israel had been a
state, there had been 26 successful revolutions and at least 42
unsuccessful attempts in Arab countries. A treaty with one ruler
would not necessarily bind his successor. As for past agreements,
Herzog pointed out that the Arabs had refused either to contract
a final peace treaty or to permit Jewish access to holy places in
Arab lands, as had been explicitly required by the 1949 armistice
agreements, and that the United Nations had proven helpless to
enforce these provisions. The United Nations had gradually developed a vested interest in keeping the two sides apart rather
than bringing them together and had acquiesced without demur
to Nasser's 1967 request to withdraw its forces. Finally, the American refusal in 1967 to honor its 1957 guarantee to insure passage

of the Tiran Straits was a catalyst for the June War. Herzog queried, since Israel can afford to take no risks, upon what can it rely? On treaties with Arab governments who have failed to date to honor most of the numerous treaties signed one with the other? Or on the traditionally cynical Soviet undertakings? Or on international guarantees which have to date proved to be utterly valueless? He preferred a deterrent posture at the present borders to the disadvantages of withdrawing and allowing Arabs and Soviets closer to Israel proper.[43]

In response to such reservations, Rogers conducted his most specific press conference to date on the Middle East and outlined in detail the American position on guarantees. According to Rogers, the American interest in guarantees stemmed from its determination to play a responsible and appropriate role in maintaining regional peace. The decision to participate in a peacekeeping force would be contingent upon the desires of the other parties and the nature of the operation. It did not intend to dictate the composition of the force or how it would be used, and would prefer that the local parties themselves work out satisfactory security arrangements. He stated that the United States was not thinking of bilateral guarantees at the moment and would prefer to participate in a multilateral force composed of more than forces of the four big powers; yet the United States was prepared to play a leading role in providing whatever guarantees the local parties desired. Despite the current congressional climate inhibiting overseas commitments, Rogers felt confident that Congress would support such deployments under appropriate circumstances—when the time was appropriate, the government could request congressional approval and thus give the present formulation a higher degree of credibility. Moreover, Rogers argued that Soviet forces were already in the region in strength and that American participation in a U.N. peacekeeping operation would be the most feasible means of countering their presence and inducing their eventual withdrawal. Various aspects of peacekeeping operations had been considered at the four-big-power talks, but not bilaterally with the Soviets. The four-big-power deliberations should not outrun progress toward a peace settlement, yet it was important to have this vehicle available in the appropriate form if it was desired. United Nations peace-keeping operations had had a spotty record, ranging from success in Korea to failure in the Sinai, but the chances were better than they had ever been for peace in the region, and a U.N. peace-keeping force was, Rogers stated, probably the best instrument available.[44]

With these remarks, the United States attempted to reassure Israel that its proposals concerning guarantees were not meant as a substitute for negotiations or a mutual accord. Negotiations would have to determine what was to be guaranteed before all parties could agree to the best manner for its protection. Guarantees would not be wielded to force an Israeli capitulation on the borders issue and then to impose compliance. Moreover, Rogers's assurances that the local parties would determine what was to be guaranteed also appeased Israel's demands that it must have a decisive voice in influencing the force's composition and juris-diction. The American position on guarantees sufficiently relaxed Israeli concern on this matter that the attention of both parties could be more sharply focused on the immediate question—an interim settlement that would allow a reopening of the Canal.

Characteristics of the Fourth Round

There were several notable hallmarks of the fourth phase of the international efforts to secure peace in the Canal War. First, pri-marily as a result of the cease-fire violations and the compound-ing crisis of confidence between the two great powers, Washing-ton conducted a comprehensive examination of its relations with the Soviet Union. The review concluded that the U.S.S.R. had sought advantages through the advocation of détente and had not cooperated sufficiently to deserve its opponent's confidence. Accordingly, the United States adopted a policy of endorsing détente only when progress was registered in resolving mutual differences. Under the new approach, the two-power talks were suspended during the initial cease-fire period, and they have never been formally resumed. This did not imply a curtailment of consultation on specific issues through normal diplomatic channels, but it did terminate the privileged position that the two great powers had reserved for themselves. Moreover, exchanges between the two on general Middle Eastern problems were confined to the less effectual four-big-power talks. While the two-power talks had been informal in nature, they had proven to be a mutually beneficial avenue of communication, and the Nixon administration had attached high prestige to this almost institutionalized forum. The unannounced suspension of the talks revealed Washington's embarrassment at having invested so much in a dark horse that had become lame.

A second feature was the decline in the diplomatic maneuvering room of the Soviet Union. There was little difference between the Soviets and the Arabs about the type of settlement to be sought; their chief concern was the procedure to be used in securing an accord. Moreover, after the Soviets had raised the level of the military balance roughly to parity, their influence in the outcome was substantially reduced. Their main function became negative, insuring that the confrontation remained within manageable limits, without the proper leverage among the belligerents to propel forward movement. This handicap became a distinctive feature of the Canal War: the Soviets could wield important influence in their sponsored state up to the point that their military aid could produce results; beyond that mark their influence declined.

An even more important characteristic was that the Soviets began at this juncture to realize the harsh realities of their policy of regional polarization. By seeking inroads into local politics through gaining influence in individual states and manipulating this influence to enhance tensions and force local opponents to choose sides, Moscow had unwittingly limited its options as the crisis along the Canal had reached a crescendo. Its one-sided policy had strictly limited its authority to one of the belligerents —the weaker of the two. Its only influence over Israel was negative or deterrent. Since it was Israel, not Egypt, that was now pacing the progress toward peace, the Soviet Union had partially forfeited its ability to shape the nature of the final settlement.

A fourth notable aspect of the fourth round was the expansion of American-Israeli disputes, covering by this time all issues under discussion. The United States disagreed with Israel: (1) over Egyptian willingness to accept a peace accord, with the United States being more optimistic; (2) over the diplomatic role the United States should play, with Israel preferring a strong but silent partner; (3) over the specific arrangements that would provide Israel the greatest possible security, with Israel preferring self-reliance.[45] The credibility of the American guarantees was the underlying theme throughout this period. In a masterful display of diplomacy, Tel Aviv was able to minimize and deflect American indignation over the shootdown of the Soviet MIGs. Israel skillfully diverted the attention of the other actors to the issues of violations and guarantees. The Israelis were so adroit that the other actors finally dismissed the shootdown, despite the fact that it was the key reason for the collapse of the Second Rogers Peace Plan.

The American failure to restore the military balance in the wake of the Soviet violations of the cease-fire created the most serious deterioration in American-Israeli relations since 1957. When Rogers raised the issue of international guarantees for Israeli borders before the dust had settled over what the Israelis had regarded as a show of bad faith and indecision, it further flamed the Israelis' sense of insecurity. The issue of guarantees struck at the basic differences between the two states on Israel's proper borders. Here the distance was so wide that both agreed that the only possible bridge was to attempt an interim settlement that might nurture greater confidence and understanding before attempting further progress toward a final accord.

The agreement to seek a partial settlement was evidence of the degree of mutual influence and common interest the states enjoyed. The United States was Israel's only friend, yet it did not maltreat that friendship, despite its attempts to formulate a balanced position between the two sides. It was this policy of antipolarization that allowed the United States to expand its common ground with both sides at the same time that the Soviet authority was diminishing.

Probably the most significant feature, then, of the fourth round was the assumption by the United States of the diplomatic initiative, and its reluctance to share it with the other great power (it did not consult bilaterally with the Soviet Union on guarantees or on the interim settlement). At the time of the beginning of the cease-fire, few analysts predicted that American prestige would have risen as high as it did in Cairo in less than one year. Few foresaw the change in climate that would permit the first visit of an American secretary of state to Egypt in 18 years. Almost no one envisioned the United States becoming the main mediating force in the Canal War.

A final feature of this fourth period stemmed from the purely military aspects. On 30 July 1970 the I.A.F. had vented its frustration over the loss of seven aircraft during the battle for the west bank and its defeat in the contest for air superiority by downing four Soviet interceptors. This was another turning point in the Canal War: it promoted greater Soviet involvement than ever with the accompanying political consequences. Such a direct affront to a great power minimized the effectiveness of Moscow's earlier deterrent posture and demonstrated to both the Soviets and the Arabs that Israel was prepared to accept the consequences of escalation if its political terms were not met. Indeed, it was a challenge to Soviet prestige of a similar magnitude to the Arab defeat in 1967: in the June War Soviet equipment had been lost by Soviet-trained Arabs, but in 1970 the losses were inflicted against Soviet combat crews. A challenge of this scale could weaken Soviet prestige among its sponsored Arab states and undermine their confidence at the bargaining table; it could also compromise Soviet authority at the two-power talks and even jeopardize its world stature. Accordingly, Moscow decided to accept the weight of international censure for its perfidy regarding the cease-fire and to construct a defensive system that would insure deterrence by its credibility, not by its mere presence. The effectiveness of the Soviet defenses introduced for the first time a military stalemate. Parity of its sponsored state had not been attained, but Israeli technological superiority had been largely neutralized. The combination of Arab and Soviet combat forces had more effectively than any time in the past 22 years denied Israel the option of employing its military facility to serve its political interests.

The United States quickly recognized the implications of Israel's mistake: it had prompted the Soviet cease-fire violations and had destroyed the prospects for a favorable outcome of the Second Rogers Peace Plan. Throughout the autumn of 1970 Washington was at a loss as to how to handle the Israelis. Not until after the pique over the Israeli shootdown had worn off in Washington could the United States turn to the substantive issue of guarantees. But the shootdown was to color American attitudes toward Israel during the next moves toward settlement.

7
The Quest for a Partial Settlement:
February–July 1971

The fifth phase of the efforts to resolve the Canal War, which would be characterized mainly by negotiations aimed at an interim agreement, opened with a new Soviet escalation of its military commitment to Egypt. Between January and May 1971 the Soviet Union expanded its air protection of Upper Egypt from scattered point defenses to a more systematic area defense. Apparently, Moscow had concluded that military pressure was the only form of argument that Tel Aviv would respect, and that even greater Soviet contributions to Egyptian defenses were required to force Israel into a more flexible stand. This assumption was evident in a government statement in *Pravda* on 28 February complaining about the lack of progress toward settlement, accusing Israel of intransigence and the United States of complicity. It warned that the alternative to progress would be renewed fighting, which would require continued Soviet military assistance. Accordingly, a massive airlift was launched on 15 March, and by mid-1971 Moscow had deployed some new types of equipment to Egypt that were not yet in general use even in the Soviet Union.

The 1971 Arms Race
The total free market value of the Soviet equipment supplied to Egypt had increased between 1967 and mid-1971 by an estimated $2 billion to some $4.5 billion (not including the equipment retained under Soviet control, such as advanced aircraft and electronic gear). By June 1971 it was estimated that:

over 200 Soviet pilots were flying 150 MIG-21J aircraft;

Soviet troops were manning 75–85 SAM sites (although some were apparently withdrawn in March);

4,000 additional Soviet technicians were servicing related equipment;

150 new LUNA surface-to-surface missiles, with a range of up to 75 miles, had been deployed along the west bank;

the Soviets had taken over control of six operational airbases at Al Manpura, Jiyanklis, and Inchas north of Cairo and at Cairo West, Beni Suef, and Aswan to the south;

a local command structure had been established similar to that of Central Europe and had been given major responsibility for providing early warning to the combined Soviet-Egyptian forces;

three SAMLET naval surface-to-surface missile sites had been constructed around Alexandria;

sufficient amphibious equipment had been delivered to land an entire division on the east bank;

the latest electronic jamming equipment had arrived;

new electronic frequencies had been introduced into radar and missile-guidance systems, reducing their susceptibility to electronic countermeasures;

the latest Soviet MIG-25 interceptor had been requested.[1]

The subsequent deployment of the MIG-25, which became operational only in 1970 and had not yet been delivered to Warsaw Pact nations, caused widespread concern in the West. These aircraft were assigned a primary role of providing reconnaissance against Israel. However, in the event of a major outbreak along the Canal, they could be employed against the I.A.F. While the MIG-25 has greater speed and altitude capabilities than the F-4 fighter-bomber, these assets would be of marginal value at the lower altitudes where the F-4 is most likely to operate. Indeed, the F-4 has a maneuverability edge over the larger Soviet aircraft that can be critical when it is flown by highly qualified pilots. Nonetheless, the MIG-25's superior avionics were an important new asset, and its Mach-3 plus engine thrust affords valuable acceleration at any altitude. The significance of the small number of 25s, however, was largely symbolic: the technological gap between the Egyptian-Soviet forces and the I.D.F. was in danger of being closed, raising for the first time the spectre of Israel losing its qualitative superiority over its opponents.

While the Soviet buildup was unprecedented, Egypt was at the same time levying a record military effort. On 3 June 1971 Cairo announced a defense budget for 1971–1972 of $1.56 billion, $175 million over the previous year's total and 26 percent of the entire national budget (for the first time approximating Israeli figures and percentages for defense spending). The announcement claimed that such heavy spending was required because of the overall increase in military operations. Nearly a million men were allegedly under arms (this figure was considered high by the authoritative IISS) and 415 combat aircraft were now operational. Despite this monumental effort, Sadat revealed that he had negotiated the Soviet-Egyptian Friendship Treaty in May 1971 because his country required even more arms and equipment than it had anticipated, particularly the latest electronic gear. He estimated that the military budget for the next fiscal year would either increase or remain at the same record level, even if the cease-fire were to hold or a settlement were to be reached.[2]

One basic disadvantage for Egypt was its limited military-industrial base and its consequent heavy reliance on foreign imports to meet its needs. Israel, on the other hand, had created an impressive indigenous base for its war effort. It produced over 75 different types of explosives and propellants, 100 types of ammunition ranging from small arms to missile warheads, 50 types of weapons ranging from small arms to jet aircraft, and over 250 weapons-related products. Israel produced 90 percent of its light and medium weapons needs and in 1969 exported $40 million worth of these products to 35 countries. It produced a medium cargo jet aircraft and a light jet trainer and had designed its own modification of a Mach-2 Mirage. It had designed and produced its own surface-to-surface missile and a ground attack missile. These improvements were the result of the government's consistent emphasis on military research and development—to which approximately 3 percent of the gross national product has been allocated annually.

Nonetheless, Israel had to rely on outside sources for 35 percent of its heavy equipment. France and Britain supplied most of these needs during the 1950s and 1960s, but now the United States has become almost the exclusive source. During the first half of 1971 the United States undertook to offset Soviet arms shipments to Egypt with a $500 million loan for the purchase of 200 M-60 105-mm gun tanks, M-109 155-mm self-propelled howitzers, M-107 175-mm self-propelled guns, M-113 armored personnel carriers, Ch-53 Sikorsky helicopters, additional Hawk surface-to-air missiles, and twelve additional F-4 Phantoms. This new equipment allowed the I.D.F. to shift its older model equipment to reserve units and to standardize the weapons inventories of these units. For example, over 18,000 captured Soviet trucks, 1,500 BTR-40 and BTR-152 armored personnel carriers, and a large number of T-54 tanks and self-propelled guns were assigned to reserve echelons.[3] Thus, as a result of recommissioned war booty and massive American aid, Israel was far stronger militarily than ever, and still enjoyed a substantial qualitative superiority over the Egyptian armed forces. As General Bar Lev, the Israeli chief of staff, said during the 1971 Israeli Independence Day ceremonies, "In the 23 years of our independence, I do not remember a year such as the one just ending in which our armed forces augmented their fighting power in such quantity and quality." [4]

It is now clear, however, that this steady arithmetic progression in the buildup of Israeli military strength was partially offset by the Soviet escalation during the spring of 1971. The Soviets reportedly directed in the autumn of 1970 one of their air defense authorities, Colonel General of Artillery Vassily V. Okunev, former commander-in-chief of the Moscow Air Defense District, to assume responsibility for Egyptian air defense.[5] Okunev apparently identified the most serious deficiency in the Egyptian defenses after the positions along the Canal and Delta had been consolidated as the 500-mile stretch of Nile Valley from Cairo to

Aswan. By May evidence had mounted that the Soviets had assumed responsibility for missile and aerial defense of this region. Thus, Moscow was actively participating in the defense not only of vital urban centers and front line positions, but of almost the entire country (80 percent of the Egyptian population lives on only 4 percent of the land).

While basically defensive and deterrent in nature, the dimensions of the latest Soviet additive partly balanced Israel's technological superiority. The Soviet decision was intended to neutralize Israeli military pressure and inhibit American counteractions; but, despite this seemingly limited goal, the fact is that the arms race in the Middle East had reached proportions unanticipated even one year earlier. For the first time, the Soviet Union had relegated its commitment to modernize the Warsaw Pact armed forces to a lower priority than the active defense needs of a noncommunist, nonallied country. This reversal of priorities could have had implications for the East-West confrontations in both Europe and the Middle East and could only have been possible after the success of Ostpolitik. The creation of a massive Soviet military base in Egypt was then the first major outgrowth of Moscow's renewed overseas strategy and the result of its establishment of a naval presence in the Mediterranean and the expansion of its commitment to the Arab cause.[6]

The qualitative and quantitative improvements in the military equipment and weapons systems of Israel and Egypt were such that by the fourth anniversary of the June War both sides enjoyed roughly equal defensive capabilities and only limited offensive resources. In these circumstances the latest Soviet escalation represented the high point of Moscow's military responsibility in Egypt. Given the scale of the existing Israeli threat, the latest escalation was the maximum commitment the Soviets could provide without crossing the threshold between defensive and offensive weapons and responsibilities. Unless they were prepared to accept the onus of posing as a potential aggressor against Israel, they could not significantly increase their obligations beyond what was assumed during the spring of 1971, and Article 8

of the Soviet-Egyptian Friendship Treaty explicitly confined Soviet obligations to providing equipment and training. The restraints inherent in this posture must have been an important
reason for Podgorny's cautious counsel in January not to resume
a war of attrition. More important, the knowledge that the Soviet military commitment had reached its outer limit provided
for the first time a degree of certainty in the calculations of the
other parties about the implications of decisions they would have
to make in subsequent negotiations. (For example, such estimates
were reportedly an important factor in the refusal of the United
States to supply additional F-4s as late as Sisco's July visit to
Israel.)

Equally significant, and possibly providing a reason for the Soviet decision to make its latest escalation, was the questionable
authority that its military posture in the Middle East could command in the diplomatic negotiations. The Soviet buildup had
already achieved its purpose of deterring Israeli strategic attacks
and defeating the I.A.F. over the west bank. The latest escalation
appears to have been designed more as cement for its influence
in Egypt than as pressure against Israel. The degree of influence
that the Soviet Union could command in Egypt became an issue
of major concern throughout the fifth round, as did the level of
American influence in Israel. Thus, the relationship between
great-power influence and the formation of national policies of
sponsored states was an underlying problem during the attempted
negotiation of an interim settlement.

Background to the Idea of a Partial Settlement
The question of reopening the Canal was first raised as an interim solution in November by General Dayan. He was convinced that Israel must regain the political initiative it had lost
because of the battle for the west bank and the Soviet military
buildup. In his words, "We have demanded total peace, and this
the Arabs were not ready to grant us. The Arabs have demanded
total withdrawal, and with this we are not willing to agree. So
let us have an arrangement that would give us something less

than total withdrawal." [7] However, Dayan framed his suggestion (it was never a formal plan) in terms that were unsupportable by the Israeli cabinet, unappealing to the Arabs, and unacceptable to the United States.[8] The most serious stumbling block to this semiofficial Israeli initiative was the American veto. Dayan foresaw that the issue of withdrawal was directly related to the existence and nature of outside guarantees. (This relationship had given rise in Israeli thinking to the notion that guarantees were meant as a substitute for a unilateral strategic defense.) Dayan envisioned American supervision as a physical presence before the Israeli withdrawal and a Soviet supervision of Arab compliance. When Dayan presented his plan in Washington in December, it was pointed out that an American assumption of such duties would legitimize the Soviet presence along the Canal without providing any assurance of its ultimate withdrawal or diminution. At the outset then, the attempted initiative was halted over the question of guarantees.

The Dayan suggestion had several other inherent weaknesses. It implied a high degree of permanency. The idea of "more territory" in exchange for "more peace" carried a strong inference of a de facto settlement, an acceptance of demilitarized zones rather than a preference for a de jure peace agreement. There was no clear relationship expressed between the de facto standoff and the Jarring mission, Resolution 242, or a peace settlement. Was it to be considered a separate body of stabilizing procedures? Or a set of preliminary confidence-building measures for future contacts? Or a substitute for superfluous and irrelevant negotiations? The suggestion might have met Israel's minimum security demands but it completely failed to meet the Arabs' minimum territorial requirements.

Nonetheless, from the Arab point of view the Dayan suggestion offered several points to commend its serious consideration. It aimed at creating some disengagement between the two sides instead of perpetuating the existing confrontation; it presupposed increased great-power involvement in a "cooling off" stage as opposed to their present status as protectors; it could enable Egypt to become less dependent economically on outside assistance; it could strengthen its international political standing; it would relieve Cairo of the dilemma of whether to reopen hostilities and accept the inevitable additional Soviet aid; it could ease tensions without the risk of provoking a great-power confrontation that would endanger local interests; it could provide a first step toward reducing the Soviet presence; and it would allow the new Sadat regime time to consolidate its domestic position and formulate its own options and initiatives toward Israel.

These specific advantages had a natural appeal to the new regime, but several broader objectives could also be realized through an interim settlement. The increasing military buildup was draining the country of physical resources and emotional energies. Social and economic progress was stagnating, and a sense of profound frustration was evident throughout the society. A partial agreement could relieve the war burden and allow Sadat to demonstrate that he was seeking an honorable settlement, thereby restoring momentum to the proclaimed social revolution.

Second, an interim accord might distract radical opinion from the controversial proposed federation between Libya, Syria, and Egypt and would permit a consolidation phase without eliminating an important justification for its creation—the Israeli issue. A third objective would be to relieve the army's frustration, since the new set of Free Officers that had replaced the purged cadre shared a deep sense of bitter humiliation over the defeat in the June War. The army still consisted of the same fellaheen soldiers and petit bourgeois officers who viewed rank as a means to privilege, but they were now better trained and equipped and not inclined to the euphoria of May 1967. More than ever the newly reconstituted army recognized its limitations, but it would not wait indefinitely for the politicians to prove that the war had not been lost, a fact confirmed by the attempted right-wing coup in May 1971. What was particularly dangerous at this juncture was that the army had regained a large measure of public confidence; had the coup succeeded, it would probably have received a significant degree of popular support. An interim accord that did not sacrifice hopes for a final settlement would ease this tension within the military establishment. Finally, the conclusion of a favorable interim accord could demonstrate to the public that the government had formulated a viable peace doctrine that was both just and attainable. Tying the reopening of the Canal to a partial restoration of lost territories would obviously suit Egyptian opinion. In the past the Canal issue had been firmly secured to the refugee question; this reversal of priorities would signal that Egyptian honor was more important than Palestinian rights. (Sadat confirmed the bisecting of this traditional linkage when he stated for *Newsweek* that his formula for the refugee question was compensation and referendum, not the restoration of political rights.) On the other hand, the return of the lost territories would be proof that the war was not lost, and a partial return would demonstrate that the government had "won" a significant battle without bloodshed, a publicly attractive reward. More than any other single factor then, the conclusion of a partial accord could enhance Sadat's domestic position.

With these probable aims in mind, Sadat tested great-power reaction to a partial agreement. According to Sadat, the issue was discussed during the January visit of Soviet President Podgorny. Moscow apparently did not oppose the proposal, and Soviet Ambassador Vinogradov held daily consultations for the next several weeks with his Egyptian counterparts. Sadat also sent a personal letter to Nixon on 30 January through a private envoy, Major Khaled Fawzi, who held a series of confidential meetings with senior American officials. The aim of Sadat's query was to explore the American attitude toward an Israeli withdrawal and great-power guarantees. In his own words, he "insisted on calling on the Big Four powers to assume their duties and responsibilities to preserve peace in view of . . . their direct interest in the crisis." [9] Rogers's reply to Riad reaffirmed a disavowal of territorial conquest but refrained from a commitment on guarantees— a disappointment to Cairo. Both the British and the Israeli Foreign Ministries noted this expansion of American-Egyptian collusion and its seeming endorsement by the Soviets. Indeed, when Sadat broke his silence on 4 February, there was widespread speculation in all four capitals as to whether it was Moscow or Washington that was responsible for encouraging Cairo.

Sadat's Proposal and Israel's Apprehensions

Speaking to the Egyptian National Assembly on 4 February, President Sadat announced that Egypt would extend the cease-fire for 30 days to 7 March. He also said that Egypt was ready to reopen the Suez Canal if Israeli troops were to make a partial withdrawal from the east bank. Initially, he envisioned a partial withdrawal as a pullback of all Israeli forces to a line from El Arish on the Mediterranean coast west of Gaza to Ras Mohammed on the Red Sea. This was to be an interim withdrawal, leaving Gaza and Sharm el Sheikh temporarily in Israeli hands, and was to be followed by a total pullback to the former Mandate borders. The extension of the cease-fire, which Cairo repeatedly said it would never make, was designed to provide time to test Israeli reactions and to get talks underway on this specific proposal. If an interim accord was reached, the cease-fire would then be extended another six months.

On 9 February Mrs. Meir told the Knesset that Israel was prepared to start negotiations aimed at reopening the Canal, but not on the terms outlined by Sadat. She said that Israel favored opening the Canal to free shipping including that of Israel, but that Israel would not withdraw from the present cease-fire lines until a settlement had been reached. Most significantly, Mrs. Meir tied any partial withdrawal to American guarantees. She stated:

The government of Israel has not adopted any conception with regard to guarantees. The government of Israel will be prepared to discuss additional security arrangements only after agreed security borders, specified in a peace treaty, have been determined. . . . On March 17, 1969, and May 5, 1969, the early stages of the four-power talks, I clearly stated in the Knesset that the four-power talks were an invitation to blackmail, so long as the illusion was implanted in the hearts of the Arab leaders that a solution was possible without negotiations between the Arab states and the State of Israel. . . . Recently, however, the United States has declared its readiness to discuss additional guarantees in the four-power forum. I shall not withhold from the Knesset the fact that I view this readiness to enter into such a discussion at this time and within the framework of the Four Powers with grave concern, even after the United States has notified us that it is opposed to guarantees as a substitute for an agreement between the parties. . . . We still demand firmly that the United States government should refrain from supporting moves that may be exploited to facilitate efforts to evade peace.[10]

Mrs. Meir then commented that "in the course of the entire speech, the president of Egypt refrained from saying that Egypt was ready to make peace with Israel—plainly, clearly—peace between Egypt and Israel," and implied that this was a contributing factor in Israel's disinterest in Sadat's terms. Cairo labelled Mrs. Meir's statement an outright rejection of the Sadat "peace gesture" and a fresh confirmation of Israel's determination to impose adverse conditions on the Arabs. Nonetheless, Sadat followed up his initial offer by specifying in the *Newsweek* interview of 15 February and his 7 March speech that if Israel withdrew its forces to the El Arish–Ras Mohammed line he would reopen the Canal to all international trade within six months and extend the cease-fire. He would also guarantee subsequent free passage through the Tiran Straits by accepting an international peacekeeping force at Sharm el Sheikh.[11] But he insisted that Egyptian armed forces be allowed to cross the Canal. Most important, Sadat confirmed Cairo's willingness to sign a peace treaty with Israel. Thus, with apparent great-power acceptance, Sadat launched a proposal for partial settlement and removed a key Israeli objection by agreeing to seek a final settlement. In fact, the partial agreement was, in Cairo's view, to be linked explicitly with the conclusion of a final peace settlement, a salient omission from Dayan's original suggestion.

At the outset of the fifth round then, the initiative had clearly been seized by Egypt. The decision to negotiate an interim accord on a partial withdrawal brought about a focus on concrete proposals that could produce definitive results. Moreover, the Sadat peace gesture unquestionably killed the Khartoum formula; yet it triggered no exceptionally adverse reaction in the Arab world. The reason for this relatively calm Arab response was that King Hussein had won the September civil war by destroying the Palestinians' major combat formations, while his small air force had defeated two Syrian tank brigades. As a result, the Palestinians were seriously disorganized, were disillusioned with both their own leadership and their principal sources of external support, and were no longer a viable military factor in Middle Eastern politics. (Paradoxically, despite the increased latitude that the defeat of the Palestinians provided Sadat, he led the Arab reaction against Hussein's decision, in July 1971, to eject forcibly or imprison all "disloyal" Palestinians, a move which eliminated almost all the guerrilla factions in Jordan and greatly improved the prospects for a favorable outcome to Sadat's peace gesture.)

The Israeli government had been completely surprised by both the 8 February Jarring initiative (see chapter 6) and the 4 February Sadat peace gesture. As the impact of the dimensions of these two moves began to register, an examination was immediately made of what had happened. The conclusion was reached (erroneously, as it turned out) that Washington had shifted its center of gravity, that it had sponsored both Sadat's and Jarring's enterprises as instruments to impose the distasteful Rogers Peace Plans on Israel. Mrs. Meir and many of her cabinet colleagues were convinced that Israel faced a Jarring-Rogers-Sadat collusion that might at any time be expanded to include Moscow, Paris, and London and thus bring about an almost total isolation of their country. This view became the dominant influence behind Israel's moves during February and March.

The Israeli embassy in Washington urged that the cabinet's draft to the Jarring mission be shown to the State Department before being dispatched to the United Nations. The United States suggested that the last line in paragraph four, stating that "Israel will not withdraw to the pre-June 5, 1967, lines," should be deleted. They commented that this view had been expressed repeatedly before and would only add a negative tone to the present document. The American response convinced Mrs. Meir of the accuracy of her interpretation of Washington's intentions, and she consequently insisted that the statement remain in the text.

The Americans viewed this obstinacy with surprise; such provincialism was uncharacteristic of the normally sophisticated Israeli thinking. But Mrs. Meir reaffirmed her demands, charging that the United States intended to impose the Rogers Plan and to substitute four-big-power guarantees for secure borders. After repeated American assurances that this was not the case and that the American position was much closer to the Israeli than to the Egyptian position, Washington became seriously alarmed. For the first time the United States began to question the credibility of Israel's claim that it sought a peaceful settlement. The Israelis seemed to be increasing their demands almost in proportion to the scaling down of Egypt's terms. (Indeed, Cairo had informed the United States that it no longer required the return of all territory if some plausible alternative formula could be found and that it was prepared to enter into direct negotiations over the reopening of the Canal.)

This quasi-crisis between the two states was due entirely to mistaken Israeli assumptions and their highly restricted view of the legitimate interests of outside powers; yet the Israelis persisted. Mrs. Meir's 13 March statement on borders in *The Times* received a mixed reaction in Washington. While it was encouraging, the State Department wondered why she had not submitted these views to Jarring the month before rather than to a newspaper. That same day Rogers conducted his most extensive press conference yet in an effort to dispel Israeli misconceptions. Mrs. Meir ignored his explanations and later warned that "Israel is becoming the object of strong pressure" and that "Israel cannot trust what Rogers offers us." It was in this climate that the cabinet instructed Eban to take a hard line during his March visit to Washington and his unprecedented confidential briefing to American senators. Eban reported that only "direct talks can rescue the Jarring mission." [12] Finally, on 3 April Dayan, who had been counselling prudence to that time, told the Labor party convention that he preferred a retention of Sharm el Sheikh and continued tensions to complete withdrawal and outside guarantees. The convention fully endorsed the cabinet's hardening position.

In light of this deterioration in relations with its sponsored state and of the growing impasse in the negotiations over Sadat's initiative, Washington decided that extraordinary measures would be required to restore communications with Israel and to promote talks on Cairo's offer. Accordingly, the White House concluded that Rogers should personally travel to the Middle East, the first secretary of state to visit the region in 18 years. But Rogers's personal efforts to regain Israeli confidence were only partially successful. Israeli fears of American capitulation, false though they were, had left a mark. Even after Sisco's subsequent visit to Israel in July, it was evident that the apprehension of collusion or excessive American pressure remained a major undertone in Israeli thinking and that this fear presented a formidable obstacle to reconciliation because it fostered intransigence. The procedural aspect of the issue, or how best to advance the stated desires of both sides, had thus eclipsed both the Jarring mission and the Sadat peace gesture and contributed to the hardening Israeli position.

The Increasing American Role
The response in February of both parties to Jarring's initiative indicated the futility of using the good offices of the United Nations. Unfortunately, Jarring's endeavor had dealt with a general and total settlement; as such, it was difficult to fraction out a single issue for detailed treatment. Yet both sides had agreed to the Rhodes formula for conducting talks. It gradually became clear that a new avenue was required for implementing the indirect exchanges. The United States was reluctant to reactivate the two-power talks and thereby contribute to Soviet prestige and influence. In these circumstances, the responsibility for mediating

or chairing the indirect talks gravitated toward the United States. The precise nature of the American jurisdiction and its relationship to the talks or the two sides was never defined, however, and remained a matter of substantial controversy throughout the period. Nonetheless, neither party could afford to allow a procedural question to impair the prospects for reaching an accord.

While the circumstances surrounding the assumption by the United States of an active mediation role were partly fortuitous, it was also a result of a calculated decision for which there were ample reasons. Washington was convinced that Cairo was more prepared than ever before to reach an agreement. President Nixon stated in his 17 February press conference, "Egypt has been more forthcoming than we expected and I believe that Israel has been somewhat forthcoming." [13] Later, in his Foreign Policy Report to Congress, he commented,

We are encouraged by the willingness of each of the parties to begin to look to the larger interest of peace and stability throughout the Middle East. There is still the risk of war, but now—for the first time in years—the parties are actively calculating the risks of peace. The policy of the United States will continue to be to promote peace talks—not to try to impose a peace from the outside, but to support the peace efforts of the parties in the region themselves. One way to support those efforts is for the United States to discourage any outside power from trying to exploit the situation for its own advantage. Another way for us to help turn a tenuous truce into a permanent settlement is this: the United States is fully prepared to play a responsible and cooperative role in keeping the peace arrived at through negotiation between the parties. We know what our vital interests are in the Middle East. Those interests include friendly and constructive relations with all nations in the area. Other nations know that we are ready to protect those vital interests.[14]

Nixon then elaborated the specific reasoning behind the American decision to take a more direct part in the Middle Eastern crisis. "First, the stakes involved are too high for us to accept a passive role. Second, we could see nothing resulting from our restraint but the steady deterioration of the situation into open war. Third, it would have been intolerable to subordinate our own hopes for global peace and a more stable relationship with the Soviet Union to the local animosities of the Middle East." He then defined the direction of the pending American effort when he stated that the conflicting interests of the parties could be reconciled if the three conditions were met: "judgment on each side that the other is willing to make and live up to commitments that could produce a just and lasting peace; judgment on each side that the other will be able to keep its commitments; judgment on each side that the world community can provide realistic supplementary guarantees of whatever agreements may be reached." Nixon also observed that the lack of mutual confidence between the two sides was so deep that only supplementary guarantees could add an element of assurance. Such guarantees, coupled in time with a reduction of armed strength on both sides, could give the agreement permanence. He then commented on the role of the great powers: "Throughout most of 1969 we had attempted to engage the Soviet Union in developing a basis for Arab-Israeli negotiations. . . . The Soviets have insisted that the major powers make these judgments [on the terms for agreement] and, in effect, impose them on the parties." The United States had rejected this approach and had consistently maintained that the provisions must meet the legitimate concerns of both sides. In other words, the Nixon administration was increasingly optimistic about the prospects for securing an interim solution despite the inability of the great powers to collaborate, and it was sufficiently encouraged to assume the risks associated with lending its prestige to a more active diplomatic endeavor.

Moreover, there was also a calculation that by employing its willingness to "play a responsible and cooperative role," the United States could improve its relatively limited influence among the Arab states. Indeed, the more positive antipolarization policy inherent in a mediation role could demonstrate the seeming frailty of Soviet relations with the Arabs and even constrict Moscow's influence. Yet there was also the possibility that the Sadat government might not be able to withstand Soviet pressure and might feel compelled to increase its dependence on the Soviet Union. Always in the background then was the danger of miscalculations by all parties. Secretary Rogers made this point clear in a television interview:

Miss Drew: How dangerous do you now think the situation is, that there is not an official cease-fire?

Secretary Rogers: Well, I think that the situation has been and is dangerous in the Middle East.

Miss Drew: Is it more dangerous now that the cease-fire has expired?

Secretary Rogers: I think probably it is, because there's greater danger of miscalculation. I think there is a reticence on the part of both sides to renew the hostilities, and I think both the Soviet Union and the United States—I know the United States is exercising restraint on the parties.

Miss Drew: Is the Soviet Union also?

Secretary Rogers: I think there is some indication that they are. Yes. But we can't be sure. But there always is the danger of miscalculation, and that would be—if that happened, the situation itself is so explosive that it's very dangerous indeed.[15]

Under these circumstances, the United States informed both sides that it would undertake to formulate a proposal that might be mutually acceptable. On 29 March it presented to representatives of both sides a plan to reopen the Canal. It prescribed a two-stage withdrawal and reopening process. The first phase called for dredging of the Canal in return for Egyptian acceptance of a continuing cease-fire with Israel and a token pullback of Israeli troops from the east bank. The plan also envisaged a later stage of reopening the Canal in exchange for Egyptian willingness to allow Israeli shipping through the waterway. Israel would then withdraw its forces 25 miles from the Canal.[16]

Reactions to the American Initiative
According to the authoritative *Jerusalem Post,* the Israeli cabinet rejected the American plan because it failed to provide for a formal termination of the state of belligerency and a mutual military withdrawal as proposed in the original Dayan scheme. Israel was prepared to consider an interim settlement provided it did

not grant Egypt a strategic advantage and that final withdrawal of all Israeli forces would not be required until peace had been accepted by both sides.[17]

After a hurried trip to Moscow, Sadat elaborated on the Soviet-coordinated view of the American plan. He said Egypt was ready to start clearing the Canal as soon as there was a partial Israeli withdrawal. Egypt would then send its troops to the east bank and would accept a formal extension of the cease-fire for a limited period, during which Dr. Jarring could draw up a timetable for the implementation of Resolution 242. Egypt would accept practical measures for separating the two forces during the cease-fire period, but reserved the right to resume fighting if Jarring's efforts failed. Moreover, Egypt would reject the demilitarization of the Sinai unless the Negev was also demilitarized. Finally, Cairo could not publicly discuss any form of Israeli control over Sharm el Sheikh, including leasing or joint administration.[18]

Addressing her Labor party convention on 4 April, Mrs. Meir rejected Sadat's terms for reopening the Canal. The United States then asked Israel on 7 April for its own terms for reopening the Canal. While the Israeli reply was under consideration, Eban expressed the most conciliatory remarks yet in a press interview:

Although Egypt and the U.S.S.R. gain more than anybody from the Canal being open, there could be a sufficient benefit for the United States and Israel to make a balanced plan possible. . . . Egypt is more likely to agree to a Canal opening than to the kind of overall settlement that Israel would accept. . . . In the climate created by that agreement, perhaps in greater leisure and with less pressure and intimidation, you could continue to explore the possibility of a further step toward withdrawal. We do not tremble at that word provided that the withdrawal is in the context of peace and of agreed boundaries. . . . We say that this Canal settlement itself must not commit us to anything beyond it. But we also do not say it is the end of the story." [19]

His reference to the Canal settlement marked the first time an Israeli official implied that the government had made a decision to accept an interim accord—Mrs. Meir had so far agreed only to discuss the issue. (Six weeks later Eban commented even more hopefully, "Such an interim settlement would be a test case in miniature, a laboratory for a final peace—if it is respected. If such an interim agreement can be negotiated, the whole psychological situation will change.")[20]

On 20 April Israel handed the United States a note containing its terms and sent Deputy Prime Minister Yigal Allon to Washington to discuss the document. Allon listed the main provisions at a press conference: a termination of the state of belligerency between Egypt and Israel; an agreement that the east bank of the Canal would not be occupied by either Egyptian, Soviet, or federated forces (meaning troops from the new federation of Egypt, Libya, and Syria); and an agreement to continue negotiations under Ambassador Jarring toward an overall settlement in the Middle East.[21]

The United States responded favorably. A State Department spokesman commented that the Israeli proposal "offers a basis for further negotiations," [22] and a partial thaw resulted in the mild Cold War between Israel and the United States. On 24 April, however, Riad issued a statement rejecting Israel's terms. The main point of contention at this juncture was the distance between Israel's insistence on preserving its security requirements along the Canal and Egypt's demand that it be allowed to exercise all aspects of its sovereignty over both banks. Both the United States and Israel agreed that Soviet forces must be barred from the east bank, but they could not agree on the extent of an Israeli pullback or on the type and nationality of troops that should man the Bar Lev fortifications. Israel did not want international forces in the front lines or between Egyptian and Israeli troops. It sought an arrangement that would be self-enforcing for both sides. The United States reportedly argued that Egyptian police and lightly armed soldiers should be allowed to cross, but no heavy equipment or major combat formations, and that Israeli combat units should be withdrawn 25 miles, leaving only sentries to guard fortifications and preclude espionage or sabotage. This arrangement would allow Israel to return promptly in the event of a threatened invasion.[23] Differences on these matters did not augur well for a satisfactory visit to the Middle East by Secretary Rogers.

In early May Rogers visited four Arab countries and Israel. It was the first time since 1953 that a ranking American official had set foot in Egypt—a country with which the United States had not had diplomatic relations since 1967. Under these conditions, American prestige was highly committed to a favorable outcome. In departing for his visit, Rogers stated three reasons why the Canal should be opened to international shipping:

1. It would provide additional stability in the area for a period of time.
2. It would prove to the Arabs and the Israelis that it was possible to live in peace.
3. The climate for negotiations through U.N. Representative Jarring would be improved.[24]

In Cairo Rogers again heard Egypt's general terms as stated in Sadat's 1 May and 1 April speeches. Sadat again pressed for a more definitive statement of the American stand on key problems. He reiterated his willingness to reach an interim and final agreement with Israel, but emphasized that there must be a firm linkage between the two—a partial accord could not be a substitute for a permanent settlement based on Resolution 242. Sadat showed some give on the territorial issue. On 9 June he commented, "I am not concerned about Israel. What I am concerned about is the position of the United States. In December 1967 the United States sent us a note recognizing the borders between Egypt and Israel as international borders. I asked Rogers: Are you still of the same opinion? And he told me: Yes." [25] When both agreed in principle that Cairo should retain sovereignty over the Sinai up to the armistice borders, Sadat was prepared to make concessions on the administration of Sharm el Sheikh—an international lease of the fortress from Egypt to be held under great-power auspices. In return, however, he insisted on maintaining Egyptian armed forces on both banks of the Canal as a visible demonstration of Egyptian sovereignty over the Canal.

Sadat reported that the United States had responded favorably but had not formulated its final position and had asked for more time.

In sharp contrast to the productive sessions with Sadat, Rogers's first encounter with Mrs. Meir was publicly labelled by a State Department spokesman as "animated." On 9 June she revealed to the Knesset the terms she had presented Rogers for a partial settlement:

"1. The fighting would not be renewed. Egypt would clear and operate the Suez Canal.

2. No Egyptian and/or other armed forces would cross to the eastern side of the Canal.

3. There would be free passage for shipping in the Canal, including Israeli ships and cargoes.

4. Means of deterrence against the danger of violation of the agreement would be assured.

5. Removal of I.D.F. troops from the water line would not be a stage leading to further withdrawal before peace.

6. Maintenance of the arrangement would not be dependent upon the Jarring talks, but it would also not be incompatible with the furtherance and aim of these talks.

7. The new line held by the I.D.F. would not be considered the permanent boundary.

8. The permanent boundary between Israel and Egypt would be determined in the peace treaty to be concluded between us and Egypt, and Israel would withdraw to it." [26]

There was no give in these terms, and their tone registered a hardening reminiscent of the Israeli position in February, clearly a disappointment for Rogers.

After the stormy Meir-Rogers encounter, Dayan asked cabinet approval to meet with Sisco in the company of Meir's personal assistant and a tape recorder (these provisions indicate that the prime minister knew and acquiesced in Dayan's views and aims, and that the subsequent charges of a sellout by Dayan were unfounded). Initially, Dayan had argued that it would be mutually advantageous if the Canal were reopened. At this time, however, he was convinced that it was the only hope for averting renewed hostilities. He had concluded that Sadat would harden his stand by insisting upon demonstrating Egyptian sovereignty over the Sinai, making compromise increasingly difficult. Dayan proposed a unilateral I.D.F. pullback (not a mutual withdrawal) to roughly the line of the Mitla Pass, slightly over 20 miles from the Canal. This was the next best defensible position on the peninsula and would bring any hostile beachhead within range of Israeli artillery. He agreed to drop demands for passage of Israeli ships through the Canal but proposed instead the right for ships chartered by Israel to pass freely. Egyptian army engineers would be allowed to cross the Canal for operation and maintenance of the Canal, but would not be permitted to bring heavy weapons. Sharm el Sheikh would be administered under U.N. auspices under a double lease from both Israel and Egypt, allowing Cairo to continue its claims of sovereignty and Tel Aviv to influence the administration of the fortress.[27]

Dayan's offer was sufficiently promising that Sisco returned to Cairo immediately after Rogers's visit in Israel to convey the new position. Sadat later related his favorable reaction to Donald Bergus, the American representative in Cairo, who relayed his views to American officials in Paris. Rogers subsequently expressed his optimism over the results of his tour. Sisco later reported that the prospects for an interim settlement had improved because of progress registered by both sides on five problems; Egypt and Israel had agreed that:

1. It would be mutually advantageous for the Canal to be reopened.
2. If reopened, it should be administered by Egypt.
3. There should be some troop withdrawal from the Canal's east bank under conditions favorable to both sides.
4. Fighting between the two sides should not resume.
5. An interim Suez agreement should not be an end in itself, but a step toward implementing Resolution 242.[28]

Internal Egyptian Developments

Despite these benchmarks the Arab position was soon to harden, as Dayan had anticipated. Three main obstacles remained: the linkage between the interim settlement and a final accord; Egyptian military presence on the east bank as a manifestation of its sovereign rights; and the practical control over Sharm el Sheikh. But the chief reason for Egypt's failure to follow up its initial favorable response was the eruption of a major domestic crisis that related specifically to Cairo's Canal policy. Forty-eight hours before Rogers arrived in Cairo, Sadat had dismissed and imprisoned his vice president, Ali Sabri—widely regarded as Moscow's protégé in Cairo. Initially, it appeared that Sadat's action was timed to coincide with the Rogers visit and was designed to impress the United States with Cairo's independence from Moscow. But the dismissal had a momentum of its own, and any beneficial side effects were fortuitous.

The episode marked the closing of the first round in the political succession crisis following Nasser's death. Opposition to Sadat on the part of some of the class-oriented members of the leadership was first noticed after he issued a decree on 28 December 1970 abolishing the practice of arbitrary seizure of property for political and other offenses. His diplomatic initiatives of 4 and 15 February worried others. Moreover, his "friendship offensive" to elicit American support for his initiative was viewed with alarm by the pro-Soviet faction. But the federation with Libya and Syria was the first issue that triggered moderate adverse public reactions and opened the possibility for either harnessing or deposing Sadat.

The federation agreement of 17 April provided for a common constitution, legislature, judicial system, president, and national flag, and a unified military establishment with power to direct units to any of the three federated Arab territories. No political party from one state would be allowed to operate in the other states, but foreign policy moves were to be carefully coordinated. Finally, the agreement was to be submitted to a plebiscite on 1 September. There were several notable trade-offs in the deal:

Libya received assurances of Egyptian protection against internal subversion; the new moderate Syrian regime agreed to subordinate its foreign policy to the common standards; and Cairo promised full political consultations in return for a promise of Libyan subsidies in case those from Kuwait and Saudi Arabia were suspended.

A union of this scope naturally precipitated a national debate. The majority supported Sadat's stand on the Israeli question, viewing it as conciliatory and honorable. They were pleased both with the important dividends forthcoming from the rapprochement he was engineering with Turkey and Iran and with the confidence that Western European countries were manifesting by financing a Suez-Mediterranean pipeline. The war remained the main block to new economic and social progress, and the federation would allow Sadat to negotiate with Rogers for the first time from a position of strength. A strong minority, led by the pro-Soviet faction of the government, held that the federation plan would unduly tax Egyptian resources. The country was on the threshold of major social, economic, and diplomatic developments that would only be diluted by diversion of Egypt's superior administrative skills to the interests of other states. The new oil discoveries would compensate for those lost in the Sinai and would make Egypt an oil exporter; natural gas discoveries in the Red Sea and the Delta would provide the foundation for a petrochemical industry; iron ore from the Bahriyah Oasis for the Hulwan steel complex would soon make Egypt the leading steel producer in the Middle East; and the Aswan High Dam would permit the electrification of every village in the Nile Valley and introduce a genuine social revolution. Critics also added a nationalist touch to their arguments by stating that the emphasis on Arabic culture that would arise naturally from the union would serve to diminish the millennia of Pharaonic history that had been at least as influential to shaping national character.

Both views were aired during the 25 April plenary session of the 150-man Central Committee of the Arab Socialist Union, Egypt's only political party. Sabri's tactics were to create sufficient opposition to selected provisions that Sadat would be forced to return to the other states and seek revisions, thereby diminishing his authority abroad and encouraging calls for his resignation for misleadership at home. Sadat effectively cancelled debate, however, by appointing a committee to review the agreement. He then canvassed the loyalty of the military chiefs before dismissing Sabri and receiving unanimous approval by the Central Committee for the federation agreement. After Sabri had been interned in the notorious Abu Zabal concentration camp where successive waves of communists had previously been incarcerated, Sadat proceeded to dismantle Sabri's power base throughout the government and party. It later became apparent that a left-wing party within the party had been organized by the pro-Soviet faction, whose threatened elimination triggered in part a second coup attempt. (In this context "left wing" indicates a desire for a political settlement with Israel along the lines advocated by the Soviet Union and solidarity with Moscow on other issues; "right wing" indicates a desire for a military solution and a reliance on national or Arab resources—such as the federation.)

Sadat learned of the plot and struck first, dismissing then arresting War Minister Fawzi, Minister for Presidential Affairs Sharif, Minister of Interior Gomma and the ministers of information, power, and housing. While some of the plotters were ideologically affiliated with Sabri, most of the conspirators represented the far right wing. Thus, the political spectrum presented by both coup attempts required a thorough purge of the leftist and rightist elements throughout the entire political apparatus. Sadat acted swiftly. The entire Ministry of the Interior was purged and the East German technicians, who were supposedly training Egyptian security police but were, in fact, conducting electronic intelligence and espionage against the Sadat faction, were dismissed. The entire A.S.U. party leadership units or basic cells were dissolved, and new nationwide elections for membership in 5,720 cells were held on 1 July. Those army officers implicated with Fawzi were cashiered or court-martialled. Some observers concluded that Sadat's days were numbered because of factionalism and continuing opposition, but the comprehensive scope of the purges freed Sadat from challenge on both his right and left flanks.[29]

The immediate post-June War era had been a time of political revolutions throughout the Arab world. The same phenomenon occurred in the wake of Nasser's death, which introduced a protracted period of change. The August 1967 army plot against the government was not, however, directed against Nasser, his image, or his accepted position as paterfamilias. The officers sought mainly to restore deposed army chief Amer to his former position. The plots four years later, however, were directed against Sadat himself. Sadat's countercoup succeeded in large part simply because the conspirators did not formulate realistic alternative policies. The contrast between the attempted coups in the two periods indicates the scale of the changes that followed Nasser's death. The passing of Egypt's great anticolonial leader with his 18 years of tradition and personal charisma propelled the country into the postrevolutionary period of growing modernization, with all its inherently destabilizing forces. Sadat and his successors will have to face a vastly different set of problems in governing a modernizing Egypt than did Nasser.

The coup attempts and the purges had an immediate impact on Egyptian-Soviet relations. There is no evidence linking Moscow with either coup attempt. But, despite the lack of a direct connection between Moscow and Sabri's decisions, Sadat exclaimed when he publicly burned the East German tapes that Soviet intelligence collection against his regime must have informed Moscow of local political conditions. When Moscow did not act to curb Sabri, Sadat must have begun to harbor suspicions about Soviet intentions and the degree of infiltration that the policy of assimilation between Arab Socialist and Communist parties had already permitted. Accordingly, Sadat did not inform the Soviet embassy of his intended actions against either Sabri or the Gomma-Fawzi plotters. He did not meet with the Soviet ambassador until 21 May, and throughout the crisis the Soviet news media maintained an embarrassed silence. Yet the carefully cultivated Soviet political structure designed to insure Cairo's reliability was being decimated. Cairo's participation in plans for the proposed federation, which Moscow strongly opposed, must have been viewed as further evidence of Sadat's growing independence and indifference to Soviet interests and admonitions. Such bold ventures after only six months in office indicated a dangerous trend. Furthermore, Moscow was clearly alarmed at the remarkable appeal the American mediation efforts were having in the Arab world. The more balanced American approach was not only endangering the Soviet policy of polarization but was also undermining its utility in Moscow's principal sponsored state. Finally, Sadat himself had become an enigma to be reckoned with. As Dayan, one of Israel's leading Arabists, stated on 3 April, "Who knows what Sadat is? And who knows what his stand will be in another month or another year?" Will he be a warlord or a peacemaker? In these circumstances Moscow felt that decisive action was required to insure Sadat's continuing dependence and to foreclose his option of soliciting American support.

With only 48-hours' notice, President Podgorny arrived in Cairo on 25 May at the head of a large Soviet delegation that promptly went to work on a Soviet-Egyptian Friendship Treaty that was signed two days later. Opinions varied about the treaty's importance. Mrs. Meir described the treaty to the Knesset as giving the Soviet leaders control over Egyptian policies and introducing an era of "colonial servitude" for Cairo.[30] On the other hand, President Nixon told a press conference that "the treaty will have effect only in terms of how it might affect the arms balance. In the event that this will be followed by an introduction of more weapons into the Middle Eastern area, it can only mean a new arms race and could greatly jeopardize the chances for peace. We trust that that is not the case." But he cautioned that it was too early to make a definitive assessment.[31] President Podgorny repeatedly praised it as a truly historic turning point;[32] but Sadat was noticeably cooler in his acclaim at the signing ceremonies. Later, Sadat justified the treaty by saying that Egypt required more sophisticated military equipment than it had anticipated.

He claimed that the envisioned aid would be a major contribution to Egypt's modernization plans.

In light of this mixed reaction, it is worthwhile to compare the Egyptian treaty with the friendship treaty that Moscow had negotiated with Rumania in 1970, which is regarded as the most moderate accord signed among the Warsaw Pact nations. Article 1 of the Egyptian treaty cites the principles of international behavior that should govern the conduct of both nations in their mutual relations and stresses nonintervention in domestic affairs; it is almost identical with the provisions of the Rumanian treaty. Article 2 outlines the goals of Egyptian development, specifying that it aims only at reconstructing society along socialist lines. This is a weak formula and cites neither "revolutionary democracy" nor the Soviet model for development. Articles 3 and 4 condemn imperialism and pledge the parties' willingness to seek peace. Articles 5 and 6 pledge Soviet agreement to continue supplying technical assistance and their mutual accord in sponsoring cultural exchanges. The consultation clauses outlined in Article 7 are far looser than those of the Rumanian treaty. The Egyptian treaty specifies that regular consultations will be held and that, in the case of threat, the parties will contact each other without delay so as to be able to act in concert against the threat. Article 8 explicitly limits Soviet military assistance to equipment and training; it does not specify active Soviet participation in Egypt's defense, nor does it provide for naval bases. Article 9, reminiscent of the 1930s Litvinov Protocol, provides that neither party will participate in an alliance against the other. Finally, Article 10 states that the treaty provisions are not incompatible or contradictory with any other obligations assumed by either party. This standard provision is also contained in the Rumanian treaty and insures that the Soviet Union can compartmentalize its commitments; but it also raises important legal questions about the treaty's jurisdiction over the obligations of the federated Arab states. At face value then, the Egyptian treaty was more limited in its requirements and obligations than any other treaty the Soviets had recently negotiated, including the 9 August

1971 Friendship Treaty with India. The provisions of the treaty only confirmed the de facto relations between the two countries that had existed for several years; they did not enhance Soviet authority over Egyptian policy; on the contrary, they spelled out limitations to the Soviet military presence and, for the first time, specified prohibitions against Soviet interference in Egyptian domestic affairs. Nonetheless, the most important aspect of the treaty was its manifestation of Soviet sensitivity about its preferential position in Egyptian policy and its indications that this position was not to be abused with impunity by Egyptian leaders.

In deference both to Soviet sensitivity and to pressing domestic problems (the need to reorganize the A.S.U., conduct national elections, draft a new constitution, and hold a nationwide referendum on federation), Sadat decided to adopt a new hard line on Canal policy. His 20 May speech indicated that he had made his last concession for the time being. He did not reverse earlier offers, but it became clear that, until Israel responded more favorably, Sadat would focus on consolidating his domestic power base. Yet this very consolidation process required that Sadat be able to demonstrate to the Egyptian people that he had won something of value from Israel. Mrs. Meir replied on 9 June with a restatement of an unyielding position. Rogers commented lamely at the time that there were still a chance for an interim agreement.[33] Thus, the optimism resulting from Rogers's visit to the Middle East evaporated in less than one month.

Diplomatic Deterioration
In an attempt to break the stalemate, the American representative in Cairo, Donald Bergus, apparently on his own initiative, presented to Riad an alternative solution that called for an Israeli withdrawal across half the Sinai in exchange for a protracted cease-fire. In an apparent attempt to create dissension among his opponents, Riad leaked the Bergus memorandum on 29 June. The proposal immediately rekindled the crisis of confidence between Israel and the United States. The State Department disowned Bergus's suggestion, but Israel remained highly

suspicious.[34] During the Department's explanation to Israeli Ambassador Rabin, the offending document was not presented and its contents were not specifically disavowed. The seriousness of the situation from the Israeli viewpoint stemmed from the fact that this was the first time the United States had defined in detail its specific position and submitted it in writing to one of the parties. This was precisely what Sadat had repeatedly requested and what Israel had insisted the United States should not furnish if it wanted to avoid charges of partiality and trying to impose a solution. Thus, the format of the Bergus memorandum was more objectionable than its particular recommendations, which Israel had already rejected.

From mid-June the diplomatic situation in the Middle East deteriorated rapidly. Dayan claimed that the region was "rushing toward war." Al Ahram wrote ominously that the Middle East was "on the threshold of grave developments." Riad charged that Rogers had deceived world opinion by falsely raising hopes of an Arab-Israeli settlement. "There were never any negotiations," he stated, "this is again American propaganda . . . poison wrapped up in sugar." But State Department spokesman Robert McCloskey replied that Washington was still not discouraged.[35]

But the differences remained wide, and Sisco arrived in Tel Aviv on 28 July to probe alternate Israeli terms. The issues discussed concerned: what kind of evacuation should be undertaken; who should cross the Canal; what kind of observer force should be involved; and what portion of territory should be released to the Egyptians. On the question of guarantees, Sisco apparently stated that an American commitment would only be valid for an overall settlement, not for an interim agreement. Yet he tried to meet Israel's terms for an indefinite cease-fire by offering an agreement with a two- to three-year armistice in return for an I.D.F. pullback of thirty miles. Mrs. Meir refused to withdraw merely for an extended cease-fire and in turn requested additional F-4 aircraft and other equipment. It was later announced by Ambassador Rabin that Israel had received $660 million from the United States in 1970 in economic and military aid but that no new agreement had been reached beyond the expiration date of 1 July 1971. The F-4 aircraft were given high priority by Israel, since the I.D.F.'s only feasible strategy in the event of resumed hostilities would be massive strategic air strikes that could saturate and penetrate Soviet defenses of Egyptian targets.[36] Sisco declined this request and reported upon his departure that no breakthrough had been achieved on any of the differences between the two sides.[37]

Dayan clarified the importance of the aircraft issue in a radio interview. He stated that he knew that Cairo's main terms for a partial settlement had been shifted to include an American pledge not to furnish additional F-4 aircraft to Israel.[38] (Suspension of deliveries of offensive weapons had to be the keystone of Egyptian guarantee requirements.) Dayan rejected a unilateral arms embargo and insisted upon reciprocal rights, whereby Israel could demand qualitative arms commensurate with Soviet quantitative deliveries. On these conditions a partial settlement on reopening the Canal could be promptly reached. Yet he firmly tied withdrawal from Sharm el Sheikh to the conclusion of a final settlement.

Characteristics of the Fifth Round

There were several notable features of the fifth phase of the settlement process. First, as both great powers sought to enhance their respective commitments to the bargaining process, they also assiduously attempted to circumscribe the implications of these obligations. The Soviet Union assumed full responsibility for the active defense of the Upper Nile Valley, but at the same time withdrew its combat crews from the missile defenses along the west bank. Advisors and technicians remained, but the crew positions were manned by Egyptians. This constriction was probably made for several reasons:

1. Egyptian proficiency was improving.

2. A reduced Soviet presence would minimize the possibility of a major confrontation with either the I.D.F. or the United States.

3. If hostilities were renewed and the Egyptian defenses were

again defeated, the Soviets could rightly claim that the consequences were solely Egypt's responsibility: Moscow had constructed the most formidable air defense system in the world and Egypt was simply incapable of handling modern equipment; accordingly, Moscow could demand even greater authority in reorganizing the Egyptian army.

4. Most important, the partial Soviet pullback from the Canal indicated a willingness to define more precisely the outer limits of its commitment to Egypt.

The United States, on the other hand, felt compelled in February 1971 to assume the negotiating initiative, yet repeatedly attempted to convince world opinion and the respective players that its efforts were not to mediate as such but merely to maintain open communications between the interested parties. In asserting that the United States was only providing its good offices, Mr. McCloskey stated, "We are not assuming the role of a middleman. . . . The United States has good relations with both countries. They confide in us and we talk separately with the two of them. We think this is a proper function for the United States. . . . We find ourselves very often extending good offices for what we hope is good reason. So our office is available but we are not assuming the role of Ambassador Jarring." [39] Yet according to official sources the United States did transmit Israel's proposal in April to Cairo, and, even more important, the renewed American efforts were opened with the presentation of its own plan for a partial settlement.[40] Finally, it attached the personal stature of its secretary of state to a favorable outcome and even proposed convening a summit conference on the Middle East. In pragmatic diplomacy, the United States clearly saw its function to be to provide a more intense mediation effort than had Jarring; yet it felt constrained to minimize its endeavors in public, lest failure impair its image in the region and undermine further efforts to reach a settlement.

Second, American reluctance to reengage the Soviets in active cooperation for a Middle Eastern solution was reinforced during the fifth period. The United States was careful not to ignore or abuse Soviet interests in a settlement, but it intentionally refused to consult in a routine manner as it had during the second and third periods. This decision produced a delicate situation: the United States needed to maintain full communications with the Soviets but was reluctant to do so in a manner that would allow them to increase their prestige or capitalize on a favorable settlement. For example, Washington did not consult with the Soviet ambassador on its proposal for a partial accord,[41] but apparently did inquire about Moscow's reactions to the idea of a Middle Eastern summit conference. Thus, American concern about securing a settlement continued to force a certain amount of interaction with the Soviets but also precluded the level of intimacy that the United States had formerly sought.

The final feature of the fifth period was the shock to Soviet influence in its sponsored state that resulted from Sadat's purges. Coupled with the eclipse of Moscow's authority with the Americans, the plateauing of its prestige in Egypt brought its standing in the Canal War to a perceptible low. Moscow had not anticipated the countercoup against Sabri and the destruction of the left-wing power base he had constructed. Moreover, when these developments occurred, Moscow was unwilling to intervene, was powerless to protect its protégé, and was unable to foster an alternative course to that selected by Sadat. The preferred Soviet policy of assimilation between communists and socialists had proven an artifice. Moscow had not genuinely abandoned its local supporters; it had attempted to rechannel their radical ambitions by incorporating their activities within the legitimate Socialist party apparatus while retaining a degree of influence over their behavior and loyalties.

The friendship treaty was a manifestation of this frustration and helplessness and marked a new expediency in Moscow's relations with radical Arab political movements. Like so many other expediencies in recent Soviet relations with the Arabs, it was intended to legitimize Moscow's interests and behavior in the region at the cost of circumscribing its involvement in domestic affairs. Articles 1 and 8 were clearly self-denying provisions that could be cited by a determined Arab leader to constrain Moscow or abrogate the agreement in the event of further Soviet meddling or renewed sponsorship of a pro-Soviet faction and a communist substructure. The treaty also restricted Soviet security obligations to Egypt, while still providing for long-term technical assistance. Thus, while the treaty served as an important precedent in Soviet relations with radical Arab movements, it represented a decline in Soviet influence in its sponsored state. Whether Moscow would be able to manipulate the accord to offset the constraints on its authority that Sadat had recently imposed would depend in large part on the latitude Sadat could nurture in seeking alternatives to the many critical problems he faced. Sadat's options, in turn, now depended increasingly on Washington's willingness to argue the Arab cause convincingly in Tel Aviv. Indeed, for the first time since the Soviet Union had become actively engaged in Egyptian defenses, it was conceivable that the United States might be able to reverse this involvement and minimize Soviet influence in Egyptian and Canal policy.

8
Interim Maneuvering on the Road to War: August 1971–August 1972

Round six of the political efforts to solve the Canal War opened with the eclipse of yet one more American enterprise. The first American initiative in October 1969 had dealt with package settlements, and the second in June 1970 had sought merely a ceasefire. Peace efforts in the spring and summer of 1971 were directed toward securing only a partial agreement reopening the Canal. This last endeavor was Washington's most sustained attempt to mediate in the Canal War, and its failure had a serious impact on subsequent American interest in the problem and on its mediation role in general—meeting one of Israel's long-standing complaints.

The Failure of the Idea of a Partial Settlement
Sadat had first proposed a partial settlement in February 1971, and his flexibility had thrown Israel onto the diplomatic defensive. He quickly scored some notable diplomatic successes, but the dual domestic crises in Egypt and the Sudan in May and July (see chapter 10) introduced several uncertainties concerning Cairo's relations with the Soviet Union and the durability of Sadat's domestic power base, compelling him to adopt a cautious stand on the Canal negotiations. In light of his earlier demonstrations of good faith and sincerity and his present precarious domestic situation, he now expected understanding and more dynamic leadership from Washington. He wanted the United States to take the ball, allowing him to assume a lower profile in the entire proceedings and to mend fences at home and in Moscow.

Washington followed up Rogers's May visit by sending Michael Sterner, the head of the State Department's Middle Eastern Division to Cairo in July. He reportedly told Sadat that if Egypt would maintain the de facto cease-fire, the United States would further its preliminary proposal made in March with more specific recommendations for implementing those portions of Resolution 242 relating to the Canal. In other words, the United States would expand its role as a mediator and formulate its own position on all negotiable points. Sadat agreed and the United States proceeded to develop its ideas on outstanding points in the partial accord to present to Israel—the more recalcitrant party at that time.[1]

(It is interesting to note that the Nixon administration had initially held that the American function in the crisis was mediation. Upon taking office, Nixon pledged to confront the crisis "with a more active strategy, putting forward our own ideas, consulting actively with other outside powers having interests in the area, and employing a broad range of tactics."[2] Early American initiatives suggest that this sense of mission remained close to the surface of official thinking, despite Israeli aversion to the idea.)

During his stormy ten-day visit to Tel Aviv starting on 28 July, Sisco presented the first detailed official American proposal. It called for a two-stage withdrawal of I.D.F. troops over a two-year truce period. In the first phase I.D.F. units would pull back to defensive positions in the mountains 25 to 40 miles east of the Canal, a line Dayan had accepted in May. A token 750-man Egyptian militia force would be allowed to cross the Canal and a U.N. force would be stationed as a buffer between the two, an even less onerous formula than Dayan had presented.[3]

The Israeli side was, however, incensed that the United States had adopted a mediation role and therefore presented an unusually tough position. It accepted a two-phase drawback, but the first stage would be only a thinning of existing forces and the second would be a pullback to existing fortifications only several miles behind the Canal. No definite timetable was attached, but authoritative Israeli sources anticipated the second stage would be completed in ten to fifteen years. Most important, the Israelis refused to allow any uniformed Egyptian troops to cross the

Canal. This position was publicly expressed by Eban on 12 August to leaders of the Labor party. He also raised some other questions: Would a partial agreement be a separate accord from the peace treaty as the Israelis demanded, or the first step toward a final settlement as the Arabs insisted? What would be the duration of any cease-fire connected with a partial settlement? Would Israeli ships be allowed to use the Canal before a final settlement? What type of supervision would be afforded areas vacated by the I.D.F.? [4]

Sisco did not present the Israelis with a written brief or a formal proposal covering all items, but the details of the "ideas" he discussed suggested that the United States was attempting to assert more positive leadership in the negotiation process. Once again the Israeli press lectured the United States on the evils of an externally imposed solution. Sisco's proposals, coupled with the Bergus affair, led Tel Aviv to conclude that American impatience and initiative was going to bypass or negate its cherished aim of direct talks with the Arabs. Accordingly, Israel hardened its position on the main issue, the sovereignty of the east bank. The argument for denying any uniformed Egyptian personnel access to the east bank was that it would be counterproductive to Israel's high priority aim of eventually demilitarizing the entire bank. Once Egyptian troops were present and the flag was flying, they would be hard to dislodge.

It was a foregone conclusion that this rationale would be unacceptable to Sadat. He had to have some visible means of demonstrating the return of the east bank to Egyptian sovereignty or the entire exercise would likely backfire. Sadat told Nixon in his reply note carried by Sterner that he would have to have indications of progress on the Israeli side by the end of August, because important decisions on Egypt's entire foreign policy would be required in early autumn. Heikal later confirmed this urgency and explained the reasons for Cairo's edginess. Moscow had informally told Cairo that it was seriously concerned about the anti-Soviet overtones of the government repressions of leftists and communists in May and July in Egypt and the Sudan and that it was reappraising its overall Middle Eastern policy. Egyptian leaders concluded that this was no idle threat and that the Soviet Union was actively seeking alternative courses of action in the region. If movement toward a partial agreement slowed and if Egypt could not retain the initiative it had launched at such high costs in domestic turmoil and subsequent Soviet reaction, then Cairo would have to seek some new options.[5]

But at that juncture the die had already been cast. On 19 August Dayan publicly called for formal establishment of permanent Israeli administration over the occupied territories. This alarming demand was later officially rescinded by the Foreign Office, but the flag was already up. The three heads of the Arab Federation met in Damascus and issued a war cry. Robert McCloskey criticized both sides for extremism, but his lukewarm comments signalled the end of the third American attempt to seek a settlement.

In a national broadcast on 16 September Sadat formally acknowledged the turn of events by announcing his decision to suspend further talks with the United States. He strongly condemned Washington for duplicity. After asking for more time in May and again in July to advance its mediation, the United States had not communicated with him in two months (meaning it had not reported on the results of the Sisco visit to Israel). Furthermore, in its silence the United States had been guilty of falsely encouraging optimism in the progress of the talks. Egypt, he stated, was abandoning the Rogers-evoked "quiet diplomacy" and would work out with the Soviet Union a joint strategy for the advancement of their common interests. As a first step he called for "open diplomacy," whereby all parties would submit full reports on their respective positions to Ambassador Jarring and the Security Council.[6]

New Obstacles and False Starts

Three trends were discernible during the opening phase of round six. First, the issue of sovereignty over the east bank had become the obstacle to a partial settlement, and Israel had successfully used it to blunt the American mediating initiative. Washington therefore had no important diplomatic bargaining counters when Tel Aviv began later in the year to mount pressure for additional arms and aircraft. Mrs. Meir stressed this point when she told the Knesset on 26 October that a dangerous change had occurred in American policy. At first the United States had opposed allowing the Egyptian army to cross the Canal. Now Rogers accepted it. She also charged that the United States was encouraging Arab intransigence by its refusal to sell Phantoms to Israel, and she implied that the United States had attempted to tie political concessions to the sale. "Israel is not prepared to agree to political conditions that harm our security, even in return for promises of vital military equipment." [7] American policy had begun to drift.

Second, Dayan's alarming demands were the first official pronouncements reflecting the growing expansionist mood of the country. Public opinion polls later revealed that an unprecedented 80 percent of those polled approved the tough line and believed that any territorial concessions should be the subject of a referendum. The rising public sentiment against concessions was to become a major input in Israeli policy up to the October 1973 War.

Finally, the first signs of serious reservations on the parts of both Cairo and Moscow about the utility, durability, and future of their mutual bondage were now visible. It was certainly too early to measure the differences, and signs of ambiguity persisted. For example, after his denunciation of the United States, Sadat stressed the importance of future cooperation with the Soviet Union. Yet throughout the next year, the disillusionment of both partners was to accelerate rapidly.

After the failure of the Sisco visit, Washington tried to keep interest in a settlement alive by diverting attention to restarting the Jarring mission and securing a new definition of its own role. In an exchange of notes in November on this issue, Sadat was markedly cool and Israel declined to reply until after yet another aircraft request was met. Before accepting the suggestion three months later, Israel took precautions to preclude the reason for Jarring's failure one year earlier, namely, his assumption of a mediation role. Israel's acceptance of a new Jarring mission was made contingent upon assurances that he would not table any issue or procedure without prior Israeli approval. According to Mrs. Meir, Tel Aviv wanted "no surprises" from Jarring this time.[8] In other words, Israel insisted upon veto powers over the introduction of any new issues or approaches.

The American acceptance of these terms doomed Jarring's efforts from the start. Paralysis was apparent after his first round of visits in February: Tel Aviv was militarily confident after Washington's pledge to increase its total aircraft inventory by one-third and was therefore not in a mood to negotiate; and Cairo had just battled its way through the arms self-sufficiency imbroglio with Moscow. Jarring met with the U.N. ambassadors from the two sides in May in New York and concluded there were insufficient grounds for him to resume his efforts. Thereupon the valiant but futile Jarring mission was finally relegated to history.[9]

Sadat decided to shift attention during the fall of 1971 back to the U.N. General Assembly—either an act of desperation or a stall, pending more momentous developments. The United Nations had contributed little since Resolution 242 and nothing since Jarring's 8 February 1971 aide memoire, and this was obvious to all parties. The Egyptian campaign was opened with a renewed call by Sadat for a partial accord, while Riad qualified Egypt's acceptance of the Jarring mission with the demand that Israel first agree in principle to troop withdrawals. Eban replied that Israel favored reactivating the Jarring mission but would not agree to unconditional withdrawal before negotiations. (At the same time Mrs. Meir was insisting in Washington on veto rights over Jarring's activities.) On 13 December the General Assembly adopted Resolution 2799 (XXVI) calling for Israeli withdrawal from *all* territory and a reactivation of the Jarring mission to promote an agreement on the basis of the aide memoire which was so objectionable to Tel Aviv. Clearly such efforts were extraneous and distracting from the central negotiating apparatus that had emerged over four years. Little progress could be expected until the parties came to grips with the key issues in both military and political spheres.

In the wake of Sisco's unsuccessful July visit to Israel, the United States concluded that it could not make a worthwhile contribution to a possible settlement unless it had the trust and confidence of both parties. Coupled with Washington's continuing preference for local solutions over externally imposed ones, the new American line indicated a gradual, resigned acceptance of Israel's definition of the proper function of foreign powers. From October through January the United States attempted to hammer out with Israel (primarily in talks between Sisco and Ambassador Rabin) a precise formula defining the upper limits of American participation in any proceedings related to a partial settlement. On 30 January 1972 Eban told the Israeli cabinet that the two sides were still trying to define the differences between the American insistence upon some degree of mediation and the Israeli demand that Washington's role be confined to "good offices," an exclusively intermediary role with no rights for independent initiative.

On 2 February Israel announced acceptance of a "new U.S. plan" for seeking a partial accord, the so-called proximity talks, which was almost identical to the already proven and accepted Rhodes formula for conducting discussions. As one Israeli official commented, what had been worked out was a set of ground rules which would insure that Israel would not again be surprised by any tactic or maneuver by the American intermediary. Israel saw this as an exclusively "good offices" role, but the United States reserved the right to make suggestions on its own in the event of a total stalemate. (Before agreeing to the American bid, Mrs. Meir had authorized a renewed effort by Nahum Goldmann, former president of the World Jewish Congress, to act as mediator. Cairo declined his services.)

The Israeli aim was to place the same restraints on the United States as had been placed on Jarring. Since Israel had been denied its high priority goal of conducting direct negotiations with the Arabs, it was determined to erect the most rigid bargaining framework possible. If it was to give up this privilege of dealing from a position of military strength, Israel insisted on a format that would afford the Arabs as few bargaining options as possible. In other words, the formulas for both the proximity talks and the Jarring mission were designed to force the Arabs to deal with Israel on its terms, thereby compensating for the downgrading of Israel's military supremacy. (The United States had concluded that Israeli intransigence on procedures was the main obstacle to forward movement and had concentrated its efforts at reducing Israeli obstructionism, neglecting and apparently only sporadically informing Sadat of the progress of the Washington talks. The formula for proximity talks was apparently never submitted to Cairo for approval, and during this period Sadat reached his decision to seek arms self-sufficiency. When the Israeli accord on the new formula was announced, Sadat was on his way to Moscow, convinced that an entirely different approach would be required to secure a settlement.)

The American position on the proximity talks represented a capitulation to Israeli demands and apparently reflected "election-year jitters." Not only were Israeli terms accepted nearly intact, but the former American leverage was allowed to deteriorate. In November, early in the political talks with Israel, the United States signed a memorandum of understanding under which it agreed to provide technical and manufacturing assistance for local production of the specialized military equipment and arms requested by Israel. Initial requests included diesel-engine transmissions for tanks, nose-wheel steering mechanisms for jet aircraft, and J-79 jet engines. In other words, the United States had agreed to supply advanced technological expertise for Israel's arms self-sufficiency program. (It appears, however, that requests will be confined to equipment already in the Israeli inventory.)

The rationale justifying this move was that it would redress the American image as Israel's chief arms supplier and would lower tensions with Tel Aviv. At the same time it would not significantly diminish American influence with Israel since arms deliveries had not proven an effective source of influence anyway. Finally, it would not hurt American influence with the Arabs since it was already at a low ebb.[10] But such reasoning proved woefully wide of the mark. This misperception of the Arab reaction was brought home by Sadat's March speech in Khartoum on Arab arms self-sufficiency, in which he charged that the United States had agreed "to produce modern weapons in Israel." He was technically wrong, of course, but he accurately reflected Arab apprehensions over the new development.

From a more realistic viewpoint, the November memorandum did represent a victory for Tel Aviv's campaign to break away from any linkage between arms deliveries and political concessions. Mrs. Meir made this clear in an interview with C. L. Sulzberger:

Mr. Sulzberger: One has the impression reading the newspapers that there is, shall we say, an understanding in one or another form with Washington that, in furnishing more Phantoms, Israel is more disposed to enter into negotiations or talks, whatever you wish to call it, with Egypt.

Mrs. Meir: We want two things. We want to be strong enough to defend ourselves and we want to negotiate not from a position of weakness. One is not dependent upon the other. There is no deal, there is no linkage. Israel's position is on the merits of the case. When we are negotiating with the United States [about] under what conditions we are prepared to negotiate (indirectly, to my sorrow) with our neighbors, we are negotiating on that. When we demand or ask for Phantoms to be delivered to us, we are negotiating for something which we believe is essential to our security. We refuse to acquiesce to a linkage between the two things, and certainly we are not going to be the ones that will institute a linkage.[11]

The American negotiating position during the winter of 1971–1972 clearly indicated acceptance of the Israeli stand on all procedural matters and a resignation on substantive issues. As Rogers told Allon before departing for the Soviet-American summit conference, the United States was no longer interested in formulating package deals or initiating new plans, but merely in creating an atmosphere that would be conducive to negotiations. Washington apparently underestimated the continuing primacy that arms procurement played in Middle Eastern politics. This neglect may have been due to the growing sophistication of Israel's own arms industry. The I.D.F. had become sufficiently saturated with normal armament that it enjoyed the luxury of focusing its interests on improving quality and exploring the utility of exotic weaponry, such as shaped-charge warheads for extremely large bombs, "smart bombs" such as the Shrike, and elaborate electronic countermeasures (ECM) equipment. Two new submarines were contracted for from Great Britain and two military versions of the Boeing C-130Es were purchased for conversion to electronic intelligence-collection platforms. Israel had developed its own TV-guided, air-delivered missile, Luz, and had modified the American Ryan Firebee drone as both an ECM-jamming drone and an attack drone armed with 500-pound bombs and antiradiation homing devices. Work had also been initiated or accelerated on an advanced tank, a gunboat equipped with surface-to-surface missiles, and antipersonnel radar.

Despite these general improvements, Israel remained hypersensitive to its long-term procurement difficulties. It could not become completely self-sufficient without an almost superhuman national effort, and Israel saw little need for such sacrifices. Besides, foreign arms purchases were important means for preserving international ties and avoiding the isolation that Israel has always dreaded. Thus, in the autumn of 1971 Israel mounted a concerted effort to gain American guarantees of long-term procurement rights, primarily of electronic equipment and aircraft. This expanded inventory of advanced systems could allow Israel to request licenses under the November memorandum for an even wider range of equipment.

For example, the construction of the Canal air defense wall, which was superior to any electronic threat experienced in Vietnam, spurred the United States into a triservice countermeasures effort. Between 1965 and 1970 the United States had spent $2.5 billion on ECM research, development, and equipment procurement. In 1971 and 1972 expenditures in these areas increased substantially. A new generation of sensors, jammers, standoff antiradiation weapons, and drone delivery vehicles were developed to provide an improved combination of penetration aids and techniques. Israel could not hope to match this industrial capability and therefore sought assured access to its products and processes.[12]

After its experience with French perfidy over the sale of aircraft and gunboats, Israel was anxious about future aircraft procurement. By the end of 1971 it had developed and was testing three different fighter-bomber prototypes—one similar to a Mirage 5 with American engines, to be delivered in late 1973; a second, an enlarged Mirage fuselage with American J-79 (F-4) engines; and a third, undesignated, all-weather interceptor.[13] Israel also produced a gunship version of the Arava STOL transport and had specialized in helicopter night-illuminating systems. Nevertheless, the Israeli aircraft industry was relatively small, employing only 14,000 people, and remained totally dependent upon the United States for high-performance engines.

Israel acknowledged that it did not need additional aircraft in the immediate future but would later require more F-4s and A-4s to bridge the gap until local aircraft production could meet I.A.F. needs. It also sought some means of institutionalizing engine procurement as an indispensable component for its domestic industry. The United States was reluctant to meet these requests, and from July through the end of November 1971 the State Department repeated the American refusal to consider aircraft purchase orders for the time being.[14] Once again there were two main reasons for this position: the hope of using the aircraft issue to soften Israel's political stand; and apprehensions about the impact that more arms would have on the Soviet posture. The deadlock continued until Prime Minister Meir visited Washington in December.

Mrs. Meir told an airport press conference upon her return

from Washington that she had succeeded in gaining assurances of long-term military aid and that this commitment was not tied to Israeli political concessions. But not until 2 February did Israel announce its decision to accept a three-month-old American proposal to restart negotiations with Egypt over a partial agreement that would allow reopening of the Canal. And only on 6 February did the United States unofficially announce that it would sell Israel 42 F-4s and 90 A-4Ns over a three-year period and that it had reached an official understanding on the sale of licenses and technological know-how for local production of advanced weapons.[15]

Assistant Secretary of State Joseph Sisco testified before the House Foreign Affairs Committee on 20 March 1972 that the reason for the unprecedented new arms sales policy was the Soviet Union's failure to respond to an American call for arms restraint, forcing the United States to act to maintain the existing arms balance. This explanation was both inaccurate and irrelevant. To continue to blame Moscow for the arms race was factually incorrect and politically unwise. It had been more than a year since the Soviets had agreed to new arms sales, and their self-imposed restraint in weapons supply was, in fact, responsible for the crisis that had already developed with Cairo.

The central issue from the Egyptian point of view, however, was not the sale of F-4s but the granting of licenses for advanced weapons, which were regarded by both sides at the time as the single most vital component in the arms race. Psychologically, the production of American weapons in Israel demonstrated a greater commitment to Israeli superiority than any prior move. Industrially, it allowed the Israelis to divert sizeable resources to other military requirements. Politically, in providing Israel with the capacity to produce its own aircraft, including the vital engine component, the United States had erased any hope of using aircraft as a means of affecting future Israeli policy; this was viewed by Cairo as one more manifestation of American resignation from Middle Eastern affairs and the Arab-Israeli dispute.

The Question of Arab Arms Self-Sufficiency
At the same time that the United States and Israel had reached an impasse on the talks formula in the fall of 1971, the Soviet Union and Egypt were also headed toward a confrontation. A serious point of dispute was the degree of Soviet support for India during its offensive against Pakistan. When hostilities broke out on 3 December, the Soviets redeployed MIG-21 and TU-16 aircraft and SAM units from Egypt to India. The numbers were not large, a squadron of each, but Cairo viewed this action as more than symbolic and raised the following objections:

1. Soviet arms and combat crews were being employed against a Moslem state.
2. Moscow had provided sufficient aid to India for it to achieve its aims but had failed to afford the same level of assistance to Egypt after four years of comradely friendship.
3. India's objective was basically national aggrandizement, while Egypt's was more legitimate, the restitution of lost territory.
4. There was more danger of a great-power confrontation in the Indian Ocean because Pakistan was a formal American ally and Israel was only a friendly state.
5. Soviet actions (including an airlift to India of spare parts from Egypt) had depleted Egyptian reserves and forced cancellation of Cairo's planned offensive.

(These views were publicly aired during the March Egyptian-Soviet Seminar; see below.)

The veracity of the charges is less important than the fact that they were made by top Egyptian leaders. They unquestionably reflected the extent of frustration and consternation over what Cairo regarded as Soviet perfidy. When Meir publicly expressed satisfaction with her talks in Washington, the Egyptians became even more anxious. With Egypt no longer able to claim first priority among recipients of Soviet military aid, what recourse would it have if the United States granted Israel more arms? Under the existing Soviet ground rule of supplying only defensive arms, Cairo feared that Soviet military aid had reached its outer limits in the spring of 1971 when the Soviets assumed air defense responsibility for Upper Egypt. There were few conceptual innovations or hardware additives that the Soviets could now offer that were not offensive but could still advance Egyptian aims.[16] Given these limitations, which Cairo believed were self-evident, the Egyptians were embittered when the United States honored Israel's request for a quantum jump in aircraft and licenses for local production. It is obviously too simplistic to view each incremental arms agreement in terms of a linear cause-and-effect relation. Besides the threat factor, political considerations, domestic pressures, budgetary restraints, arms specifications, and numerous other inputs must be assessed with each move. But the United States has consistently maintained that the cyclical effects of escalation could be broken by mutual accord among suppliers. And it was the gap perceived by the Egyptians between Moscow's announced upper limit on defensive weapons and Israel's attainment of almost unrestrained access to the American arsenal that forced the crisis of confidence between Cairo and Moscow.

During the latter part of 1971 Sadat's domestic political position had become so tenuous that he tried to relieve some of the pressure by waging a war of nerves against both Arabs and Israelis. For example, he repeatedly claimed that 1971 would decide the outcome of the Canal War. Vice President el-Shafei stated publicly on 20 October that Egypt had mobilized 800,000 troops for total war: "By the end of the year there will be either peace with justice or total war between Egypt and Israel." And on 26 October Prime Minister Fawzi said in a public speech, "We are facing a major test at present in which we will have to decide . . . the timing of the battle. There will be no other way but to rely on our military strength, our faith, and our determination." On 20 December Sadat addressed an A.S.U. meeting and said that the war of attrition with Israel would be resumed; and authoritative Egyptian sources predicted that this would happen in March 1972. (To ease around the former 1 January 1972 deadline for the resumption of hostilities, the A.S.U. officially declared on 28 December its full support for war in 1972.)

In November Sadat also attempted to rekindle interest in a partial settlement, but he was turned down by Mrs. Meir while she was still in the United States. He offered nothing new and his gesture was regarded by Israel as a gimmick to complicate Mrs. Meir's talks with President Nixon. By January Sadat's domestic political position had substantially deteriorated. Student and worker unrest focused on demands for more assertive leadership and more effective war preparations. Protesters were disillusioned by Sadat's inability to reopen the war according to his own prescribed timetable and were demanding positive action. Even Heikal, his trusted confidant, publicly warned of growing disenchantment and a credibility gap between his pronounced intentions and actual developments. Furthermore, the defense burden could not be continued indefinitely. Total financial indebtedness to the Soviet Union had reached nearly $5 billion and was increasing at the astonishing rate of $5 million per day.[17] These funds had purchased ten additional TU-16 bombers, the new SAM-6 mobile missile system, a new naval base and airbase at Mersa Matruh, and a new airfield at Aswan—both for use by the Soviets. But most of the funds were being consumed by operational costs and hard currency payments for the 17,000 Soviet advisors, technicians, and dependents in Egypt. Clearly, Sadat's position had become desperate, and some dramatic or drastic measures would be required to restore his political stature.[18]

Sadat could not turn to fellow Arabs for the kind of succor he needed. Syria was still obsessed by the guerrilla question. Libya provided vocal bombast and reportedly agreed to transfer some of its French Mirage fighters to Cairo. But Jordan was regarded as politically unreliable and was negotiating for as many as 24 F-5E fighter aircraft from the United States. Iraq was opening negotiations with the Soviets on a friendship treaty that would elevate it symbolically to the stature of Egypt. It was in such circumstances that Sadat arrived in Moscow on 2 February 1972.

To counter domestic pressures, Sadat had to show progress in recovering the lost territories. This feat would require either "decisive" weapons, as the Egyptians called them, or greater self-sufficiency and a corresponding diminution of foreign restraints.

Sadat went to Moscow with an "either-or" presentation that obviously angered his Soviet hosts. He later revealed that he had first requested MIG-25s as the "decisive" counter to the F-4 during his March 1971 visit to Moscow. The Soviets had replied that the aircraft was so complicated that Egyptian pilots could not be trained within a reasonable time, but they finally agreed to supply their own aircraft and crews. Because of Sadat's insistence, the Soviets sought an alternative and convinced Ali Sabri that Sadat was betraying Egypt to the Americans. When Sabri's May coup attempt failed, President Podgorny had presented the completely unexpected friendship treaty and insisted that Sadat's acceptance was necessary as evidence of his reliability. The Soviets sweetened their demands with the promise of prompt MIG-25 deployments. Four MIG-25s finally arrived in the early fall and conducted their first reconnaissance sortie against Israel on 10 October.

Sadat returned to Moscow in October 1971 to press the Soviets for more vigorous action. Four aircraft were only a symbolic gesture that contributed little to Egypt's operational capability. The Soviets promised additional deliveries by the end of the year. When these were not made, Sadat requested on 11 December a further audience in the Kremlin. The Soviets did not reply until 22 December and then stated that he could not be met until February, two months after his deadline for a resumption of the fighting. The urgency in Sadat's mission was enhanced by the announcement on 6 February of the new American commitment to Israel.[19]

The impression soon emerged that, as *Al Ahram* had predicted, it had been the most serious conference to date between the two countries.[20] (Ominously, an unsuccessful armed attempt to free Ali Sabri from prison was made during Sadat's visit, illuminating the degree of tension between the two countries.) In interviews in December and March with *Newsweek* magazine, Sadat was quite candid in his bitter complaints about the enormous burden caused by his dependence upon the Soviets. These were the first hints of a change in Egyptian policy and set the tone from the Egyptian side for the meeting. In light of real or alleged domestic pressure for a resolution of the Canal War, Egypt would have to have a major contribution to its military preparations. Sadat therefore renewed his argument for an offensive capability and an effective counter to the F-4 that would deter Israeli strategic strikes. He also argued that, since Israel was moving toward greater self-sufficiency and organizing its military industries on a long-term basis, the Arabs should adopt a similar stance. Greater Arab self-sufficiency would partially relieve the defense burden and would increase popular identification with the war effort, both critical needs.[21] The Soviets publicly responded at the Cairo seminar in March (see below) that Arabs could not expect to defeat the Israelis in the near future, and they were, of course, reluctant to accept the rationale for greater self-sufficiency for their own reasons.

On their side, the Soviets probably wanted further reassurance of Sadat's fidelity in light of the continuing internal unrest and the alleged failure of the oft-demanded Soviet program for domestic reform. The communiqué stressed Soviet insistence upon seeking a political settlement and refrained from expressing support for Sadat personally. It mentioned "considering" military cooperation only, not prescribing the usual firm promises. Finally, it expressed the need for reactivating the Jarring mission and omitted any reference to saber rattling.[22]

But the central issue was Sadat's demand for arms self-sufficiency. Upon his return, he toured other Arab capitals, including those of the Maghrib, seeking endorsement and funds. He then met on 10–11 March with the first session of the 60-member Federal Assembly of the Arab Federation, and on 16 March he called an emergency session of the 1,700-member A.S.U. National Congress. Sadat apparently encountered some minor opposition since he publicly threatened to resign unless his solution to the "no war, no peace" dilemma was fully endorsed. He won unquestioned support and marked the occasion with the expulsion of a top Soviet general for offending Egyptian honor by rude personal conduct.

Moscow had anticipated the growing concern in Cairo and

launched a countercampaign. After the beginning of the year, visiting Arab delegations were systematically counselled against pursuing a militant line. They were told that the combined Arab armed forces could not defeat Israel and that to attempt to do so at this time would be injurious to the prospects for a political settlement. Moscow undoubtedly estimated that it was acting in the Arabs' best interest, but this radical about-face created confusion and distrust among friends and foes alike. For example, this issue caused a split in the Syrian Communist party, the most effective Communist party in the Middle East at that time. When the two factions journeyed to Moscow for a benediction, the Soviets severely rebuffed the majority group for adopting a militant posture and rejecting the "correct" conciliatory line.[23]

The most dramatic Soviet attempt to clear the air publicly with its sponsored state was the aforementioned Egyptian-Soviet Seminar, conducted in March by the Center of Political and Strategic Studies in Cairo. The cast was impressive. Among the Soviet delegation were Dr. Yevgeny Zhukov, a leading historian and member of the Academy of Science, Vasily Solodovnikov, Director of the Soviet Institute of African Studies, and Viktor Mayevsky, a prominent writer for *Pravda*. Among the Egyptian delegation were Mr. Heikal, editor of *Al Ahram*, Lutfy al-Kholy, editor of the leftist journal *Al-Talla*, and Dr. Ismail Sabri Abdullah, a Marxist and the minister of state for planning. The official purpose of the unprecedented seminar was to intensify the dialogue between the two states, but the Soviets quickly recited a long list of complaints that were allegedly inhibiting both Arab socialist development and relations between Egypt and the Soviet Union; for example:

1. the absence of a "progressive revolutionary party" to lead the Arabs and unite them against the imperialists;
2. hostility to communism by some socialist Arab regimes (mainly Libya and the Sudan);
3. the persistence of a strong petit bourgeois class in Egypt, obstructing "socialist transformation"; and
4. the inability of the Palestinian guerrilla groups to unite and agree on ultimate aims.

The Egyptians responded with charges that certain Soviet policies were injurious to the Arab cause:

1. Moscow's insistence that the Arab-Israeli dispute be settled by political means and not by war;
2. the ambiguous Soviet attitude toward assisting the guerrillas;
3. Soviet endeavors to promote communist ideology in Arab countries; and
4. the Soviet policy of permitting an increasing number of Russian Jews to emigrate to Israel.

This exchange was unique and was notable for its candor and frankness on both sides. The list of charges and countercharges covered all the basic factors in the Arab-Soviet difficulties. The Soviets did not wince at revealing them; but, more significantly, the Egyptians did not accept them in a subservient manner. Having already confronted the Kremlin with the arms self-sufficiency decision, the Egyptians apparently had enough confidence to speak straightforwardly at the seminar. The dialogue neither intimidated the Egyptians nor convinced the Soviets; it did not clear the air as it had been intended to do. But it did demonstate to both sides the dangers of a continuing deterioration in relations. From this point on, the alert signals were clearly visible.

At the same time that Sadat cautiously began conditioning the Arab public to the impact of arms self-sufficiency, he also revealed that he had reopened communications with Washington. On 30 March he announced that contacts had been resumed, and on 25 April he stated that he had written to Nixon and informed him that Egypt would grant certain naval facilities to the Soviet Union in its Mediterranean ports. (This announcement coincided with the publicity related to the negotiations for a Sixth Fleet "home port" at Piraeus.) Washington responded politely that these facilities were Egyptian, that their use was an internal matter, and that the United States did not wish to intervene. Further, it was confident that the government of Egypt could exercise its own will and was independent of outside powers.[24]

One aim in querying Washington at that time was to explore the American attitude toward the Middle East prior to the Soviet-

American summit conference in May. Washington's discreet response apparently held no cause for undue alarm. More to the point, Rogers had decided to adopt a change in American priorities and had assured Israeli Ambassador Rabin that the Middle East would be a low interest point in Moscow. The United States had already sketched the position it would take at Moscow in the State Department's 1971 Annual Report: sustained efforts would be made to achieve an interim accord and the historic enterprise of gaining Soviet agreement on regional arms limitation.[25] These probes revealed, as was later confirmed, that the Nixon administration had decided to place the Middle East on the back burner during the election year; it foresaw no dramatic changes and would try not to contribute to any.

On 16 March Sadat made his dramatic announcement in Khartoum that Egypt would soon be producing sophisticated weapons with which to confront Israel. President Moamer Qaddafi of Libya followed on 28 March with a statement that the Arabs would soon be able to manufacture advanced weapons on their own soil. Finally, Sadat disclosed to the Central Committee of the Arab Socialist Union in April that the Federation of Arab Republics had decided to reduce its reliance on imports from the Soviet Union, to which strings had been attached, by establishing arms industries that would produce as much as possible locally. (The strings he referred to were Soviet demands for naval facilities.) He revealed that Libya was acting as the principal negotiator with Western countries for military industrial plants.[26]

Thus, the issue had finally been broached with the Soviets, and Egypt was launched on a program of arms self-sufficiency. Clearly, Egypt's educational, managerial, industrial, and financial resources were too limited to expect an arms boom. But Libya's seemingly inexhaustible wealth promised to provide shortcuts. Nonetheless, it remained to be seen how extensive actual production would be. With this significant decision made, however, a question arose as to what role the Soviets anticipated playing in this new defense program.

Moscow's role had become one of the most crucial issues of the five-year Canal War: it was in danger of losing the preferential position in Arab politics that it had acquired from its status as sole arms supplier in an interminable conflict. This strategy of trading arms for influence had succeeded because of the Arabs' limited ability to procure arms in the West or to manufacture them domestically. Sadat's determination to "go it alone" posed a menacing new dilemma for Moscow, reminiscent of China's decision in 1959 and 1960 to seek greater self-reliance. How could Moscow continue to monitor and influence Arab military aspirations? What leverage could be established that would allow it a voice in strategic decisions concerning Arab industrial and military developments? Could favorable Western responses to Arab orders for industrial plants reintroduce Western influence into the arms sector of local economies at Soviet expense? No wonder the February Moscow conference was labelled the most serious to date, and no wonder the Soviets reverted to an earlier strategy of currying an alternative power base in the Middle East through precipitously concluding a friendship treaty with Iraq and supporting Baghdad's challenge to Western oil companies.[27]

Military Developments
As tensions began to erupt in the wake of the breakdown of the American mediation initiative, both sides had begun to express their frustration in military exchanges. On 11 September 1971 the I.D.F. downed an Egyptian SU-7 over the Sinai with ground fire. Egypt retaliated on 17 September by shooting down an Israeli C-130 electronic intelligence stratocruiser fourteen miles east of the Canal with a SAM missile. On the eighteenth Israel returned the fire by shelling SAM sites on the west bank. Open exchanges then abated, but the Soviets entered the confrontation by conducting MIG-25 reconnaissance flights near or over Israeli-held Sinai (see figure 1). The MIG-25s were flying at altitudes of 70,000 to 80,000 feet and at speeds of Mach 2.5 plus. Israeli F-4s could not close with the Soviet planes and an urgent plea was sent to the United States for a high-acceleration air-to-air missile that could counter the new threat. In the interim the I.D.F. began launching

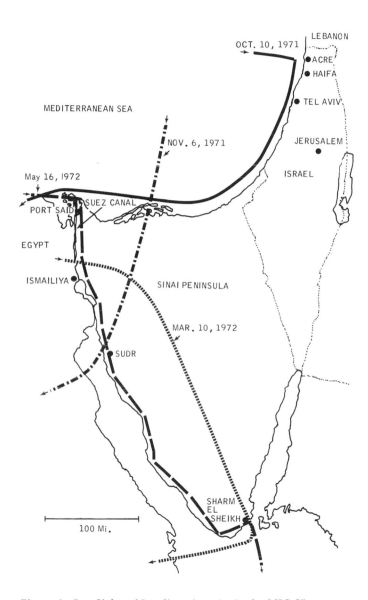

Figure 1. Overflights of Israeli territory by Soviet MIG-25s.

Teledyne Ryan 124I reconnaissance drones over Egypt.[28] Sensitive about hostile overflights, the I.A.F. reacted quickly on 13 June 1972 when eight Egyptian MIG-21s flew 25 miles north of the Sinai, and the Israelis downed two, the sixty-eighth and sixty-ninth MIG-21s and the one hundred fourteenth aircraft shot down since the June War by Israel.

Both sides demonstrated quick reactions, indicating professionalism and high morale. Yet the upper limits of the prescribed contingency actions were strictly observed. Generally, it appeared that the military on both sides of the Canal were prepared and confident. On the Egyptian side there were repeated well-founded reports that front-line officers were eager to resume the fighting, assured that the balance was swinging in their favor.

The Soviet-Egyptian military buildup during the five-year Canal War had indeed been impressive. It had demonstrated that the Soviet Union could export major air defense systems, including radar-filter and flight-coordinating centers, without depleting Warsaw Pact defenses. Overlapping radar and weapon densities far exceeded those of North Vietnam, long regarded as having the toughest defenses prepared since World War II.[29] The introduction into the Egyptian air defense system of the SAM-3, SAM-4, and SAM-6, and the SU-11 and MIG-25 and their respective supporting radar systems diversified the electronic spectrum and seriously compounded the countermeasures problem. Yet the control factor for systems turned over to the Egyptians remained a tough problem for the Soviets. There were reportedly ten Soviet advisors in each Egyptian front-line tank and artillery battalion: two in battalion headquarters and two in each of the four companies. There were probably more Soviets assigned to air defense units because of the higher maintenance requirements. (The United States seldom had more than one advisor per battalion in South Vietnam.) But even such a heavy concentration did not give the Soviets the ability to block determined Egyptian military efforts.[30]

The Jordanian Initiative

As the tempo of Soviet-Egyptian relations quickened, Cairo received a jolt on its Arab front that compromised both its bargaining position with Moscow and the solidarity of its arms self-sufficiency program. Jordan has never played the key role in the struggle against Israel, but it has always played an important secondary one. In the 1947 war its British-trained army had turned in the only creditable Arab performance. Its resistance against Israeli reprisals in 1956 had been instrumental in diverting Israel against Egypt in the Suez War. Amman's antiguerrilla policies in 1964–1967 had earned it the hostility of its Arab neighbors, but had forced them to receive the brunt of Israeli reprisals. King Hussein's decision to join Nasser in May 1967 was the linchpin in a united Arab front and as much as any other single factor was a precipitating catalyst for the June War. Hussein's ambivalent attitude toward the guerrillas after the June War was a stimulant both for Palestinian communal organization and for its diversification; yet when the guerrillas tried to overthrow him for accepting the Rogers cease-fire bid, Hussein effectively countered and virtually annihilated the main guerrilla fighting units, ridding Jordan of its most virulent problem.[31]

On 10 March 1972 Hussein again acted unexpectedly by announcing a plan for the future settlement of the Israeli-occupied West Bank of the Jordan. His scheme called for the creation of two semiautonomous states—two Germanies in one nation, or East and West Bank entities with the right of a referendum for the West Bank. As announced, the plan presumed a state of peace, but Israeli and Egyptian reactions indicated their fears that it was being offered as a bargaining counter.

Mrs. Meir angrily denounced the proposal as another Arab concoction, but the government hastily improvised counteractions. Existing and future plans for consolidation of the occupied territories, which had previously been denied, were now openly discussed with the foreign press. A new town of Ophir was to be built outside Sharm el Sheikh, where five tourist hotels were already flourishing. New kibbutzim were to be added to the 22 already operating in the new territories. Arab agricultural communes were being built near El Arish and infrastructures were springing up on a monthly basis. But most important, for the first time since the June War maps began to circulate depicting the new Israel with the earlier suggestions of the Allon Plan as sovereign territory. They included Sharm el Sheikh and connecting land links, and a wide strip of the West Bank with only a narrow land strip connecting Nablus and Hebron with Jordan proper.[32]

Israel's reaction to Hussein's proposal had the unexpected result of coalescing heterogeneous domestic groups into an active progovernment lobby and strengthening the growing swing to the right in Israeli politics. The religious and conservative parties now found common cause with war-weary moderate circles who saw advantages to settling things on at least one front. These sentiments were bolstered by the unexpected awareness that Arabs and Jews could live together peacefully on the West Bank. The unprecedented Arab prosperity, the collapse of the guerrilla movement, the successful communal elections under the Israeli authorities in March 1972, and the increasing personal Arab travel to Jordan were cited as evidence of the growing success of peaceful coexistence. Under the threat of a resumption of instability posed by Hussein's plan (the king went to Washington on 27 March to elicit support), more and more moderate Israelis began thinking of a prompt solution. Thus, after five years Israeli intentions toward its eastern front were beginning to take shape. It appeared only a matter of several years rather than decades before the West Bank would be formally incorporated into Israel along the lines of the Allon Plan or a suitable compromise accepting portions of the Hussein scheme[33] (leaving, of course, such issues as Arab civil rights and integration as outstanding grievances).

While Hussein may have been acting to forestall de facto incorporation of the West Bank, the mere possibility of a separate settlement with Jordan seriously compromised Egypt's position against the three other players in the Canal War. Israel would be able to deal individually with the two Arab states without undue fear of collusion. Moreover, Cairo would have to regard an accord reopening the Canal as just that and not the first step toward a final peace treaty. Egypt would no longer be able to use the issues of Palestinian rights and the restoration of the West Bank as leverage in its Canal settlement. These new uncertainties were sufficiently disruptive in Cairo's planning that on 6 April Sadat broke all diplomatic ties with Hussein and later threatened to extract severe commercial reprisals.[34]

While Sadat's fears were certainly based more on potential than actual dangers from Hussein's "defection," his actions revealed apparent concern about the growing constraints on his own policy options. In the wake of the February Moscow conference, the Soviets had openly cultivated other Arab states by signing a friendship treaty with Iraq in April and publicly endorsing that country's expropriation of Western oil companies as "a great victory for Arab peoples." [35] Moscow then initiated a rapprochement in March with its arch Arab antagonist, Libya, by negotiating an oil agreement. Moscow agreed to provide technical assistance if the operations of Western oil companies should be reduced and to buy Libyan oil if Western markets should be denied.[36] At the same time a summit conference was held in Algeria at which Moscow attempted to restore warm relations. Yet such developments were again only potential constraints.

The tone of euphoria in Sadat's speeches during April and May, in which he spoke of new horizons and condemned the Soviet Union, the United States, Israel, Jordan, and his own political opponents on the right and left all with the same brush, had the ring of whistling in the dark. Signs of domestic unrest had again begun to appear. On May Day student riots again broke out, and by 16 June Heikal was warning of a serious public disenchantment about the "no peace, no war" predicament. Fifteen members of a subversive group, the Arab Vanguard Organization, including a former employee in the office of the president, were arrested but given light sentences. The prominent Beirut newspaper *An-Nahar* printed in July a copy of a note reportedly submitted to Sadat in April by ten eminent Egyptians who had previously held responsible government posts. It complained that the existing policy of "overdependence on the U.S.S.R." had contributed nothing to the liberation of lost territories. Finally and most alarming, morale and discipline were again becoming problematic among Egyptian military officers, especially in the air force, forcing Sadat to make several unscheduled tours of combat units to restore confidence.[37]

The Expulsion of Soviet Advisors

It was probably Sadat's probing of army attitudes that provided the most conclusive domestic reason for his decision to ask for the recall of Soviet military advisors and technicians. Sadat has acknowledged that his confidence in the Soviet leadership had deteriorated to a point where he felt compelled to return to Moscow again in April—before the Nixon conference—to insure that the Soviets would not formally codify their seeming reluctance concerning arms deliveries. On 1 June Sadat sent Brezhnev a seven-point questionnaire about further weaponry. A follow-up query was dispatched on 15 June after no Soviet reply was received. Finally, on 7 July Moscow responded. In a letter delivered by Ambassador Vinogradov, the Soviets vigorously attacked publisher Heikal and War Minister Sadek as being behind the worsening relations, but completely ignored Sadat's questions. In the ambassador's presence, Sadat made the expulsion decision and issued the appropriate orders.

On 18 July Sadat announced to the Central Committee of the A.S.U. that his government had terminated the service of Soviet personnel. Sadat's three statements were: "A decision to end, with effect from 17 July, the mission of the Soviet military advisors and experts who came at our request. Our sons in the armed forces will replace them in everything they did. Second, the military installations and equipment which were established on Egyptian soil after the June 1967 War are considered the private property of Egypt and are under operation of our armed forces. Third, a call [will be made] within the framework of the Egyptian-Soviet

Friendship Treaty for an Egyptian-Soviet meeting at a level to be agreed upon later to hold consultations concerning the future state [of military cooperation]." [38]

Sadat's announcement was one of the most dramatic decisions of the Canal War, and it mirrored the Sudan's expulsion of Soviet advisors one year earlier. It affected all the other players and had an immediate bearing on their policies toward the Canal War. The immediate questions that arose were the effects the expulsion would have on the prospects for a political settlement and on Egyptian military effectiveness. In her 26 July policy statement to the Knesset, Mrs. Meir made the following summation:

> The Soviet Union stationed in Egypt more than 7,000 advisors, experts, and instructors in all armed forces, and close to 10,000 additional military personnel to operate squadrons of MIG-21 and other aircraft, SAM-3 and SAM-6 batteries, and personnel in various command formations. The Egyptian demand for evacuation affects the entire establishment of advisors and experts, but not the instructors. On the other hand, the demand for evacuation also affects Soviet operational units which are integrated into the Egyptian air defense system. It appears that the SAM-3 batteries and perhaps also the interceptor squadrons have been handed over to the Egyptians.[39]

The military implications of the expulsion influenced the policies of all the players in the following year, and arguments about the technical proficiency of the Egyptian armed forces figured prominently in the assessment. The question of whether the Soviet advisory mission should have been terminated sooner or later was clearly irrelevant to the larger issues. First, Arab proficiency requirements for maintaining and operating sophisticated equipment were not as high as those of the Soviets. The preferred mission of their present equipment was set-piece warfare, which is far simpler for operational purposes than mobile or strategic warfare. Further, Egypt had sufficient redundancy in weapons systems to compensate for a degree of inefficiency. Finally, the Soviets apparently did not turn over the latest generation equipment, especially in electronic warfare, thereby placing a ceiling on proficiency requirements. Thus, if vital maintenance servicing and spare parts could be assured, termination of the advisory mission would probably have only a marginal adverse effect on operational capabilities.

The combat proficiency of Egyptian troops was a separate issue. In set-piece warfare, they would probably perform satisfactorily. For set-piece tactics to operate fully, however, Cairo's strategic deterrence would have to be effective. Without an independent and credible Egyptian strategic force, the presence of Soviet interceptor pilots had been a greater deterrent than all the Arab defense forces combined. The resumption of full responsibility for Egyptian air defenses by Cairo was probably based in part on the confidence that the Soviet deterrence could be preserved indirectly, i.e., that, since the Soviets had once demonstrated their commitment to protect vital Egyptian centers, Israel must now anticipate that they would reintervene if the threat should reappear.

Finally, a more fundamental issue was the motive and timing of the decision. By Sadat's perfunctory announcement and the precipitous evacuation, it was clear that the demand was not a routine termination of a training mission, which could have been handled without publicity (as it is in most other countries receiving Soviet arms). Sadat resorted to shock tactics with political objectives in view. Although somewhat conjectural, several motives can be suggested that collectively may indicate why Sadat acted as he did. First, the manner rather than the content of the demand suggests that Sadat was engaging in brinksmanship. He explicitly tied the evacuation to "excessive Soviet caution." In his 24 July speech he clearly identified the failure of the Soviets to provide "decisive weapons," with which Cairo could break the "no peace, no war" deadlock, as a crucial Egyptian grievance against Moscow. His aim was probably to increase his freedom of maneuver in dealing with the Soviets and thereby increase pressure for greater receptivity for his demands. After the repeated consultations starting in March 1971 indicated continued Soviet reserve, however, Cairo probably did not place too high hopes that this tactic would fundamentally alter the Soviet position.

A separate motive has been alluded to several times by Sadat: the interaction and inactivity of the great powers. On the one hand, he denounced the Soviet Union for not pressing Cairo's interests during the Moscow summit; on the other, he bitterly criticized the United States for its indifference. As early as March 1972 reports were circulating in Israel of an alleged collusion whereby the Soviets agreed to accept a limited withdrawal of its troops in exchange for the resurrection and vigorous prosecution of the Third Rogers Plan. Sadat's anger, however, was apparently aroused for exactly the opposite reason: the fear that the two powers had failed to reach accord on a regional arms limitation but had tacitly agreed to allocate a lower priority to the Canal War until the American election or until both sponsored states showed more flexibility. Like Hanoi, Cairo relies heavily on international public opinion to advance its cause. It can neither allow the Arab-Israeli dispute to be shifted from center stage nor risk great-power distraction. Sadat's disappointment with the Moscow summit conference stemmed from his perception that great-power competition and cooperation was moving to other areas and issues, leaving him with even greater burdens in altering the status quo.

A third motive stemmed in part from the first two: the withdrawal was a logical progression in the sequence of arms self-sufficiency. The latter decision was probably reinforced by the first two motivating factors; and, once the scope of self-sufficiency was determined, financing became more critical than proficiency, increasing the pressure to reduce the hard currency payments for Soviet advisors. Egypt could not continue paying the full costs of the Soviet aid program and simultaneously launch its own ambitious arms manufacturing plans.

A fourth motive may have been mutual disenchantment about the profitability of Soviet-Egyptian cooperation. Sadat claimed on one occasion that his differences with the Soviet Union started during his first Moscow visit as president in October 1970, when "decisive weapons" were initially discussed. He has also referred to March 1971 as the point of departure, when the Arab Federation and Qaddafi's proposal for complete merger between Libya and Egypt were being considered.[40] Certainly, the recurring Ali Sabri affair, his bid for power and subsequent attempted forceful release, demonstrated mutual suspicions. The Egyptians saw the episode as a manifestation of Soviet imperial will, an attitude that was reinforced when Moscow demanded the ouster of Heikal and Sadek, two symbols of deteriorating Soviet-Egyptian relations, and insisted upon naval facilities as the price for the requested arms manufacturing plants.[41] Further, an increasing number of Egyptians began to interpret Moscow's alleged perpetuation of the "no war, no peace" dilemma as a deliberate attempt to project its own influence through a manipulation of instability.

On the other side, reports were rife of the disdain and disgust of Soviet personnel in Egypt. Sadat acknowledged in a press interview, "The Soviets themselves, I must be fair, don't want their soldiers to stay here in Egypt. Every time I try to prolong their stay I must use all my efforts to convince them. . . . The Soviets themselves don't want their people here at the SAM sites." [42] Soviet dislikes were widely known and could hardly induce cordiality and confidence among the Egyptians.

A final motive may have been Sadat's perception that the country needed a psychological lift and that his own power base required repair. Critics and detractors were charging that his options were waning. Under similar circumstances Nasser could deflect public attention with attacks on imperialists or the Hashemites, but Sadat could not. His sharp action against the Soviets, however, garnered him more public support than any other single move since he became president. His political stature rose in proportion to his lifting of Egyptian national pride. As a result, Sadat entered the sixth year of the Canal War with more freedom of action than he had ever had. The Soviet Union had been put on notice that in the future its counsel would be measured.

Initial Reactions to the Expulsion

The Egyptian position was presented by Minister of Information el-Zayyat at a 22 July press conference, where he stated that Cairo was seeking a new working relationship with the Soviet Union but did not expect a halt in Soviet arms or spare parts deliveries. He stressed that Egypt was not a part of either great-power team (consistent with this theme, Egypt ordered on 17 May 1972 a 50 percent reduction of the American diplomatic staff in Cairo), and called for a renewal of bargaining on a partial settlement. In a major policy speech on 24 July (punctuated by a SAM attack on Israeli F-4s over the Sinai), Sadat repeatedly emphasized that the Arabs were now alone and would have to achieve a just settlement of the Canal War by their own efforts; yet he too asked for peace talks. As a follow-up, the Egyptian U.N. ambassador, Esmat Abd-al-Meguid, met with the secretary-general and conveyed the impression that Egypt was prepared to give Jarring its full co-operation by a public statement welcoming the resumption of his mission in August.

Mrs. Meir responded on 26 July in an equally grave statement before the Knesset. In the most respectful tone she had ever addressed to Egypt, she reiterated in muted colors the Israeli position. She avoided the term "direct talks," but replied to Sadat's bid for negotiations with the suggestion that they "meet together as equals. . . . let us sit down together." She specifically cited Sadat's February 1971 proposed interim accord as a subject for negotiation, stating that Israel would also regard it as a temporary solution.

But temporary to what? Sadat would not accept the risks of direct talks for a temporary solution. In an address on 27 July he rejected Meir's speech as an "old tune" and focused his criticism largely on the United States. In an accurate assessment, he blamed the United States for perpetuating Israeli demands for direct talks. Washington has always backed down, he claimed, after any constructive step, falling back on the direct talks after each failure to achieve substantive agreement. Further, while the

"United States is committed to preserve Israeli superiority," Egypt was now prepared to go it alone. Sadat expressed appreciation for Soviet aid but he stressed that Egypt would not accept dependent status. (The Egyptian press had started by this time a cautious campaign to soothe Soviet anxieties by urging that the government spare no efforts to maintain Soviet-Egyptian friendship: "Soviet friendship is not only important, it is without substitute.")[43]

Behind this exchange was the apparent belief in Israel that there was no need to "rescue" Sadat at this time. Let both the Soviets and the Egyptians assess the impact of Moscow's confirmed inability to "deliver" against the odds of a strong and determined Israeli position. But the United States still held the key chips. Sadat's stand reflected bitterness and disappointment. He was now faced with two hard options: the sacrifice and hardship of the long-haul, go-it-alone program, or the necessity of an even more dramatic move to shake American passivity. His harsh attacks revealed his helpless acknowledgment that ousting the Soviets had proportionally increased American authority among all four players. As Algerian President Houari Boumédienne stated in a press interview, if the United States did not respond, as the only power that could now influence adjustment, Sadat's ouster of the Soviets would have been insignificant and might even invite military defeat. "The departure itself isn't what counts. . . . If it only means that Russians are no longer needed to the same degree in Egypt, then it is unimportant. . . . But if it is a signal that means an eventual reorientation in U.S. policy, then it could be an historic event." [44] Washington's subsequent actions, however, failed to capitalize on the opportunity or to rescue its fourth attempt at a peace settlement—the proximity talks.

Despite Moscow's efforts to give the matter the air of a routine phasing out of an overseas training mission,[45] it had sustained a setback. While it initially may have intended to perpetuate tensions, it had ultimately perceived the true dimensions of its dilemma. It had attempted to provide military parity for its sponsored state. When the upper limits of its commitments were soon reached, however, Israel still retained important military advantages. Moscow's limitations were not merely on offensive weapons systems, but also extended to late-generation equipment. If Moscow's most up-to-date systems, such as its ECM components, were defeated by the American-supplied I.D.F., it would have grave repercussions for the NATO-Warsaw Pact confrontation and the European Conference on Security and Cooperation, and could severely weaken Soviet prestige in the Third World. American ECM capabilities, for example, proved vastly superior in North Vietnam to Soviet countermeasures of ten years' vintage. To preclude such embarrassment, Moscow had to give the impression that it was withholding its latest systems from the Egyptians. Thus, when hard choices were required, Moscow had to assess the prospects of compromise to its stature in the Third World from either of two negative decisions: either accept penalties in the eyes of other arms recipients for denying a developing nation what it regarded as its ultimate security requirements; or accept the adverse consequences on the Soviet defense posture itself of a possible defeat of Moscow's most sophisticated weaponry. The Kremlin chose the former alternative and accepted an inadvertently self-imposed formula of "sufficiency" for Egyptian armaments.

Moscow also had to weigh the degree of political influence that was desirable and attainable in Canal War politics. The Soviets' past behavior had indicated a strong dislike for unstable, unpredictable, and uncontrollable phenomena which might force them onto the defensive. In such circumstances, the lack of adequate contingency planning had resulted in hasty or clumsy makeshift options. The Red Army defeat in the summer of 1941, the Cuban Missile Crisis, and the June War are examples of reversals that panicked the Kremlin. And the attempted jailbreak of Ali Sabri is another illustration of the Soviets' lack of finesse in cutting their losses. They had been able to stage remarkable recoveries in most instances because their adversaries did not exploit their advantages and were prepared to accept the status quo ante.[46]

After the expulsion, Moscow was again faced with an uncertain situation in which the earlier barometers for measuring political influence that had failed to predict Sadat's actions were of limited utility. This sudden reversal still left the Soviets several possible options. First, they could promote a reduction of differences with the United States on immediate issues in the Canal War, while leaving long-term problems at variance. Second, they could renew their earlier policy of cultivating additional Arab clients, not as a fulcrum for unseating Sadat but as a means of expanding the basis for their influence. Third, they could reduce their involvement in Arab affairs as being unproductive and shift their focus to cultivating nations in the Indian Ocean Basin, who would hopefully be more reliable collaborators in the Soviet conception of great-power influence competition. Finally, Moscow could conceivably reverse its Israeli policy from animosity to friendship, as it had done with Turkey, Iran, and West Germany; indeed, an intentional by-product of the recent unprecedented scale in emigration of Soviet Jews may be the cultivation of a new climate of relations with Israel.[47]

The Soviets seemed to be pursuing all of these options simultaneously up to the time of the October 1973 War, with particular attention being paid to reducing differences with the United States.

In the opening years of the Canal War, the operative assumption in Soviet policy was that it could persuade the United States to pressure Israel into accommodation. The United States had, however, concluded that it was imperative not to comply with Soviet intentions without some quid pro quo that could assure the ultimate reduction of Soviet influence or options, despite the fact that nonsettlement was contrary to historic American attitudes about the inadmissability of aggressive aims. The difficulty in forging a quid pro quo that would meet American aims cast Washington increasingly into the role of opposing Moscow, supporting Tel Aviv, and ignoring Cairo, while allowing the Soviet Union relatively wide latitude in devising options with the Arabs.

All four Rogers Plans were conceived within this framework, and all failed. It was Arab opposition, not American, that finally forced the Soviets to turn the corner in the Canal War. This rounding the corner, the enforcement of Moscow's sufficiency formula for Egypt and the subsequent withdrawal, had a stunning impact on the American position and showed up Washington's failure to impose a similar sufficiency formula on Israel. True, Nixon could argue in the election year that his policy of assuring Israeli supremacy had shown Moscow that the United States would not tolerate unchecked Soviet expansion, and this probably appealed to many Jewish and right-wing voters. But American policy did not contain Soviet influence; it merely stimulated Moscow to search for sounder grounds for its influence. And now the earlier premises were even less relevant than they had been, for example, when, at a time in July 1967 of overwhelming Israeli supremacy, Dean Rusk told the U.S. Senate that American pleas for arms control were being ignored by the Soviets.[48] These actual or anticipated Soviet reactions became the incremental guide for each American escalation. But Moscow's failure to secure Egyptian military parity and subsequent reluctant acceptance of sufficiency now highlighted the bankruptcy of the American notion that assured Israeli supremacy would be conducive to accommodation.

Characteristics of the Sixth Round
A central question in assessing the sixth round of the attempts to settle the Canal War is why Washington entered this phase still "high" on Nixon's sense of mission and leadership in the crisis and then collapsed into futility and passivity. There are several possible explanations:
1. election year anxieties;
2. apprehensions about Soviet motives;
3. the inflexibility of both local players and possibly a misperception about the scope of changes taking place in Egyptian policy; and
4. a malignant guilt complex, frequently exacerbated by the Is-

raelis, about earlier American betrayals of the beleagured, tiny state.

These factors repeatedly acted as constraints, forcing Washington increasingly to see its own best interests lying in a hypersensitive handling of all things Israeli. As a result, Washington appeared at the end of the sixth round to be less well equipped conceptually for the ongoing negotiations than in any of the previous phases. Washington seems to have taken to heart Bernard Lewis's advice to the Senate, "It may often be better to stand pat and do nothing rather than engage in activity. There is a common tendency, especially in the New World, to assume that action or even more activism is always better than inaction in terms both of expediency and of morality. This is sometimes the reverse of truth. In a situation of deadlock, a burst of febrile activity can often lead to a weakening of one's own stand to the advantage of one's immobile and more stupid perhaps, but more patient, opponent." [49]

Continued immobility at this juncture, however, proved the wrong alternative. At no other time during the Canal War had there been a more propitious opportunity for dynamic leadership. At no other time were the sponsored states in a better position for mutual accommodation. Yet at no other time were the consequences of diplomatic inactivity so grave—namely, Arab preparations for arms self-sufficiency independent of foreign restraints and the prospects of unilateral Israeli actions to solidify the status quo.

9
The October War and Its Aftermath: August 1972–January 1974

The rigid positions that had developed in the Canal War received a major jolt with the Egyptian suspension of the Soviet Military Advisory Mission. The United States had insisted that the expulsion of the Soviet military forces from Egypt was a precondition for a durable settlement. When this was achieved by Arab rather than American action, Washington was unable to move decisively to introduce fluidity into the local players' positions. (The Egyptians argued that this was the most forceful move yet toward settlement, but the Israelis insisted that it merely vindicated their policy of localizing solutions and failed to make a gesture toward adjustment.) With the Soviets in seeming disgrace, only the Americans could have moved the confrontation toward settlement. But the apathy resulting from repeated Israeli vetos of American good intentions and the constraints arising from the forthcoming presidential campaign precluded any American initiative at that time.

But even with the seeming American paralysis, Cairo was able to retain important advantages from its draconian measures. It had challenged the sincerity of its great-power patron by threatening to seek alternative sources of supply if its aims were denied. When the United States and Israel failed to respond to Egypt's initiative, Moscow was forced to resolve its differences with Cairo. The resulting closure between the Soviet Union and Egypt was the turning point that led to the resumption of hostilities. Both parties now realized that military parity could not be achieved by such deus ex machina devices as strategic weapons or political manipulations. Moscow finally concurred with Cairo that any political settlement must be the product of the battlefield. Both then agreed upon a formula for renewed hostilities, which prescribed only a conventional attack for the limited war aims of recovering Israeli-occupied territories. With this agreement, acknowledged several times in 1973 by Sadat, the initiative passed to the Arabs.

Preparations for October

Sadat realized that renewed fighting could no longer be confined to artillery barrages, since technological advances on both sides precluded such low-level hostilities. The Arabs would clearly have to orient themselves more to Israel's type of war. The establishment of Arab military parity now required an escalation in battlefield performance heretofore inconceivable in localized warfare. Therefore, Sadat gained Soviet approval for a two-fold strategy. Moscow agreed to provide a limited surface-to-surface missile capability which would deny Israel its strategic option of bombing targets in the interior by the threat of retaliation. Two SCUD-B battalions were deployed to Egypt, manned by Soviet crews to insure that they would be launched against Israeli cities only as retaliatory action. Additionally, Moscow agreed to improve the Arabs' tactical capabilities by providing its latest armored, antitank, and air defense weapons. Moscow's renewed active participation in the Arab cause required modification of its policy of sufficiency. The Soviets finally accepted Sadat's argument that Israel must be deterred from attacking Egyptian cities in any renewed fighting. This retaliatory capability could not be used indiscriminately and was to remain under exclusive Soviet control. By mutual agreement, the new formula for Soviet participation was to provide sufficient equipment to assure battlefield equivalency.

Round seven in the Canal War was the best orchestrated and coordinated Arab undertaking in 25 years. It opened in February 1973 when Egypt launched a final effort to move the political stalemate off dead center. Sadat's national security advisor, Hafez Ismail, visited London, Bonn, Moscow, Washington, and the United Nations to explore any new suggestions for inducing an Israeli withdrawal. Sadat was prepared to consider any terms, except direct talks. At each stop Ismail received sympathetic hearings and expressions of satisfaction about the flexibility of the Arabs' bargaining position, but no new recommendations were forthcoming. Mrs. Meir then visited Washington and told the National Press Club that she would only consider direct talks with the Arabs and that the Golan Heights and Sharm el Sheikh were nonnegotiable. Several days after the reiteration of this inflexible stance, the United States announced the sale of an additional 48 F-4s. While Israel had accepted in principle the American suggestion for proximity talks, the aircraft sale cancelled the prospects for such talks because it confirmed Israel's insistence on dealing from strength. The aircraft issue signalled the collapse of Ismail's diplomatic undertaking.

On 26 March Sadat indicated that a corner had been turned. He announced to the National Assembly that he was taking over the premiership in order to strengthen the war effort. He told the deputies: "The stage of total confrontation has become inevitable, and we are entering it whether we like it or not. The military situation must be made to move, with all the sacrifices that this entails. We must tell the world that we are here and that we can dictate our will." [1] But first military preparations would have to be completed and Arab unity consolidated. He reiterated these warnings and expectations several times during the summer, but his candor and lack of inflammatory commentary deluded observers conditioned to radical anti-Israeli invective. The general assessment was that such calls to war had been heard so frequently in the past that they could now only be aimed at bolstering Sadat's domestic position.

The achievement of Arab unity has always been the principal obstacle to Arab action against Israel. Syria had never accepted Resolution 242 or the right of Israel to statehood, and it still cherished the hope of ultimately dissolving the Jewish state. Such radical goals were antithetical to Egypt's basic interest in securing a compromise political settlement through a demonstration of military parity. In 1973, however, Cairo began to see both its immediate and long-range goals in terms of the restoration of national honor through *only* the recovery of Israeli-occupied Sinai. Even this aim seemed to be open to compromise: alternative dispositions of Gaza and Sharm el Sheikh apparently could be tolerated. Finally, both Syria and Egypt had broken diplomatic relations with Jordan over Hussein's proposed plebiscite for the West Bank. The issue, then, in achieving Arab unity was to establish a consensus on war aims, whether they encompassed the recovery of occupied territory, the elimination of Israel, or the establishment of conditions compatible with genuine self-determination. Sadat's first task was to win Syrian President Asad's approval of his limited war aims.

The following partial chronology from press accounts indicates the intensity of contacts among the parties on what may be presumed from delegation composition to have been political and military matters.

2–5 April
Egypt's war minister, General Ahmed Ismail visits Damascus for the first joint strategy meeting.

21–22 April
Arab chiefs-of-staff meet in Cairo

8 May
General Ismail visits Damascus after returning from Baghdad

19 May
Sadat visits Damascus

6 June
A Syrian military delegation visits Cairo.

12 June
Sadat visits Damascus for talks with Asad.

18 June
Abdul Rifai, Hussein's personal envoy, flies to Cairo.

30 June
Rifai visits Damascus.

2 July
Syria's foreign minister goes to Cairo and announces that the
two countries have developed a joint Middle Eastern policy.

19 July
Rifai returns to Cairo with a formal message from Hussein to
Sadat.

28 July
Jordan's Prime Minister Zaid Rifai visits Saudi Arabia's King
Faisal.

5 August
Egypt's Major General Abd-al-Latif Najjar holds talks in Damascus with Syrian military leaders.

6 August
Sadat's personal envoy, Hasan Khouli, visits Amman.

10 August
Khouli leaves Amman with Rifai for Damascus and top level
discussions.

15 August
Egypt's Foreign Minister Mohammed el-Zayyat flies to Damascus.

29 August
Syria's defense minister, General Tias, visits Amman.

10–12 September
A summit conference is held in Cairo between Egypt, Syria, and
Jordan.

12 September
Egypt and Syria reestablish diplomatic relations with Jordan.

This frantic diplomatic activity suggests that hard negotiations
took place between Cairo and Damascus in April, May, and
June over the political aspects of the war effort. By the end of
June a compromise had been reached whereby Syria agreed to
Sadat's limited war aims of recovery of territory and he, in turn,

accepted Damascus's demands that concrete measures be undertaken to insure a prompt resumption of hostilities, that is, that military preparations be accelerated along a fixed timetable progressing toward a specified D-day. Since Jordan had already lowered its expectations regarding the "liberation" of the West Bank, negotiations up to that point were confined to the bilateral level. But when consensus was established on political objectives, it became essential to introduce Amman into discussions about strategic and tactical problems. Hussein apparently made it clear that he was unprepared to conduct a general assault against the West Bank for several reasons:

1. It was heavily populated by Jordanian citizens, and civilian casualties would be excessively high.
2. A lightning drive toward Jerusalem would be out of the question because it would require an uphill attack over easily defended terrain.
3. The Arab Legion had proven its valor during the June War and had suffered the heaviest casualties of any Arab army, reducing the need for demonstrative performances.
4. Jordanian civilian and military targets are few and extremely vulnerable to Israeli air attack.

Apparently because of this vulnerability factor, Hussein stated several times that Jordan would not participate in Arab military operations unless there was a 50 percent chance of an Arab victory. During the negotiations in August this nebulous commitment was refined to specific obligations. The Syrian and Egyptian armies were to attack under the guise of annual fall maneuvers. In the event that Syrian forces reached the crest of the Golan Heights, overlooking the Jordan River Valley and Sea of Galilee, Jordan would strike northwest across the Jordan River in the direction of Beit Shean to tie down Israeli reinforcements. The Syrians were apparently not to enter Israel proper, and the Jordanian incursion into the relatively unpopulated extreme northern corner of the West Bank was to deflect the I.D.F. counterattack and ease Israeli anxieties about Syrian intentions. At the same time the Egyptians were to attempt a land-grabbing operation with the three inland passes as the major goals. This was apparently the limit of the Arabs' strategic objectives. A cease-fire at that time would confirm the primary overall objective of demonstrating Arab military parity.

With accord roughly along these lines, it became necessary to insure broader Arab support. It could be expected that the more radical Palestinean factions and their supporters would attempt to sabotage any effort to reopen hostilities for only limited war aims. Thus, Qaddafi of Libya and the Palestinean leaders were intentionally excluded in the war planning. (After the fighting erupted, Qaddafi openly stated his disapproval, despite his formal alignment with Syria and Egypt in the Arab Federation, by denouncing the campaign as an "operetta war.") The Palestineans were a more serious problem. To preclude leaks to the radicals, details of the planning were not discussed with other Arab countries. (Iraq was only informed generally that plans were going forward and was unprepared when hostilities broke out.) The Palestineans rightly charged that they had been intentionally excluded from the planning, and they accused the "plotters" of hatching plans for surrender and concessions. All three countries at the September summit meeting agreed to take coordinated action to neutralize radical Palestinean opposition to their plans —a momentous decision for Syria. Sadat dropped charges against dissident students and intellectuals, while Hussein made the unexpected and potentially dangerous gesture of granting general amnesty. At the same time Syria closed a Palestinean radio broadcasting station that had been virulently anti-Hussein. Apparently, Yasser Arafat, the "majority" leader, was informed at the latter stages of the preparations, and his aid was solicited in preventing outbreaks of euphoric emotion when hostilities began.

A major factor in the Arabs' achievement of surprise was that Sadat did not repeat the political error that had led to Nasser's military defeat. Nasser had counted on military deterrence and political leverage by gaining Arab unity. The degree of cohesion he sought required the acceptance of the lowest common denominator of all Arab aspirations, including those of the most radical factions. Incorporation of the radicals' demands concerning the annihilation of the Jewish state was sufficiently ominous to prompt Israeli preemptive attack. Sadat chose just the opposite course. He concluded that a successful military operation would require agreement on a highest common denominator that would preclude participation of the radical fringe. This more prudent course contributed in large part to the deception of the Israelis about the impending attack.

The Question of Foreknowledge
The most recent Arab-Israeli hostilities, the so-called October War, will probably have a more significant impact upon future military armaments and tactics than the Spanish Civil War had upon World War II weapons and tactics. The three-week encounter was as decisive in destroying myths and misconceptions as the earlier June War had been in creating them. The results of the June War compelled all modern armed forces, including those of the great powers, to make basic changes in tactics, planning, and equipment, most notably in insuring aircraft survivability. Because of its greater scope and intensity, the October War will have a more profound impact.

One important question that demands detailed examination is the amount of forewarning provided by the Israeli intelligence service. The basic premise of Israel's defense policy is that an accurate and timely strategic-political warning will allow sufficient time for mobilization. A strategic-political warning was expected in several forms, such as a deterioration of political relations, an increase in incidents directed against Israel, an upsurge in third-party warnings of an impending attack, and an increase in belligerent statements by the heads of neighboring states. None of these occurred in the months preceding the attack.

What did occur was an Egyptian-sponsored reconciliation among the central figures in the Arab world. Two events should have received close Israeli attention. First, by late summer Egyptian President Sadat had persuaded the conservative oil kingdoms, particularly Saudi Arabia, to link oil production to a Mid-

dle Eastern settlement. Second, on 12 September Sadat and
Syrian President Asad reconciled their differences with Jordanian
King Hussein in Cairo and reestablished diplomatic relations.
Although the impact of these political changes upon the Arab
capability to wage war was substantial, Israeli officials misread
Sadat's intentions for inspiring them. They concluded that the
shift in Arab support toward Egypt was the result of Egyptian
concessions necessitated by internal pressures for diplomatic action aimed at securing a Middle Eastern settlement. The military
impact of these actions was purposely minimized. American
Secretary of State Kissinger told a press conference on 24 October
that the United States had consulted with Israel on several occasions about new developments indicated in their respective intelligence reports. Both concurred that hostilities were unlikely,
and both were surprised by the Arab attack. This failure to correctly interpret political events deprived the Israeli Defense Force
of the required warning necessary to achieve mobilization. As a
result the I.D.F. had to fight with only its forward units alerted.

If the Arabs did not signal their intentions clearly to Israel at
the strategic-political level, they did do so at the tactical-military
level. Since August 1970 the Israeli intelligence services had accurately reported the military preparations of Arab forces along
the Suez Canal and in the Golan Heights. Along the Canal,
Egyptian intentions were initially screened in late September
1973 by annual fall maneuvers, which had been scheduled months
in advance and were well-known to the Israelis. In the Golan
Heights, however, the Syrian buildup obviously improved its
capacity to attack. Furthermore, the movement of Jordanian
troops north to the border with Syria without apparent Syrian
concern indicated that a political change had occurred. As 6
October approached, military indicators of hostilities increased,

Nine days before the war Egypt actually brought rubber rafts
and pontoon bridging equipment to the Canal's edge in an exercise maneuver. At the beginning of the month Israel noted that
both Egypt's and Syria's air defense systems went on alert. Egyptian troops continued to enter the Canal area and soon exceeded

the number forecasted for the exercise. On 2 October Syria mobilized its reserves. On 3 October the Soviet Union began a hasty airlift of Soviet dependents from the two Arab states. This development, monitored by both Israel and the United States, was not anticipated, and the Soviets themselves diverted some aircraft in midflight for the evacuation. On 5 October the Egyptians began a major exercise toward Suez.

On the morning of the attack Israel warned both Egypt and Syria not to attack at 6 P.M. as then scheduled. It also warned the United States of the impending attack at 6 P.M. The Arab response was to move the ground attack forward by four hours, launching it at 2 P.M. on 6 October after a two-hour artillery barrage.

From these known developments it can be assumed that Israel knew several days in advance on a tactical-military level that Egypt and Syria were preparing to attack. In affirmation, Israeli Foreign Minister Abba Eban, Israeli Ambassador to the United States Simcha Dinitz, and Israeli Defense Minister Moshe Dayan all insisted that Israel had had several days warning of the attack but did not preemptively strike Egypt and Syria for political reasons. Certainly, a preemptive strike such as that executed in June 1967 would have evoked a chorus of international criticism and necessitated undue political risk, a fact recognized by many Israelis. Military considerations were, however, probably more decisive. A preemptive attack would not have altered the military balance. This time the Arab forces were in fortified positions, their aircraft were protected in semihardened airfields, and their air defenses were on alert. An Israeli preemptive strike against ready troops in prepared positions would not have seriously degraded the Egyptian or Syrian attack capability.

But the key question remains: Why did Israel fail to take the precautionary measure of mobilization? Mobilization did not commit Israel to military action. In fact, even a partial mobilization of Israel's five reserve brigades would have materially assisted in controlling the Arab assault. Instead, Israel gave leave to many regular army tank and artillery crews so that they could observe the Yom Kippur religious fast.

In light of the information provided by the intelligence services, it seems highly doubtful that the I.D.F. did not recommend mobilization to the Israeli political leadership. The prospect of facing Arab forces at odds worse than one to six would have militated strongly for some sort of increased readiness posture. That the I.D.F. was not permitted to mobilize until the morning of the attack appears most indicative of emphatic political restraints. Whatever these constraints were, Israel's failure to react militarily until the morning of the attack in large measure dictated the outcome of the battles.

The Syrian Front

The war on the Syrian front (see figure 1) was given first priority by Israel for several reasons. Most important, the Golan Heights did not contain the necessary area for an Israeli defense based on trading space for time. Israel could not afford to fight in the Sinai and then turn its attention to the Heights. A successful advance of two or three days could cover the 25 miles to the crest of the Heights, overlooking the Huleh Valley 4,000 feet below. At its widest, the Israeli portion of the Heights was only 26 miles, and this provided only limited room for maneuver.

Second, the Syrian advance scored stunning successes during the first two days and penetrated some 21 miles, within three to five miles of the crest. This high ground constituted the last key terrain between the Syrian forces and the vital Bnot Yaakov bridge in Israel proper, from which Israeli settlements could again be shelled. Retaking the crest would be an even bloodier operation than it had been during the June War. East from the crest, the Syrian plateau sloped downhill all the way to Damascus, giving geographic momentum to any Israeli counterattack. Therefore, the crest had to be held.

A third reason for shifting north was the relatively small size of the Syrian army and air force. While holding in the Sinai,

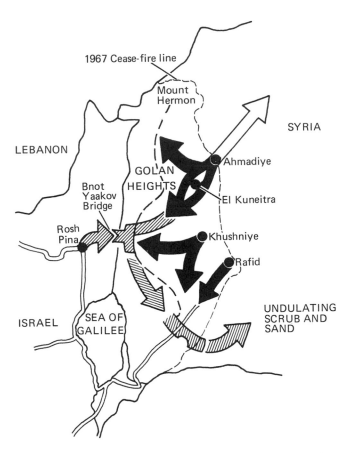

Figure 1. The Golan Heights battlefront. The solid arrows indicate the direction of movement of Syrian armored divisions on the first two days of battle. The cross-hatched arrows describe the Israeli counterattack on the third day. The white arrow indicates the direction of Israeli movement by the fifth day.

Israel could fight Syria at better than one to one odds and then, with its northern flank secured, it could devote its efforts to the much larger Egyptian armed forces. Further, concentrating the weight of Israel's military strength in the north would have a deterrent effect against Jordanian intervention. Finally, the proximity of the political target of Damascus, roughly 30 miles from the cease-fire line, enhanced the value of military action against the Syrians. There was always the possibility that a successful Israeli counterattack would interdict the capital and force Syria out of the war. Even if political advantages were not gained, the position of Damascus as the key Syrian supply base was enough to justify an attack.

The 1967 cease-fire line is located from 10 to 26 miles east of the crest. Israel had constructed a fortified outpost line along this boundary, while one to three miles further east the Syrians had built a strong defensive line consisting of minefields, bunkers, trenches, and gun emplacements. The Syrians also had a much longer and more intensive line 24 miles from Damascus, stretching from Jassem in the south to Beitima and Beit Jann at the base of Mount Hermon. Syria's attack force in the first defensive line consisted of three infantry divisions, one armored brigade, one independent infantry brigade, and several artillery regiments, for an estimated total of 60,000 men and 800 of Syria's 1,400 tanks. A final defensive line screening Damascus reached from Batroune on the highway to Beirut through Katana to Kissoue on the road to Amman and was manned by elite Syrian Guards units.

The backbone of the tank forces were Soviet T-54 and T-55 tanks. Both tanks weigh 36 tons, have a four-man crew, and mount a 100-mm gun as the main armament. The main gun has a total of 43 rounds and fires a fin-stabilized shell which is less stable than Israeli spin-stabilized rounds and is subject to severe ricochet. The T-54/55 rounds, therefore, have reliable accuracy to only 1,000 meters against an Israeli accuracy with the same reliability of twice that distance. Syria also possessed Soviet T-62 medium tanks, the newest in the Soviet inventory. The T-62 has the basic characteristics of the T-55, the major difference being the 115-mm smoothbore main gun on the T-62. This gun fires a fin-stabilized round with a reliable accuracy to 1,500 meters.

On its side Israel had an estimated 1,900 tanks in active service and in reserve. This figure included 400 American M-48s, 250 Ben Gurions (modified British Centurions), 600 Centurions, 200 Ishermen and Super Shermans, 100 modified T-55s, and 150 American M-60s. All Israeli tanks fire a standard 105-mm main gun with a tungsten-head, armor piercing (APDS) shell. The American models have a fire-control computer system that assures a high percentage of single-shot kills.

Syrian artillery consisted of Soviet 122-mm, 130-mm, and 152-mm guns with ranges of 14, 16, and 11 miles, respectively. Syrian armored infantry vehicles consisted of the 6-wheel, 18-passenger BTR-50. Israel had a substantially wider assortment of artillery, including 350 American 105-mm and 155-mm guns, 175 self-propelled howitzers, 900 120-mm and 160-mm mortars mounted on French AMX chassis, and varying numbers of 122-mm, 130-mm, and 240-mm guns. In antitank weapons it had 90-mm antitank guns, 106-mm jeep-mounted recoilless rifles, American TOW, and French SS-10/11 antitank missiles. The I.D.F. had about 3,000 armored personnel carriers including some French and British models, but consisting mainly of American M-2s, M-3s, and M-113s.

Syria deployed an extensive air defense system composed of surface-to-air missiles (SAMs) and antiaircraft artillery (AAA) in support of its defensive lines, military airfields, and major cities, particularly Damascus. These two systems were composed of Soviet SAM-2, SAM-3, SAM-6, and SAM-7 model missiles, and Soviet 23-mm, 37-mm, 57-mm, 85-mm, and 100-mm antiaircraft (AA) guns.

The SAM network provides all-around air defense from ground level to high altitudes. The SAM-2 is a two-stage guided missile with a 28-mile range, a minimum effective height of 1,000 feet, and a maximum ceiling of 90,000 feet. Six missiles comprise one battery and are usually deployed in a star formation around a central radar. Specially designed missile transporters are located near each launcher; these have a ready round and can reload the launcher in five minutes. The SAM-3 is a two-stage guided missile with a 15-mile range, a 500-foot minimum ceiling, and a 40,000-foot maximum. The SAM-3 is considered a medium-altitude defensive weapon. Four missile launchers, each with two missiles, comprise a battery. The SAM-6 is a single-stage guided missile effective from less than 100 feet to 100,000 feet with a 25-mile range. This is the latest Soviet air defense missile and has good to excellent performance characteristics, with both optical and radar guidance. One tracked armored carrier mounts and fires three missiles. Because the carrier is highly mobile, its vulnerability is lessened.[2] The SAM-7 is a shoulder-fired, infrared-guided missile which can be carried by infantrymen. It has a range of less than 4 miles and is effective from ground level to 10,000 feet. Additionally, Syria had vehicle-mounted SAM-7 multiple launchers configured to fire four or eight missiles either singly or in salvos. The SAM-6 and SAM-7 combine to provide a low-altitude defense and, because of an organic, terminal, infrared-guidance capability, they are less susceptible to electronic jamming. Syria's SAM inventory was much smaller than Egypt's, but it consisted of approximately 300 SAM-2, SAM-3, and SAM-6 launchers. The SAM-7 is an individual, lightweight weapon, and Syria probably had hundreds in its inventory. However, the number of infantry trained to fire the missile was unknown.

Complementing the SAM network was an extensive AAA system. Of primary importance were the Soviet four-barrelled, fully automatic, 23-mm AA gun, the ZSU-23-4, and the two-barrelled, fully automatic, 57-mm AA gun, the ZSU-57-2. The ZSU-23-4 is effective from ground level to 16,000 feet and has a 4.2-mile range. Each gun fires 1,000 rounds per minute. The ZSU-57-2 is effective from ground level to 27,000 feet and has a 7.2-mile range. Both are mounted on tracked armored carriers, which permits them to remain near the front of an advancing field army. The 37-mm, 85-mm, and 100-mm AA guns are single-barrelled, towed weapons. The 37-mm has a 6-mile range and 21,000-foot ceiling, the 85-mm a 9.3-mile range and 32,000-foot ceiling, and the 100-mm a 12.6-

mile range and a 45,000-foot ceiling. The 37-mm AA gun is used in support of the field army, while both the 85-mm and 100-mm AA guns are used for point defense of airfields, cities, and other vital locations.

Tactically, the two missiles and the gun systems are designed to be used together. Elements of both systems are normally deployed in close proximity to provide high-, medium-, and low-altitude defenses. The SAM system is usually used to protect a particular target, such as a defensive line, city, or airfield. An AAA system is then deployed to assist in the defense of the SAM sites. Together, well planned SAM and AAA systems provide a formidable air defense system.

On the other side, the I.D.F. has adopted a substantially different air defense strategy for several reasons. First, it places high confidence in its manned aircraft in the air defense role. Second, in fast-moving ground and air battles it is difficult for gunners and SAM operators to identify and engage hostile aircraft. For protection of forward ground units, the I.D.F. has some 300 20-mm, 30-mm, and 40-mm AAA weapons. In point defense around military and civilian targets, the I.D.F. has 10 SAM batteries with 60 American Hawk missile launchers.

In the air, Soviet-built aircraft constituted the bulk of the Syrian Air Force (S.A.F.). The primary aircraft throughout the war was the MIG-21 with a maximum air speed of Mach 2.2 and a combat radius of 348 miles. For comparison, the I.A.F. depended upon the American F-4 Phantom with a maximum speed of Mach 2.4, a combat radius of 1,000 miles, and a maximum payload of 16,000 pounds. The French Mirage III, with an air speed of Mach 2.2 and a combat radius of 745 miles, was the primary I.A.F. interceptor. Thus, the Mirage III could counter the MIG-21, while the F-4 can carry eight times the MIG-21 bombload. The secondary aircraft of the S.A.F. and I.A.F., respectively, were the Soviet SU-7 and the American A-4 Skyhawk. The SU-7 has an air speed of Mach 1.2, a 5,500-pound payload, and a 1,000-mile range. The A-4 is slower at Mach 1.0, but it carries a maximum of 10,000 pounds and has a combat radius of 2,000 miles.

At the start of the war, Israel had 513 combat aircraft, including 160 A-4s, 120 F-4s, and 35 Mirage IIIs.[3] Syria had 326 combat aircraft, including 200 MIG-21s and 30 SU-7s. Egypt was credited with 620 aircraft, of which 210 were MIG-21s and 80 were SU-7s. The attacking Syrian force was met by the three regular infantry brigades normally allotted to the Golan Heights. These units occupied the outpost line and a series of fortified strongholds extending west to the crest of the Heights. There is evidence that a fourth armored or mechanized infantry brigade was in the area, having been mobilized in the week preceding 6 October to conduct a campaign in southern Lebanon against the Palestinean guerrillas in retaliation for their successful closing of the Jewish rehabilitation center at Schöngau Castle, Austria. Including Israeli paramilitary and border forces, the initial defense force could not have been larger than 20,000 men and 200 tanks.

The Syrian attack was preceded by a heavy artillery barrage that began at 11:58 on the morning of 6 October. An estimated 700 artillery guns and mortars participated in the barrage. Simultaneously, commando units executed helicopter-borne raids on key Israeli positions, such as the Mount Hermon radar station. Over one-half of the Syrian helicopters in these raids were destroyed in flight. At 2 p.m. the Syrians attacked the Israeli outpost line. United Nations observers reported three initial Syrian crossings of the 1967 cease-fire line, one at Ahmadiye in the north, a second at Khushniye along Highway 41 connecting El Kuneitra with Damascus, and a third to the south in the Rafid area.

Israel's immediate response was to launch massive air attacks while ground units fought a delaying action. Hundreds of sorties were flown by the I.A.F. against the advancing Syrian columns and SAM and AAA sites in the first defensive line. The northern Syrian columns split, with one part swinging north to capture Mount Hermon and the second by-passing El Kuneitra and pressing up the Bnot Yaakov road to the crest. The central column also split: one part driving west to the Bnot Yaakov bridge and the rear of the Israeli defenders and the other swinging south to link up with the Rafid column advancing along the alternative route onto the Heights. By nightfall the deepest penetration was 21 miles, conducted by units at Hushmiyir south of the Rafid column. This advance, however, had lost over 100 tanks.

In an unexpected development the Syrian forces conducted night operations and continued to advance. Israeli reserve units were committed to the battle upon arrival, even if only in company or battalion strength. In the early morning hours of the seventh the I.A.F. returned to the battle with hundreds of planes flying six, seven, and eight sorties during the day. Given the relatively short distances involved, I.A.F. aircraft could carry maximum ordnance loads. Meanwhile, the Israeli ground forces were continually being strengthened.

For Israel the seventh was the critical day that determined whether Syrian tanks would reach the crest of the Golan Heights before a counterattack could be launched. The southernmost penetration was within two to five miles of the vital crest at dawn, while the middle and northern penetrations were at points ten miles deep. But as the day wore on, Israel steadily gained the upper hand. El Kuneitra was heavily contested throughout the day but remained in Israeli hands. The southernmost column was stopped by a massive concentration of artillery and tanks. By afternoon, despite the very heavy fighting, some mobilization units arriving in the area were being withheld from combat and assembled at Rosh Pina for a counterattack planned for the next day.

In preparation for the counterattack the I.A.F. concentrated on the air defenses along the first and second Syrian defensive lines. By nightfall of the seventh the I.A.F. had penetrated the first-line air defenses; by the following night the I.A.F. had seriously damaged the Syrian air defense infrastructure, but at the cost of almost 30 aircraft (over one-fourth of the I.A.F.'s total aircraft losses of 110 during the war).

On the eighth Israel counterattacked with at least nine brigades, the equivalent of three divisions, using approximately 700 of Israel's 1,900 tanks and the bulk of its aircraft. To this point the S.A.F. had conducted only defensive patrols over the country's interior, but now it too was committed. Fighting was extremely heavy on the eighth and into the ninth, with Syria launching counterattacks north, west, and southwest from El Kuneitra. By nightfall on the ninth Israel had recovered the 1967 cease-fire line. Israel claimed the destruction of over 400 Syrian tanks and Syria's forward air defense system in less than four days, while losing only 100 tanks itself.

Sometime during the ninth Syria began moving her two armored divisions west to the first defensive line. By the tenth Syria had reconstituted her front line with parts of the line held by remnants of her three infantry divisions. This deployment left her with minimal reserves and in a critical position. The I.A.F. now claimed mastery of Syrian skies, and large unit movements during daylight were constrained. Political targets in Damascus and oil refineries and power stations in Homs were hit. This was the opening of a strategic bombing campaign against Syria. The I.A.F. struck strategic Syrian targets in stated retaliation for 20 firings of Soviet FROG-7 surface-to-surface missiles (SSM) against settlements in northern Israel. The FROG-7 SSM can deliver a 1,100-pound warhead, either nuclear or conventional, over 40 miles.

By 11 October Kuwaiti troops and a Moroccan brigade had been committed to the Syrian line. Iraq had placed all its forces at Syria's disposal on the seventh after reestablishing relations with Iran the same day and thus securing its eastern flank. By the tenth over 18,000 Iraqi troops and 100 tanks were available in Syria for commitment, with over 150 tanks still in transit. But this contingent arrived too late to be deployed en masse or to alter the outcome.

On the eleventh Israel launched a general offensive and penetrated six miles along Highway 41 onto the Syrian plateau. The attack pierced the Syrian defensive line and inflicted heavy losses upon the two Syrian armored divisions. The ground attack was accompanied by hundreds of I.A.F. sorties. By the next day Israeli tank units had advanced to the second Syrian defensive line, centered on Saasa, 18 miles southwest of Damascus. Two Iraqi bri-

gades were committed, and the Israelis promptly destroyed 30
to 40 of their assembled 200 tanks. Although Israel stated that
the Syrian forces staged an orderly rearguard and delaying action
back to their second defensive line, it also claimed the destruction of 400 more Syrian tanks, for a total of 800 tanks since the
outbreak of hostilities. Israel acknowledged the loss of 50 to 100
of its own tanks in the advance.

Beginning with the S.A.F. commitment in an offensive role on
the eighth, air engagements quickly rose between the I.A.F. and
both S.A.F. and Iraqi aircraft. The I.A.F. clearly demonstrated its
superiority in these engagements. From the eighth onward the
I.A.F. destroyed in air battles from 10 to 20 Syrian and Iraqi aircraft each day, usually without the loss of a single Israeli aircraft.
Their most successful day was 12 October, when the I.A.F. and
Israeli ground forces downed 29 Syrian aircraft.

One objective of Israel's Syrian offensive was to destroy as large
a proportion of the Syrian armed forces as possible. As a secondary objective the I.D.F. sought to reach a dominating position
around Damascus. By 13 October, one week after the war's start,
Israel had destroyed over 55 percent of the Syrian armor and
30 percent of its air force. But Israel's advance had also ground to
a halt on the thirteenth without fully realizing either of its objectives. Israeli forward elements were coming under extremely
heavy artillery fire along Highway 41, while 50 percent of Syrian
air defenses remained intact, including some 40 SAM-6 launchers.
Syrian army resistance stiffened, firmly holding the hills before
Saasa and blocking access to the open terrain around Damascus.
The Israeli penetration was a large bulge in the north toward
Damascus that tapered off to the cease-fire line in the south. The
bulge was being held by two Syrian infantry divisions and one
armored division, all three somewhat rebuilt with Soviet equipment airlifted in since the tenth; meanwhile, the Moroccan
brigade held the Mount Hermon positions north of Beit Jann,
while one Iraqi armored division and a small contingent of
Kuwaiti troops were stationed north of El Harra. To the south,
part of Syria's remaining third infantry division held the line

with the assistance of at least one Iraqi brigade. The Jordanian 40th Armored Brigade and a Saudi brigade were also committed to Syria on the thirteenth and were located south of Jassem.

The contingents from Syria's Arab allies began a series of strong counterattacks both north and south of the main Israeli penetration to relieve the pressure on the defensive line at Saasa. These counterattacks continued up to the Syrian acceptance of the United Nations cease-fire on 23 October. At no point had Israel seriously penetrated Syria's second and more elaborate defensive line, positions that were still stoutly defended and being continually reinforced by Arab allies. Heavy damage had been inflicted on the Arabs, but Damascus had not been interdicted, and to do so would certainly have required a sustained I.D.F. effort with heavy losses.

Israel's original battle plans prescribed a breakthrough at Saasa and then a sweep to the right, outflanking the third defensive position and cutting the road to Jordan between Kissoue and the impassable lava beds south of Rhabarheb before turning north and cutting the highway to Iraq behind Duma and thus virtually encircling Damascus. But after the fourteenth the Israelis concentrated their efforts upon deepening the flank penetrations, particularly in the north, to bring them on a line with Saasa. This operation included the capture of the hill Tel el Sharmes south of Saasa and a final costly assault by one crack Israeli paratroop brigade on Mount Hermon, the successful seizure of which gave Israel control of the commanding terrain feature west of Damascus, overlooking the northern sectors of the Syrian lines.

The Soviet airlift was increasingly felt as more and more artillery pieces were deployed in the continuing Syrian barrage against Israel. But the American airlift, beginning on the fifteenth, also made a difference for the Israelis. Repeated Syrian, Iraqi, and Jordanian armor attacks were repulsed by American tube-launched, optically tracked, wire-guided (TOW) antitank missiles with their maximum effective range of 3,000 meters. The I.A.F., meanwhile, maintained a defensive watch over the 300-square-mile area Israel had seized and occasionally conducted heavy ground attacks to break up pending Arab attacks. By the twenty-second one Saudi brigade and a second Jordanian brigade had also taken up positions in Syria, with the Saudis in the front line. But the stalemate remained essentially unchanged after the fourteenth (see figure 2). In the early morning Israel was forced to deploy some units and the bulk of the I.A.F. against the mounting threat in the Sinai.

The U.N. cease-fire went into effect on 23 October on the Syrian front. Tank losses were estimated at 900 for Syria, 125 for Iraq, 20 for Jordan, and 250 to 300 for Israel. Additionally, Syria lost 185 aircraft and Iraq lost 20, compared to I.A.F. losses of 50 to 60.

The Sinai Front

The major operation of the October War was fought in the Sinai. By virtue of its size Egypt had been Israel's chief antagonist since 1948 (see table 1). After the Canal cease-fire of August 1970, Egypt began improving its military posture. Two massive efforts were undertaken first to deploy an effective air defense system to prevent a repeat of the June War air battle, and then to create the military infrastructure necessary to launch and support a cross-canal operation in strength.

Egypt's first major effort involved the construction of the world's largest air defense system. During the months of September and October 1970 Egypt violated the U.N. cease-fire terms and with Soviet assistance moved several score SAM launchers into the 50 kilometer cease-fire zone west of the Canal. Although this was the largest single buildup, Egypt continued to improve and expand the air defense system until the October War. By 6 October there was one SAM-2 battery positioned every two miles along the 106-mile west bank of the Canal. Additional batteries were deployed at Suez City and Port Said for a total of 360 SAM-2 launchers. A SAM-3 battery was colocated at each site, for a total of 240 launchers and 480 ready missiles. Together, the two missiles occupied a prepared site with revetments, control bunkers,

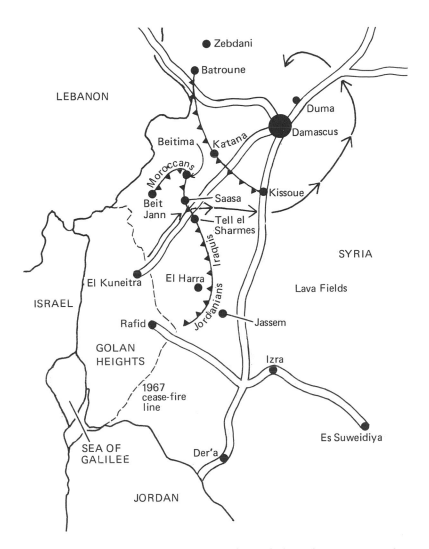

Figure 2. Strategy in the Golan. The spiked lines indicate the Syrian lines of defense. The arrows show the flanking move around Damascus planned by the Israelis. They were, however, halted at Saasa, the first main line of defense.

Table 1 Comparative Strengths of Israel, Egypt, and Syria

	Israel	Egypt	Syria
Population	3,180,000	35,700,000	6,775,000
Length of military service	3 years (men); 20 months (women)	3 years	30 months
Estimated GNP (1972)	$6.85 billion	$7.5 billion	$1.93 billion
Defense budget for fiscal 1972	$1.474 billion	$1.737 billion	$216 million
Defense spending as % of GNP (1972)	18.2%	20.2%	11.5%
Defense spending per capita (1972)	$404	$43	$38
Total armed forces strength (navy included)	30,000 regulars; 85,000 conscripts; 300,000 when fully mobilized (within 72 hours)	298,000	132,000
Air Force			
Strength	15,000 regulars; 1,000 conscripts; 20,000 when fully mobilized	23,000	10,000
Army			
Strength	11,500 regulars; 83,000 conscripts; 275,000 when fully mobilized	260,000	120,000

| Major formations | 10 armored brigades; 9 infantry brigades; 9 mechanized brigades; 5 parachute brigades; 3 artillery brigades.* *7 brigades (2 armored, 3 infantry, 2 parachute) at full strength; 5 brigades (1 armored, 4 mechanized) at about 50%; rest at cadre strength | 2 armored divisions; 3 mechanized infantry divisions; 2 independent armored brigades; 2 independent infantry brigades; 1 airborne brigade; 1 parachute brigade; 5 infantry divisions; 6 artillery brigades; 26 commando battalions | 2 armored divisions; 3 infantry divisions; 1 armored brigade; 1 mechanized brigade; 1 infantry brigade; 2 commando brigades; 1 reconnaissance battalion; 3 parachute battalions; 7 artillery regiments; 12 SAM batteries with SAM-2s and SAM-3s |

Source: *The Military Balance: 1973–1974*, IISS, London.

concrete radar housings, and sandblast walls. Each site also contained buried storage bunkers for stockpiled missiles.

The SAM-6 system was not colocated with the permanent SAM sites discussed above. To do so would have denied the SAM-6 the advantages derived from its mobility. Rather, the carriers were initially dispersed behind the Canal in sand revetments and moved as the situation dictated. In anticipation of the canal crossing and the need for forward air defense, additional sand revetments were prepared nearer the Canal and left empty for later occupation once the east bank was secured. Although the number of SAM-6 carriers in Egypt was unknown, it was estimated to be near 240, with 60 carriers deployed in five batteries around Cairo alone. Egypt probably positioned over one-half of its total inventory within the 50-kilometer-wide Canal zone, giving it at least 120 carriers with 360 ready missiles.

Since the SAM-7 is an individual weapon, there is no way of estimating the size of the Egyptian supply. The figure, however, would be in the thousands. Considering only the SAM-2, SAM-3, and SAM-6 capability then, at the start of the war Egypt had deployed not less than 1,200 ready missiles within the 50-kilometer Canal zone.

To the SAM totals must be added the AAA systems. Around each permanent SAM site were located ZSU-23-4 and 37-mm towed batteries. Near the Canal Egypt massed hundreds of ZSU-23-4 and ZSU-57-2 AA guns. Due to their mobility most of these guns crossed to the east bank and provided air defense for divisions and brigades, while some protected the pontoon bridges. Egypt also deployed a number of 85-mm batteries near airfields west of the Canal. On the sixth Egypt probably had almost 1,000 AA guns within the Canal zone. Together, the SAM and AAA weapons constituted the densest area air defense in the world.

Egypt's second major effort was the construction of the necessary infrastructure to launch and support a cross-canal invasion in strength. Preparations were concentrated in two areas west of the Suez Canal; in the north between Qantara and Great Bitter Lake and in the south between Little Bitter Lake and Suez City.

Some preparations were also undertaken around Port Said. During the three years from August 1970 until the October War, Egypt had constructed in-depth fortifications west of the Canal. Concrete gun emplacements, sometimes with steel reinforcement, and ammunition storage bunkers had been constructed. Drive-in revetments for artillery and tanks had also been built. Trenches had been dug for thousands of troops. Command post bunkers with elaborate communication nets had been emplaced. Air defense radars had been integrated into a national air defense warning network. At potential crossing points, Soviet bridging equipment had been stored in dispersal areas.

All of these fortifications were continuously, but lightly, manned. Once or twice a year, during maneuvers, Egyptian units would move to and occupy the Canal fortifications, familiarizing themselves with the area and equipment. The annual fall maneuver scheduled for the weeks preceding the attack on 6 October was typical of past exercises.

Opposite the Egyptian forces west of the Canal, the Israelis had also been busy, constructing three parallel lines of fortifications known as the Bar Lev Line. The first line east of the Canal consisted of a minimum of 25 evenly spaced steel and concrete bunkers. Each bunker contained 30 to 40 troops with a few tanks, mortars, and machine guns. Each bunker was in communication with bunkers north and south and also with the two lines to the east. This line was neither intended nor considered to be impregnable, although the bunkers themselves were designed with 17-foot-thick ceilings to take a direct artillery hit. In fact, this line was only a fortified outpost line with the dual mission of reporting any major canal crossing and thwarting small Egyptian raiding parties.

The second line lay approximately five to ten miles east of the Canal and consisted of company-size strongholds. Fortifications at the strongholds were much more intensive, and this line was Israel's first defensive position, although that term is a slight misnomer. The purpose of the strongholds was to slow down any attack and to channel it between them. The strongholds were designed merely to position the attacking force to the best advantage of Israeli armored brigades in the counterattacking force. The third line, which was attacked in the war only in the Mitla Pass area, was composed of very heavily fortified positions on the western face of the Sinai plateau that extends generally from north to south. These positions guard the Ismailia, Giddi, and Mitla Passes and the key access routes to the Sinai interior. In the Sinai interior, approximately 50 miles east of the Canal, were Israel's two regular armored brigades.

The concept of the Bar Lev Line was to report, direct, and fix an attacking Egyptian force into the area desired for the Israeli counterattack, which would be conducted by at least the two armored brigades and a paratroop brigade stationed in the Sinai. Since the lines themselves were well fortified and protected, the I.D.F. did not deploy any air defense weapons near the Canal in their support. The first Israeli SAM and AAA systems were located in support of the mobile armor brigades and I.A.F. Sinai airfields. The Israelis did not expect to use the systems heavily, however, because they were confident that the I.A.F. would detect and engage the Egyptian Air Force (E.A.F.) before the latter could conduct its ground attacks.

In late September the Egyptians moved into their canal fortifications. The main body of this force consisted of five infantry divisions and several independent armored, infantry, and artillery brigades that had been organized into two corps. The Egyptian II Corps, consisting of three infantry divisions, deployed north of the Great Bitter Lake. The Egyptian III Corps, consisting of two infantry divisions, was situated south of Little Bitter Lake. Each corps had at least two independent artillery brigades. The estimated size of this force was 70,000 men, 600 tanks, and over 1,000 artillery pieces. Also employed, but located in various areas near airfields, were several commando regiments.

Unlike the Syrian forces, the Egyptians carried hundreds of antitank (AT) weapons such as the Snapper and Sagger wire-guided missiles, rocket-propelled grenades (RPG), and 57-mm, 85-mm, and 100-mm AT guns. The Snapper is a Soviet missile with a high explosive, shaped-charge warhead and a range of one mile. It can be mounted in groups of three on an armored infantry carrier. The Sagger is also a Soviet missile with a range of 1.5 miles. It can be vehicle-mounted in groups of six or carried by infantry. The manpack version requires a three-man team to carry the launcher, fire-control equipment, and two complete missiles. The RPG is the standard Soviet squad antitank weapon. It is a shoulder-fired, 40-mm, rocket-propelled grenade with an effective range of 300 meters against moving targets and 500 meters against stationary targets. The 57-mm, 85-mm, and 100-mm AT guns have ranges of 5, 9, and 12 miles, respectively. The 100-mm AT gun can be employed in an artillery role if necessary.

The Egyptian canal crossing was conducted in Soviet textbook fashion as a deliberate assault river crossing. From the execution, it is evident that extensive training occurred well before the attack. Ground reconnaissance of crossing sites, probably the most crucial factor, had been conducted for three years. Every topographical detail was mapped out and analyses had been made to determine the best sites. Following the selection of sites, approaches to them were prepared. Israel, in fact, had photographs revealing the construction of each site's road network over one year before the assault. Each crossing site was integrated into the layout of the large-scale fortifications adjacent to the bank. These fortifications permitted the main body of Egyptian forces to move within one to three miles of the Canal in the weeks prior to the attack.

At exactly noon on 6 October the Egyptians commenced hostilities with a massive artillery barrage along the length of the Canal (see figure 3). Coupled with this were heavy air attacks on Israel's Sinai airfields, conducted on a north-south, rather than an east-west axis. Simultaneously, teams of frogmen swam the Canal and dismantled or destroyed Israeli sensors and communication lines on the east bank. Egyptian infantry units also brought forward and prepared rubber rafts for the crossing. At 2 P.M. infantry companies rushed the Canal and crossed by rafts to the east bank. Once ashore, they scaled the 100-foot-high sand embank-

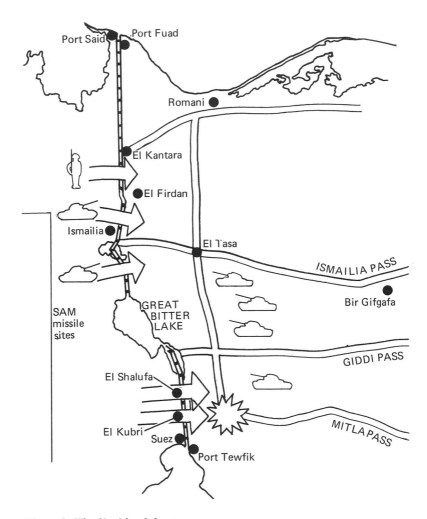

Figure 3. The Sinai battlefront.

ment the Israelis had constructed to deter a canal crossing. Fanning out, some attacked the Israeli bunkers while others moved east into the desert and set up a narrow belt of antitank defenses. At approximately 2:15 the Egyptian artillery shifted its fire to the second Bar Lev Line to the east. The artillery fire was replaced by direct infantry and tank fire from Egyptian units on the west bank. Within ten minutes of the crossing the Egyptian flag was flying east of the Canal for the first time since 1967. (See figure 3.)

Engineer troops, meanwhile, lowered hoses into the Canal to supply their giant water cannons. Strong streams of water were used to wash away enough sand from the embankment to make it traversable for tanks and armored vehicles. When these gaps neared completion, the first wave of infantry, in amphibious armored personnel carriers, entered the water and crossed to the east bank. Exiting the Canal, they drove through the gap and moved east several hundred meters, where they discharged their troops. Meanwhile, the rafts continued to ferry infantry troops across, particularly Sagger AT missile teams.

After 30 minutes pontoon bridge construction was started, and motorized barges and ferries were placed in the water. While engineer troops assembled the heavy folding bridge sections at a rate of six or seven meters a minute, the rafts and barges carried the first tanks across. Also, some earthmoving equipment was ferried across to widen the gaps created by the water cannons. Simultaneously, PT-76 amphibious tanks mounting a 76-mm main gun swam across and reinforced the first T-54/55 medium-tank companies that had been ferried over. With the tanks across, a second wave of armored infantry carriers swam the Canal and expanded the east-bank bridgeheads. By 3:30 P.M. the Egyptians had opened their first pontoon bridges for traffic, and the tank units soon crossed the eleven assembled bridges.

During this opening phase Egypt conducted a series of commando raids against Baluza (along the northern coastal road), El Tasa (the I.D.F. forward headquarters), Bir Gifgafa Air Base, Sharm el Sheikh, and other key installations. Egypt had 20 commando battalions regarded as their elite troops. Israeli air defenses shot down most of the helicopters, killing the commandos before they reached their destinations. Only at Sharm el Sheikh did the commandos see action. After a brisk naval bombardment, many of the helicopters were destroyed when they landed, and the commandos were driven into the Sinai wasteland.

The Israelis immediately reported the artillery barrage and canal crossings. The 30 to 40 men in each outpost deployed in the bunker and into the supporting trenches and opened fire on the Egyptians along the opposite bank. Israeli units further back occupied their strongholds, and Israeli artillery batteries began returning fire, directed by the outpost line. Within hours, however, the Egyptians were swarming onto the east bank, and all the outposts were under heavy attack. The outpost line reported by late afternoon that the situation was critical, and some fell into Egyptian hands. The two Israeli armor brigades began moving west through the passes and assembled at the base of the Sinai plateau.

The Egyptians, however, were moving slowly east, deliberately establishing defenses in depth for the inevitable Israeli counterattack. The Egyptian attack did not approach the second Bar Lev Line at this point. Instead, by continued pressure on the Israeli outposts, the Egyptians forced Israel's hand, and by dusk the two armored brigades were moving to the attack. Throughout the night of the sixth and into the seventh, they attacked the five Egyptian bridgeheads, located south of El Kantara, south of El Firdan, south of Ismailia and Timsah, at El Shalufa, and at El Kubri north of Port Tewfik. But the I.D.F. was blocked by hundreds of AT weapons. The Egyptians were able to stop the Israeli night attacks without committing Egyptian tanks and with heavy Israeli losses.

Throughout the seventh and eighth Egypt continued its crossing. Israel continued to launch a series of uncoordinated battalion-size counterattacks using regular units and reserves as they became available, while the I.A.F. attempted to destroy the bridges. Both actions proved very costly and forced the I.D.F to

abandon any hope of defeating the Egyptians first before turning
against Syria. In the first three days the Israelis lost 300 to 400 of
their 900 tanks earmarked for this sector, with well over 200 of the
losses to Snapper and Sagger AT missiles. Included in this total
are the 96 tanks of the much heralded 190th Israeli Tank Brigade,
whose commander was captured and interviewed on Egyptian
television. The I.A.F., while attempting to knock out the Egyptian bridges and SAM sites, lost over 20 aircraft. On the eighth
the I.A.F. claimed that 9 of 11 bridges were destroyed, but they
were quickly repaired. By the ninth Israeli spokesmen were con-
ceding that the Egyptians had crossed a substantial force and that
no quick victory was possible.

The I.A.F. was also forced to reconsider its tactics. The Soviet-
supplied Egyptian and Syrian air defense systems had downed
about 50 I.A.F. aircraft by the ninth, or almost half of Israel's
total air losses for the October War. The SAM-6 was exacting its
heaviest toll against I.A.F. aircraft supporting Israeli ground
forces. Aircraft not downed by SAM-6s were subjected to heavy
AAA fire, particularly from the 23-mm and 57-mm AA guns. In
fact, 95 to 98 percent of the I.A.F. losses were to air defense systems, and over half of these losses were to AAA. To counter the
air defense network, the I.A.F. limited its Canal attacks after the
ninth to the northern or southern ends in an attempt to "roll up"
the SAM and AAA systems from the extreme flanks. Formerly, it
had attacked heavily in the central Canal zone and had even
flown parallel to the Canal in an attempt to maximize the number of strikes at each bridge or SAM site. Paralleling the Canal,
however, increased exposure to the Egyptian air defense, thereby
increasing the probability of a hit. After the ninth, if it became
necessary to conduct ground attacks in the central sector, the
I.A.F. sought to remain perpendicular to the Canal and to limit
the time spent within the Egyptian air defense envelope. (The
I.A.F. tried the same tactics in Syria. But to hit the system in a
flank position, Israeli aircraft had to overfly Jordan, which
prompted a Jordanian reaction and the downing of two I.A.F.
aircraft. Fearing that further violations of Jordanian airspace

would force Amman into the war, Israel confined its flights to the Heights and accepted the heavy cost of frontal attacks on Syrian defenses.)

The ground battle in the Sinai became stalemated by the ninth as Egypt penetrated to the strongholds of the second Bar Lev Line. The Egyptians were now in control of the entire 102-mile east bank of the Suez Canal, and their penetration varied in width from three to eight miles. Egypt and Israel continued to parry, but neither launched a full-scale offensive as the first week of hostilities came to a close. East of Suez, the Egyptian III Corps was able to push as deep as ten miles toward the Mitla Pass. To support the east-bank operation, Egypt also moved a few SAM-6 batteries across the Canal. Israel, meanwhile, assembled a force of at least fifteen brigades, or the equivalent of five divisions, to oppose the Egyptians. This force numbered at least 60,000 men and 500 to 600 tanks.

On 14 October Egypt launched a massive offensive along the entire length of its bridgehead. To assist in the attack, Egypt's two armored divisions were moved east to the Canal. The Egyptian plan was to conduct a frontal attack with the aim of achieving limited territorial gains, which would increase Egyptian maneuver area east of the Canal, and possibly seizing the key Giddi and Mitla Passes. In support of this attack, the E.A.F. conducted its first large-scale ground attacks.

The attack was a costly failure and resulted in an Israeli tactical victory. In air battles the I.A.F. downed 28 E.A.F. aircraft on the fourteenth without loss. Despite the SAM envelope the I.A.F. conducted its own ground attacks with good results. Where the Egyptian advance toward the Mitla Pass reached east of the SAM envelope, the I.A.F. was extremely effective in destroying Egyptian armor. On the ground Egypt chose to disperse its tanks along the entire front in support of its infantry, instead of concentrating them to seize key strongholds or terrain features. Israel, on the other hand, formed two armor-heavy, multibrigade task forces and dispersed the remainder of its forces between strongholds.

One task force struck just north of the Great Bitter Lake, while the second attacked from the Mitla Pass area.

The subsequent battle raged through the fifteenth, with each side employing over 600 tanks in the largest tank battle since World War II. Sometime during this period, Egypt crossed some of its divisional armored brigades to the east bank, thereby increasing its force to nearly seven divisions and increasing its committed tanks to possibly 1,000. Israel, meanwhile, also brought in additional reserves, probably from the Jordanian front. These units, in turn, were relieved by units from the Syrian front.

The Egyptian attack clearly failed. Egypt lost a minimum of 220 tanks, while Israel lost 50 to 100. In the two days the E.A.F. lost over 40 aircraft, while the I.A.F. lost about five. The successful repulse of the Egyptian offensive can be considered the turning point on the Sinai front because it forced the Egyptians to the defensive while demonstrating how vulnerable their forces were when operating beyond their air defense envelope.

More important, the battle demonstrated the decisive leadership edge of the Israelis and its importance to the outcome of tactical operations. After breaking through the forward Egyptian defensive line on the fourteenth, the northern Israeli task force discovered a weak spot south of Ismailia and north of the Great Bitter Lake. Immediately, ground commanders called in the I.A.F., which then conducted numerous ground attacks against forces east and west of the Canal. When darkness came, the armored task force continued its push west to the Canal, almost reaching it before being heavily engaged. The battle raged all night, but by dawn on the fifteenth the Israelis were at the Canal. Throughout the day the I.D.F. fought to expand the corridor and made slow but steady progress. In the confusion of the battle the I.D.F. used an infiltration tactic similar to techniques used against the defenses of El Arish in 1967. A company made up of fifteen captured T-62 tanks with Egyptian markings infiltrated a retreating armored column and was waved across a bridge by Egyptian Military Police. The Israeli company immediately established a defensive perimeter, and the Egyptians, realizing their error, blew up the bridge to prevent the company's reinforcement. The canal crossing was not entirely fortuitous and unplanned. Press reports on the eleventh revealed that numerous Israeli amphibious vehicles and bridge-laying tanks were already on the roads near the front. The press speculated then that they were probably destined for some flanking movement.[4]

Egypt recognized the breach in its lines on the west bank and rapidly moved its armored divisions to cut off the Israeli penetration, expecting the Israelis to remain east of the Canal and roll up the Egyptian bridgehead by attacking north and south. To do so would have meant heavy Israeli casualties, a price unacceptable to the Israeli command. Instead, the local Israeli commander, Major General Arik Sharon, decided to relieve the beleaguered company on the west bank by a daring crossing of the lightly defended Great Bitter Lake.

The night of the fifteenth was critical for the I.D.F. Before dawn several hundred commandos and two tank companies of twenty tanks total were ferried to an area west of Deversoir. Upon landing, the Israeli party pushed north and west, overwhelming some isolated Egyptian forces and bypassing others. They moved straight to the Egyptian SAM sites closest to the Lake, overran them, and destroyed several AAA sites. The Israeli ferries continued to cross the northern end of Great Bitter Lake into the morning of the sixteenth, bringing infantry and tank reinforcements.

While the crossing was being conducted, Israeli tank units engaged the Egyptian armored divisions in the fiercest fighting of the war in an effort to maintain the gap through which the Israelis were reinforcing their west-bank incursion. The Egyptians, with the commitment of their armored divisions, had over 500 tanks between Ismailia and the Great Bitter Lake, or over two to one odds. The only certain way to stop the Egyptians would be heavy I.A.F. attacks at dawn, but these would be extremely costly unless at least part of the air defense systems west of the Canal could be destroyed. By dawn the Israeli force on the west bank had destroyed at least two SAM sites plus additional AAA guns and had slightly cracked the Egyptian air defense envelope. The destruction of these sites permitted the I.A.F. to launch hundreds of sorties against the two Egyptian pincers without heavy losses. As the day progressed, the Israeli force west of the Canal overran at least two more sites. By nightfall on the sixteenth the I.A.F. was pouring through the air defense gap and the two Egyptian pincers were falling back both north and south along the Canal. Many of the 220 Egyptian tanks destroyed during the fourteenth and fifteenth were in this area, with another 75 to 100 destroyed by the night of the sixteenth.

Israel expanded the penetration with reinforcements on the sixteenth, finally crossing them on its own pontoon bridge. Continuing success against the Egyptian forces on the west bank probably caused Israel to devote greater efforts to the crossing than were originally intended, and the general pattern of this operation quickly evolved. The Israelis moved rapidly north to cut the northern Cairo-Ismailia road, destroy SAM and AAA sites, and capture the Abu Suweir Airfield. They also turned west to cut the southern Cairo-Ismailia road and capture Fayid Airfield. Egypt, in the meantime, was forced to withdraw armored units from east of the Canal to counter the Israeli thrusts. The Egyptian 21st Armored Division attacked south from the Ismailia area, while the Egyptian 4th Armored Division attacked northward, west of the Great Bitter Lake. Additionally, one mechanized infantry division was moved east from Cairo to limit the Israeli push westward.

Despite a stiffening Egyptian defense by the eighteenth, Israel increased the size of its bridgehead. The destruction or capture of additional SAM and AAA sites slowly decreased the effectiveness of Egypt's air defense, while I.A.F. effectiveness improved. Between the eighteenth and the twentieth, Israel destroyed over 200 Egyptian tanks west of the Canal and pushed south toward the Cairo-Suez City road. The E.A.F. was committed to the air defense role as the air defense envelope protecting Egyptian ground forces was slowly neutralized. In the ensuing battles the I.A.F.

downed about fifteen E.A.F. aircraft daily, usually without loss. The Egyptian II Corps between Kantara and Ismailia in the north moved a large number of medium- and heavy-artillery pieces to the rear of the central sector. They were overrun by the Israelis, however, before they could be employed. By 20 October Israel had at least 300 tanks and 10,000 men west of the Canal, including one paratroop and two armored brigades.

During this period the Egyptians attempted a series of attacks in the II Corps sector on the east bank north of Ismailia to divert I.D.F. efforts from the west-bank penetration. These Egyptian attacks were held to minimal gains by heavy-artillery battles extending through the daylight hours. The two and one-half infantry divisions of the II Corps and their approximately 200 tanks were contained within their bridgehead by the relatively smaller Israeli forces.

West of the Canal the Israelis pushed south against increasingly lighter Egyptian resistance. By the time of the U.N. cease-fire of 22 October forward Israeli elements had cut the Cairo-Suez City road. Israel had destroyed over one-third of Egypt's fixed SAM sites west of the Canal. Israeli units were firing on Egyptian III Corps units east of the Canal from positions west of the Canal and south of Little Bitter Lake. The I.D.F. claimed the destruction of over 450 tanks west of the Canal between 16 October and the cease-fire. And to the north, both roads connecting Cairo to Ismailia were cut.

The resumption of hostilities on 23 October provided an opportunity for Israel to improve its somewhat weak tactical situation. By that day's close the Israelis had encircled the Egyptian III Corps by seizing Egyptian territory south to Adabriya. An estimated 20,000 men and over 2,000 tanks of two infantry divisions comprising the III Corps were trapped. Israel claimed the destruction of all SAM and AAA sites south of Ismailia, and the I.A.F. dominated the skies above this sector of Egypt.

The situation remained generally unchanged after the twenty-third despite several attempts by the Egyptian III Corps to break out of its encirclement. Total Egyptian losses were approximately

950 tanks, over half of which were accounted for by the cross-canal operation, and 225 aircraft. Israel lost approximately 600 tanks, including 300 to 400 in the first three days, and about 55 aircraft. Egypt's two armored divisions had ceased to exist as effective fighting forces, and Egypt had begun using its units earmarked for the defense of Cairo to stop the Israeli west-bank operation.

The Effect of the Arab Allies
Jordan's military role in the October War was limited. Inadequately equipped for modern aerial warfare, Jordan received both Syrian and Egyptian approval to remain aloof from the fighting unless victory should come within sight. Nevertheless, Jordan's position as a possible belligerent forced Israel to maintain three brigades in the hills of the West Bank. These three Israeli brigades, however, would probably not have altered the outcome had they been committed to the Egyptian or Syrian fronts. Undoubtedly, there were political reasons for Jordan's commitment of its 40th Armored Brigade, and later its 99th Armored Brigade, to the Syrian front after the Israeli counteroffensive. Neither brigade reversed the Israeli advance; but the approximately 8,000 men and 150 tanks did assist Syria in holding its second defensive line until the cease-fire. And, as expected, the Jordanians fought commendably and reaffirmed their status as the best-trained Arab forces.

Similarly, the roles of Iraq, Kuwait, Saudi Arabia, Morocco, Tunisia, Algeria, the Sudan, and North Korea were not significant because they did not materially affect the outcome of the war on either front. Iraq committed more than one armored division with 20,000 men and 250 tanks to the Syrian front, the largest force sent by any Arab ally. Saudi Arabia sent one mechanized brigade of 2,000 men to Syria; Morocco committed one infantry brigade of 2,000 men; and Kuwait dispatched one company of 200 men. Iraqi losses were heaviest, as its troops were poorly trained and led. Saudi and Kuwaiti units fought well. Initially, the Moroccans fought tenaciously; but after the second week they quarreled with the Syrians, and several hundred disaffected troops deserted to Lebanon. Morocco provided one brigade of 2,000 men for the Sinai front; Tunisia and the Sudan each sent about one thousand men; Kuwait committed one battalion of 600 men; Algeria supplied one squadron of MIG-21 fighters; and North Korea had at least 30 pilots in Egypt when hostilities erupted. Moroccan, Tunisian, Algerian, and Sudanese troops did not see reportable service, but the Kuwaiti battalion was annihilated. A few aerial dogfights occurred between Israeli and North Korean pilots, but no losses were reported by either side.

Military Lessons from the October War
The most recent outbreak of hostilities in the Arab-Israeli conflict has been graphically portrayed in the world press as one of the most intensive limited war engagements of small powers in recent history. The Egyptian air defenses were the most elaborate ever constructed and the tank battles were conducted on a scale not witnessed since World War II. Both sides seemed equally committed to the attainment of their war aims. Equipment levels, troop proficiency, officer leadership, and logistical support on both sides had improved substantially during the five years since the Arabs' last defeat and had incorporated wide-ranging innovations. Armaments and tactics employed during the war, therefore, are likely to have a major impact on future military operations of all major powers.

Probably the most significant lesson was that of the continuing need for military and political vigilance to insure readiness and prevent tactical surprise. Despite numerous indicators, the Arabs achieved a high degree of tactical surprise—only regular garrison units in forward positions were on alert, and a low-key Israeli mobilization began only on the sixth. In Mrs. Meir's words, Israel nearly lost the war in the first several days; Israeli leadership did not take the political decision to mobilize in time to prevent serious reversals on both fronts. Israel has consistently based its defense policy on the doctrine of maintaining a minimum standing force which can be augmented by the rapid mobilization of highly trained reserves. But even with the excellence of its national mobilization capability, the Israeli Defense Force requires adequate warning of its opponent's intentions if it is to deploy sufficient troops to forward positions. To insure sufficient warning, Israel has developed an intelligence service of legendary competence. But both the intelligence professionals and the political authorities minimized the prospects of hostilities because of their almost uniform perception of beneficial changes in the international situation.

Israel's political strategy after the June War was highly consistent and adroitly managed. Repeated Soviet interventions in various forms were intended to underwrite Arab military parity and to deter the I.D.F. from attack until battlefield equivalency could be convincingly demonstrated. When these constraints became apparent, Israel adopted the position that it would negotiate with the Arabs only in circumstances where their political leverage would be reduced to a point where their military buildup would be irrelevant. In other words, Israel wanted to force the Arabs into a political straitjacket with no more freedom of maneuver than they could exercise from their militarily inferior position. This line required that Israel maintain its military superiority and prevent any external attempts to reach a political settlement that violated its terms for negotiation. Tel Aviv had successfully blocked the efforts of both great powers, primarily the United States with its repeated Rogers Peace Plans, and was convinced that apathy had replaced initiative in Washington's Middle Eastern policy. Egyptian President Sadat's expulsion of the Soviet combat troops in July 1972 and the Americans' inability to exploit the opportunity convinced Israeli leaders that both great powers had been effectively checked. Without massive political or military support from the external powers, Israel was confident that the Arabs would not launch an attack. This error in political judgment was in large part responsible for the decision not to mobilize Israeli reserves until hostilities were imminent.

Israeli domestic critics have frequently charged that Israel should have repeated its June War tactic of conducting a preemptive attack against the deployed Arab forces. But substantial changes in the Egyptian air posture had occurred in the five-year interval. The establishment of the world's densest area air defense system, coupled with semihardened airbases with aircraft housed in concrete dispersed hangars, combined to make an effective Israeli preemptive attack impossible. During the first week of hostilities the Israeli Air Force attempted to destroy Egyptian aircraft on the ground, but with futile results. The I.A.F. also used standard tactics of attempting to render airbases unserviceable by cratering runways. But the use of quick-drying cement effectively countered these efforts. In short, the inability of the I.A.F. either to destroy Syrian and Egyptian aircraft on the ground or to render their bases inoperable forced the Israelis to achieve air superiority by aerial combat.

The air war provided additional unexpected developments for the I.A.F. Among military experts the I.A.F. is generally regarded as being perhaps the world's finest air force, especially in its pilot proficiency and ground support. It had repeatedly defeated Syrian and Egyptian attempts to establish a credible air defense system and had maintained unquestioned supremacy over Arab pilots. Indeed, only several weeks before hostilities the I.A.F. baited and ambushed two flights of Syrian interceptors and downed a total of nineteen aircraft. With this previous experience, the I.A.F. was surprised by the effectiveness of the Soviet-supplied air defense system and the Arabs' proficiency in operating it independently of Soviet crews. In particular, the relatively old I.A.F. electronic-countermeasures equipment was unable to jam the radar acquisition and tracking frequencies of the much-heralded SAM-6 and the ZSU-23-4 and ZSU-57-2 AAA systems. Moreover, decoy flares were ineffective against the optically-aimed, heat-seeking SAM-7 missiles.[5] Arab crew proficiency was high, allowing all systems to be operated under conditions of heavy usage. After three weeks those systems that had not been destroyed were still operable against the I.A.F. Even in the later stages Syrian and Egyptian SAM batteries were able to fire salvos rather than single missiles. The ripple-fire technique made aircraft evasion difficult and minimized electronic countermeasures,

which had to cover as many as seven frequency bands simultaneously.[6]

To the I.A.F.'s credit it learned quickly from its initial errors.
At the outset it attacked parallel to the Canal in order to gain
maximum time over target per sortie. Due to high attrition rates
and the failure to inflict serious damage on the Egyptian bridgeheads, more selective tactics were used, whereby a crack in the air
defense wall was sought by saturation raids conducted along
flight paths perpendicular to selected points. These efforts also
failed, and the I.A.F. thereafter confined its operations outside
the stationary Egyptian air defense envelop. When the I.A.F. was
forced to attack the Syrian air defense network on the eighth and
ninth, it could not flank the system by overflights of Lebanon
and Jordan for fear of expanding the conflict. It had to use a
frontal assault that cost thirty aircraft, but it did manage to open
a wedge in the first of the three Syrian fortified lines. By the end
of hostilities 40 Syrian SAM-6 batteries were still operational.
On the Egyptian front the air defense envelope was not cracked
until I.D.F. tank units operating on the west bank on the night
of the fifteenth physically overran SAM and AAA sites. In coordination with ground forces, the I.A.F. was then able to roll-up
systematically the air defense system from flanking positions by
saturating individual sites with nearly omnidirectional attacks.

Because of the Arabs' confidence in their air defense system,
their air forces were not committed to the air battle until the
SAM network was broken. This was due in part to the difficulty
of having aircraft operating in the barrage air defense environment, in which radar-guided and optically-aimed systems are hard
to integrate for the purpose of identifying friendly aircraft. The
Arabs may also have calculated that by holding their aircraft in
reserve they could later engage a weakened I.A.F. with greater
success. However, when the Arab aircraft were committed, they
lost heavily to the Israelis, suffering as high as 20 to 1 kill ratios.
The Arabs, however, demonstrated such personal aggressiveness
and proficiency in ground support that sustained operations
could be conducted.

In close ground-attack operations, the I.A.F. was able to inflict heavy losses against Arab mechanized units operating beyond the air defense envelopes. Indeed, the I.A.F. will probably be credited with the major responsibility for the halting of Syrian columns on the sixth and seventh only a few miles short of their military objectives. The seventh was the crucial day and the I.A.F. flew hundreds of sorties and turned aircraft around sometimes in seven minutes. During the offensive of the fourteenth and fifteenth the I.A.F. was again most effective in the Sinai against Egyptian supporting columns when they were beyond air defense ranges. It was less effective in supporting engaged units because of the identification problem. The experience of the October War suggests that the Soviets and Arabs have excelled in constructing and operating a static air defense network; but, despite the mobility of the SAM-6, SAM-7, and the ZSU antiaircraft-gun series, they failed to provide adequate air protection for their maneuver battalions in the field. The simplest explanation may be the difference between indiscriminate barrage fire from fixed batteries and the controlled fire required for field operations. If accurate, this would suggest that the deficiency stems from logistics and training rather than weapons sophistication.

There was a significant difference in the strategic aspect of the conduct of the air war on the two fronts. Israel repeatedly sought the psychological Achilles' heel that would impair the determination of both Syria and Egypt. Accordingly, Israel launched a series of strategic raids against political and economic targets in Syria. The country's economic infrastructure was severely damaged, but there is no evidence that military or civilian morale was adversely affected. If anything, the raids galvanized Syrian resolution. On the other hand, it is important that Israel was deterred from conducting similar strategic strikes against Egypt, as it had in 1970 in the Nile Valley. The presumed reason for Israel's withholding on this option was Sadat's announcement on the sixteenth that he had surface-to-surface missiles for retaliation against I.A.F. strikes. These were not Egyptian SSMs as claimed, but two battalions of Soviet SCUD-B SSMs which had departed the Soviet Union with crews on 12 September. Their arrival in Egypt was a fairly open secret. (After Israel's violation of the 22 October cease-fire, Moscow sent two additional battalions.) Western press sources began speculating that the missiles might have been accompanied by both nuclear and conventional warheads. Whether this was true or not, Israel could not afford the risk of testing Soviet intentions; even a conventional missile attack on Tel Aviv would have been an unacceptable consequence for a raid on Alexandria.

In summary, the air war is likely to have important consequences for other military powers. Air superiority will have to be won in the future in the air and not on the ground. Only multiple nuclear strikes can now render an airbase inoperable for an acceptable period of time. Paradoxically, it was the I.A.F. in 1967 that had demonstrated aircraft vulnerability to ground attack, but it was denied further benefits from this tactic by its opponent's countermeasures. After assessing the reasons for the 1967 defeat of the Arab air forces, other military powers, especially the Soviets, launched major campaigns to insure aircraft survivability. But new constraints on the use of air power are now apparent. In the ground-attack mission, for example, the availability of large numbers of air defense weapons and inexpensive missiles will require a greater number of aircraft to inflict the same degree of damage. The cost-effectiveness of fighter-bomber aircraft may soon be seriously questioned. The expense of modern aircraft may either prohibit an attacker with a limited aircraft inventory from conducting large-scale ground attacks or necessitate employment of inexpensive lightweight aircraft with markedly reduced payloads. The air defense threat will also require increasingly sophisticated ECM equipment, greater use of drones for reconnaissance and electronic-support missions, and employment of standoff air-to-surface missiles with ranges of 20 to 50 miles (such as the American SRAM). But there is no reliable countermeasure against the optically-aimed, portable, heat-seeking missiles, which will soon make attack aircraft vulnerable to forward infantry patrols. Thus, there may soon be sound grounds for returning the close-ground-attack mission to artillery and gunships and reserving fighter-bomber aircraft for interdiction and hardened targets. The ground war provided several unexpected developments as well. The Israeli government and defense officials believed that the post-June War lines of the Golan Heights and the Suez Canal were the most defensible borders Israel could secure against its neighbors. They insisted that these borders must not be negotiated away without a durable peace. They proved not to be as secure as had been envisioned, but they did provide sufficient depth that the I.D.F. could trade space for time when caught without adequate warning. Some Israelis argued that the ground war confirmed the necessity of maintaining these "strategic" borders, while others pointed out that this could only be justified if Israel expected a war of attrition or annihilation. But if in fact the war was waged from the Arab side, as was alleged, only for the recovery of Arab honor and lost territories, then Israel was fighting merely for land it had been attempting to exchange for security for the past five years. In this case Israel fought the wrong war, at the wrong time, for the wrong aims. The incongruity between these extremes suggests that a greater consensus on security policy is now required: Israel must now accept a formula for secure borders that puts more emphasis on political stability than on military defensibility. Mutually agreed borders mean just that!

The fortifications along these lines reflected differing concepts of operation and a high degree of ingenuity on both sides. On the Golan Heights Israel had constructed only a thin line of fortified bunkers and tank positions that would be adequate to block minor incursions. A major attack was to be countered by the maneuverability of armored units on terrain that favored the Israelis. Syria had constructed a line of heavier fortifications several miles behind the armistice line. It was to provide protection for the forward air defense system and several mechanized divisions. Ten to twelve miles behind it was the main fortified echelon with heavy-artillery revetments. A third echelon had been constructed eight to ten miles from Damascus. The first line held sufficiently well for the three retreating mechanized divisions to pass through in good order while the two armored divisions controlled this position. The armored divisions covered the retreat and then withdrew to the second, the Saasa line. This echelon was never seriously breached at any point by the I.D.F.

In the Sinai the Bar Lev Line of three coordinated defensive positions functioned exactly as designed. The first echelon along the Canal reported and constrained the Egyptian attack. Its principal function was to channel any major incursions into desirable areas for I.D.F. counterattacks. The second echelon was to refine this process by pinning the Egyptians down with artillery main thrusts while armored units maneuvered for flanking attacks. The third line contained a series of battalion-sized fortresses and was only reached in the area of the Mitla Pass.

On the Egyptian side of the Canal, massive fortifications had been constructed for the protection of at least five divisions and supporting equipment. The effectiveness of these defensive works cannot be adequately assessed, however, since they were turned and overrun by flanking maneuvers. Both sides underestimated the value of the Canal as a complement for their fortification plans: the Egyptian crossing was well planned and well rehearsed, and the Israeli opportunity crossing was planned and ingeniously executed, contributing to the collapse of the Egyptian III Corps. In short, the fortifications on both sides reflected the respective military preferences: the Arabs sought set-piece engagements of attrition in which their superiority in numbers could be brought to bear if their initial forward thrusts failed, and the Israelis opted for a war of movement in which they could destroy or neutralize as much of the enemy force as possible. The effective use of static defenses is widely regarded as a novel innovation. With the rising costs of advanced weapons, the adoption of similar combinations of static and mobile defenses may become appropriate for an increasing number of smaller states.

The use of fortified positions revealed changes in the roles of the traditional combat arms—infantry, armor, and artillery. The

Arab initiative in tactics forced the Israelis to a surprising degree to fight on Arab terms. Israeli overconfidence also played a role in the initial Arab successes. The uncoordinated and piecemeal Israeli counterattacks, especially in the Sinai, were indicative of poor planning and excessive confidence in I.D.F. proficiency. The initial I.D.F. setback, the loss of up to 350 tanks in the first three days on the Canal front, forced an immediate reappraisal and the replacement of several prominent commanders. More methodical operations were then undertaken, initially on Egyptian conditions.

The reason for this shift was that Arab emphasis on static warfare placed a higher priority on localized firepower superiority than on speed and mobility. Movement out of fortified positions was made by infantry armed with self-protection antitank and antiaircraft missiles. Initial attacks by both Syria and Egypt were conducted by infantry divisions only, with their respective two armored divisions held in reserve. The Arab conception of the offensive use of tanks was best illustrated during Egypt's 14 October offensive. Armored vehicles were spaced equidistantly behind slowly advancing infantry, leapfrogging antitank-missile crews forward. Israel had to counter with infantry and smoke screens, but was eventually able to mass and counterattack at times and places of its choosing. With infantry screens, tank breakthroughs were not costly, and I.D.F. armored units then rolled up the flanks or sought tactical advantages in the rear of the advancing line.

The Arab use of armor in a defensive mode was best demonstrated on the Syrian front. On the night of the seventh Syria's two armored divisions moved forward to the first line of defense to cover the retreat of the three mechanized divisions and to slow the I.D.F. advance.[7] On the ninth and tenth they fought largely from fortified positions, and only began the general withdrawal on the eleventh. Arab tanks were, in general, outclassed by the Israeli armor. The American M-60 tank was superior to the Soviet T-62 in gun range, accuracy, and shell penetration. In open terrain the Syrians attempted to close quickly so their rapid-firing guns could compensate for range and accuracy limitations. But the M-60 and other Israeli tanks were equipped with a computerized rangefinder that assured a high percentage of first-shot kills. Thus, in open engagements the Syrians lost heavily. But the remaining elements of any unit were able to fall back to the next fortified position, sacrificing mobility but strengthening the line's firepower. Thus, Israel was able to destroy over 50 percent or 850–900 of Syria's tanks and 30 percent of its aircraft at a cost of 250–300 tanks and 50–60 aircraft, but it was unable to mount a sustained attack on the Saasa fortifications.

The Arab concept of operation restored the infantry to the forefront after a period of secondary importance dating from the advent of the tank. The tank was intended to be primarily a defensive weapon, used for exploitative purposes only rarely. (Even in the initial Syrian attack, tank units fanned out prematurely to screen flanks, while support infantry seized ground.) Because of its need for movement, the I.D.F. was compelled to draw out the Arab tanks and to create its own area of maneuver and initiative. The success of these operations was due in part to the field maintenance service of the I.D.F. armored units. Hundreds of captured vehicles and tanks were integrated into Israeli service within a matter of days. Meanwhile, the Israelis repaired over 10 percent of their own tank losses within three days, and another 10 percent within one week. Of Israel's total of 900 tank losses, over one-third had been returned to service before the cease-fire. This support aided in destroying five Arab armored divisions (two Egyptian, two Syrian, and one Iraqi). But Israel was unable to achieve its full military objectives—partly because of the Arabs' use of fixed defenses and partly because of the political intervention of the great powers. (Against fortified positions, incidently, the artillery of both sides was relatively ineffective; it was, however, able to inflict heavy casualties against moving columns and entrenched infantry, suggesting a slightly modified role for artillery in the future.)

Developments in several peripheral areas also deserve mention. Contingents from other Arab states generally performed well.

They were often underequipped and were sometimes committed piecemeal. On the Syrian front, however, they did contribute to the containment of the Israeli drive, with the Jordanian 40th Armored Brigade sustaining its reputation as the best-trained Arab tank unit. Indeed, the degree of command and control and lateral unit coordination on this front suggests that the making of a workable united Arab command is technically feasible.

The helicopter proved highly vulnerable in hostile territory and over open terrain. Both sides attempted to use helicopter-borne commando raids. Almost 50 percent of the helicopters were destroyed in the air. None of the raids was successful, indicating the limitations of helicopters where they cannot use terrain cover effectively for evasive action.

Little attention has been devoted to the naval battle of the war. Nevertheless, the Israeli navy played an important role against both Syria and Egypt, sinking 43 vessels of all classes. The Syrian navy was rendered virtually inoperable and the Egyptian units, except those blockading the Red Sea in conjunction with Soviet vessels, were eventually confined to home ports. Israeli naval supremacy was the result mainly of the Gabriel surface-to-surface missile with a 20-mile range. The Soviet-supplied subsonic Styx missile mounted on Arab warships was a relatively easy target for Israeli ship-mounted AA guns and apparently inflicted no losses. The Gabriel reportedly had a 90 to 95 percent reliability and accounted for over 85 percent of the losses, with the I.A.F. credited with the remainder. After gaining local superiority, Israeli gunboats attacked Syrian and Egyptian port and naval facilities and struck the air defense systems west of the Canal.

The brilliance and ingenuity of the Israeli crossing to the west bank is generally regarded as exemplifying the flash and daring expected of the I.D.F. It was a hard-fought battle with the Egyptians on the defensive and forced to fight the Israelis' type of war. Nearly one-half of Egypt's total of 950 tank losses occurred on the west bank, while Israel apparently lost about 100 tanks. The encirclement of the Egyptian III Corps is the stuff of tactical victory; it is not, however, a source of military lessons upon which future doctrines can easily be constructed.

With this acknowledgment of Israel's localized success, several conclusions can be offered. The infantryman, armed with cheap antitank and antiaircraft missiles, has regained some of his historic importance. The tank must now be adapted to confront this new threat. Well-constructed defensive positions in suitable terrain, bristling with antitank and SAM missiles and supported by artillery batteries, may nullify the mobility advantages of the air-tank team upon which military doctrine for the past quarter century has been based. To restore the importance of fast-moving armored forces where geographic limitations have been imposed, new methods of breaching these positions will have to be developed. Unless aircraft can penetrate static air defenses, the utility of tanks' exploitative capacity is limited. The most immediate solution would appear to be a redoubling of emphasis on self-propelled artillery and mobile air defenses for its protection. But such interim suggestions merely indicate that the entire doctrine for localized warfare should be reexamined in detail. Indeed, part of the Arabs' pride in the outcome of the war resulted from the growing acknowledgment that their innovations in tactics and adaptations of Soviet equipment were significant contributions supporting the school of thought that localized wars are governed by concepts often independent of the general standards and that they should be studied in a separate context.

Wars, as Clausewitz noted, are extensions of politics. As such, the three combatants in the October War fought for political aims. Egypt and Syria launched their attacks to move the Middle Eastern confrontation off a political dead center. Militarily, they limited their objective to the seizure of territory occupied by Israel in 1967. Egypt further limited its military objective to the seizure of the east bank of the Suez Canal. Militarily, Syria failed and Egypt partially failed. Politically, however, both Arab states were successful. The Israelis had slumped into political and military lethargy following the protracted Canal War; and their failure over 25 years to reach a political solution with the military instrument had stunted their estimation of the value of military applications for political ends. The political surprise of the October War was no less than the military surprise; and, as a whole, Israeli objectives seemed reactive rather than assertive. Politically, Israel hoped that a decisive military victory would force the Arabs to the negotiating table. Militarily, the I.D.F. sought to repel any Arab invasion while inflicting maximum losses on the attackers. The I.D.F. did not succeed in either aim. The Soviet resupply of Syria deprived the I.D.F. of a tactical victory and stalemated that front. The Egyptians were able to hold their own until the cease-fire. In sum then, it appears that the Arabs succeeded in advancing their political aims as a result of the October War.

Toward a Final Solution of the Arab-Israeli Conflict
As Henry Kissinger later admitted, the United States and Israel were taken by surprise both militarily and politically by the Arab attack. Washington's immediate reaction was to seek a meeting of the U.N. Security Council on 7 October to establish the grounds for a cease-fire. The Soviets took the position that Israel was responsible for the fighting, though it did not accuse it of initiating the attack. Specific denunciations and inflammatory remarks were withheld, giving the impression that the Soviet Union was keeping the door open for further contacts but was unprepared at that time to explore a cease-fire. As Kissinger later observed, there was no consensus on a cease-fire or on the appropriate role that the Security Council should play.[8]

On 8 October President Nixon sent a personal message to General Secretary Brezhnev in an effort to define some common position for joint action to end the fighting. In a public response Brezhnev praised the Arabs, abused the Israelis, and reiterated hopes for peace, but he notably omitted any reference to a cease-fire. The next day, in an open message to Algeria, Brezhnev cited the assistance the Soviet Union was giving the Arab side and called on all Arab states to support the Egyptian and Syrian armed forces energetically. The level of Soviet aid and participation in the war became the critical issue from the American viewpoint. If the Soviets were to undertake a major resupply effort, or if they were actually to dispatch combat troops, the prospects for an early end to the conflict would be sharply reduced. On 10 October State Department spokesman Robert McCloskey announced that the Soviet Union was conducting a major airlift of supplies to Egypt and Syria. He warned of the dangers to détente if the great powers became involved. Kissinger also publicly stated that détente could not survive irresponsible action in the Middle East. Most NATO countries declared their neutrality and an arms embargo for both belligerents; only France continued to sell arms to the Arabs. The Europeans were not important sources of supply for either side, but their noninvolvement was more symbolic than real, indicating Israeli isolation and Washington's vulnerability as a sole supplier for one of the belligerents. American SR-71A reconnaissance aircraft and intelligence satellites had provided almost continuous coverage of the tactical situations and revealed the extent of Egypt's reserves. At the same time Eban told Kissinger that the unexpectedly heavy bombardment had reduced Israel's munition stocks to dangerously low levels, especially of 105-mm tank shells.

On 10 October an Israeli 707 was photographed while reportedly loading Sparrow and Sidewinder missiles and electronic equipment at Oceana Naval Air Station. Two days later, after numerous press reports of other clandestine flights, the United States announced it was conducting an airlift to furnish munitions and heavy equipment to Israel as a counter to the massive aid delivered by the Soviets. On 14 October Washington announced its decision to furnish combat aircraft as replacements for losses incurred during the first week of hostilities. As the first American C-5As and C-141s began operations, Brezhnev told visiting President Boumédienne of Algeria that the Soviet commitment between 10 and 15 October had amounted to 280 flights that had delivered 4,000 tons of equipment.

Thus, during the first week the only common ground discernible between the two external powers was their mutual intention that their sponsored states should not be subjected to defeat and humiliation. Both great powers saw a military stalemate as the most realistic approach to a durable political settlement. Kissinger quickly grasped the importance of acknowledging the achievement of Arab military parity by means other than a prolonged contest of arms. By the end of the first week the Arabs had unquestionably demonstrated this renewed military capability. Even Israeli authorities were warning that they were fighting a new enemy and that the public should not expect quick or easy victories. In Kissinger's view a protracted war would inevitably hurt Israel more than the Arabs, because of the disparity in population sizes, and would thereby endanger the prospects for a durable stalemate. Thus, an end to the fighting with the least possible losses on both sides was seen as an essential factor for an early political settlement. Further, the curtailment of external arms deliveries was crucial in demonstrating great-power understanding about the need to encourage a cease-fire.

After insisting for nearly six years on basing its Middle Eastern policy on the necessity of guaranteeing Israeli military superiority, Washington's acceptance of the virtues of a stalemate was a significant concession to Soviet policy, for during the same period the Soviet Union had been just as tenacious in its determination to insure Arab military parity. The cruel calculus of the battlefield had forced the United States to abandon its former stand; it was, however, more difficult for Israel to accept the futility of attempting to deal with the Arabs from a position of strength. After the first week of fighting it was clear that, no matter who won in the immediate tactical contest, the Arabs would never again be humiliated. Israel had achieved only its minimum goal on the Syrian front; stout Arab resistance at the Saasa line had prevented a breakthrough to Damascus. The achievement of the maximum Israeli war aims, the destruction of Arab resistance and the reduction of Damascus to hostage status, would have required heavy Israeli casualties. The Soviets were confident at that point that they had little to lose and much to gain from maintaining their position. If the Israelis rejected the stalemate, the Soviets would once again rearm and retrain the Arabs, with the assurance now that their efforts in the past few years had effectively reduced the technological gap upon which Israeli superiority had heretofore been based. Ultimately, Israel would have to compromise, and the Soviets would receive general acclaim from Third World countries for their indisputably correct line in challenging the imperialists.

After the Israelis had severely mauled the Arabs on the Syrian front and began shifting the center of gravity to the Sinai front, the Soviets were justifiably apprehensive about the genuineness of the American commitment to a military stalemate. Further, the Soviets had witnessed on several earlier occasions the difficulties in gaining Israeli compliance with mutually agreed great-power positions. Israel seemed determined to achieve the same degree of military victory it had enjoyed after the June War and thereby attempt once more to impose its terms on the Arabs. The Soviets must have been alarmed by what they probably viewed as Israel's rejection of the constantly repeated lesson that the Soviet Union was determined to guarantee Arab military parity, and that a mutually accepted military stalemate was the only position from which political talks on a final settlement could begin. Therefore, during the second week it became imperative to provide sufficient aid to allow the Egyptians to hold their gains on the east bank and to fight the I.D.F. to a standstill. Soviet ship-delivered arms were now arriving at Latakia and Alexandria, and 45 flights landed per day in Egypt and Syria. In Washington there was growing concern about the escalation of Soviet involvement. Kissinger hinted on 16 October that, if the Soviets deployed troops to the Middle East, the United States would do likewise. The warning was made in the context of a rapid naval buildup in the region by both great powers.

A key factor in psychologically defusing the Israeli war effort could have been a statement of Arab war aims. In marked contrast to the June War the Arabs had minimized prewar publicity of their intentions. This lack of Arab bravado was a major factor in misleading the Israelis, who had become accustomed to Arab proclamations of their intention to destroy the Israeli state. The lack of bombast indicated that the Arabs joined in the fighting were seeking only limited aims. Indeed, the denunciation of the war by Libya's Qaddafi and his refusal to support the Arab cause was a strong indication that the Arabs were not seeking radical solutions. In what may have been one of the most serious tactical errors of the war, Syria never formally voiced its war aims or confirmed that it sought only the recovery of the Golan Heights. Sadat publicly proclaimed the Egyptian position on 16 October, but only after the decisive battle of the east bank had blunted any hopes of an Egyptian breakthrough to the Sinai passes. Sadat insisted that the Arabs were seeking not the extermination of Israel but only the restoration of national honor and the recovery of Arab lands lost in the June War, just aims in his view. But to make known the Arab goals after the turning points on both fronts smacked of insincerity for many Israelis. The Egyptians were still in a strong position at that time and controlled the territory they had sought through the partial political settlement of 1971. Had the Arabs announced their objectives at the outset, rather than at a time when the hoped-for stalemate seemed imminent, it might have had an impact on Israeli public opinion. The Israeli government has demonstrated a keen sensitivity about public morale and determination and might have felt compelled by this tactic to seek an earlier cease-fire. Thus, Sadat's belated announcement of Arab moderation had no perceptible effect on the Israelis' publicly acclaimed intentions "to break their bones."

Premier Kosygin's arrival in Cairo before Sadat's speech to the National Assembly indicated that Moscow had concluded that military parity had now been effectively demonstrated and that a cease-fire should be sought. (Moscow had maintained steady intelligence coverage of the conflict by launching and deorbiting four Cosmos satellites, Number 596 on 3 October, 597 on the sixth, 598 on the tenth, and 599 on the sixteenth.) According to *Al Ahram* Kosygin and Sadat met five times during the four day visit, but no joint communiqué was issued after Kosygin's departure on the nineteenth. This omission gave rise to press speculation that serious differences had emerged between the two, but it more probably reflected a Soviet desire to maintain a relatively low profile as the conflict began to reach the decisive stages. Kosygin was undoubtedly concerned with Israel's developing salient on the west bank and apparently did not share Sadat's conviction that it could be contained and neutralized. After hard bargaining, Sadat reluctantly accepted Kosygin's terms for a cease-fire, which included a partial Israeli withdrawal, a demilitarized zone on the east bank, and the reopening of the Canal. But the Israelis were now on the west bank, and their terms would undoubtedly stiffen. The question was now how much pressure the United States could put on Israel. After Kosygin's return to Moscow, Brezhnev urgently requested that Kissinger be sent to Moscow to negotiate the terms for a cease-fire.

Before Kosygin returned to Moscow, Nixon announced that the United States had extended $825 million in aid to Israel since the start of the war and that he would seek congressional authorization for a total of $2.2 billion in immediate assistance. This was a spectacular move, called by Mrs. Meir "generous indeed." It must have appeared to the Soviets as being more consistent with Nixon's former position of guaranteeing Israeli superiority than with the secretary of state's acceptance of a military deadlock. Kissinger may have justified this magnanimous gesture in Moscow by arguing that American reassurance to Israel in the form of long-term military aid would induce greater Israeli pliability for a negotiated settlement. However, based on their previous experience with Israel, the Soviets probably feared that an escalation of the American commitment to Israeli military superiority would increase intransigence rather than flexibility. The demonstration of such solid congressional support would reduce fears of international isolation, an important deterrent upon which the Soviets probably counted, and could restore Israel's determination to deal from a position of strength. Such an eventuality was particularly alarming in view of the I.D.F.'s penetration of the west bank and the vulnerability of the Egyptian position to this unexpected development.

After two days of hard bargaining Kissinger and Brezhnev reached a cease-fire agreement. The jointly sponsored Resolution 338 was adopted by the Security Council on 22 October 1973 by a vote of 14 to 0. It called for an immediate in-place cease-fire effective 1650 GMT, implementation of Resolution 242, and immediate negotiations to insure peace. Kosygin flew to Cairo and Kissinger to Tel Aviv to explain the great powers' position on the agreement. On the twenty-second both Egypt and Israel accepted the cease-fire, and Moscow proclaimed Resolution 338 a victory for détente.

Israeli forces on the west bank had already severed the Ismailia-Cairo road, and during the night of 22–23 October they concentrated their armored units for a final drive in the south to cut the Suez City-Cairo road and gain control of the port facilities, thus isolating the city and the Egyptian III Corps entrenched on the east bank. After heavy fighting throughout the twenty-third Israel achieved its objectives and once again accepted the cease-fire. It seems irrelevant to argue about who opened fire first on the morning of the twenty-third. As the day wore on it was clear that Israel would not be deflected from its military objective by American or international pressure. (Similarly, in the June War Israel disregarded a U.N. cease-fire until it had secured the Golan Heights.) On the twenty-third Israel again demonstrated its determination to deal with the Arabs only from a position that commanded their military respect. Entrapping the III Corps and placing 20,000 Egyptians at Israel's mercy would give Tel Aviv the political leverage it wanted. As in the case of the July 1970 Israeli attack on Soviet pilots, the cease-fire violation on the twenty-third was an unquestionable indication to the Arabs and the Soviets that Israel was determined to conduct political negotiations only on its own terms. As Major General Peled told the I.A.F. pilots on 21 October, the Israeli objective was to "bring the enemy to the point where we can dictate the terms of a cease-fire." [9] Israel partly achieved this goal through its actions on the twenty-third.

By the morning of the twenty-fourth the Soviets were in a difficult position. Israel had gained the upper hand and Washington was unwilling or unable to act as a restraining force. An Israeli armored dash to Cairo seemed a distinct possibility. Moreover, Soviet aid had reached 13,000 tons via the airlift alone, while American deliveries had only amounted to 8,000 tons. But the American supplies included vital ECM equipment and Shrike antiradiation missiles, giving the I.A.F. distinct advantages in the air battle. After gaining complete air superiority over the lower half of the west bank, the I.A.F. could once again conduct strategic attacks in the Nile Valley, just as it was presently doing in Syria with devastating effect. American delivery of 38 F-4s as replacements for combat losses indicated that strategic raids were a definite possibility, and the crushing effect such raids would have on Egyptian public morale and Sadat's domestic position now had to be taken into account.

On 24 October Sadat asked both the United States and Soviet Union to send military observers to the Middle East to verify cease-fire compliance. The Soviets apparently concluded that compliance was no longer the question, but that the military posture of the two sides would again have to be redressed. As in January and August 1970 the Kremlin decided that a balance in the military situation could only be restored by some form of direct Soviet involvement. Deployment at that time of Soviet SAM crews, pilots, and air defense controllers had deterred Israeli attacks, but they had not provided sufficient leverage to open negotiations. Stronger constraints were now needed. A powerful combat presence on the ground to preclude further "adventures" seemed necessary if the Arab position was to be maintained. Only a muzzle-to-muzzle confrontation of political proportions that Tel Aviv could not accept could bring about the military stalemate Moscow sought. Accordingly, Moscow diverted transport aircraft assigned to the seven airborne divisions that were already on alert from the airlift operation back to assembly points, in preparation for the possible movement of major Soviet combat forces into Egypt.

At the same time the Soviet Union strongly criticized Israel for its continuing provocations and the United States for its apparent perfidy in seeking a stalemate and then encouraging Israel by pledges of massive military support. On the evening of 24 October Brezhnev sent a personal note to Nixon expressing these views and apparently suggesting that the desired military posture, whereby neither side could impose its will upon the other, could best be created if both great powers introduced military forces. In the event the United States declined, the Soviets reserved the right to initiate whatever measures they deemed necessary to achieve this end. The tone and content of this note were strongly reminiscent of the January 1970 Kosygin note to Nixon warning that the United States would have to either restrain Israel from conducting strategic raids against Egypt or accept the necessity of an increase in Soviet arms deliveries to Cairo.

With the prospect of Soviet combat troops being deployed to Egypt, Washington had to make a difficult decision. As Kissinger later stated, it was equally inconceivable that the United States would introduce its own combat forces into the conflict or that it would countenance the use of troops from any other great power. Yet Israel had sought unilateral advantages by violating the cease-fire that Kissinger had helped to negotiate, and these advantages contravened the premise of the Soviet-American agreement about the basis for forward movement toward a durable settlement. Paradoxically, the United States once again found itself in the hopeless position of attempting both to deter further Soviet involvement in Egypt and to extend credible guarantees to Israel. Bold action would have to be taken against both Israel and the Soviet Union if the United States was not to duplicate its 1970 performance and accept a political stalemate over a military imbalance.

The United States slowed its airlift into Israel and announced in low tones that it would have to reconsider the entire issue of arms deliveries. It voted in favor of a Security Council resolution calling for a restitution of the 22 October cease-fire lines, and it agreed to dispatch unarmed observers to inspect compliance with the cease-fire. Finally, on 25 October the president called a phase-three alert of all American armed forces.

It is important to note that these measures were signals directed at all the other actors in the October conflict. They were aimed against Israel as much as they were against the Soviet Union. In their consideration of possible Soviet reaction, it was reportedly argued during the 24 October session of the National Security Council that the adoption of half measures that would necessitate subsequent escalations in force postures would probably be both misleading and ineffective. It was also argued that the development of a situation that could be labelled the most serious great-power confrontation since the Cuban missile crisis was necessary to convince Israel that further provocations would have grave implications for American interests far beyond the confines of the immediate hostilities. During Kissinger's press conference on the twenty-sixth, he specifically tried to moderate the domestic reaction to the alert by insisting that no confrontation had erupted with the Soviet Union. But the credibility of American intentions to act firmly to move hostilities toward political discussions was accepted by the other parties, and none saw an advantage in resorting to unilateral action until Kissinger's diplomatic moves could be assessed. For example, in the wake of the alert, Mrs. Meir asked for and received a prompt audience with Nixon and Kissinger to explore the nature of continuing American commitments to Israel.

On the twenty-sixth Brezhnev also signalled Soviet moderation. In a major policy statement before the Moscow World Peace Congress he praised the durability of the great-power détente but condemned Israel for the continuing tensions. The Soviet aim in the explosive Middle East, he claimed, had been consistent from beginning to end: to create conditions conducive to true security for all nations in the region.

As is known, on 22 and 23 October, on the proposal of the Soviet Union and the United States, the Security Council of the United Nations twice adopted resolutions providing for an immediate cease-fire. Both times Israel, while talking about bowing to the resolution of the Council, in fact perfidiously violated it and continued aggressive actions against Egypt, seizing ever new territories of that country. Israel completely ignored the Security Council's demands for the withdrawal of troops to positions they held on the evening of 22 October. It is hard to see what Israel's rulers had in mind in pursuing this adventurist course. . . . Here apparently a part is played by outside patronage. . . . Calculations to insure the peace and security of a state by the forcible seizure and retention of the lands of others are wild calculations inevitably doomed to failure. . . . [Such a course] will only lead to still further international isolation of Israel and will give rise to even more hatred of it by neighboring peoples.[10]

This one-sided rebuke against Israel indicated Soviet interest in moving forward on the political front. (It should be noted in passing that there was little the United States could have done militarily to deter the airlift of 50,000 Soviet airborne troops that would not also have escalated tensions to a point where serious damage would have been inflicted on the détente process. The implications for great-power détente were probably more persuasive constraints against Soviet actions than the alerting of American nuclear forces.)

Instead of stalling, as in September 1970, until the impact of the cease-fire had had a chance to cool the tempers of belligerents and the United States could more accurately measure Soviet intentions, Kissinger immediately conducted a series of diplomatic consultations on the Middle East. His immediate task was first to consolidate the cease-fire, by removing the source of the continuing outbreaks of hostilities, and then to construct the cease-fire in a manner that would contribute to political negotiations.

Since 1967 Israel had consistently refused to accept the presence or function of U.N. peacekeeping forces on its borders. Nevertheless, on 25 October the Security Council adopted a resolution calling for establishment of such a peacekeeping force. The United States insisted that both great powers refrain from participation, but Moscow argued that, without a Soviet presence, Israel would only be deterred if one of the Soviet Union's Warsaw Pact allies participated. Washington finally agreed that forces from Canada and Poland should be included in the noncombatant functions of logistics and engineering. With these provisos, the Soviet Union agreed to accept its share of the financial obligations for maintaining the force, a thorny problem in earlier great-power relations. Israel raised no objections in principle and merely asked that participating states be chosen from among those that maintained diplomatic relations with Israel. However, by the end of the war only two African nations retained full relations with Tel Aviv and many Asian states had severed ties, leaving mainly European states that would fit Israel's requirements. The formation of a European force would undermine the representative facet of the international enterprise. Accordingly, Secretary-General Kurt Waldheim asked Kenya to furnish troops, which it did on 15 November without restoring diplomatic relations and without Israeli objection. Thus, Israeli adjustment to the necessity of a peacekeeping force was its first diplomatic concession and may have been an immediate consequence of the American alert.

The precise functions of the U.N. force now became the major obstacle to further movement. When Kissinger started his Middle Eastern tour, the two sides seemed deadlocked. Under an agreement reached between Moscow and Washington, 125 truckloads of food, water, and medical supplies were allowed through the Israeli lines to the III Corps. But that agreement had expired, and the Israelis refused to allow any more supplies through until the Egyptians furnished a complete list of their prisoners. Cairo insisted it would not proceed on the prisoner-exchange issue until the Israelis withdrew to the 22 October lines and thus released their hold on the III Corps. Israel refused, but Mrs. Meir suggested in Washington that some form of disengagement of military forces was conceivable, provided the Egyptians did not seek a military advantage and lifted their naval blockade of the Red Sea and Israel's vital oil route to Iran. By the time Kissinger ar-

rived in Cairo, enough give had developed in both positions for
a compromise to emerge. A six-point plan was acceptable to both
sides and included:

1. scrupulous observation of the cease-fire called for by the Security Council;
2. immediate discussions to settle the question of a return to the 22 October positions within the framework of an agreement on a disengagement and the separation of forces under U.N. auspices;
3. daily shipments of food, water, and medical supplies to Suez City;
4. movement of nonmilitary supplies through Israeli lines to the III Corps;
5. replacement of Israeli checkpoints on the Cairo-Suez City road by U.N. checkpoints, with Israel participating in the supervision of the nonmilitary nature of the cargo; and
6. an exchange of all prisoners as soon as the checkpoints had been established.[11]

To increase the durability of the cease-fire, Kissinger convinced
Sadat of the value of restoring complete diplomatic relations
with the United States, affording Egypt greater maneuverability
and allowing the United States to act in a more impartial manner. Kissinger told both sides, however, that the United States
would withdraw its support from either side if it resumed hostilities. This provided powerful leverage against both belligerents, since the United States held the important cards for promoting peace. Once the Arabs were able to demonstrate effectively
that they would not be humiliated again, the Soviets' function in
the conflict was largely fulfilled: they did not have enough authority among all the local belligerents to move them toward the
conference table; only the United States could perform this task.
But the Soviets seemed content at the time to allow the United
States once again to assume the forefront position. They may
have calculated that, based on the precedents, the American
initiative would eventually lose momentum and Washington
would then be forced to accept concerted great-power action.

The Cairo Agreement was a relatively precise, explicit schedule for disengagement. It broke down, however, soon after Kissinger departed on 30 October for Peking and the Far East. At issue were both the level of Israeli participation in the supervisory process and progress on the prisoner exchange. Cairo insisted that the wording of the agreement was clear and that the checkpoints would have to be transferred to U.N. auspices before any prisoners would be exchanged. Israel refused to relinquish the posts to the Finnish contingent of the U.N. force and proceeded to destroy or set up alternative sites wherever the United Nations created control points. After a week it was apparent that there was no give in the Israeli stand and that the prisoners would have to be returned before the siege of Suez City and the III Corps would be lifted.

In light of the suffering of the civilians and wounded, Sadat finally agreed to a compromise whereby the prisoner issue would be resolved first and thereafter the Israeli troops would withdraw to distances within machine gun range of U.N. control points and would furnish inspection teams to assist the U.N. force. The blockade of the Red Sea had already been quietly lifted. (The blockade did not have to be formally lifted because it had never been officially proclaimed.) This eased tensions along the ceasefire line. But in the first test of negotiating strength the Israelis had bested the Egyptians; its hold on the III Corps had proven effective. The distinct impression of foreign observers was that, as Mrs. Meir's had proclaimed, future negotiations would be long and difficult. (To the Egyptians' consternation, Israel announced on 20 November plans to construct an earthen causeway across the Canal to supply its units on the west bank, indicating that Israel viewed its new military posture with an eye toward permanency.)

The next hurdle was devising a forum for convening political talks. Israel had consistently asserted that it would participate only in direct talks with the Arabs as an indication of their de facto acceptance of the existence of the Israeli state. The Arabs had, in turn, refused to participate in such talks without a prior statement of Israeli terms and a prior withdrawal of Israeli forces from Arab territory. Israel had also systematically rejected all attempts by external powers, particularly the United States, to introduce initiatives for reaching a settlement. Both sides had paid heavy prices for past "no win, no lose" compromises, and it had been clearly shown that neither side could impose its will on the other (Israel's 2,412 dead would be the equivalent proportionally to 168,000 American dead). These penalties induced an awareness on both sides of the need for adjustments short of total victory. Israel quickly and quietly accepted the importance of Washington's position in the new confrontation and dropped its earlier denunciation of externally imposed solutions. Resolution 338 and the Cairo Agreement were the product of Kissinger's initiative, imagination, assertiveness, and diplomatic skill in devising balanced compromises. At the same time the Arabs relaxed their refusal to meet directly with the Israelis. Military commanders of both sides met repeatedly at the main checkpoint on the Suez City-Cairo road to negotiate the prisoner exchange and the disengagement.

On 18 January 1974 Israel and Egypt signed a disengagement accord that corresponded roughly to the Egyptian bargaining position in the 1971 negotiations for an interim agreement. Both sides were to withdraw designated forces to predetermined lines according to a fixed timetable. Israel was to pull back all of its forces from the west bank and from the edge of the east bank to a line approximately thirteen miles inland. Egypt was to withdraw the 1,200 pieces of artillery it had deployed on both banks, but was allowed to leave 7,000 lightly armed troops and 35 guns on the east bank as a symbol of sovereignty. Air defenses in the Canal zone were to be reduced, and armored units were to be withdrawn completely from the zone. In an unprecedented move, both Israel and Egypt agreed to allow American reconnaissance satellites and aircraft to monitor their compliance with the accord, thereby eliminating a shortcoming in the August 1970 ceasefire bid. A U.N. peacekeeping force was to be stationed in the gap between the two forces on the east bank. When the disen-

gagement was completed, Egypt was to begin operations to reopen the Canal, without making any concessions on the question
of Israel's right of passage.

Thus, Egypt gained the main objective it had sought in 1971,
and Israel lost the leverage it had earned by its cross-canal operation. Equally important, Israel gave up strategically and politically valuable ground won in the June War without receiving a
parallel Egyptian concession. This gesture of goodwill established
a precedent for the return of some of its pre-1967 territory that
Syria would later demand as the price of a cease-fire and a disengagement on the Golan Heights. Until withdrawals had been
achieved on both fronts, the peace talks scheduled for Geneva
could not begin.

The most plausible means of productive bargaining is an international conference under the aegis of the two great powers with
the interests of all belligerents adequately represented, including
the Palestineans. Under this format the issue of direct talks can
be avoided, and the presence of the great power will reduce the
tendency to stall and haggle over minor points (see chapter 10).

It was the suggestion of a great-power-sponsored peace conference that triggered the initial enmity of the Europeans in the
Security Council, mainly the French and British. Such an exclusive conference was viewed as an attempt to reach a great-power-
guaranteed peace settlement in a region where European states
retain vital interests. Europe's sense of exclusion in early October
was compounded by Washington's failure to inform its NATO
allies of its unilateral declaration of alert or of its decision to
ship military hardware stored in West Germany to Israel. Spain,
France, Italy, Turkey, and Greece proclaimed strict neutrality
and refused overflight rights and landing permission for U.S.
aircraft destined for Israel. When confronted with the partial
Arab oil boycott, the nine E.E.C. states promptly issued a statement supporting the Arab demands for the return of the occupied territories. The result was a crisis in Atlantic relations.

Paradoxically, the Soviet Union had emerged from the June
War with a challenge to its leadership by some of its Warsaw Pact

allies that had ultimately led to the Prague Spring, a painful experience that it now systematically undertook to avoid repeating (see appendix 1). On the other hand, after the June War the U.S. position had received the general endorsement of its allies, but now, in the wake of the October War, the United States witnessed its first informal censure by the Europeans for its unilateralism. The question of the appropriate role of the great powers in the Geneva talks therefore came to assume great importance, and its answer could well have repercussions beyond the confines of the Middle East.

The October War may have introduced the degree of fluidity into the Arab-Israeli conflict that was never present in the longer Canal War. If it does not, for whatever reasons, this local confrontation is likely to assume new dimensions in regional tensions and in great-power influence competition on a scale completely unexpected in September 1973.

10
On the Roles of Great and Small Powers in Regional Confrontations

The history of the attempts by the four key players to reach a political settlement to the Canal War presents a consistent record of misunderstandings about the correlation between military power and political negotiating strength and of erroneous assumptions about the interests of great powers and sponsored states in the specific terms of settlement. The period was marked by Moscow's cautious exploitation of American unimaginativeness and indecision and also of local intransigence to enhance and consolidate its influence in the most susceptible Arab states. However, the countercoups by Sadat in Egypt and Numerei in the Sudan (see below) and the establishment of the Arab Federation demonstrated the brittleness and lack of elasticity in Soviet influence among Arab states. And at the same time as this decline in Moscow's political influence, a remarkable resurgence in Washington's prestige occurred in the Arab world. Both phenomena were unpredicted by all four players, and the uncertainties associated with these rapid changes have tended to reinforce circumspection in the policies of each government. The general nature of political influence and its application among great and small powers in a variety of crisis settings will require further exhaustive study and analysis if it is to help to provide reliable guidelines for future policy formation. Such a comprehensive undertaking would require uninhibited access to confidential government archives and lies beyond the scope of the present project.

This chapter will be confined to a summary and analysis of the principal trends that emerged during the first five years of the Canal War and the most notable changes that were observed during the last year. Plausible reasons for these evolutions will be offered before discussing the most feasible solutions to the Canal

War that these modifications are likely to accommodate. Finally, several generalizations will be submitted about the nature of great-power–small-power relations observed in the Canal War that might be germane to other regional conflicts. Observations will be extended to the great-power adversary relationship and the changing nature of détente that has emerged during the Canal War.

Initial Negotiating Positions: 1967–1970

At the outset Israel's policy was based on the premise that Egypt was patently unwilling to accept its existence and that it had no genuine partner willing to share ultimate responsibility for its national survival. Consequently, Israel felt little compulsion to behave as a partner itself or to position itself for political negotiations. It consistently refused to formulate its peace terms, relying instead on employment of whatever military measures were necessary to bolster its policy of *forcing* the Arabs to negotiate. This remained Israel's preferred policy even when specific measures (such as the deep-penetration raids) damaged both the prospects for negotiations and its world image. And when the negotiations were on the verge of starting, Israel viewed the talks mainly from a military perspective and, accordingly, took actions to reinforce its ability to deal from a "position of strength" and to test American determination.

Israel expected real peace and real independence in the presence of a weak Egypt and a trembling Jordan; yet neither government could negotiate a durable settlement from such an inferior posture.[1] Paradoxically, although only a dozen Jewish settlements could now be directly threatened by Arab armed forces and Israel proper was safe from direct assault, the fact that the Arab armed forces were also less vulnerable to massive destruction raised the overall dimension of the military contest. Accordingly, Tel Aviv had to decide between a major military escalation to restore the credibility of its former reprisal strategy and a dilution of its political demands—and it chose the former option.

This policy preference was a reflection of the siege mentality and "capitulation neurosis" that has characterized the Israeli leadership since 1967. Tel Aviv's refusal for three years to accept Resolution 242 in principle and its insistence on direct negotiations represented the defiant stand of a victor, not the pliable position of reconciliation its leadership often professed. Given any other option, the demand that the Arabs should listen directly to Israeli proposals for settlement, especially when these were issued from a position of admitted military superiority, sounded too much like an attempt to dictate surrender terms to be acceptable to them as a negotiating procedure. Israel's unwavering pursuit of this policy revealed a serious underestimation of the Arabs' refusal to compromise on what they regarded as their national honor and dignity. Israel also misjudged the potential level of outside support that the Arabs could solicit.

The capitulation neurosis and the level of misunderstanding of the Arab side were well illustrated in Mrs. Meir's January 1970 offer to negotiate. After destroying Egypt's air defenses and in the wake of first deep-penetration raids, she called for secret talks with Nasser, but he opted for a secret flight to Moscow instead. Insistence on capitulation led to a strategy of forward defense and continuing escalation to insure unquestioned military supremacy; but this strategy proved self-defeating. With each escalation the Soviet Union moved into a more prominent position in the defense of Egypt; each increase in Israeli military pressure resulted in a quantum jump in Soviet participation. As a consequence of this strategy Israel was effectively denied its former military options in the Canal War and was forced onto the defensive for the first time since 1967. Moreover, the Soviet Union had intentionally left the limits of its involvement imprecise, increasing the deterrence against further Israeli escalation.

Israel's acceptance of the near-inevitability of its status as a garrison state diminished the prospects for its accepting a compromise solution. Yet even if the Israelis had accepted the moderate Arab terms for peace, it would have been uncertain how long the settlement would have lasted, given the strong likelihood of Israel's continued policy of nonassimilation of its non-Jewish inhabitants and continuing regional instability. In a region where turmoil is equated with normalcy, self-defense has a higher priority than in areas where noninfringement is taken more for granted. After 25 years it was apparent that this cycle of instability could only be rectified by some form of great-power intervention.

In the words of Nahum Goldmann, leader of the World Jewish Congress, the most serious implication of this war policy was the impact it had had on Israel itself. Its hard line had also eroded much of the international sympathy that had been earned in 1967 when Israel had defended itself against threatened annihilation.[2] A basic axiom of Israeli foreign policy has been that it must maintain cordial relations with at least one great power, and preferably sympathetic ties with a group of lesser states as well. But Israel's policies alienated first Britain and then France, its former chief allies, leaving the United States in the difficult position of becoming increasingly Tel Aviv's sole foreign supporter and confronting Israel with the prospects of international isolation and estrangement from the Diaspora.

These developments pressed the United States into assuming an increasingly prominent role in Mediterranean affairs, and Washington approached its new responsibilities gingerly. This was the first regional great-power confrontation since the Soviet Union had achieved strategic nuclear parity, and the relationship between theater forces and strategic reserves remained confused. Both great powers were newcomers to the Middle East, and there were no precedents or accurate guidelines for assessing the value of their respective national interests. No vital great-power interests were involved; but how important should the vital interests of supported states be in great-power relations? Finally, this was the first protracted confrontation in which both great powers acted independently of their respective alliances, and this raised major uncertainties about the limits of each power's willingness to make unilateral decisions that could affect those alliances. These unique features in the four-power confrontation understandably induced caution and circumspection into Washington's approach to its new role as a regional power. The cautious American policy, however, did not fulfill its expectations. The chief fallacy in this position was the failure of the United States to appraise objectively the political position of its sponsored state. It took an ambiguous stand on both the territorial and refugee questions. On the one hand, the United States did not accept the right to conquered territory; on the other hand, it advocated insubstantial territorial acquisitions by Israel; the difference between these two positions was to be left to the contestants. Did the United States endorse military acquisition of territory or not? Clarification of this ambiguity would have facilitated the bargaining process by reducing the leverage each party could claim in asserting its own interpretation. Likewise on the refugee problem, the United States advocated both compensation based on individual choice and the restoration of the Palestinians' just claims, clearly contradictory proposals, and yet it refused initially to negotiate with the Palestinians or to have their interests represented by the Arab governments. The United States conveniently sidestepped these issues and left solutions to the contestants, thus relegating a settlement to the outcome of the military contest.

Likewise, the United States took an unclear stand on the preferred levels of violence and the means for minimizing hostilities. It did not devise a credible formula for "sufficiency" in its aid to Israel, nor did it impose constraints on the use of these weapons as it had on other military grants. Indeed, this confusion encouraged a policy of preserving Israeli military supremacy under the guise of stabilizing the balance. In Nixon's words, the United States "will do what is necessary" to insure the existing "balance." Such ambiguity appeared to be intentional, based on the assumption that as long as Israel maintained a decisive military advantage over the Arabs its security would be guaranteed without serious risk of American involvement and a possible great-power clash. Equating sufficiency with superiority, of course, co-

incided with Israeli views that the Arabs could be forced to negotiate. The similarity of views was attested to in Nixon's private
pledge to supply replacement aircraft shortly after the "no aircraft now" decision and before any appreciable improvement had
been made in the Arab military posture. Washington's problem,
then, was to devise a formula to afford Israel a defensive force
large enough to deter renewed Arab offensives effectively and yet
too small to allow a pressing of Israeli military advantages. American arms deliveries should perhaps have been tied directly to
actual combat losses, not to long-range estimates with consequent
excessive delays in deliveries. As Israel complained, only equipment on hand contributes to deterrence, not that in the pipeline
or promised. The failure to devise such a solution allowed the
Soviets to assume the initiative by contributing their own formula
of assured military parity to the negotiations.

A frequently overlooked principle of international politics is
that rival nations with sufficient determination and resources will
not negotiate from a position of inferiority about issues relating
to important or vital interests. Robert Herrick has conclusively
demonstrated that a key reason for the Soviets' delay of nearly two
years in accepting a firm date for opening the SALT talks was
their insistence that the United States refrain from public assertion of the superior American strategic posture. Moscow did not
participate in the talks until after Washington had made an unequivocal statement that it would not enter the talks from a position of strength.[3] The same logic held for the status of Egypt, the
state that Moscow was committed to support. It is paradoxical
that it was only the increasing Soviet military threat that convinced Washington in both instances of Moscow's seriousness in
gaining recognition of its parity and that of its sponsored state.

The chief reason for the American dilemma was that it never
challenged the claim that air superiority over the Canal was vital
to Israeli survival. This supposition has now been proved an
anachronism that has served mainly to demonstrate the weakness
of substituting military strategy for foreign policy. The exaggerated value of air power resulted from an inaccurate assessment

of its relationship to the respective air and ground battles in 1967. The prompt conclusion of the air battle resulted in uninhibited Israeli air attacks against enemy armored forces after the I.D.F. breakthrough had already been achieved. But this would have occurred on almost the same scale anyway because of the Egyptians' inability to conduct low-level intercepts against high-performance aircraft. The air battle also eliminated any air threat to Israeli armor, but this was never a serious challenge. The gravest danger was Egyptian artillery, which was neutralized primarily by Israeli armor rather than by its air power. Thus, the conclusion of the successful air battle was an important contribution to the total collapse of the Egyptian armed forces, but it was not the prerequisite for the victory by the ground forces that many analysts have claimed. Air superiority during the June War was less a necessity than a luxury. Washington's failure to perceive this led to its own entrapment on the escalator of its policy of supremacy.

As Israel's relative superiority over Egypt increased from the fall of 1969 to the spring of 1970, its diplomatic position hardened, correspondingly reducing the amount of political constraint the United States could exercise and illuminating the fundamental contradiction in American Middle Eastern policy. When Israel expanded its strategy of limited offensive to strategic warfare, its dependence upon the United States was substantially heightened, reinforcing Arab claims that Israeli goals could not be achieved without major American contributions and thereby reducing further whatever modicum of American influence was left in the Arab world. While the Nixon administration entered office with the pledge to pursue a balanced policy toward Arabs and Israelis, its unequivocal stand on Israeli supremacy compromised these good intentions.

With Israeli supremacy the cornerstone of its policy in the Middle East, Washington had few options when Moscow insisted that military parity was the only basis for a durable settlement. Without a formula for sufficiency each military escalation forced the United States into closer alignment with Israel without improving its political options against either contestant. The disproportionate political profits earned from its military aid was dramatically illustrated by Israel's attack on the Soviet pilots. This completely unexpected development led to disgusted comments that paraphrased Mrs. Meir's earlier admonition to Washington, "that the United States has the right to demand that Israel not conduct its policies at the expense of American interests." The American pique over Israeli high-handedness did not constrain Tel Aviv's successful effort to shift emphasis from the substantive aspects of a political settlement to the issue of guarantees. By the end of 1970 it was evident that the United States was on the defensive in its Middle Eastern policy. It had been able to preserve only a few options and a minimum degree of influence; its leverage among all three players was probably less than at any time since the June War.

Thus, the American failure to define the limits of its responsibility to support Israeli political interests, despite its protests to the contrary, led to the supposition that Washington was prepared to defend any Israeli borders, regardless of how Tel Aviv defined them. And the failure to set upper limits to American military aid without privately disavowing these limits contributed in large part to both the escalation in fighting and the deterioration in its relations with the Soviet Union, the only other player on whom the United States could exercise constraint.

Meanwhile, the seemingly interminable rivalry among Arab leaders provided repeated opportunities for Israeli diplomatic coups. Since World War II Egypt has played the dominant role in Arab politics and has assumed a heavy burden for the repeated Arab failures. Egypt used its strategic location and cultural heritage to assert its position as the regional "great" power. Cairo laid claim to the mantle of the protector of Arab rights from the Atlantic to the Persian Gulf and asserted its right to represent these interests in world councils. These claims were seldom accepted by other Arab leaders, and the resulting struggle for leadership and the manipulation of power politics without either real military strength or great-power support led to incessant

Arab infighting and ultimately to three disastrous confrontations with Israel. In the wake of each contest Israel exploited the widening fissures in the Arab ranks to consolidate its position. The list of Arab failures in the past twenty years attests to these observations. The Arabs failed to prevent the establishment of Israel or to contain it within its legally prescribed borders; they were outmaneuvered in 1949 on certain territorial adjustments; Israel gained admission to the United Nations in 1949 without making any concessions on the frontiers or the refugees, as the Arabs had sought at Lausanne; by 1955 both Syria and Egypt were outmaneuvered by Israel on the issues of the demilitarized status of two frontier salients; in 1956 Egypt lost control of the Straits of Tiran; in 1964 the Arabs collectively failed to prevent Israel from utilizing the disputed Jordan River waters; the Arabs also failed to discourage mass immigration into Israel, to prevent large-scale external investments and massive German reparations, and to block Israel's ascendancy in the international community of nations.[4]

Malcolm H. Kerr has concluded from this record that three main disabilities have prevented the Arabs from either pressing their claims effectively or adjusting the substance of their claims to political realities. "One of these disabilities consists of the lack of military and economic means by which to bring direct pressure on Israel itself, coupled with the lack of general political leverage over those great powers upon whose goodwill Israel is dependent. The second disability is the failure of the Arabs to draw up any meaningful plan for a solution to the problem, on the basis of which to prepare a negotiating position. The third disability, closely related to the first two, lies in the division among the Arabs themselves."[5]

Since 1948 the Arabs have failed to develop their resources and capabilities to advance their claims and have remained almost totally isolated from public sentiment in countries that could provide political options to their growing dependence upon the Soviets. The experience of the Canal War illustrated that the Arabs were incapable of adequately helping themselves and that the degree of their military prowess had become directly proportional to the level of Soviet participation.

A further underlying reason for Arabs' ineffectiveness was their inability to agree on fundamental strategic objectives. They were unable to decide between a policy of destroying the state of Israel, negating its Jewishness, or containing its expansionism; each of these goals would have required different implementation plans. Lacking a mutually agreed aim, they were unable to formulate a consistent strategy, and their unity often seemed to be based solely on the conviction that Arab honor needed to be vindicated and the assertion that they had the patience and physical resources to absorb any Israeli counteractions. Before the October War the Arabs demonstrated neither the will to make peace nor the determination to conduct war, and their vacillation between the opposing aims of destruction and containment denied them leverage against their opponent and sympathy with states that could provide the needed pressure. Moreover, the lack of Arab focus had diluted the concentration of the interested parties on the basic issue at stake: What kind of Israel should the Arabs accept, and on what terms?

This complete lack of agreement on the Israeli question encouraged many Arab states to accept a "no war, no peace" situation. The militant states, however, opted for a policy of restitution of Arab dignity through military posturing. The difficulty was that Israel viewed these militant poses as a manifestation of hostile intent, and the Arabs paid a steadily increasing price for their "war of attrition" through a growing dependence upon external support.

Yet it was the level of Soviet support for the Arab cause that finally countered Israel's ability to earn important political gains through a policy of intransigence and exploitation of Arab disunity. But the precise level of Arab influence over Soviet policy remained unclear. Nasser made major concessions toward an accommodation during his last visit to Moscow. It is not known whether this was due to Soviet pressure or to his own assessment that the time was ripening for movement toward a political settlement. His acceptance of the American peace initiative may have been a result of both influences. Moreover, it seems more certain that the Soviets did not have sufficient authority over Nasser to coerce him into accepting decisions that he regarded as contrary to Arab interests. He was clearly as important to the advancement of Soviet ambitions, if not more so, as the Soviet commitments were to his aims. Furthermore, Soviet policies toward other Arab states during the time of the Canal War indicated that Moscow had abandoned its former policy of playing off Arab leaders against one another. An attitude of mutual respect and cooperation seemed to have developed over the past two years between Nasser and the Kremlin that was more durable than that between Nasser and any other Arab government. Indeed, a key obstacle in advancing the Soviet-Egyptian position was now the unreliability of the other Arab governments.

An important reason for the Soviets' gradual reliance on Nasser over other Arab leaders was the collapse of radical Arab movements and of nonalignment as instruments for challenging Western "imperialism" in the Middle East. The proliferation of local nationalism and the failure of Soviet economic aid to produce political profits all contributed to the disintegration of nonalignment after the abortive Second Afro-Asian Conference in Algiers in 1965. Third World nations could no longer pose as the "conscience of the world" or as intermediaries in local disputes. The unproductive summit meetings in Yugoslavia in 1969 and Tanzania in 1970 registered the futility of their efforts to establish a new line of action or to reactivate a sense of identity.[6] With the rapid erosion in international influence of a regional entity it had initially encouraged, Moscow had no other option but to shift the weight of its political force to direct channels with selected governments—a choice that had been made long before by Western states.

With the death of Nasser in September 1970 the Soviet position underwent another reexamination. No other Egyptian had the stature at home or abroad to counterbalance the rising Soviet influence effectively; and Soviet sponsorship of potential candidates like Ali Sabri merely intensified internal disorders without solidifying Soviet influence. Yet, from the Soviet viewpoint the successful outcome of the Canal War would depend in large part on the preservation of a receptive Egyptian terminal for the Cairo-Moscow axis.

Evolution in Bargaining Positions: 1970–1973

Sadat's remarkable recovery against both domestic and foreign challenges to his political position confirmed that he had weathered the succession crisis and was in the process of consolidating his power base to prevent further intrigues. He had clearly assembled a more formidable alliance of political forces than any combination of possible opponents.

The May 1971 events allowed Sadat to adopt new tactics in foreign policy. He attempted to reinforce the initiative he had secured by his agreement to negotiate a peace accord with Israel and to accept a partial settlement by reopening the Canal through announcing an unyielding stand on these concessions. He had clearly taken Israel by surprise and he now forced it onto the defensive. For the first time Israel would have to abandon its standard demand that procedures for negotiations should have a higher priority than the substantive aspects of a settlement and to itemize its terms for accord. Moreover, Israel would have to make concessions of a magnitude similar to those granted by Sadat before Egypt could be expected to modify its latest offers further. Cairo had demonstrated greater tactical diplomatic skill than the normally more sophisticated Israelis. It had forced Tel Aviv into the difficult position of having to make decisions partly on Cairo's terms that would affect the course of Israel's national development. Israel had been denied the luxury, afforded by its former military superiority, of dictating both the provisions for agreement and the procedures for accord. The erosion of Israel's position of four years' tenure was a major Arab diplomatic triumph. Tel Aviv could only recover its bargaining strength by modifying its terms along lines already outlined by the Arabs.

Political intransigence and the quest for military supremacy had resulted in an Israeli diplomatic imbroglio.

In the wake of Sisco's failure to achieve any breakthrough with Israel in August 1971, Sadat sought to increase pressure against Tel Aviv by calling for a comprehensive American statement on the withdrawal of Israeli forces. This move signalled Egypt's tactics during the fall session of the U.N. General Assembly. The failure of the United States to define its stand allowed Cairo to charge that this "passive" attitude only encouraged Israeli firmness. Cairo calculated that this approach would appeal to many U.N. member states and stimulate argumentation designed to embarass the United States. Indeed, the role of the United States and its preferred position on central issues became a focal point in the deliberations on the Middle East in the 1971 session of the General Assembly. As Heikal repeatedly insisted in *Al Ahram,* the issue of Israeli aggression should be regarded as a test case for the United Nations parallel to the issue before the League of Nations of Italian aggression against Ethiopia.

Prior to May 1971 neither Egypt nor the Soviet Union had attempted to define the boundaries of their mutual interests, interdependence, or national prerogatives on specific issues. The two had agreed under Khrushchev to disagree about ideological matters and to limit cooperation to political, military, and economic matters, in a manner not dissimilar from the modus vivendi Moscow had worked out with Yugoslavia. In the wake of the June War, however, the difficulty arose of how to intensify political cooperation to an extent commensurate with the greater Soviet military involvement and yet preserve Cairo's freedom of action to the extent required by its sovereign demands. This dilemma remains the hinge for determining the nature, scope, and durability of Soviet influence in the Middle East.

After May and the elimination of the Soviet political substructure within Egypt some means were urgently required to institutionalize as much as possible the remaining level of Soviet influence. With at least four years' laborious preparation and the cre-

ation of an almost total military dependence, Moscow had failed
to establish a durable basis for its influence. Indeed, it appeared
that Soviet influence was on the verge of reverting back to the
level of the early 1960s. For example, Moscow had been unable
to control the deployment of two Soviet-equipped Syrian tank
brigades in Jordan in September 1970 or to avert Syrian attacks
in the same area nearly one year later. During the 1970 Jordanian skyjacking crisis, Moscow could not prudently restrict the announced intention of the United States to intervene if necessary. Moreover, it was unable to influence the outcome of the
repeated struggles among the Palestinians. Finally, the Soviet
Union was apparently taken by surprise by the proposal for a
federation of the Arab states. The Soviet news media refrained
from commenting for nearly two weeks on the new political
scheme, an enterprise Moscow was known to oppose vigorously.

Moscow viewed these events and the "anti-Left" purge in Egypt
with sufficient alarm to invoke a friendship treaty to buttress its
sagging position in the Middle East. But the treaty fell far short
of providing a durable institutional framework for its authority:
it neither specified a threat nor required concerted action against
that threat; it did not provide for mutual defense; it did not prescribe automatically binding commitments; and the self-denying
clauses limited Soviet responsibilities under the treaty primarily
to rectification of the results of aggression, a condition that
would be negated by any eventual settlement of the Canal War.
It is unlikely that the treaty will significantly influence Egyptian
policy or serve the purpose that Moscow had intended. Nevertheless, the mere attempt to codify and formalize Soviet-Egyptian
relations pushed the Canal War further into the great-power
arena and escalated great-power polarization in the conflict; indeed, it aided in globalizing the dispute, contrary to both powers'
intentions.

The limits of the treaty became readily apparent during the
Sudanese political crisis less than two months after the treaty had
been signed. Indeed, the deterioration of Soviet influence in the
Sudan related directly to the measure of Soviet prestige in the

Middle East and to its stature in the Canal War; therefore, it warrants more detailed examination. The Communist party of Sudan
actively participated in three successful coup attempts.[7] The
Soviet government had advised the local party to adopt a policy
of assimilation, as had its Egyptian and Algerian counterparts,[8]
but the advice was firmly rejected by party leader Abd-al-Khalig
Mahjub. In the wake of the 31 May 1969 coup by a junta of army
officers, the communists were offered participation in a coalition
government in exchange for public support. The proposal split
the Communist party; the secretary-general argued against participation on the classical grounds that the junta was only a
transitional regime to be followed by a genuine popular uprising,
that identification with the Numerei government would contami-
nate the party's image, and that an immediate takeover bid
would be premature. A large minority of the party argued in
favor of participation on an individual basis in hopes that Marxist influence would "reform the negative elements of the junta's
policies." As a result a tacit split developed between the slim
Mahjub majority that followed the standard Leninist evaluation,
and the minority that remained loyal to Moscow and accepted
assimilation and participation in the regime. But even the minority faction persisted in using standard communist tactics; for
example, Prime Minister Awadallah was deposed for publicly
advocating giving the communists a leading role.[9]

When Numerei visited Moscow in November 1970, he complained about the continuing communist attempts to subvert his
regime. The Soviets restated their preference for assimilation between the Marxists and the officers' planned single ruling party,
and they communicated this desire to the local Communist
party.[10] They also reinforced this preference by agreeing to provide a massive military and economic aid program, designed
mainly to insure public order, but at a cost of one-half of Sudan's
annual yield of 1.2 million bales of high-quality cotton. By the
summer of 1971 the Soviets had reequipped most of the Sudanese
armed forces and had provided advisors at all echelons down to
brigade level. Despite Soviet admonitions to the local party

leaders and massive aid to the Numerei government, however, Moscow could not act decisively to influence either faction as the situation deteriorated. When the local communists refused to join a genuine national united-front party, leading communist figures were exiled or imprisoned and three procommunist cabinet ministers were dismissed, leading subsequently to a full-scale government offensive.

The center of gravity in the dispute between the junta and the communists had become focused on the proposed Arab Federation. Originally, the officers had been strong supporters of the federation scheme, but in April Numerei was forced to inform the other participants that he could not endorse the plan at that time because of the severe opposition that the communists had raised. Numerei was apprehensive lest Soviet opposition to the federation project reinforce that of the local orthodox communists and produce unbearable political pressure. Numerei's reservations were reinforced by Libyan Premier Moamer Qaddafi's insistence that it was impossible to envision federation with a state that accepted a coalition with even reformed communists. After testing the prevailing winds in Moscow in April, he decided to stabilize his domestic position before advancing the federation proposal. In a major policy statement on 25 May 1971 Numerei condemned the "deviated progressive forces"; he then arrested 70 leading orthodox communists and dissolved those trade unions and societies that had been dominated by this faction. At the same time he established the only legal national political organization, the Arab Socialist Union, modeled after the Egyptian party.

The orthodox communists had forged an alliance with Marxist elements within the army, and in July they staged a coup. After four days under house arrest, however, Numerei launched a successful countercoup, and the opposition was systematically reduced. Leftist circles in the armed forces and the orthodox communists were imprisoned, and leading figures were tried and executed. Even many reform communists were purged. By 20 July TASS expressed official concern over the "hysterical bloodbath and anticommunist campaign" being conducted in the Sudan. A gradual crescendo of criticism developed in the Soviet news media against Sudanese policies, resulting in Khartoum's recall of its ambassadors to Moscow and Sofia.

These events led to the worst crisis in Soviet-Arab relations in years. Defying Moscow's request for support or neutrality, Sadat, who had also recently experienced a pro-Soviet coup over the proposed federation, openly endorsed Numerei's stand. The two leaders now shared the common bond of domestic subversion and acted in unison against the mutual threat. As the situation worsened, Moscow felt compelled to interrupt the customary holiday period and convened a summit meeting on 3 August of Warsaw Pact leaders, minus Rumanian party leader Ceausescu. Moscow was in a problematic position. It clearly preferred to support the assimilated reform Marxists, but it could not withhold criticism when venerated orthodox leaders were being prosecuted and executed. The assembled bloc leaders apparently decided that they would not reciprocate by breaking diplomatic relations or suspending economic aid. (Pact nations had underwritten an 8 percent increase in the Sudan's gross national product during the 1970–1974 planning period and were heavily committed to providing the necessary producer goods and infrastructure.) Numerei, like Sadat, was to be given a free hand in dealing with his domestic opponents, despite repeated public protests against the persecution of communists, and no further movement was to be made against the federation, whose constitution was formally signed in August 1971. Once again Moscow underscored its timidity in dealing with radical Arab movements and acknowledged a decline in its authority among key Arab leaders. Clearly, massive military and economic aid had not been accompanied by assured political authority; nor had it offset Moscow's continued identification with unconventional political movements and methods.

Reversals on such scale warrant an examination of the changes that occurred in Moscow's policy position. The Soviet diplomatic stance during the Canal War remained remarkably consistent.

Indeed, the evolution in the positions of the other three players gradually brought them to coincide more with the Soviet line than with their own original argumentation. (For example, discussion during 1971 corresponded closer to that outlined in the Soviet 30 December 1968 note than to subsequent proposals of other states. Even the 1969 Rogers Peace Plans underwent more revision than the Soviet proposal. Further, Israel accepted in the third round procedural provisions—the location and level of talks—that it had rejected during the first phase.)

The success of Moscow's military contribution to the Canal War is more problematic. From the outset Soviet military aid denied Israel the political rewards of its brilliant victory. Furthermore, its refusal to support fully the Palestinians, over whom it exercised little if any control, led in part to their temporary eclipse. Moscow's active engagement in various levels of Egypt's defense either deterred or defeated Israel's military activities over Egypt. More than any other single factor, the Soviet involvement forced a military stalemate and induced Israel's acceptance of Arab terms for talks. Through the violations of the cease-fire agreement, the Soviets erected for the first time defenses that constituted a de facto balance or stalemate. The military option had been partially denied to both contestants; yet the Arabs' political demands had not been satisfied. Also for the first time, this balance contributed to a stability and reduction of fear that made the cease-fire relatively durable. It is inconceivable that the American understanding of regional arms balance, distinctly favoring Israel, could have made the same contribution.

While Soviet cease-fire violations were the dominant factor in insuring Arab-Israeli parity and military stability, they were also the direct cause of the lapse in Soviet influence with the United States and the ultimate loss of diplomatic initiative to its adversary. The diminution of its stature in Washington, coupled with the crisis of confidence with its sponsored Arab states between 1970 and 1973, did not seem to augur well for the durability and scope of Soviet authority in the Middle East. Nonetheless, the fact remains that the Soviet Union was the power that finally redressed the military imbalance and created a climate favorable for negotiations, thus underscoring its standing as a major regional power whose interests cannot be ignored in any final settlement—a notable success story, despite its uncertain future. Soviet success was due largely to its decision of the early 1960s to abandon the national liberation movements as political liabilities and to construct the physical foundations for a viable overseas strategy that could support its political ambitions in areas close to the homeland. At the same time it adopted a policy of penetration marked by the establishment of friendly relations with its southern neighbors and consolidation of its influence through the extension of more realistic economic and military aid to potentially pro-Soviet governments.[11] This revised foreign policy allowed the Soviet Union to enter the June War period in a stronger diplomatic and strategic position than it could have attained if it had continued to support radical political movements. The June War upset this strategy, however, and imposed severe restraints on Moscow's Middle Eastern policy that were eventually offset by the adoption of three major assertions:

1. the affirmation of its responsibility to guarantee Arab military parity and assure that the bargaining would be conducted from a position of political equality;
2. the isolation of the Warsaw Pact countries from its Middle Eastern involvement at the expense of concessions to their respective national grievances (see appendix 1); and
3. acceptance of bilateral talks with the United States on selected topics of mutual interest, including the Middle East.

The broader transformation in Soviet foreign policy over the past decade was due in large part to changes in the overall nature of Soviet political objectives (e.g., the attainment of strategic nuclear parity and emergence of more responsible global commitments). Yet the evolution of Moscow's Middle Eastern policy during just the cease-fire period suggests that many of the restraints that prompted the earlier changes still plague Soviet planners (e.g., they have not been able to rid themselves of the legacy of supporting radical movements).

A remarkable aspect of Soviet policy has been its correlation with the traditional Russian perspective of the role the Middle East should play in its global strategy. The Middle East has remained an arena for confronting its primary world rivals and challenging their international influence and prestige. The enhancement of Soviet regional stature has not been a product of a grand design; rather, Moscow has moved adroitly with events. This is not to say that it has failed to seize local or tactical initiatives or has not sought a more facile theoretical framework for its foreign policy. Moreover, at no point in the Canal War or in its rivalry with the United States has the Soviet Union appeared to assume an offensive role; it has even restrained its sponsored state from offensive posturing. (The presence of only 150 Soviet pilots, for example, is not enough for sustained offensive operations against Israel; the figure would need to be about 500.) In general, then, Soviet policy has remained more responsive than assertive.

A chief reason for the lack of an aggressive spirit in Moscow's new strategic posture in the Middle East relates to the difficulties of translating the advantages of its conventional military parity with the United States into political profits among its sponsored states. Problems in projecting naval power ashore have partially neutralized the political influence of the rival powers' military postures, for, as Curt Gasteyger has pointed out, great-power navies may inhibit or deter each other but, without a land presence in client states, significant influence is remote.[12] For example, the presence of the Sixth Fleet in the Mediterranean for twenty years has not induced friendliness among the Arab states (Jordan is strongly pro-American and yet is unexposed to the American naval presence). Indeed, Arab anti-imperialism reached its peak before the advent of the Soviet squadron, when the Mediterranean was still an "American lake."[13] Furthermore, similar firepower advantages have been enjoyed by former great powers over client countries, yet they felt compelled to fight their way into the interior in order to protect their principal commercial salients and assure their dominance of the seaways.

Not even a permanent great-power land presence has restrained local governments. The closure of American and British bases in Libya and the withdrawal of British forces from east of Suez eliminated the last Western military presence from the Arab world. The physical location in or near Arab states of Western military forces more powerful than those of any combination of local countries has not induced assured local support for Western policies. The history of Western involvement in the Middle East, therefore, provides no clear precedents for relating military force directly to political influence within smaller states, and the Soviet expulsion from Egypt also fails to provide better insight.

Moscow's penetration of the Mediterranean and the historic limitation imposed on the application of great-power military strength in this region have contributed to a degree of military parity between the United States and the Soviet Union (see appendix 2). American accommodation of the military consequences of the Soviet penetration and determination to preserve an asymmetrical deterrence in the lower spectrum of conflict while coupling the tactical nuclear threshold with its strategic deterrence, may be considered to define the probable military parameters of great-power relations in this region for the next five years.

The collapse of the Western military presence in the Arab world and the establishment of rough parity between the great powers have provided no guidelines for measuring the relevance of the former vast Soviet military presence in Egypt to the exercise of political authority. Moscow's most massive military overseas undertaking in history, its subordination of Warsaw Pact priorities to its Middle Eastern commitments and its acceptance of responsibility for filling the gap between Arab proficiency and Israeli technology by direct participation, represented the most significant obligation the Soviet Union had ever accepted with a noncommunist state. Yet the sheer dimensions of the Soviet participation became an inhibiting factor; the more exclusively Soviet the Egyptian military establishment became, the more Soviet prestige became committed, giving Egypt important leverage in advancing its independent aims. As Moscow has sought a "sole arms source status" among its sponsored states, it has plummeted into the same pitfalls that "imperialists" experienced earlier. The mere scale of the Soviet and Arab military buildup inhibited the erection of a politically reliable apparatus carefully nurtured over many years. Indeed, it is now safe to assume that Moscow will have to conduct its arms diplomacy according to the same ground rules that govern Western policies in the region. When the first cease-fire was extended and there appeared to be a definite possibility for some form of settlement, the Soviet land forces in Egypt became partially redundant, and they soon became yet another victim of nationalist Egyptian outbursts against foreign presences.

Israel also experienced an unexpected change in its preferred strategy for securing a political settlement. It applied a form of the theory of "compellance," [14] or the continuous escalation of military pressure, against the Arabs to secure its terms for settlement. This strategy was based on its confidence that without foreign intervention the I.D.F. could defeat any combination of Arab forces. (Both Arabs and Israelis suffered from the illusion that they possessed political and military assets that would eventually allow a decisive breakthrough; yet with each escalation the means for success became progressively more dependent upon outside powers.) The fallacy in Israel's strategy of compellance was that it failed to prescribe accurately that point in escalation that would precipitate external intervention. The effectiveness of the subsequent Soviet intervention negated the aims and merits of the strategy and denied Israel the prospect of the successful use of its military options. Clearly, Israel gained far less than any of the other players through its use of military operations; its compellance strategy had proved counterproductive and underwent the most drastic change.

From the Israeli standpoint, there were several serious implications resulting from the repeated escalation in the Canal War. First, there was the possibility that, despite the withdrawal of Soviet advisors, Moscow's military influence would remain high in the region either until the Canal was again internationalized and Arab-Israeli tensions had subsided to a point where regional stability was reasonably assured or until the Soviets had been countered by an equally powerful or reliable military force. Second, the Soviets had finally demonstrated the falsity of Tel Aviv's repeated allegation that air superiority over the entire Canal zone, including the landward approaches to the west bank, was vital to Israeli security. The freedom of maneuver that the Israelis claimed as vital was desirable for constraining Egyptian resumption of hostilities and for employing their military superiority for maximum political profit; but it was not crucial to Israel's survival, and Israeli persistence in this line of reasoning resulted in repeated escalations.

Finally, Israeli-American relations were seriously undermined by the Israeli affront to the Soviets. During the three-week interval of the initial cease-fire violations, Washington was probably as puzzled and disgusted with Israeli audacity as with Soviet duplicity. A reassessment was needed of both Soviet and Israeli motives. Had either intentionally sabotaged the American peace bid? If not, what measures were required to reactivate the initiative?

From the perspective of the United States, the repeated Soviet interventions raised new dangers. The chief threat was not the destruction of Israel, but the probable increase in Moscow's political terms for a settlement and for its withdrawal—terms that would likely be unacceptable to both Israel and the United States. The United States was also trapped by its policy of maintaining Israeli military superiority. Such a policy could no longer be applied to counter an integrated Arab-Soviet defensive system without requiring superiority over Soviet arms in general, an awesome prospect. Thus, the United States found itself in the uncomfortable situation of having to supply additional arms for the defense of territories it did not desire and whose protection carried the risk of a long-term infringement on other important American interests in the Middle East and throughout the world.

Before the October War it had been customary to minimize the Arabs' military position and the advantages inherent in their military posture. But, given the norms of Arab psyche and their capacity to absorb human losses, the program announced in 1972 for improving war preparations raised the possibility that such a strategy might provide sufficient compensation for Israel's technological prowess to risk hostilities. Israel would continue to benefit politically from the Canal War only as long as the military stalemate existed. But Sadat's decision to opt for Arab military self-sufficiency was a firm indication of his determination to overturn the stalemate and to minimize the imposed Soviet constraints.

By the end of 1971 the Soviet military aid to Egypt had produced a degree of equality that was propitious for movement toward a political settlement. But American contributions to Israel's arms self-sufficiency were followed by demands for like treatment by the Egyptians. Moscow was in a dilemma: if Arab arms self-sufficiency gained momentum, Soviet military and political involvement would be correspondingly reduced; if hostilities were resumed and proved inconclusive or detrimental to the Arabs, they would probably not turn again to Moscow after tasting the freedom of even partial self-sufficiency; and, if the war were terminated, the raison d'être for Soviet military aid and presence in the Arab world would be sharply reduced. The end result was a series of frantic Soviet efforts to convince Cairo that its commitment to military parity had been for deterrent, not offensive, purposes. The Soviets' fallback position was to point out to the Egyptians that they could not expect victory over the I.D.F. and therefore should not resume hostilities—an argument that was rejected by the Arabs. As Qaddafi charged, the U.S.S.R. was directly responsible for the stalemate because it would not provide "decisive" weapons and it had no confidence in Arab capabilities.

Thus, the most striking single feature in the military aspect of the Canal War on the fifth anniversary of the June War was the remarkable leverage Egypt had been able to amass in its dealings with both friends and foes. It had demonstrated a will of its own and sufficient determination to introduce new pressures to achieve its political aims in the Canal War. The stratagem of expelling Soviet advisors, in fact, had as great a political as a military effect on the outcome of the war. Both Cairo's inability to force the military deadlock off dead center and the futile American efforts at mediation had revealed that greater mutual goodwill or a substantially stronger military posture by one side would be required before a solution would be possible. For two-and-a-half years the Soviet presence had been the key deterrent against Israel—a factor used repeatedly to justify increased American arms deliveries. In view of the gradually increasing Soviet presence and the accompanying threat to the Sixth Fleet, Washington was unable to withstand Israeli pressure, even though it recognized the cyclical effect of each arms concession. Sadat apparently concluded that an important by-product of the Soviet expulsion would be the elimination of the chief obstacle to more determined American efforts to reduce Israeli intransigence. The United States had long held that the elimination of the Soviet presence in Egypt was the essential quid pro quo for mutual arms reduction along the Canal and a stable settlement. Those terms had been met by 1972.

Could the forfeiting of the Soviet deterrent for the time being induce a reduction in kind by the I.D.F. and ultimately engender an atmosphere of mutual force reductions along the Canal? Israel's initial reaction to the expulsion was the expression of a feeling of vindication: its policy of guaranteeing its position of strength had borne fruit and had bolstered its tough bargaining position without jeopardizing important interests.[15] Accompanying the self-satisfaction was the confidence that the I.D.F. could hold the Sinai indefinitely, although such a move carried with it the possibility of increased international isolation. Sadat had again seized the initiative and had introduced conditions calculated to increase American interest in seeking a settlement. Israel also had to calculate whether Soviet interest in a settlement that would reopen the Canal had reached a new high point. Finally,

Israel had to contemplate the costs of renewed fighting that might result either from Egyptian domestic pressures or from Sadat's ouster.

These calculations were contingent upon American reaction to Sadat's initiative. When Washington proved incapable of responding to the Soviet expulsion, Tel Aviv felt reassured. Of the four actors the United States had perhaps the greatest incentive at that juncture to renew interest in a political settlement. But the United States had become indifferent after repeated Israeli vetoes of its well-intentioned enterprises and was distracted by the upcoming presidential elections. This seeming paralysis forced Moscow and Cairo to reconsider their alleged differences. The interests of neither power could be advanced by estrangement. The terms of reconciliation therefore became the focal point for the next phase of Canal War hostilities.

After the August 1970 break in the American policy of coresponsibility with the Soviet Union for Middle Eastern stability, the United States assumed a policy of unilateralism that became counterproductive. The United States attempted to capitalize on concessions offered by the Egyptians and inadvertently assumed a mediation role without first achieving the precondition of demonstrating impartiality. While the possibility of alternative political settlements diminished, the United States became Israel's sole source of weapons and the single guarantor of Israeli supremacy, leaving Tel Aviv in the comfortable position of being able to reject both political concessions made by the Arabs and pressure raised by the Americans.

Israeli insistence that its security required dealing with the Arabs from a position of military strength was the prime factor in prolonging the conflict. A resumption of hostilities after six years of fruitless attempts to start negotiations was the harsh price the Israelis had to pay for not learning the lesson that their demand for essentially an unconditional surrender ran counter to their true security interests. The Soviet Union had guaranteed the Arabs' military option to the same extent that the United States had guaranteed Israeli superiority. The Soviets were in the advantageous position of being able to reinforce their commitment to Arab military parity contingent only on the avoidance of a great-power confrontation. Prudent diplomacy with the United States and adequate checks against recurrent Arab recklessness were the brakes the Soviets needed for the continuance of their policy. Arab demands for parity and Soviet escalation in commitments were the immediate reasons for the resumption of hostilities.

Yet the American commitment to the continued existence of Israel is probably stronger than it is to that of any other state that is not a legal ally. Even the majority of protestors against the Vietnamese war would probably accept the necessity of American military involvement if the viability of Israel was ever threatened. But the only time American intervention was even probable to fulfill this requirement was during the 1947–1948 war, when Israel was still a weak, embryonic state with uncertain ties with the outside world. It was clear then, as it is now, that the United States would have acted unilaterally if necessary to prevent the annihilation of the new state. Paradoxically, with each subsequent round in the Arab-Israeli conflict, Israel has been stronger and better prepared to defend itself, and the threat to national survival has been proportionally reduced—even in the October War when the Arabs presented their best military performance. Each successive round since 1948 has been fought for tactical advantages that could lead to strategic objectives. Thus, the probability of American intervention has been progressively reduced. The only plausible scenarios for a direct American commitment of combat forces centered around the unlikely possibilities that the Arabs might achieve a decisive advantage or that the Soviets might undertake an assault on Israel proper. This assurance against direct involvement was the result of the consistent American policy of guaranteeing Israeli supremacy.

The consequence of this train of events was that Israeli intransigence systematically estranged its former chief supporters abroad, France and Britain, and forced it into the increasingly isolated position that Ben Gurion had warned against and that

Moscow had felt would be necessary as a prerequisite for political compromise. As Israel became ever more dependent upon the United States both materially and morally, each government became hypersensitive about political pressure. With almost ritualistic precision both sides would announce before and after each Israeli request for additional arms that weapons would not be used to advance American political aims in a settlement. American sensitivity was due to earlier predicaments about extending commitments and then failing to honor them and also to its increased responsibility as the sole source of all the vital components in the Israeli defenses. Inevitably, this increasing dependence led to growing tensions and suspicions about the appropriate aims and tactics of each partner. Indeed, General Dayan expressed the opinion on 20 October 1973 that the United States had withheld advanced weapons systems and was therefore to blame for the "technological advantages" enjoyed by the Arabs during the October War.[16] Thus, the United States accrued greater leverage over Israeli policy from the October War than from any other episode in the twenty-five-year-old conflict. Yet, in the final analysis, its responsibility for Israel's preservation had diminished. In this shift in influence, Israel could now employ only limited pressure against Washington. Yet the United States did not exploit this unexpected dilemma of its sponsored state; it continued to exercise restraint.

When repeated Soviet interventions denied Israel the ability to use the weight of its military power in shaping the political negotiations, Tel Aviv sought to impose constraints on the Arabs' political options that would inhibit or channel negotiations as rigorously as if the full pressure of its military authority could have been exercised. In other words, Israel's strategy was to construct a negotiating framework in which political and military authority could be equated and freely transposed from one dimension to the other. Its diplomacy was directed specifically to preventing any "shocks" or jolts to this precise bargaining structure. This formulation led Israel to the conclusion that Washington had become the prime source of unbalancing influences.

Accordingly, the United States was perceived as Israel's chief opponent in the negotiating process, not Egypt or the Soviet Union. Israeli diplomacy was directed to the systematic erosion of the American role in the settlement and of its proposals for solution: from package agreements, to cease-fire arrangements, to partial accords, and finally merely to creating an atmosphere conducive to proximity talks. Indeed, the Fourth Rogers Plan was confined to a discussion exclusively between the United States and Israel on Washington's prescribed function. When this exercise proved largely barren, Israel correctly concluded that indifference and apathy now permeated American Middle Eastern policy. The perceived effectiveness of Israel's preventive diplomacy against further American initiative led to the erroneous conclusion that the Arabs had finally been checked. With both great powers now excluded from direct involvement, the Arabs were isolated and unable to act independently. Israel confidently held the upper hand and was determined to perpetuate the status quo until fatigue or domestic unrest induced flexibility in the Arab stand. Israel's tenacious diplomacy against the United States was the main contributing factor to the success of the Arabs' surprise attack in October. Tel Aviv was confident that without direct support from one or the other great power the Arabs would not resume hostilities.

This diversion of Israeli attention forced the I.D.F. to fight the wrong war for the wrong objectives and without achieving a settlement on its terms. The scale of Israel's misjudgment tended to reinforce the unquestioned assumption that Arab war aims were once again to eliminate Israel. But the Arabs sought specifically to reverse the imagery of the June War, when international opinion strongly supported tiny, besieged Israel fighting for the just goal of preserving the Jewish homeland from decimation. The radical Arabs were intentionally banned from planning and interfering in the conduct of the war. The majority position was confined to the limited objective of recovering Arab territory. If the Arabs had failed to adhere to these constraints, the entire character of the war would have been changed. They could not seek world support for their "just demands" and would have undermined the moral grounds for precipitating an international oil crisis. Israel was forced to fight some of the greatest air and tank battles in history to defend "Arab" lands. It paid a heavy toll in blood and money for territories it had attempted to negotiate away for six years. There is no doubt that the Israeli right-wing parties are correct in arguing that Tel Aviv needed the 1973 borders as an adequate defense in depth against the radical Arabs' intentions. But this reasoning is irrelevant in the context of limited Arab goals. Israel paid an unacceptable price for not bargaining and then fighting for land it intended to return—clearly a wrong war for wrong objectives, and an error that is finally being corrected at the bargaining table.

The destabilizing factor in Israel's bargaining position was the Soviet Union's revision of its policy of arms sufficiency for the Arabs. The shock of Cairo's expulsion of its advisory mission was sufficient to convince Moscow that the entire fabric of its 20-year-old Middle Eastern policy was likely to become a funeral shroud. Arab arms self-sufficiency was not attainable in the near future, but Soviet interests were most immediately endangered by Arab indifference. In light of Sadat's determination, adjustment became imperative. Accordingly, Moscow apparently agreed to the long-standing Egyptian demand for the equipment necessary to deter decisively the Israeli strategic option. Just prior to hostilities, on 12 September,[17] the Soviet Union shipped two battalions of SCUD-B surface-to-surface missiles, with a 180-mile range, to Egypt. The I.A.F. was thus deterred from launching strategic attacks. (As a manifestation of outrage reminiscent of August 1970, the U.S.S.R. reportedly deployed two more SCUD battalions to Egypt after Israel violated the 22 October cease-fire.)[18] Probably more important, however, Moscow concluded that Arab training standards had improved to a point where line units could effectively handle advanced equipment. Thus, Moscow made two major concessions that it had heretofore denied the Arabs:

1. effective deterrence against Israeli strategic escalation, even if it meant deploying SSMs to Egypt; and

2. sufficient quantities of technologically advanced weapons and equipment to establish battlefield equivalency.

The I.D.F.'s failure to detect these basic shifts in Soviet policy and afford them appropriate weight compounded Israel's conviction that *both* great powers had been eliminated from direct involvement. Despite Tel Aviv's disastrous judgments before the October War, the brilliance of Israeli diplomacy was demonstrated by the facile tactical adjustments that were made in the prenegotiation bargaining. Israel quickly moved to seize the initiative from the Arabs, who seemed so dazzled by the new fluidity that they clutched minutiae for security.

Adversary Relations and Great-Power Détente in the Middle East

Before the prospects for a settlement are assessed, the changing nature of great-power relations should be discussed within the context of both the Canal War and their relevance to a durable peace. Models for influence competition, adversary relations, or appropriate behavior will be avoided. An effort will be made merely to relate the experience of the Canal War to the broader framework of recent East-West developments and to derive generalizations appropriate to a possible accord.

In light of previous observations about the interrelationship between political and military factors in the four-power tactical play, several assumptions should be made about the nature of the confrontation and those long-range characteristics that will tend to remain relatively constant influences in shaping future policy. Particularly in the Middle East, the prevailing long-term influences are frequently overlooked in the urgency of tactical maneuver, a deficiency that must be corrected in analyses of adversary policies. Moreover, there are several uncertainties that call for prudence in both decision-making and subsequent critiques that should be outlined while enumerating the long-term influences.

The first uncertainty that should introduce circumspection into the analysis is the unknown dimension of both great powers' long-term ambitions in the Middle East. Karl Marx observed in 1867,

"The policy of the Russians is ageless. . . . Its methods, its tactics, its maneuvers may change, but the polar star of its policy—world domination—is a fixed star." Fifty-seven years of communist rule have resulted in dramatic changes in the Soviet Union's foreign policy aims and the conduct of its diplomacy. The major changes in the interwar years and the Cold War era have, however, provided only limited insight into the transformation presently underway and its most likely orientation during the 1970s.

The mid-1960s can be typified as a period of Soviet diplomatic retrenchment. Moscow abandoned its strategy of rolling back Western influence wherever and whenever an opportunity arose and sought to be more selective and systematic in providing a reliable basis for its own influence. It was no longer compulsory that every leftist revolution succeed or that every radical movement be Sovietized. This retrenchment was due to:
1. a change in Soviet leadership;
2. a recognition of its inability to support physically its former ambitious strategy;
3. the eclipse of the Chinese ideological challenge; and
4. the effectiveness of Western resistance.

Consequently, the Soviet Union constricted its horizons to contiguous zones of influence and accepted the losses inflicted on its prestige as a revolutionary center by its reduced support for radical movements throughout the world. Furthermore, it adopted programs to construct a strategic conventional military capability to match its growing strategic nuclear posture and to neutralize the containment barriers, thereby allowing this new strategic capability to be exercised beyond its continental confinement. Finally, it launched a major construction effort designed to insure nuclear parity with the United States, reducing the utility of America's vast strategic resources in the conduct of diplomacy.

The late 1960s were marked by growing uncertainties in both the West and the East about the scope of these changes and the precise nature of Soviet aims. The June War, the Prague Spring, and the Ussuri River clashes appeared initially to be either diplomatic reversals or renewed demonstrations of Moscow's limitations. They more than offset the enhanced prestige it had earned by eliminating twenty years of asymmetric American strategic nuclear deterrence. Moscow responded to these new setbacks by attempting to insure greater stability in its immediate security zones in Eastern Europe and the Balkans in order to guarantee greater predictability in the conduct of its foreign policy. It therefore sought to "compartmentalize" its foreign policy, completely isolating each individual issue and area, so that it would not have to face domestic or intra-Warsaw Pact repercussions of its foreign-policy decisions. (For a further discussion of Soviet compartmentalization see appendix 1.)

In contrast, American foreign policy has become a hybrid of earlier isolationism and contemporary global responsibilities. Since its inception, America has generally pursued a policy of isolation that has only gradually been modified during the last fifty years. Wilsonian optimistic faith in the fundamental reasonableness and single-mindedness of all peoples characterized American views on international affairs during this period. Americans regarded foreign problems primarily from a moral point of view, seeing them in black-and-white terms and placing a high degree of confidence in signs of good faith from other nations. The United States believed that, given good faith, permanent solutions to world difficulties could be found. And so the United States went to war four times during this period, not merely in defense of national interests, but to preserve higher human values espoused by other peoples. This expansiveness was due to America's insular perspective, similar to the British historic position, which encouraged isolation and a reliance on natural defensive barriers, but which facilitated the extension of popular thinking to the global dimension once parochial views had been accepted as anachronistic and led to a universalist approach to foreign policy.

More than in any other regional confrontation, great-power rivalry in the Middle East illustrates the dichotomy between the fundamentals of American and Soviet foreign policies. In the Middle East political vagaries and geographic diffusion are incompatible with the concepts of both powers: the Soviets' continental spheres of influence and the Americans' universalism. Moreover, the lack of any significant conceptual advantage by either power and the urgency of regional demands have already compelled a partial adjustment of their respective philosophies. For example, the Eisenhower Doctrine of January 1957 was propounded as an extension of the Truman Doctrine and implied firm offers of assistance to any endangered Middle Eastern state that resisted communism. The generosity and universality of the Eisenhower Doctrine were designed to protect the interests of the entire region by extending the umbrella of ultimate weapons for the defense of human rights. It did not, however, prescribe the limits of the American commitment in any given situation. Conversely, it allowed the Soviets the tactical option of expanding their commitments without having to supply actual physical protection. The Soviets could not rival the level of the American guarantee at that time, but they showed little desire to do so since their commitments were flexible and no vital interests were involved. With minimal interests and obligations, Moscow had nothing to lose and much to gain by encouraging local authorities to exploit the difference between the upper limits of any crisis, which were always controlled by Washington, and the lower intensity of the actual confrontation. Once local leaders perceived this disparity, it was used to gain maneuverability, while the Soviets received credit for advancing the interests of their protégés.

The basic incompatibility of the concept of spheres of influence, with its inherent requirement of cultivated dependence, and the universalist approach, with its notion of sponsoring local viability and self-determination, has been a key factor in the rise of the Cold War. One of the most challenging questions about the present confrontation in the Middle East is whether the press of events will direct attention away from the manipulation of parity and toward an adjustment of these incompatible concepts of international domain and an examination of the impact any accommodation might have on the broader issues of the East-West détente. Both powers, however, are experiencing constraints on their foreign policies that will inhibit sweeping renovations. In the wake of America's introspection over its Asian policy will come an inevitable assessment of American policy in other regions. The most striking feature of the present American retrenchment in its international commitments is not the alleged regression to isolationism but the growing awareness that a more definitive understanding of national interests and appropriate responsibilities is now required. While fostering priorities that preclude isolationism on critical issues, this process is likely to result in a more precise grasp of the limits of American influence and a more conservative estimate of the desirability of projecting this influence into less important areas.

But a strong inducement for modifying American aims in the Middle East is that the United States has primarily defended other states' interests in this region for the past twenty years—not its own. America's governing circles are presently rejecting the role of universal defender of freedom. A basic optimism still governs American foreign policy, however, and it is expected that the Soviets will one day not behave as Russians, reducing the need for direct American involvement. This partially explains Washington's relative ease in accepting Moscow as coresponsible for Middle Eastern stability.

On its part, the Soviet Union has effectively challenged the American concept of global foreign relations and has gained general recognition of its shared responsibility for Middle Eastern stability, but it has not succeeded in imposing its formula for international conduct on either regional powers or its adversary. The soundest generalization, then, about both great powers' aims in the Middle East is that they have been and will continue to be the product of fundamentally divergent concepts of international relations, introducing far-reaching uncertainties into the nature of the confrontation.

The second major area of uncertainty in the great-power contest in the Middle East stems more directly from the linkage between domestic influences and foreign-policy objectives. Many Western analysts have concluded that the Soviet system is experiencing a political decline. Paradoxically, the country is reportedly stronger militarily but weaker politically than under Stalin. The collective system of government is supposed to be inherently unstable, and the arbitrary demonstration of Soviet authority over its allies is likely to perpetuate the unreliability of these allies. Finally, the Soviet economic model is deemed the source of a continuing East-West technological gap that will doom the socialist states to permanent economic inferiority. The permanence of these domestic contradictions in Soviet foreign policy has been summed up by Richard Lowenthal as the outward expansion of an inwardly declining society.[19] These assertions have been the subject of a wide-ranging debate about the future of Soviet society which is relevant to a foreign-policy analysis because of the complete lack of consensus in both the East and the West about the nature of the Soviet Union in the 1980s.

The future development of the West and the long-term character of American society are also a subject of mystification for both powers. There are undoubtedly many stabilizing and tranquilizing institutions and common beliefs within American society, but the unique nature of the present social turmoil is not clearly understood by Americans, much less by authoritarian socialists. Without firm historic precedents that might aid in defining how far these pressures might move toward disrupting traditional institutions, the Soviets tend to view the future of the United States as being governed by cyclical choices between increasingly drastic or radical options that will, in general, increase instability and unrest. Thus, each great power is experiencing a degree of frustration in determining its adversary's future social aims, foreign-policy objectives, and views on international behavior. Furthermore, neither power has a theoretical advantage over its opponent in analyzing the other's posture and limitations.

Additional uncertainties emerge when the military dimension

of the great-power confrontation is considered. One of the most serious unknowns centers on when and how the Soviets might conceivably use their regional military forces. Many Western analysts have viewed the Soviets' quest for naval parity, their invasion of Czechoslovakia, and their military buildup in the Middle East as being detrimental to the prospect of their dealing in "good faith." Such manifestations of militancy seemed to show Moscow's determination to reestablish military power as the prime means for protecting important national interests, a position that had been eroded since its use of brute force in Hungary and its retreat from Cuba under strategic duress. These developments were also seen as shattering the Kremlin's image as a collective of stable, middle-of-the-road, aging politicians and as replacing it with an image of unpredictability. The Soviet leadership clearly displayed a willingness to manipulate both national resources and international conventions to meet military requirements. But this is not new. While the Kremlin decreed forceful measures against Hungary and Czechoslovakia, it is important that it did not do so in the equally alarming cases of Yugoslavia in 1948, Poland in 1956 and 1970, Albania in 1961, Rumania in 1964–1968, or China during the 1960s. The Soviets' record for accepting setbacks is longer than the ledger of their use of force to prevent reversals. Unfortunately, the full record of the Kremlin's past use of force provides no clear guidelines to indicate what issues and levels of tensions the Soviet Union would regard as necessitating military solutions.

On the American side, the aftermath of Vietnam will make it difficult to determine under what conditions the United States would intervene in the Middle East. Moreover, there are several physical aspects of the Middle East's military balance that will influence intervention decisions by either great power. First, the growth in Middle Eastern defense budgets—the highest percentages of GNP in the world—has resulted in improved combat effectiveness for both Arabs and Israelis. New conflicts fought with more advanced weapons would make containment more difficult. Second, both sides have already accelerated changes in the nature of the arms race by calling for better and more expensive weapons systems, as well as for an ever growing number of them. Finally, should external intervention be required in a climate of arms escalation, the foreign powers will have to calculate on employing forces equal to the weapons they have supplied, raising the dimensions of Middle Eastern conflicts to heretofore unanticipated levels.[20] Thus, improvements on both sides will have an uncertain effect upon escalation, regional stability, the degree of great-power control, and the level of possible intervention.

The uncertainties surrounding the use of force are further compounded when military power is related to the complex nature of political influence in the Middle East. In the atmosphere of strategic parity and multipolarity that now pervades the region, the nature of political influence has become more diffuse than under the conditions of either asymmetrical deterrence or bipolarity. The sources of influence, such as economic incentives, political coercion, and the threat of military power, can no longer be employed on an either/or basis. Each type of influence has now assumed a variety of forms, applications, and inferences not formerly regarded as germane. Furthermore, the cultivation of a recipient and the intrusion of external pressure have been complicated by the spread of nationalism and the priority now placed on national solutions to local grievances. Nationalism tends to foster isolationism and a political inversion that reduces the sense of urgency about establishing a commonality of interests with foreign states. The most significant aspect of this new atmosphere is that it applies equally to both great powers; neither has an inherent advantage in the use of military pressure for the intrusion of its political influence.

These main questions about the four-power confrontation contribute to the most complex uncertainty yet in Middle Eastern politics: the changing nature of great-power–small-power relations and the appropriate innovations necessary to promote the national interests of the respective parties. The basic challenge to both great powers is to devise a formula that acknowledges the changing nature of great-power–small-power relations and that provides protection for the interests of both. Military operations in Czechoslovakia and Southeast Asia indicate that while the great powers can act independently to protect vital national interests, they are less apt to act alone to achieve less important goals. Broad multilateral moral and material support is still sought when coercive options are deemed necessary; therefore, the demands of small nations must be considered before combined action can be attempted. Thus, the underlying features of great-power–small-power relations in matters of collective security continue to be the great powers' traditional desire for combined action and the small powers' demands for adequate protection. The dramatic changes that are occurring in force-employment concepts for regional operations center on the accommodation of these persisting security requirements to diverging national interests and new methods for applying and controlling force.

The partial dismemberment of contemporary alliances and the current preference for political assurances over collective-security treaties do not negate the utility of military pacts. Some agreements still satisfy the most urgent needs of the signatories; however, new approaches are clearly required in the Middle East. Middle Eastern nations have demonstrated little propensity for promoting collective defenses, and new ones are required to attract their approval, preferably of an ad hoc nature with limited membership, scope, and duration. Yet, except for solutions of the Canal War, neither great power is likely to be attracted by other durable regional security arrangements, leaving the issue of small-power security highly tentative and increasingly subject to "self-help."

None of the integrative factors required for community-building are present in the Middle East in sufficient intensity to warrant optimism about the imminent development of either a viable community or reliable spheres of influence. There are no ethnic, political, or geographic lines that will naturally accommodate the erection of spheres. Neither opponent can establish viable, geographically cohesive entities within which it can exercise decisive authority at critical junctures. Acceptance of this fact would be a turning point for each power in redefining the concepts of both spheres of influence and of the risks of great-power miscalculation and overcommitment, which could further intensify local antagonisms. The principal goal that should be stressed for the great powers is, thus, the urgent necessity to preserve the scope and intensity of their mutual probings of interests and issues within the acknowledged limitations of the policy constraints peculiar to the Middle East.

But there is no assurance that the great powers will equally perceive the value of further consultations in reducing genuine Middle Eastern tensions, despite detailed discussions of the issue at the first two Soviet-American summit meetings. Indeed, there is a serious danger that they may not be able to restore the degree of cooperation that was experienced formerly in the two-power talks, much less expand their collaboration to other issues and areas. In view of this uncertainty, the durability of an Arab-Israeli settlement may depend increasingly on the will of the local contestants. But the Arabs' propensity for intrigue and subterfuge minimizes the prospects for unity and the formulation of a constructive policy for regional stability and development. The very hopelessness of earlier Arab endeavors augers well for assertive Israeli leadership in regional matters when peace is restored. The success of Israeli leadership, however, will depend mainly on the extent to which secularization can be introduced and minority grievances ameliorated. Then, as a modern, industrial state, Israel could transmit the tranquility to its neighbors that is so vital to its own social progress.

Toward a Settlement Reflecting These Changes

Several observations may now be made, about the contemporary political situation in the Middle East and about the national character and aims of the four interested parties, that are relevant to a mutual accord.

First, Moscow's specific aim is to reduce Western influence and enhance its own as much as possible, but it has no grand design to implement this strategy. Moscow is unlikely to alter its opportunistic tactics, but it is likely to become increasingly circumspect in committing its prestige to risky adventures. Thus, the Soviet Union is apt to capitalize on the renewal of the two-power informal dialogue while striving for some institutional means to consolidate its political authority among friendly governments at a level proportional to that of its military assistance.

A second observation is that Moscow will continue to regard Washington as its ultimate antagonist in any important regional crisis, and its manipulations of local factors will be calculated in terms of probable American responses. An underlying factor in any Soviet estimate must be the American global posture and the feasibility of decoupling the local crisis from a strategic American response. Furthermore, the reasons for Moscow's reluctance to date to become involved militarily in a major Middle Eastern conflict are also likely to dictate restraint in the future. Therefore, the Soviet military presence in the Middle East will continue to be used primarily for deterrent and political purposes.

Third, there are, however, several disadvantages inherent in Moscow's present posture in the Middle East: it enjoys remoteness, but it also suffers from a lack of identification with reliable, like-minded regional states. Indeed, the modernization process is gradually amplifying the antagonisms between the Soviet model for economic and political development and those preferred by Middle Eastern governments.

Fourth, despite the charges and recriminations resulting from the cease-fire violations, the suspension of the two-power talks, and the resumption of hostilities, progress was registered by the dialogue that will continue to govern the positions of the great powers. They remain in agreement on the desirability of reaching an eventual settlement, the necessity of securing peace, the right of Israel to exist, the enforcement of freedom of navigation in international waterways, and the appropriate negotiating procedures. These have been the primary casus belli for four wars, and mutual accord on these issues is an important move toward an eventual settlement. Important outstanding differences remain on the questions of the final definition and guarantee of Israel's borders and the disposition of the refugees' claims. The unpredicted rise in American prestige among the Arabs that has resulted from Henry Kissinger's "shuttle diplomacy" has, however, increased Moscow's incentive to expand the great-power dialogue as much as possible.

Middle Eastern states are no longer really client states. A fifth observation is that, although the degree of dependence on external powers may remain relatively high in individual cases, this dependence has not in the past been consistently translatable into positive great-power influence on national policy. Thus, both great powers may gradually lose their flexibility in relations with sponsored states, which will be correspondingly increasing their freedom of movement.

Sixth, it was the nature of Middle Eastern politics and the local sources of tension that made the June and October Wars inevitable, and this fact ultimately reduces the relevance of great-power intervention to regional stability. The relationship between local conflicts and local solutions has become more direct, despite the increasing great-power involvement. Given this situation, if both great powers remain relatively balanced militarily, they are likely to try to capitalize on their remoteness and to keep their respective long-term commitments intentionally imprecise. Such ambiguities may initially foment instability, but eventually they will reinforce the direct relationship between local tensions and local settlements.

A seventh observation relates to Arab cohesion and unity of purpose. While there are numerous uncertainties related to Arab politics, there are also several constant factors that contribute to assumptions about the role of Arab politics in the four-power confrontation. The declining strategic value of the Middle East and the proliferation of national interests have multiplied Arab views of the world and of appropriate policy options. No single set of circumstances seems sufficiently ominous to induce cohesion or consensus within the Arab world, the 1973–74 oil crisis notwithstanding.

A further major observation concerns the nature of the Jewish state and its function in regional developments. The root of Arab-Israeli tensions is the confrontation between separate cultures and opposing philosophies. Contemporary Arab political thought is committed to a deterministic belief in the historically inevitable revival of Arab national identity and the eventual victory over the Jews on the Palestine question. The deterministic grip of these views provides the matrix for the concepts and strategy of the declining but still relevant concept of Pan-Arabism.

The Jewish national character presents the very reverse of determinism, typified by individualism, elitism, and a totally personal approach to life. Through the centuries Jewish identity was never saved by numbers or majorities, but by conviction and quality. Today, as historically, the Israelis live individually and as a state in a marginal situation with regard to all the surrounding societies. This marginalism is a basic quality of the Jewish nation. Zionism holds that a Jew will never be allowed to fulfill himself in a gentile society; he must live, therefore, in an independent Jewish society. The possibilities of spiritual fulfillment, accordingly, are preserved by the perpetuation of Judaism in the politically autonomous state of Israel.[21]

The deep cleavage between Arab determinism and Israeli individualism suggests that hope for accommodation between the two cultures is remote without some extenuating pressures. While a state of war need not persist, the degree of possible adjustment over the next decade is probably not large. Since a parallelism of views on major issues between Arabs and Israelis is not feasible, tensions may remain relatively high and foreign interests insecure.

These assumptions also relate to the nature of internal Israeli politics. By necessity the political apparatus must gradually absorb a greater proportion of Sephardic Jews, and the average age of political figures will slowly be lowered. But both changes will take time and will contribute little to the immediate outcome of the present confrontation. In view of the solidarity of the Euro-

pean-oriented ruling hierarchy, public opposition to any given
foreign policy is more likely to be expressed in the news media
and on the streets than in the Knesset. The recent, unprecedented
phenomenon of public protests will probably take on increasing
importance before greater liberalism is introduced into the establishment's policies. This trend is unlikely to split the country;
however, grievances on all matters are likely to be viewed as complaints related to the war, and the government is unlikely to
enjoy again the degree of popular consensus it had during its
first 25 years.

A final observation relates to Arab-Israeli relations within
Palestine. While the occupation of the Arab territories has been
painful, it has been less onerous for both sides than either anticipated. For the first time in the history of Palestine, Jews and
Arabs were not thrust together after the June War as separate
ethnic and religious communities so hostile to each other that a
foreign presence was needed to preserve stability. Both sides felt
equal in self-respect, civic discipline, and cultural richness. Israeli
military government of these territories is probably the most en-
lightened in modern history, but it remains nonetheless a military
administration. Yet an unofficial coexistence has emerged, prescribed on a day-to-day basis by the immediate demands for
normalcy that have overridden the cultural cleavages that separate
Jews and Arabs on the regional scale. The most integrated elements among both the Arabs and the Jews, not the more militant
and separatist factions, have finally taken the lead in outlining
this de facto relationship.

This gradual, tortuous return to normalcy has been accompanied by several paradoxes. On the one hand, Arabs within
Israel remain a potential security problem that still places the
highest demands on I.D.F. resources, yet the Arabs have become
an unexpected source of valuable manpower vital to Israeli industrial expansion and an important internal market to stabilize
this growth. On the other hand, Jewish consciousness inside and
outside Israel has never been greater. The sudden revival of Jewish consciousness in the Soviet Union and the fresh waves of West

European immigrants are demonstrations of the deep roots that Zionism has retained. This manifestation of renewed Jewish pride is a reflection of Israel's ideological attraction, not expulsion or prosecution. Yet the increased Arab participation in the economic structure of Israel and the rise in Jewish awareness have not proven incompatible. It remains to be seen whether a multinational society controlled by Israeli institutions and in possession of powerful military and economic resources can conceive of itself as a nonrefugee state, a genuine multicultural, multinational, multireligious society with a modern, universally acceptable political philosophy and political identity of its own. It can be assumed, however, that intercommunal strife is likely to decrease as the rewards of normalcy become more apparent. While mutually acceptable integration may remain elusive, de facto coexistence is a foreseeable feature of life in Palestine.

In light of these conclusions about the conduct of the Canal War and assumptions about the four-power confrontation, what recommendations can be made that would promote a durable settlement? Because of the numerous plans and suggestions for agreement that have been made, there is little new that can be offered. Only a shift of emphasis that reflects recent changes is plausible.

Great-power global interests are now involved, and the relative strength or moral certitude of the belligerents' respective stands will become increasingly irrelevant if the two giants decide to test each other's determination in this new arena. Moreover, parochial interests are likely to diminish in value if the favored giant loses face, becomes disinterested, seeks compensating concessions in other areas, or agrees to accommodate its rival's demands. Both great powers have the resources available to present the adversary with a fait accompli that could result in hard choices between escalating the arms race and being the first to use military force. Therefore, an important, if not dominant, aim of any settlement must now be the reduction of both great powers' involvement in the confrontation.

One general measure that could advance a durable settlement

would be the provision of security guarantees for the borders of both belligerents. Egypt now appears to be as concerned about guarantees as Israel, and the search for these assurances should help convince the friends of both states that each places a higher priority on security than on territorial adjustments or claims. From the Egyptian side security requires that Israel relinquish its capability to launch an incursion, while, from the Israeli side, security requires that the Soviet presence and the technological advantages afforded the Arabs be neutralized. Thus, the role of third parties is paramount for both sponsored states.

Alan Dowty has pointed out,

> If past experience is a guide, third-party guarantees are believable, if at all, only when the guaranteeing power or powers have themselves a concrete interest in the preservation of the agreement or state being guaranteed. Generally, such a motive is supplied by mutual jealousy among the outside powers; as each fears and checks the ambitions of the others, the independence of the threatened states is guaranteed. . . . many U.S. alliances in the Cold War have been of this nature. Two difficulties affect the application of this experience in the Middle East. . . . First, the outside powers were often more successful at balancing among themselves than at preserving the independence of the "guaranteed" states. . . . Second, the guarantees were usually against each other and not against local rivals of the guaranteed states.[22]

If this view is adopted, the first objective should be to devise guarantees that would remove the entire issue as much as possible from the arena of great-power rivalry. The June War demonstrated that the great powers can deter each other but cannot control the local forces of either sponsored state. The U.N. Emergency Force was intentionally designed to preclude great-power involvement, but its precipitous departure indicated that the forces of guaranteeing states cannot easily be isolated from the national interests of any state. Firmer interests in preserving peace by a wider variety of states should be itemized in legally binding commitments, surmounted by the assurances of one or more great powers. Recent Middle Eastern developments suggest that modifications have occurred that may accommodate

these aims. The resurgence of American influence in both sponsored states has increased Washington's stakes in seeking a balanced settlement and has opened new possibilities for the assertion
of American leadership. On the other hand, the unpredictability
of Soviet influence may prompt Moscow to seek better means for
institutionalizing the Soviet position in the Middle East. Finally,
both sponsored states have been largely denied the military
option in their respective strategies, increasing the necessity for
reaching a political adjustment.

At the outset Israel must be convinced that there is a credible
alternative to maintaining military superiority over its opponents
as the key instrument for insuring its survival, and Egypt should
be offered an option to its continuing dependence on a single
external power as the only means for protecting its vital interests. The United States should unilaterally assure both belligerents that it will satisfy their respective requirements for valid
guarantees of their security needs—not just those of Israel—after
they have reached a mutually acceptable settlement. (This could
be accompanied by a similar guarantee from the Soviet Union,
although it need not be.) It must, however, be attached to a
stringent warning that the United States will not remain in-
terminably embroiled in a deepening crisis. The promise of assured American commitments to both countries must be firmly
tied to unquestioned indications by each side of its willingness
to reduce tensions and reach an accord, or to the prospect of
mounting American disinterest and withdrawal from the regional
confrontation.

The guarantees should not involve great-power peacekeeping
forces, as was suggested in *Pravda* on 14 October 1970. The great
powers' military presences must be reduced. Circumstances that
could mitigate the reintervention of Soviet combat forces in Egypt
must also be avoided if accord is to be reached. The final agreed
borders should be demilitarized and patrolled on both sides by
U.N. observer teams that would be subject to withdrawal only
by a positive U.N. Security Council vote and in accord with specific bilateral treaty provisions (see below). The teams could be

aided by unmanned electronic sensor devices, which have been employed successfully in this capacity in Southeast Asia, and supported for active combat purposes by forces from medium powers, on-call or stationed in Cyprus. Static defenses would be permitted beyond demilitarized zones that could be defined as the outer range of medium artillery, or approximately ten miles. Because of limited airspace, Israel would again be allowed to overfly the West Bank of Jordan, as before 1967, provided the flights were not conducted in a provocative manner. All parties would be permitted to conduct aerial surveillance of the demilitarized zones. The stress of this proposal should be on locally conducted reconnaissance, monitored periodically by great-power surveillance, with appropriate American sanctions against violations of the demilitarized zones or the peace agreement. The credibility of the American deterrent will depend in large part on the prior publication of its intended responses to breaches of the peace (e.g., reference to the Security Council, consultation with the Soviet Union, recommended joint action with U.N. forces, or unilateral military operations if necessary).

A unilateral American guarantee is not as untenable as some analysts have suggested. It would rest on the reasonably sound premise that both sides had already established the outer limits of their tolerance. For example, explicit in the accord would be a pledge by each side to allow the other to live in peace without violence and to insure its peaceful intentions by seeking non-military solutions to disputes. Furthermore, Israel has now firmly established that it considers interference with its shipping through the Canal and the Tiran Straits as a threat to its vital interests; it need not occupy Sharm el Sheikh to reconfirm this site's tripwire function in a regional confrontation, especially since the Arabs have now demonstrated that they can blockade the Red Sea at any other point. Arab violations of this aspect of a peace treaty would clearly invoke either American reprisals or an Israeli attack. Meanwhile, the Arabs have confirmed their willingness to recognize roughly the 1967 borders, and Israeli expansion beyond them would clearly be a casus belli for them. In other words, the border aspects of the peace agreement would be largely self-enforcing. The more difficult question for an American guarantee is the extent to which it would cover the more fundamental sources of Arab-Israeli tensions.

Explicit in the guarantee should be the pledge to extend assistance to both sides on beneficial and mutually acceptable terms. Implicit should be the understanding that the United States is ready to aid any nation engaged in the complex process of modernization. This aid-and-security guarantee cannot cover policies that unquestionably contribute to international tensions. An Arab challenge to Israel's right to exist would automatically negate its claims to American aid and protection. On the other hand, pursuit by Israel of territorial ambitions or a discriminatory civil-rights policy should result in a similar American reaction.

The self-enforcing features of the American security guarantee could be strengthened by a unilateral decision to curb the regional arms race. Any form of guarantee implies that the United States must abandon its policy of insuring the military superiority of one side against the other. A new formula of "sufficiency" must be adopted that is commensurate with the defensive posture of both antagonists. The United States must convince Israel that it is not only unprepared to defend Israel's territorial ambitions, but it will no longer support its prior policy of strategic operations. The guidelines for the new sufficiency strategy should require an end to Israel's preferential treatment and a clear discrimination in the nature of the arms supplied, accompanied by strict limitations on their employment similar to the restrictions the United States applies to other arms recipients. The arms and equipment should be purely defensive and incapable of posing an offensive threat. This voluntary restraint would parallel Moscow's refusal to date to supply major strategic systems to the Arabs and Britain's cancellation of all offensive-weapons sales to the Middle Eastern states, and would contribute to a scaling down of any future fighting.[23] Furthermore, a unilateral restraint could prove a more durable damper on hostilities than a cease-fire in which all parties strive to advance their respective postures. To insure a reasonable chance of success, however, American efforts to induce Israeli acceptance of military parity with the Arabs must be accompanied by convincing assurance of American security guarantees for the final settlement.

To add credence to great-power (or powers) guarantees that do not envision in-place combat forces, the military discipline for the guarantees should be provided by medium powers. The best qualifications for these powers should be that they have no overwhelming interest in either Israel or the Arab World, but have sufficient interest in the region as a whole to place a high priority on the preservation of peace. Such countries as Norway, Finland, India, and Australia are friendly to both sponsored states and have a keen desire to keep the Canal open and retain access to Arab oil. A manageable number of states in this category should be elicited to provide military forces for the entire spectrum of contingencies. In keeping with the reduced military profile envisioned in the postsettlement period, however, these forces should be earmarked and placed on on-call status with only token elements deployed to bases in Cyprus and Turkey. If tensions rise, the on-call forces could be deployed to the staging areas, and the token elements could be deployed directly to the demilitarized zones. Token elements and deployed on-call forces should be assigned to a U.N. Command and financed directly from the regular U.N. budget. As in nineteenth-century treaties the specific commitments of each participating state should be negotiated with the guaranteed states. Such treaties should include precise provisions governing the sizes of contingents, types of infringements, recourse of the guarantor, termination of the treaty, and withdrawal of forces (by the mutual consent of the guaranteed states). The precision of the treaties and the remoteness of the enforcing units should enhance local security while minimizing infringements on sovereignty and strengthening the self-executing aspects of the settlement.

The rationale behind this composite formula for guarantees also supports the argument that Israel should abandon its strategies of offensive operations and reprisals and adopt a doctrine of dynamic defense as an *interim* measure to a final accord. The strategy of reprisals has been Israel's preferred option because it allows the optimization of military pressure and the economization of resources. This strategy, however, has not produced the desired results. It has humiliated and infuriated the Arab governments and has introduced the most tangible element of unity yet among the Arab peoples, but it has not inflicted unacceptable damage. The adoption of a dynamic-defense strategy, in which Israel would substantially increase its border security with light static defenses and would voluntarily refrain from attacks on neighboring territory, would shift the onus for invasion onto the guerrillas or regular Arab armies. An abandonment of the policy of holding Arab governments responsible for terrorists' activities and inflicting reprisals against civilians could have the paradoxical effect of heightening the psychological pressure on neighboring regimes to act more effectively in controlling the guerrillas. If Israel were to accompany this change with determined effort to counter individual infiltrators, the demonstration of responsibility toward a regional problem would exacerbate the onus for harboring terrorists.

Moreover, a dynamic-defense strategy would be considerably less expensive and could serve as an interim measure in converting the economy to long-term peacetime pursuits. The construction of only anti-infiltration defenses would require an initial budgetary outlay, but not in excessive amounts and far less than what has been provided by other states that have physically secured their borders. Furthermore, a partial demobilization could be expected without impairing the I.D.F.'s reliance on its reserve cadre, a sector that gives Israel a distinct advantage over any Arab army and that will undoubtedly remain the muscle of the I.D.F.'s fighting capability. Israel is not likely to be surprised again. Lastly, as a tangible move toward a peacetime footing, a dynamic-defense strategy would lower the profile of hostilities, and would contribute to a climate conducive to negotiations and a durable settlement.

An important side benefit of this reduced profile would be the possibility of cultivating additional features of military détente, such as:

1. establishment of a tactical "hot line" between air defense commands and control posts to notify the opposite sector in the event of an inadvertent airspace violation;
2. implantation of unmanned electronic surveillance devices, remotely operated, to provide data about military marshaling activities in selected areas;
3. exchange of military attachés;
4. creation of procedures or facilities for selected joint operations (e.g., air-sea rescue); and
5. creation of a joint committee to discuss provision and implementation of mutual military reductions.

These and other possible measures could be employed to demonstrate confidence and then implement détente.

The last substantive issue that warrants detailed elaboration is the refugee question. Justice requires that all persons involuntarily dislocated by the four regional wars be granted a free choice to return to Israel or accept reparations. At present most Arabs within the camps have little option but to return, since any move would provide them more security and stability than they now have. Yet a large increase in the non-Jewish population of Israel would exacerbate tensions, not relieve them. An equitable solution, then, centers on providing the refugees with a viable option to returning to a society with which they will not be able to identify and in which they will probably find themselves isolated from the mainstream of national life. An international rehabilitation program should be undertaken on a larger scale than schemes previously proposed or conducted by the United Nations. A fund of $1 billion could be established from contributions by the Arab states, Israel, Western Europe, and the great powers to provide resettlement incentives, such as transportation costs to the labor-hungry markets of Western Europe, capital for small businesses, and funds for advanced education. The undertaking should be successfully underway before a referendum is held so that the viability of the choice between the camps, Israel, and resettlement is as visible as possible. Given these alternatives, the number of refugees demanding repatriation would be small, and many Israeli Arabs might ultimately elect to emigrate. Thus, the refugee problem could be the least burdensome aspect of the entire dispute, if it can be separated from the question of Jewish assimilation by creating genuine options and incentives for Arab dispersal.

The specific provisions of a final accord should include the following points:

1. Israel would be recognized by the Arab governments as a sovereign state with the right to peaceful existence, free from the threat of violence. The Arab governments would guarantee the right of passage through the Suez Canal and the Tiran Straits, pledges imposed by an international Montreux-type convention.[24] On its side, Israel would accept the obligation to refrain from the use of force against its neighbors. All parties would accept the provisions of the U.N. Charter, including the full responsibilities of peaceloving states and the obligation to settle peacefully all disputes.

2. Upon assignation Israel would agree to withdraw all armed forces behind mutually agreed borders and appropriate demilitarized zones. Partial withdrawals prior to the final disengagement would be scheduled as demonstrations of good faith. The borders would be regarded as binding on all parties and would be guaranteed by one or more great powers and by a group of medium powers under treaties negotiated with the guaranteed states. Supervision of this provision would be entrusted primarily to a U.N. Observer Team, responsible ultimately to the Security Council.

3. Borders would roughly parallel those of 4 June 1967 with the exceptions of minor adjustments of the Jordanian-Israeli boundary. East and West Jerusalem would be governed by Jordan and Israel under joint rule, with the sanctity of the various holy shrines provided by extraterritoriality, as in the case of the Vati-

can, and monitored by the U.N. Observer Team. Pending Syrian acceptance of the peace accord, the Golan Heights would remain under U.N. custody, but eventually would be demilitarized. The Gaza Strip would be turned over to U.N. administration for a period not exceeding five years, pending the gradual resolution of the refugee problems. Its final disposition would be the subject of a plebiscite.

4. An appropriate and just solution of the refugee problem would be recognized as primarily an international responsibility. An international rehabilitation fund, to which Israel would contribute, would be established to encourage resettlement. Two years after the rehabilitation program was underway, the remaining refugees would be given a choice between returning to Israel and reparations. The West Bank of Jordan would be guaranteed a referendum to determine its political future (i.e., reaffiliation with Jordan, political independence, or a degree of autonomy between both Jordan and Israel). The present Jordanian-Israeli cease-fire line would be demilitarized. The West Bank's border with Israel would be open, with guaranteed duty-free access to the Mediterranean Sea.

5. The format of the accord would be determined by the respective parties, but need not be a formal peace treaty. A formula similar to the West German-Soviet and West German-Polish treaties, or normalization accords, may be both more desirable and more durable.

In light of the heavy responsibility the United States would undertake under the above proposed settlement, a more active and determined American policy would be required, both to assure stability and to contain Soviet influence. Traditionally, American Middle Eastern policy has pursued three objectives. First, it has sought to curb the growth of Soviet influence in this region. This aim should resurface as the primary reason for American involvement in Middle Eastern matters. Renewed efforts should be made to exploit local anxieties over the Soviets' military involvement and to reaffirm Western solidarity with Iran,

Turkey, and Yugoslavia, countries that control Soviet access routes to the Middle East. A stronger NATO defense posture in the Mediterranean should be encouraged and new initiatives explored to induce a closer identity of views between the United States and its NATO partners on Middle Eastern matters. On the other hand, friendly Arab governments should be enjoined to preserve an independent position and to block further Soviet efforts to polarize the region.

The second American aim has been to limit great-power involvement in Middle Eastern affairs. After adopting unilaterally a policy of arms restraint, modeled on an announced formula of sufficiency, the United States should seek Soviet compliance in adopting a similar formula for its arms recipients and eventually establishing a regional arms ceiling. If the Soviets should reject this proposal, which seems unlikely in light of their own restraint, the United States should not react as previously by escalating the local arms race. The proper response should be to confront Moscow directly for its lack of cooperation. Such ultimate sanctions as a NATO naval quarantine of Soviet arms deliveries to Egyptian ports would be an extreme measure, to be used only if the situation deteriorated. But it would effectively demonstrate Moscow's continued isolation from its traditional allies and reliable regional support, and indicate the West's determination to insist upon nonprovocative Soviet behavior.

The third American aim has been to preserve the channels of great-power communications and to explore all areas of potential agreement. This goal is more positive than the others and may be potentially more rewarding. It is also the only goal on which there is presently a degree of great-power agreement. Both powers have concurred on the value of the joint channels and have established appropriate procedures for their implementation. Agreement on procedures has led to understandings on a broad scale of substantive problems, though the utility of these understandings has been partially curtailed since August 1970. Diplomatic communications have been equally critical for the sponsored states. Israel has had limited contacts with Egypt through periodic secret talks with Hussein but has maintained no independent channels with the Soviet Union. This lack of direct communications and dependence upon American interpretations was a contributing factor to its inaccurate analyses and recurring frictions with Washington. During the spring of 1971 there was repeated speculation that Israel and the Soviet Union were exploring more direct lines, such as through their respective embassies in Geneva. Abba Eban has stated that Israel would welcome the establishment of diplomatic relations, and Mrs. Meir reportedly met secretly with Soviet envoys in Finland on this issue, but to no avail. A crucial requirement for the upcoming political deliberations is the opening of direct communications among all four players. The establishment of full diplomatic relations between Washington and Cairo in October 1973 was an important step in this direction and indicated the advantage in flexibility the United States had gained over the Soviet Union.

These three basic objectives remained elusive during the Canal War. There is no facile means for advancing all three simultaneously, but institutional innovations could be envisaged that would provide better assurance than heretofore that they would not be neglected. The most imaginative suggestion advanced so far is a modification of a call for an international conference made first by Lord Caradon, British ambassador to the United Nations, and approved in December 1973. The scheduled Geneva Peace Conference could be of historic importance in overcoming the past deadlock and advancing the interests of all the parties.

There are several advantages to the conference technique. It will appease Israeli demands for direct talks without imposing on the Arabs the connotation of a victor–vanquished bilateral confrontation. The presence of both sponsoring powers will provide each local state with assurance that it will not be subject to direct or indirect coercion by its rival's sponsor. On the other hand, it is plausible that both local states will view the conference as a suitable vehicle for manipulating the interests and position of the great powers to their respective or mutual advantage. Indeed, it is highly probable that the smaller states, as at the Geneva Disarmament Conference, may quickly find greater common ground between themselves on some issues than with their respective sponsors. Such eventualities would add significantly to the durability of a settlement by enhancing the local formulation of the adjustment.

This reasoning raises the question of the great-power input to the conference. Since August 1970 suggestions about conferences or even less formal gatherings have sent shudders through most American diplomatic circles. There has been a general fear that great-power participation in a regional conference would measurably heighten Soviet prestige and influence and not necessarily provide assurances of good behavior. Inherent in such arguments is a residual fear of the Soviet propensity to seek influence through foreign meddling. To admit the Soviets to a Middle East Conference need not be to whitewash Moscow's past behavior and future interests in trying to manipulate international developments. But to reject the conference idea because of reluctance to include the Soviet Union is to return the settlement procedures to the triangular American mediation enterprise that has proven so barren. It should be reemphasized that the local states have been utterly incapable of resolving their differences and are even less likely to do so without a Soviet regional presence and a degree of great-power parity. An indefinite period of "no war, no peace" cannot be ruled out—a situation that would favor influence competition rather than cooperation of the weaker great power. If a durable local adjustment is to be expected, Soviet interests must be incorporated.

Since April 1969 Washington has recognized Moscow as being coresponsible for Middle Eastern stability. The withdrawal of that recognition in August 1970 has not markedly improved American authority, advanced prospects for an accord, altered Soviet regional standing, or lowered Soviet terms for solution. Finally, the inclusion of the Soviets in a conference, in which they have an important vested interest, could prove a viable means of inducing good behavior. Those with long memories will recall the frequent times in the past when Moscow used an international gathering for propaganda and subversive purposes. But today Moscow has little incentive to be obstructionist or provocative in a conference that is related directly to the protection of its political interests.

The central issue, then, in the conference idea from the points of view of three of the four possible participants is whether a formal or informal four-power dialogue would strengthen Moscow's position in the Middle East. If successful, there is no doubt that the Soviet image as a peaceloving nation would be magnified, but no more than that of its equally responsible rival, the United States. Participation in resolving local disputes, however, contributes only to image-building. It is not the stuff from which a concrete basis for reliable influence can be constructed, as the Soviets found out in their mediation experiment at Tashkent. In instances where great-power–small-power relations are not based on a wide variety of integrative factors, as is the case in Soviet-Arab relations, political influence is more durable when it is based on mutual security interests or common threats to vital concerns. Such joint interests do not exist between Cairo and Moscow and would be precisely opposed to the aim of a Geneva Conference: the codification in part of both great powers' regional interests at the lowest possible level.

Thus, there would appear to be important incentives in convening the conference at the earliest possible date. The dangers of overcommitment, from the American standpoint, will be substantially smaller in the conference forum than when it places its national prestige on an unsuccessful mediation effort. And surely the opportunities for irresponsible Soviet conduct at a conference will be fewer than they are at the various disarmament forums, where the United States has fully accepted Soviet partnership. Indeed the U.S.S.R.'s prime goal in the Middle East to date has been to gain general recognition of its stature as a major regional power. It has predicated this recognition on achieving regional parity with its chief rival and insuring local military parity for its sponsored state. In the final analysis it is only the rival great power, not the local states, that can grant the Soviets the degree of recognition in regional affairs they desire. Further exclusion or denial by the United States may merely intensify Soviet ambitions and accelerate tendencies to manipulate local problems to achieve these ends. Thus, American extension of the degree of acceptance that Moscow requires is probably the best means for containing the extension of Soviet influence in Middle Eastern affairs. The least dangerous vehicle for this recognition would be joint sponsorship of the international conference, which would afford the needed imagery on a temporary basis without necessarily institutionalizing Moscow's political authority. Indeed, a settlement that stresses local self-endorsement would strengthen the American objective of reducing the regional commitments of both great powers.

In the final analysis, then, what are the prospects for a workable solution to the Arab-Israeli problem? The Canal War has provided convincing evidence that a correlation exists between military parity and political compromise among adversaries who have options other than capitulation or surrender. The degree of military parity achieved by the Arabs has now introduced a new level of fluidity into the positions of all the actors. The positions of the belligerents in particular have been eroded; they may later recalcify, but not along the former lines. The perpetuation of this new fluidity over the long term now seems probable for the axiomatic reason that the vital and important interests of all actors are closer to fulfillment than ever before:

1. The Arabs' sense of honor and self-esteem has now been vindicated as never before since decolonization. They have fought the "final war" of anti-imperialism–anti-Zionism and have forced their traditional adversary to a standstill in a battle that necessitated using the opponent's preferred terms for conflict. When a seeming "underdog" can deny a formerly overwhelmingly superior adversary its announced war aims, it will inevitably claim a victory, whatever the tactical configuration at the cease-fire. This objective seems to have been the overriding Arab goal throughout the entire Canal War.

2. The Soviet Union has now moved closer to its objective of

gaining international recognition of its stature as a regional power than at any time in the last twenty years. The Arabs, individually or collectively, cannot grant this authority. Only the United States can bestow the prestige that Moscow seeks. This has now been achieved by Washington's intentional exclusion of its allies, France and Britain, from the peace conference and by its invitation to the Soviet Union to cosponsor the gathering. Moscow's cochairmanship symbolically demonstrates American acceptance of the shared responsibility for providing the prerequisites for the long-term stability of regional adjustments. After persistently pursuing a policy of linkage between military parity and political compromise, Moscow is now enjoying its finest hour as a regional power protecting the rights of local states oppressed by "imperialistic" interests. It remains to be seen what form and role this new political splendor will take in Middle Eastern politics.

3. The United States is closer than ever to its goal of regional stability. Washington has consistently viewed Middle Eastern stability as requiring the curtailment or emasculation of the Soviet challenge and influence. A change in the American position has acknowledged the legitimacy of a Soviet presence in the Middle East. A shift has also occurred in its estimation of the role of a compromise solution. The United States had sought a localized solution but had placed a higher priority on maintaining Israeli military superiority, a policy which was self-defeating. After the October War Washington agreed with the Soviet position that stability is a function of compromise on both the political and military planes.

4. Israel's vital interests in insuring its security through military superiority and adroit diplomacy have been modified to the point that it will now accept non-self-reliant mechanisms as adequate guarantees. The question of Israeli security has been and continues to be the main issue in a durable settlement. The fact that Israel enters the peace conference apparently prepared to accept some form of political guarantees to supplement its own military preparedness indicates that Tel Aviv has agreed to internationalize the issue. The internationalization of Israeli security has finally brought a solution within sight.

If it now seems plausible that the basic interests of all four actors are within reach, what will be the impact of a durable settlement on the détente process and on great-power relations? A settlement is likely to have a profound impact on the détente process for several reasons:

1. It would demonstrate that the great powers can extend their collaboration, which has heretofore been largely confined to issues of bilateral importance and to topics of vital regional necessity.

2. A settlement would serve as another precedent for guidelines in future great-power–small-power relations, with emphasis on local solutions to local problems without small-power actions that could precipitate great-power intervention.

3. If the solution holds, continuing Arab-Israeli problems would be removed from the international limelight, reducing the prospect of either great power being able to exploit any potential advantage it might gain from a settlement.

4. If the Palestinians prove to be politically mature in their quest for national rights and if the Israelis can dissociate Palestinian justice from Israeli security, then there is a reasonable chance that future Arab-Jewish differences will revert to the issue of minority rights.

5. It remains an open question whether the precedent of great-power collaboration on Third World problems will be sufficiently durable and rewarding to provide common ground for tackling the next Middle Eastern problem—the energy crisis.

The Arab-Israeli conflict was confined largely to four actors with fairly clear national objectives. In the international energy crisis the great powers' interests transcend prestige and influence competition to the more critical problems of national economic growth and the prosperity of one's allies. Great-power competition during the Canal War legitimized the credentials of both as Middle Eastern powers. But the cooperation involved was for the vital interests of other states, not those of either great power or of their traditional allies. The energy crisis is likely to be a dominant international issue for the remainder of the decade. For the first time in détente history an economic issue of international dimensions is likely to supersede issues that have been confined largely to political and military matters. Moreover, the energy crisis is the first instance where the initiative on a major world problem has passed to developing nations. As a result the détente process is likely to receive its most definitive test over the question of "have" versus "have not" nations as it is related to future world energy needs.

In discussing the feasibility of and necessary means for shifting adversary relations from containment to cooperation, Pierre Hassner has observed, "It is characteristic of our age that old confrontations never die, although they sometimes fade away. They give way to new ones, or at least to new unpredictabilities rather than to stable settlements." [25] The four-power confrontation during the Canal War has provided abundant evidence of the scope of the regional animosities, the impact of policy errors, the risks to the national interests of all four, and the differing interpretations of a satisfactory settlement. The interests identified heretofore are likely to remain the paramount aim of each power, despite maneuvers and stratagems; and therein lies the hope for ultimate regional stability. But it was the Soviet Union that established the dominant tone for the confrontation. It sought parity for its client through both diplomacy and the physical acquisition of military resources. Moscow demonstrated that it viewed great-power diplomacy from the realistic position of political balance and that it was prepared to make important sacrifices to insure that it would not have to deal from a position of inferiority. The most germane conclusion that can be drawn from a survey of the Canal War is thus that, in the age of maneuver and potential détente, great-power negotiating positions must rest squarely on mutually acceptable estimates of their respective security. In the era of political maneuver the possibility of negotiating important issues in the context of military imbalance is over as surely as the era of assured strategic deterrence has been eclipsed. The West must now fully recognize that the Soviet Union will not accept negotiations on any critical international issue until it has the assurance that its opponent has no inherent advantages. The age of adjustment, then, is the age of equality.

Appendix 1
Eastern European Reactions to the June War:
A Case Study in Soviet
Foreign-Policy Compartmentalization

A key characteristic of Moscow's penetration of the Middle East has been the conscious and deliberate policy of eroding or reducing constraints that have impaired its flexibility or inhibited its selection of options. No other power in the region has been as systematic or single-minded in pursuing these or similar objectives. Its efforts to secure Arab military parity and a favorable political settlement of the Canal War were motivated in large part by these aims. Through Arab parity and the restitution of Cairo's political stature, Moscow sought recognition as a major regional power and latitude commensurate with this status that would provide additional avenues for penetrations and issues upon which to consolidate its presence.

Two major influences, largely external to the Canal War itself, however, remained as important constraints: the reaction of Moscow's East European allies to its ventures into the Middle East and its military strength relative to that of the only other external power that could effectively intervene at critical junctures. Both of these potentially detrimental factors had to be neutralized or offset in some manner to allow greater Soviet freedom of action. A review of the impact of the June War on the socialist camp and the alarmism promoted by some of Moscow's allies may provide indications of the extent to which the Soviet Union regards their reactions as constraints and of its preferred methods of adjustment.

The dependence of the Arab armed forces on Soviet arms before the June War tied Moscow's prestige closely to the Arab humiliation and defeat. Initially, this bondage was viewed by both friends and foes of the Soviet Union as a major diplomatic reversal of far greater proportions than, say, the anticommunist coup in Indonesia. But the decision on 6 or 7 June to rearm the Arabs and to launch a massive resupply operation soon recouped whatever loss of prestige in the Third World Moscow may have suffered because of the anti-Soviet Arab student demonstrations, for example. Yet the options that might ultimately be available were not immediately perceivable to either the Soviets or their socialist allies; indeed, both the scale of the reversal and the recovery efforts created dismay and uncertainty in Eastern Europe in dimensions that had heretofore been seen only in the development of anti-imperialist policies.

In fact, the dimensions of the anxiety that infected many East Europeans soon led to frontal assaults on the very legitimacy of the Soviet model for socialist development. First in Czechoslovakia and then in Poland the value of Soviet communism was openly attacked, and its strongest advocates were formally deposed. Moscow undertook repair work and even drastic surgery in Eastern Europe, and at the same time attempted to cure the source of its allies' apprehensions, not by reducing its involvement in the Middle East but by minimizing the scale of their concern. Moscow could not accept another challenge to communist legitimacy resulting from its activities on the world stage as a great power.

The Kremlin's initial reaction to the Israeli attack was to convene a conference in Moscow on 9 June, before the cease-fire, to which all European socialist countries, including Yugoslavia, were invited. Undoubtedly, the Soviets presented the conferees with a tentative assessment of the scale of the disaster and a forecast of the remedial efforts required to restore Arab military proficiency. The conference ended with a communiqué condemning Israel for aggression, demanding its withdrawal to the 1949 armistice lines, and announcing the signatories' determination to administer a "firm rebuff" for noncompliance. (At the same time Kosygin used the Soviet-American "hot line" to issue an identical warning to Washington.) Similar statements were issued after the second and third meetings on 12 July and 5 September, but without threats of punitive action.

On 14 July *Pravda* revealed that one of the Soviet objectives
behind convening these unprecedented meetings was to establish
a strong sense of "unity of action" in Middle Eastern policy by
the socialist countries. This Soviet motive became at once a source
of solidarity and apprehension among the socialist governments.
Some suspected that Moscow was less concerned about the fate
of its Arab clients than about seizing the emergency as a means
of reasserting hegemony over a disintegrating empire. The Soviet
Union had failed to manipulate the Chinese heresy as an instrument of discipline, and the Vietnam War had elicited only limited support among the East Europeans. Since 1963 every form of
interparty deliberation and all "burning" issues had been used to
induce a more collective response to common problems. But even
the issue of greatest concern for East Europeans, West German
revanchism, had already provided a divisive controversy. The
cold war between East Germany and Rumania had been only
partially resolved by the meetings associated with the July 1966
Bucharest Pact summit gathering, where, for the first time, a
common stand was announced on the outstanding national anti-
Western grievances of the respective members, primarily on the
German problem. Yet only six months later Rumania formalized
its "two Germanies" policy by exchanging diplomatic recognition
with West Germany and refusing subsequently to participate in
any Pact meetings, discussions, or statements that might impair
its impartial attitude toward both German states. This decision
created the worst Pact crisis since de-Stalinization, one which was
only partially resolved in 1970–1971. The 1967 Middle Eastern
crisis clearly provided Moscow a welcome opportunity to assert
its influence beyond the immediate context of the Arab-Israeli
confrontation.

Other socialist states accepted this sinister possibility at face
value but argued that there was no feasible alternative for restoring a Middle Eastern balance; yet many East European parties
saw the crisis as an amplification of their own domestic problems.
A brief case review will illustrate these divergent viewpoints. (Of
the East European countries, Albania's outright rejection of So-

viet policy since 1960 placed it beyond the pale of the socialist countries from whom the Soviets sought aid in a united Middle Eastern program. As usual, Tirana followed Peking's lead during the crisis and accused Moscow of hypocrisy by encouraging the Arabs into the confrontation and then refusing to accept the consequences. Indeed, Albania charged that the Soviets had directly collaborated with the "imperialists" in seeking a solution that would alleviate Moscow's embarrassment. Thus, Albania was able to use the crisis to attack the Soviet Union and strengthen its own independent posture in Eastern Europe.)

Soviet Self-Criticism
For the Soviet Union itself, the Middle Eastern crisis triggered the most heated internal party debate since Khrushchev's ouster. At the party's Central Committee Plenum at the end of June, the reasons for Moscow's erroneous calculations and overcommitments were debated. The secret police (KGB) was called to account for having provided fallacious estimates of Israeli and Arab military capabilities and political intentions. Some Kremlinologists and Western intelligence experts argued that the KGB had precipitated the first phase of the confrontation through circulating "unauthorized" reports in Syria of an alleged impending Israeli attack. It is going too far, however, to suggest that the Soviet backing of the Arabs up to May was the result of interdepartmental conflicts or intrigues within the Politburo itself.

The June Plenum authorized the only significant purge of the 1960s. A. N. Shelepin, a one-time contender for the party's general secretaryship, was demoted to the ineffectual position of chairman of Soviet trade unions, apparently because of his tutelage and patrimony within KGB. Coupled with earlier dismissals of V. S. Tikunov and V. Y. Semichastny, this action broke the stronghold of the KGB that had been created by the post-Beria generation. A confirmed Brezhnev protégé, Yuri V. Antonov, received the top post and has conducted a thorough screening of the entire apparatus.

The Plenum also discussed the issue of the future Soviet role in the Middle East. N. G. Yegorychev, first secretary of the powerful Moscow Party Committee, led the opposition against further large-scale outlays for the Arab cause. His reasoning struck at the roots of key Soviet policies: industrial versus consumer allocations, ideological returns from the June War, and the nature of great-power confrontations. In attempting to downgrade the commitment to the Arab cause, Yegorychev was pressing for a higher quality of life for Soviet citizens, but he was dismissed for his efforts.[1] The Plenum agreed to attempt to cut its most obvious political losses by reequipping the Arabs on the condition that they institute appropriate political and military reforms.

Despite the merits of this decision or the actual demands of the Middle Eastern situation, the crisis was a convenient vehicle for Brezhnev and Kosygin to eliminate festering opposition within the party and to insure the reliability of their security apparatus. So effective was this purge that no significant opposition emerged over subsequent emergencies, such as the invasion of Czechoslovakia.

The East European parties also used the crisis to advance individual national causes. Hungary, Czechoslovakia, East Germany, Poland, and Bulgaria closely followed Moscow's lead during the opening phases of the emergency. On 5 and 6 June they individually issued formal statements denouncing Israel for aggression and demanding a cessation of hostilities. Later they also broke diplomatic relations with Israel for its refusal to comply with the terms of the 9 June joint communiqué. Compliance with these actions was relatively simple for Hungary and Bulgaria who had no other competing foreign policy aims that would complicate their full support for the Soviet stand. In the case of Hungary, however, Moscow's distraction with the Middle East served as a welcome opportunity to accelerate domestic economic reforms. Concentration on perfecting its New Economic Mechanism during this crucial period proved a more judicious choice than Czechoslovakia's more ambitious program of comprehensive social renovation. For its part, East Germany granted unquestioned backing for Moscow, due in large part to the high priority it attached to securing diplomatic recognition from the Arab states. Indeed, East Germany placed so much value on gaining international recognition in the Third World that it could not afford at that time to deviate from the Soviet line on issues not vital to its national security.

Rumanian Defiance
The most systematic deviant from the Soviet line during the entire crisis was Rumania. Prior to the outbreak of hostilities Bucharest voiced general backing for the Arab cause but withheld comment on Nasser's moves related to the confrontation and commented favorably that trade with Israel had doubled in the past year. During the war Rumanian news media were the only sources of factual reporting in Eastern Europe. Because of the one-sided condemnation of Israel, Rumania refused to sign the communiqué of the first Socialist summit meeting. Party leader Ceausescu and Premier Maurer returned from Moscow and issued a separate statement that called for a restoration of the status quo ante and pledged assistance to the Arabs but refrained from condemning Israel and omitted a break in diplomatic relations. Rumanian editorials called for "active coexistence" between the belligerents and a settlement *without outside interference*. Finally, Rumania refused to participate in the second Pact summit and attended the third meeting only with the assurance that no statement injurious to Rumanian-Israeli relations would be issued.

When the issue was discussed at the U.N. General Assembly, Maurer met with Israeli Foreign Minister Abba Eban and then told the Special Session that *all* foreign interference in the crisis (including Soviet) must be eliminated as a precondition for opening negotiations. Moreover, Rumania voted against a Soviet draft resolution condemning Israel and actively campaigned with the nonaligned nations for an early settlement. Rumania's efforts at the United Nations, although they proved abortive, helped to create increased recognition of the validity of its claims to international independence and its role as an important representative of the smaller nations. Indeed, this general activity contributed significantly to the election of Rumanian Foreign Minister Manescu to the presidency of the U.N. General Assembly.

Rumania used the 24–26 July session of its Grand National Assembly to discuss foreign-policy issues connected to Middle Eastern developments and to consolidate the gains achieved in establishing its autonomy within the communist world.[2] Various speakers stressed the need to devise new forms of party relationships and new norms for acceptable conduct among communist parties and countries along the lines of Rumania's brand of "creative coexistence." More consultations and exchanges of information were proclaimed to be basic necessities for future relations among fraternal parties. Premier Maurer stated that it was "unnatural that methods and practices in contradiction to the standards of equal rights and noninterference in internal affairs . . . should occur in relations between socialist countries."[3] This clear warning to Moscow followed a major party shakeup not unlike that which the U.S.S.R. had recently experienced.

On 15 and 18 July Ceausescu harshly criticized the activities of the secret police.[4] In the most drastic instance of this nature during his rule, Ceausescu insisted upon the comprehensive reorganization of the nation's security apparatus, covering leadership, organization, and jurisdiction. A law embodying the reforms and curtailing the arbitrary use of police power was unanimously adopted by the Grand National Assembly. As in the case of the Soviet Union and Yugoslavia, these reforms were designed to devalue the power base of conservative elements and to garner broader public endorsement for the party by sharply censuring former Minister of Interior Alexandru Draghici, one of the most powerful members of the non-Ceausescu group of the Party Presidium.

Although the remodeling of the police apparatus had been under consideration for many months, Ceausescu introduced an important new sidelight when he concluded his criticism:

It is known that a number of shortcomings and defects still persist in various fields [of security]. . . . It is true that in recent times these shortcomings and defects have been subjected to serious criticism on the part of the party and state leadership and also on the part of the public opinion. . . . In light of the latest international events [the Middle Eastern crisis], it is even more necessary for the security organs to have the capacity to study intelligence materials very carefully and thoroughly check them in order to be certain that they are accurate and that they conform with reality, because effective measures can be decided only on this basis.[5]

These demands for accurate intelligence reporting clearly registered Rumania's displeasure with Soviet estimates on Middle Eastern developments and its former dependence upon Soviet intelligence capabilities. Foreign Minister Manescu told journalists later in The Hague that Rumania had differed with Soviet policy toward the Middle East prior to hostilities and that Bucharest's assessment had been proven correct. Bucharest concluded that it had gained considerable political profit from the accuracy of this assessment, but it was determined through criticism of opposition within the party and subordination of the security apparatus under Ceausescu to reduce further its political dependence on the Soviets in these matters.[6]

By linking its political autonomy with a more nationally oriented intelligence effort, Rumania would make a significant step toward institutionalizing its independence from Soviet hegemony, since one of the inducements for loyalty among the East Europeans had been access to Soviet intelligence estimates. This has made it unnecessary for other Pact members to mount a highly complex, national intelligence capability commensurate with the status of a completely independent, but potentially threatened, state. Earlier Rumanian pronouncements reflected a desire either to gain greater authority over Pact decisions or to redirect Rumanian resources from its commitments to the alliance, without jeopardizing its security or invoking undue Soviet wrath. In this vein, several speakers during the 1967 session of the National Assembly called for greater independence in arms procurement and an increased emphasis on national production. Thus, Rumania was able to exploit the seriousness of the crisis to reaffirm its autonomy from Moscow and to use its neutrality to launch a diplomatic initiative aimed at reaching a mutually satisfactory settlement outside the efforts of the great powers. Bucharest also appeared prepared both to lessen its dependence upon the Soviet Union for various military support activities and to pay the additional costs for a more autonomous security service. These developments suggest that Ceausescu used the Middle Eastern crisis to consolidate his standing at home and in interparty affairs as well as to further Rumania's claim to be an objective spokesman for smaller nations in world affairs.

Poland's Revival of Antisemitism

Poland, on the other hand, experienced serious difficulties during the crisis precisely because of the party's lack of objectivity and its close identity with the unpopular Soviet position. The Polish government formally denounced Israel for aggression, broke relations with Tel Aviv, voted with the Soviets at the United Nations, and conducted a vicious propaganda campaign against Israel and Jews. During this same period, however, Western press accounts alleged that "there is no doubt that almost the whole population is on the side of Israel." Prior to its closure, the Israeli embassy in Warsaw was flooded with messages of sympathy and solidarity.[7]

The government countered by staging several anti-Israeli protest meetings in politically reliable factories and publicizing the results as representative of the attitude of workers in general. Even party leader Gomulka entered the controversy by delivering on 19 July a major policy speech devoted to the Arab-Israeli dispute. He warned that a Zionist "fifth column" could emerge in Poland and cautioned Poland's Jewish population that the state would not tolerate those who displayed loyalties and sentiments toward other countries—those who "come out in favor of the aggressor, for the wrecker of peace, and for imperialism."[8]

Official acrimony was expressed by Deputy Minister of Arts and Culture Kazimierz Rusinek on 17 July: "It is no secret that many Hitlerite criminals are at the service of the Israeli government.

They live on the territory of the State of Israel. I cannot give exact figures but I estimate that there are over 1,000 experts of the former Hitlerite Wehrmacht who have become advisors to the Israeli army." [9] He charged further that the methods of Israel toward the defeated Arabs were so brutal that they equaled Hitlerite cruelty. In supporting this line, Radio Warsaw carried "eyewitness" accounts of alleged Israeli atrocities, as well as charges that Tel Aviv was conducting a campaign of genocide against the Arabs. [10]

In another vein, the military daily *Zolnierz Wolnosci* of 9 July carried an article linking a close associate of Israeli General Moshe Dayan to the Warsaw ghetto police, "without whose help the SS would have been unable to carry out so quickly the mass deportation of Jews." On 19 July it further alleged that Israel was seeking missiles and nuclear weapons and that "the military and atomic cooperation between West Germany and Israel is no secret to anybody."

The dimensions of the campaign expanded beyond mere public propaganda when it was projected into the military sphere. The minister of defense, Marshal Marian Spychalski, himself of Jewish origin, stated on 1 July before the Military Political Academy, "Without regard to their nationality, we cannot remain indifferent to those who, against the interests of our state and its security, take the side of the aggressor. There have been and there are various Jews: capitalist Jews and worker Jews, fascist Jews, Zionists, and communist Jews. . . . Yet every imperialism is evil and genocidal, be it Nazi or American imperialism, and the Israeli lackeys of imperialism are by no means any better." In two later speeches on 19 and 20 July Spychalski gave the first indication of a military split when he admitted that the armed forces were not unanimous in supporting the government's stand regarding Israel. Spychalski concluded, "In the face of this situation [Poland's stand on the crisis], a severe test was made of party and class attitudes, of the attitude toward socialism and of the ideological and political positions." [11]

In the wake of an unannounced visit on 30 June of the "political commissar" of the Soviet Armed Forces, Colonel General P. Yefimov, and on 25 July of the commander-in-chief of the Warsaw forces, Marshal I. Yakubovski, this "severe test of party attitudes" resulted in the dismissal of three top air force generals: Division General Czeslaw Mankiewicz, commander-in-chief of the Air Defense Forces; Brigadier General Tadeusz Dabkowski, deputy commander-in-chief for political affairs; and Brigadier Jan Stamieszkin, chief of staff of the Air Defense Forces. All were non-Jewish and known staunch supporters of Spychalski, but they reportedly refused to give unqualified endorsement of the regime's stand.

On 16 July First Party Secretary for Warsaw Stanislaw Kociolek acknowledged in the party organ *Trubana Ludu* that opposition also existed within the party to Poland's position on the Middle Eastern crisis and implied that severe counteractions would be taken. A periodic renewal of membership cards took place in November and December. This proved an occasion for a thorough verification of each member's qualifications and "an appraisal of the ideological and moral level of party members." Western sources estimate that over 50,000 members did not have their cards renewed, including normal attrition in a party of nearly two million.

However mild, the 1967 purge reflected the current strains within the party, stemming from breaches of discipline over the Middle Eastern crisis. Kociolek condemned "cases of conscious unpartylike attitudes, originating from premises other than socialist, state, and national reasons . . . which were observed in some instances after the aggression of Israel in the Middle East." The Middle Eastern crisis produced tensions within the party which were relieved only at the expense of an ignominious antisemitic campaign that inevitably led to a comprehensive review of the party's position on a more fundamental issue—domestic reform.

This renewed public concern led to the March 1968 student demonstrations and intellectual protests, and the subsequent repressive purges that contributed directly to the December 1970 crisis. Nearly 40 percent of the Central Committee lost their jobs in the 1968 purge, without resolving the domestic unrest. A prominent Polish economist, Wlodimierz Brus, has noted the firm linkage between these developments:

In Poland in 1968 the protest of a good part of the students and intellectuals was an expression of unrest due to increasing awareness of a retrogressive process in the political mechanism, incompatible either with socialist ideas on the liberation of the individual or with the purely pragmatic needs of social and economic development. . . . At the center [of the unrest] was the call for a restoration of the fundamental liberties of the citizen, and in the first place for an end to the practice of [providing] partial, and even downright false, information. . . . It was decided to exploit the demonstrations by students and intellectuals in order to achieve the final blocking of all actual and potential sources of independent criticism . . . and it must be said that the ideological campaign used themes never before exploited on such a wide and open scale, even during the darkest days of the Stalinist purges (we may refer above all to the so-called anti-Zionist campaign . . .).[12]

The use of antisemitism had obvious appeal to certain party segments, but it antagonized those intellectuals who were sensitive to calls for increased party democracy. In the end, Jews were dismissed from many positions of leadership and authority in the government and party, and thousands felt compelled to emigrate to Israel. But there was more at issue than antisemitism; this was merely the pretext for the last power struggle between the vestiges of the "Soviet Poles" and the "Home Poles," the two traditional wings of the party. Many of the "Soviet Poles" and their supporters were Jewish, and the ultranationalistic "Partisans" faction led by former Minister of Interior Mieczyslaw Moczar was thus able to combine anti-Soviet and antisemitic sentiments under the guise of patriotism to advance the faction's political ambitions.

While the various factions succeeded in eliminating important opponents, none gained sufficient strength to upset Gomulka's delicate balance of the rivals with the moderate majority. Such manipulation was possible because of Gomulka's lingering political authority and the rise of the revisionist-traditionalist controversy as the highest national priority, overriding feuding among the key party personalities. Gomulka's fortuitous compromises in the wake of the purges weakened the bargaining position of both rivals but failed to resolve the controversy or provide unambiguous policy guidance. Indeed, the ranks of the revisionists were sufficiently thinned so that the pace and scope of domestic reforms were reduced to the point that public unrest eventually forced the dismissal of the Gomulka faction. In Brus's view:

The link between the lack of criticism and the scope of the mistaken and arbitrary decisions is evident. The success obtained in March 1968 gave those who gained it the feeling of complete liberty to act in an autocratic manner, and this finally led to December 1970. Here we come to the true connection between March 1968 and December 1970, a link which can serve as a classical, if negative, example of the dialectical development of social processes: the stifling of the outward manifestations of conflict, without finding an effective solution to them, becomes in itself the source of intensified conflicts, while the strength, scope, and significance of the delayed explosion builds up.[13]

Thus, the estrangement of the intellectuals primarily over their claims to the right of accurate information, especially in crises such as the June War, effectively denied the party the valuable safety valve afforded by their criticism and created a credibility gap between the party and people which resurrected again in December 1970 the entire issue of the legitimacy of communist rule in Poland.

The Middle Eastern Crisis and Prague's Spring

The domestic impact of the Middle Eastern crisis was more comprehensive and immediate in Czechoslovakia than Poland, though no less decisive for the dominant clique. The crisis triggered the most serious test of will between conservative party elements and the liberal intellectuals of any controversy since de-Stalinization.

Since 1965 Czechoslovak intellectuals, primarily writers, had conducted a gradually intensifying battle with conservative factions over creative freedom. The liberals had made sufficient progress toward freer expression for party leader Antonin Novotny to recognize the potential dangers a foreign crisis could hold for his domestic confrontation. As early as 4 June he condemned Israel for its aggressive intent and broke previous records for his personal public commitments on controversial issues when he made two more major speeches during the short war.[14]

His apprehensions were justified: the crisis became the point of departure for a bitter debate on personal liberties during the Fourth Congress of Czech Writers, which ended on 29 June. As in Poland, the issues at stake were the authority of the regime to impose an official interpretation of events of intense national interest and to censure opposing views, and the recourse that was legitimately open to dissidents. Revisionist speeches delivered to the Congress prompted the inevitably sharp response by the dominating conservative majority, and the confrontation soon reached full-scale proportions. The most dramatic and courageous attack from the liberal side was made by party member Ludvik Vaculik, recipient of the 1966 Writers' Union Prize. Vaculik insisted that the highest social virtue is individual freedom of expression and demanded the establishment of a political system that would provide genuine guarantees of such freedom. He observed that under formal democracy the citizen remains upright even if the government should fall. Under a totalitarian system, the regime stands firm and the citizen falls. He stated, "I believe there are no citizens in our country any more," and bemoaned the fact that his once independent-minded nation had been "converted into a herd of faceless, scared nonentities." In criticizing the party's use of power, Vaculik complained that it had abused its authority by perpetuating and homogenizing itself, and by ejecting all alien elements that could not be assimilated. The party's goal seemed to him to be the production of an environment in which all parts would be true replicas of the whole and could be interchanged.

He denounced this program and called on artists to resist the ruling circles. "I see and I hear how Power [the ruling circles] retreats only where it sees and hears too strong a resistance. It does not withdraw when confronted by arguments; those do not convince it." [15]

Vaculik insisted that "nobody was born simply to be ruled" and demanded constitutional amendments which would provide genuine guarantees of personal rights through the establishment of an equal partnership between the governors and the governed. He brandished other taboos by praising the high degree of democracy the First Czechoslovak Republic had achieved, and he concluded that the abuses of power by the present ruling circles had nothing to do with socialism, which he espoused. Indeed, the corruption of power had contributed to the prevailing economic chaos as well as to the social abuses. In a devastating criticism Vaculik condemned the existing regime by charging that "not one human question has been solved in the course of the last twenty years" and insisting that no undemocratic system in the world can solve these problems.

These charges were the most seditious yet voiced publicly in Czechoslovakia. In reply, chief party ideologist Jiri Hendrych defended the conservative position: "In disregard of the Party Central Committee's standpoint . . . and with obvious reluctance to honor it, some contributions concealed or quite openly attacked, and defamed, the socialist system, the government, as well as the internal and foreign policy of Czechoslovakia and the Communist party . . ." He complained that the Congress had been misused and implied that it had no authority to deliberate on foreign affairs. "Freedom," he asserted, "had been mistaken for anarchy." [16]

The party member selected to give the important concluding speech, Jan Prochazka, delivered a sharp rebuttal to the arguments of the conservatives. He sided with the revisionists and reaffirmed that the writers would continue the struggle for their constitutionally guaranteed right of free expression and that they would refuse to be subordinated to either doctrine or dogma. Prochazka asserted that the useful ideas coming from the Congress would survive and the superfluous would vanish. He called for all like-minded colleagues to fight against "oppression, persecution, the poison of racism and antisemitism, against chauvinism and narrow-minded nationalism." [17]

The party reacted promptly. Disciplinary action was initiated against Vaculik and Prochazka and three revisionist playwrights, Pavel Kohout, Vaclav Havel, and Ivan Klima. Shaken by this open defiance, the ruling conservatives arbitrarily postponed the election of Central Committee of the Writers' Union until autumn, hoping to be able to erect more effective defenses. But they could not block passage of a revisionist proposal for a more liberal censorship law, and they responded lamely to the defection of Czechoslovakia's internationally best known writer, Ladislav Mnacko, who fled to Israel in part "as a protest against the [Middle Eastern] policy of the Czechoslovak government." [18]

Unlike Poland, where the conservatives were the first into the ring and actively pressed their opponents, Czechoslovakia witnessed revisionist intellectuals assuming the initiative and openly demanding some of the most far-reaching political reforms yet expressed in any East European socialist country. By October the controversy had reached the highest party forums. The Central Committee decided to strip Novotny of his party leadership, but they could not agree on a successor and he was not formally replaced until January. Prague's obedience to the Soviet line on the Middle East created the most serious domestic crisis in the regime's history, the consequences of which were resolved only by Moscow's use of force in August 1968. The irony of this sequence of events is that the present Prague regime has largely diverted its attention from foreign-policy matters in a desperate effort to redress the effects of the party's attempts in the April 1968 Action Program to institutionalize the freedom of expression and independent views that had been initially demanded on international issues.

Tito's Temporary Rapprochement with Moscow

The reaction of President Tito and the Yugoslav government to the Middle Eastern crisis initially surprised many Western as well as communist observers. Tito's apparent rapprochement with Moscow was viewed by some of his associates as a retreat from the independent position Belgrade had sacrificed so much to achieve. Tito's reaction to the crisis generated a major dispute within the party that had important ramifications for the future of the most comprehensive economic and political reforms presently in progress in the communist world.

In his reelection speech on 17 May, President Tito emphasized Yugoslavia's old and familiar channels in foreign policy. He declared that the policy of nonalignment had not outlived its utility in world developments and called for a broader approach to give the concept a renewed viability.[19] *Borba,* the leading Belgrade daily, picked up the message and urged the promotion of an expanded and progressive interpretation of the concept. This new version could incorporate states that had formerly been members of power blocs, as well as positive measures to improve the organizational integration of the original nonaligned states. *Borba* cited the Tripartite Meeting in New Delhi in February 1967, during which India, Yugoslavia, and Egypt had agreed to expand trade, coordinate balance-of-payments matters, and develop customs arrangements, as exemplary.

During the period of rising Middle Eastern tensions, Yugoslav leaders made several official visits to the region. Deputy Foreign Minister Misho Pavicevic went to Cairo following the closing of the Gulf of Aqaba and visibly associated Yugoslavia with the Egyptian stand. After the hostilities erupted, former Foreign Minister Koca Popovic visited Cairo on 11 June and Foreign Minister Marko Nikezic went to New Delhi on 13 June as Tito's personal envoys. An effort seemed underway to salvage nonalignment and to preserve Yugoslavia's leading position within this bloc. This interpretation became increasingly apparent when Tito, despite classical Yugoslav reservations about the utility of communist summit conferences and for the first time since attaining power in 1945, attended the 9 June Moscow summit gathering.[20]

Tito failed to consult either the cabinet or the Party Presidium on this radical departure from previous policy. In an interview with the Western press on 8 August, he justified this dramatic step by declaring that he went to Moscow to help the nonaligned nations.[21] Even in defeat, Tito believed that Nasser remained the pillar of nonalignment in the Middle East, and he used his dramatic flight to Moscow to restore the Soviets' faith in Nasser. Tito stated that he sought arms in Moscow and economic aid in Budapest for the Arabs because the Soviet Union was the only power that could possibly restore the regional balance. Tito clearly feared that the downfall of Nasser would permanently impair the effectiveness of nonalignment and its "moderating" influences in the Middle East and the Third World. This would leave Tito as the last of the "founding fathers" of nonalignment and would demonstrate that the concept was based more on personalities than on political realities. Tito was therefore prepared to take drastic measures to prevent such a repudiation of the basic axiom of his foreign policy, and he visited Cairo twice during the summer to promote his own solution to the crisis.

Besides the sentimental and ideological aspects of his defense of nonalignment, Tito calculated that the greatest long-term potential threat to Yugoslav interests was the possible return of the Middle East to the Cold War arena. This was similar to what had happened after the 1956 Arab-Israeli conflict and was one of the primary stimulants for the initial Yugoslav participation in nonalignment. In 1967 Tito encouraged a return to a balance of power between the belligerents and among the big powers by urging that "the Arabs have the right to defensive arms—not for an offensive," and that "the defense of the Mediterranean should be the exclusive duty of riparian states." With this aim in mind, Tito sought Soviet cooperation, and, during an August tour of the Middle East, he tried to restore Arab confidence and to revitalize the fabric of local nationalism, while at the same time cultivating realism in Arab objectives. If Arab nationalism and nonalignment could be rejuvenated, Tito estimated that the Arabs would have enough resilience to forestall major encroachments by either great power and that the prehostilities détente between Moscow and Washington in the Mediterranean might thus be restored. Only under conditions of great-power détente in its immediate geographic locale could Yugoslavia enjoy an optimum number of options in international affairs. These expectations became the political foundations of Tito's new concepts of nonalignment and of Yugoslavia's proper role in world affairs.

To this end, Tito took stringent steps to gain acceptance of his views by bitter domestic critics. His supporters alleged that a worldwide imperialist coalition was endangering Yugoslav national security. This coalition was manifested by military coups in Greece and many developing countries, pressure on Cuba, and "aggression" in Vietnam and the Middle East. Confronted with such ominous threats, "only socialist forces, together with nonaligned forces, can be bearers of the resistance [against international imperialism]." [22] Thus, in certain world circumstances nonalignment means alignment. In Tito's words, he had not abandoned neutrality; rather, Moscow had joined him for the moment because their individual interests coincided. These views were incorporated in the resolution adopted by the Seventh Plenum of the party's Central Committee on 1 July 1967, which also included a denunciation of Israel's "aggression" and a demand for the withdrawal of Israeli troops from Arab territory, as well as a decision to strengthen Yugoslav defenses.

This line was by no means universally accepted, even at the top level. During a debate on the issue before the National Assembly in July Foreign Minister Nikezic championed the moderate position. While he condemned Israel for aggression, he insisted that mutual efforts must be made by both sides. In his view, "these nations must, to an even greater extent, speak in their own name." [23] He closely paralleled the Rumanian position when he demanded that foreign powers refrain from attempting to influence developments in the crisis.

During the course of the meetings of the National Assembly and the Central Committee, it became increasingly apparent that the most serious aspect of the domestic contest over foreign policy was the impact it might have on the future of the political and economic reforms presently underway in Yugoslavia. The liberal faction of the party had succeeded in 1965 in gaining endorsement for the broadest economic reforms in the communist world. They were designed to transform the economy into market socialism based on profitability and relatively free prices. One year later the party introduced a program to reduce its direct influence in political matters and to decentralize the control and authority of the federal government. Tito's arbitrary conduct during the Middle Eastern crisis created widespread fears that the trend toward decentralization and the "legitimate withering away of the state" had been reversed for no justifiable reason—few believed that the imperialists were an actual danger. A public poll discussed at the Plenum revealed that "the population at large strongly support everything considered to be an essential component of democratic development, while only 2 percent of the people queried consider that because of the world situation the role of state institutions in society should be strengthened." [24] During the Plenum repeated pleas were made for the timely prosecution of the reforms as designed; some speakers even suggested that the process of altering the Yugoslav society be accelerated.

(A leading party theoretician, Zarko Vidovic, subsequently published an article in which he asserted that in a truly communist state the parliament must become the supreme power, stronger than the party, the government, or even the state president. In his view, Yugoslavia "is ruled not by a king or a powerful person, or a caste, group, or class; this state must be ruled by an assembly composed of freely elected representatives, mediators of people's authorities or mediators defending the rights of citizens and man." [25] He concluded his powerful indictment against Tito by arguing that a freely elected deputy in parliament has concluded a contract with his voters whereby no one has the right to impose on him views that are contrary to those of his voters.)

The economic reforms were also discussed in July by the National Assembly. During the progress report on the nation's economy and the state of the reforms, the government was sharply rebuked. Some Western analysts asserted that Minister of Finance Kiro Gligorov received the severest criticism ever administered to a communist minister.[26] The entire Economic Chamber of the Assembly, representing business and commercial interests, lined up against the government and rejected thirteen revisions of the national budget. The point of the unanimous Chamber attack was that the economy was slowing down and the reforms were being mishandled by the regime.

It would be unrealistic to conclude that the Middle Eastern crisis had as sharp an impact on internal development in Yugoslavia as it did in Czechoslovakia or Poland. It did, however, fuel the growing controversy between centralists and revisionists. In July 1966 Tito had decapitated the conservative faction by dismissing Vice President Rankovic and purging the security apparatus. Contemporary critics feared that Tito's arbitrary decisions related to the Middle East signalled a shift to the right, filling the vacuum among the conservatives and providing them sufficient authority to limit the scope of the domestic reforms.[27]

But a tacit modus vivendi emerged in which the liberals suspended attacks against Tito's Middle Eastern policy provided that it in no way adversely affected Yugoslavia's economic growth and reforms. Accordingly, Belgrade was able to provide only lip service to the common socialist aid program for the Arab states, and has refrained from further participation in Soviet-sponsored Middle Eastern projects. Furthermore, Tito has substantially reduced his personal commitment to a political solution of the crisis and has acted with greater circumspection regarding the exercise of his personal authority in domestic matters. Finally, as the involvement of both great powers in the Middle East has reached unprecedented proportions, Yugoslavia has sought to establish a position midway between the two, symbolized by its criticizing the presence of both navies in the Mediterranean, its hosting of President Nixon in 1970 and General Secretary Brezhnev in 1971. Public statements by Tito from 1970 on suggest that, with the fading of prospects for a Middle Eastern solution that would revitalize nonalignment and Yugoslavia's leadership among smaller nations, he is increasingly focusing his attention on the country's gripping domestic problems. His dramatic attempt at active personal diplomacy in the Middle East is thus likely to be his last such venture into major international controversies.

In summary, then, the June War and its consequences provided the most serious international controversy the Brezhnev regime had yet faced. Both the scope of Moscow's commitment to the Arabs and its efforts to manipulate the emergency to promote collective socialist action created chain reactions of varying magnitudes throughout Eastern Europe. East Germany, Hungary, and Rumania used the crisis to advance their respective national priorities—international recognition, economic reforms, and local autonomy. But in Poland, Czechoslovakia, and Yugoslavia, Middle Eastern developments nurtured internal unrest on a scale clearly unforeseen by the respective leaders. Where the regimes survived, in the Soviet Union, Rumania, and Yugoslavia, decisive measures were introduced to discipline the security apparatus and redefine central authority over dissident elements. Conversely, the Polish and Czechoslovak parties' inability to exercise firm authority during the aftermath of the crisis allowed the ensuing domestic turmoil to topple the ruling circles. Clearly, events related to the 1967 Middle Eastern crisis had an unpredictable impact on the domestic policies of key socialist countries.

The Soviets must have concluded that the uncertain linkage between foreign and domestic issues could prove a dangerous restraint on future Soviet diplomacy. This assessment was probably reinforced by the dual cathartic experiences resulting from the Prague Spring and the Ussuri River clashes. Moscow responded by attempting to insure greater stability and reliability in the conduct of its foreign policy. In an effort to be more systematic and, therefore, more flexible, the Soviet Union sought to compartmentalize its foreign interests and issues and to isolate each from related problems. Such compartmentalizations reduced the degree of adverse spillage from international crises into domestic affairs and permitted far greater latitude for tactical diplomatic maneuvers.

The implications of this new orientation became most readily apparent on the European scene. The Soviets agreed at a December 1969 Warsaw Pact Political Consultative Committee meeting to suspend the multilateral approach in solving East-West problems and to permit each East European state to pursue its respective grievances against the West on a bilateral plane.[28] With regard to West Germany, for example, East Germany could now concentrate on securing recognition of its legitimacy; Poland, on gaining acceptance of the Oder-Neisse border; Czechoslovakia, on securing repudiation of the Munich Pact; and Hungary, on promoting a European Security Conference, leaving the Soviet Union free to negotiate the test case for renunciation-of-force agreements. This shift to a bilateral approach did not weaken the impact of collective support for single issues, nor did it reduce the degree of coordination. Indeed, the extent of consultation between Moscow and its allies noticeably increased. Accordingly, it should not be concluded that Moscow altered its preference for centralism and adopted a genuine form of coalition politics as understood in the West. It merely allowed each ally greater responsibility in resolving highly circumscribed national problems.

The result of this new bilateralism was the successful conclusion of normalization treaties between Moscow and Bonn and between Warsaw and Bonn, plus the opening of formal negotiations between Bonn and Prague and Bonn and East Berlin on their respective problems. For the first time in over 25 years, Central Europeans are making progress in reducing their most ominous difficulties without jeopardizing the Soviet Union's strategic interests in the region.

The trade-off that Moscow earned from allowing its partners more local authority on selected questions has been a freer hand in those areas reserved for the great powers—SALT, China, the Middle East, and Southeast Asia. For over three years Moscow participated conscientiously in the SALT deliberations, which span the entire spectrum of Soviet-American strategic questions—clearly the most important arms-control negotiations ever undertaken. In 1970 Moscow adopted a policy of increasing its defenses along the Chinese border while negotiating with Peking on political differences. On the Vietnam issue Moscow continued to draw world attention to the abuses of American involvement, while refusing to allow conflict in this corner of the communist alliance to block dealings with the "imperialists" on more urgent matters.

Moscow's new freedom of action, unfettered by its allies' inhibitions and restraints, was most strikingly visible, however, in the Middle East. The deployment of Soviet combat units to Egypt and the commitment of equipment destined for Eastern Europe was unprecedented in the history of the Warsaw Pact. (In 1970 alone the Soviet Union reportedly invested $2.5 billion in Egyptian defenses.)[29] This marked the first time that Moscow had accepted responsibility for the defense of a noncommunist nation and that the Pact had received secondary priority in circumstances that could be detrimental to its members' national interests.

Indeed, on several occasions during 1970 the possibility of a great-power clash in the Middle East appeared threateningly near; and Moscow's involvement in the Middle East in the early 1970s had openly increased by quantum measures and was potentially far more dangerous for East European interests than it had been in 1967. Yet in no known instance did the East Europeans challenge Moscow's decision. The news media minimized polemics, and party leaders omitted flamboyant references to the Middle East during the Twenty-Fourth Soviet Party Congress. Even public opinion appeared by 1973 to be disinterested in Middle Eastern matters. In general, the Middle East was no longer either a prominent issue in East European politics or a factor in international affairs for either the governed and the governors. Thus, in a remarkably short time the Soviets had successfully detached East European interests from Middle Eastern affairs and had isolated regional issues within their immediate context—a noteworthy feat!

It may be concluded, therefore, that Moscow did succeed in effectively reducing the most serious restraint against its policy that resulted from the June War. It now has greater freedom of action in the Middle East than ever before; and any inhibitions it experiences are regional rather than global, with the important exception of its dealings on local issues with the United States. But even in these circumstances, the extent of its compartmentalization has forced its adversary to adopt a somewhat similar policy, thereby assuring a regional context for two-power deliberations. If successful, the Soviets may now have a greater ability to confine the results of local developments within regional parameters, whenever this is desirable. Thus, a setback in the Middle East is not likely to challenge again the legitimacy of Soviet rule in Eastern Europe and may not even be exploitable by the Chinese. On the other hand, any successes the Soviets might score would be readily exportable. The aim, then, in overcoming Soviet constraints in the Middle East has been to reduce the adverse implications of possible reversals to the smallest possible dimension, while retaining the broadest possible options for exploiting any gains that may be realized on the global scale—a manifestation of the realism and flexibility in contemporary Soviet foreign policy.

Any attempt to analyze the origins and evolution of compartmentalization must face several obvious methodological limitations. The basic substance of the problem, interparty relations in which the Soviets have important state rather than ideological interests, would naturally be a matter of unusual secrecy. The only facts available are actual events and developments which indicate that compartmentalization has occurred. No other empirical data exist that could provide insight into how the concept was conceived and executed. Indeed, it may not have been a deliberate plan, but merely the product of a nebulous desire for more freedom of maneuver or less coercion.

We do not know why the East Europeans' interest in the Middle East dropped so precipitously. It may have been the result of direct negotiations at one of the Pact Political Consultative Committee meetings, but it may also have been involuntary and unintentional. It may have been a consequence of pure dominance and recession. But the most plausible explanation is that, after the Czechoslovak crisis had demonstrated the precise limits of Soviet tolerance and after the success of Ostpolitik and the European Security Conference idea had indicated the positive gains to be achieved through adjustments on local matters, the East Europeans acquiesced in granting Moscow full privileges as a world power and agreed to focus their attention exclusively on regional interests.

If this conjecture is accurate, however, it indicates a potential danger for Moscow in that, without a formalization and even institutionalization of the concept, foreign-policy issues will remain potentially destabilizing factors in intra-Pact politics. Without a successful attempt to incorporate foreign policy into a genuine scheme for coalition politics within the Pact, the Middle Eastern conflict could again become a source of socialist tension. This leaves the issue of compartmentalization somewhat in the air with as many possible future difficulties for Soviet planners as benefits they have gained, at least temporarily.

Appendix 2
The Mediterranean Military Confrontation:
Has Parity Been Achieved?

A major policy constraint on the Soviet Union in the 1950s was the artificial nature of its claim to military authority in the Middle East. In 1955 the Soviets revealed the first sign that they had adopted a new overseas strategy when they extended $250 million in military aid to Egypt. This single act demonstrated that the Soviet economy had recovered sufficiently from the devastation of World War II to allow the use of commercial credits for political purposes. It also pointed out to the Western powers the porous nature of the containment alliance by its circumvention of the 1950 Tripartite Declaration, which had attempted to control the intensity of the conflict in the Middle East by limiting the influx of arms. Finally, Moscow's entry into competition in the field of military aid signalled a new level of regional instability. The Soviets were obviously making a deliberate effort to polarize an area that had been dominated by Western powers; and Soviet prestige among its Arab clients increased at first in rough proportion to local calculations about the importance of new arms in achieving national aims. For example, the Soviet arms deal contributed heavily to Nasser's mistaken confidence that he could nationalize the Suez Canal without precipitating the threatened Anglo-French intervention.

When the Soviets joined the United States in 1956 in demanding the withdrawal of all foreign forces, and then proceeded to rearm the Egyptians, their prestige increased even further. But the exact degree of their influence among Arab leaders and of their stature with key rivals was difficult to measure. Moscow refrained for ten years after the 1958 Western intervention in Lebanon from promoting any crisis in the Middle East that would demonstrate its comparative lack of military staying power. This was the first indication of Moscow's sensitivity about its inability to support militarily its overseas ambitions. The Congo crisis underscored this deficiency. Soviet AN-12 transport aircraft based in Algeria could not match the combined Western efforts, and the Soviet protégés in Stanleyville were effectively neutralized. Finally, the superiority of American interdiction capabilities were demonstrated to the entire world during the Cuban missile crisis. The precise limits of Moscow's conventional strategic capabilities had been openly registered. Given these reversals, Moscow recognized that political objectives abroad could not be attained merely by enhanced international authority gained through economic favors; there could be no substitute for raw military power when challenging the interests of a stronger rival.

As a result the Kremlin made two important decisions designed to overcome this fundamental policy constraint. First, it sought a limited détente with the United States, sufficient to preclude a deterioration in relations that might further damage Soviet international standing, until it could deal from a position of parity or strength. It then launched a redoubled effort to gain strategic nuclear parity with its adversary. Second, it decided at the same time to increase its conventional overseas capabilities by providing its military forces with the physical assets and training necessary to intervene in strategic areas at appropriate times. This new requirement necessitated the creation of mobile naval and air forces on a scale approaching those of the United States. Simultaneously, Moscow sought to improve diplomatic relations with those neighbors who controlled the access routes out of its continental confinement. Thus, by the mid-1960s the first indications began to appear that Moscow had given a lower priority to its former tactic of seeking political gains largely by bluff and extravaganza, and was determined to deal ultimately from a position of political equality, earned from military parity in both conventional and strategic nuclear forces.

In less than five years the Soviet Union secured American recognition of its parity at the strategic nuclear level, as evidenced by Washington's interest in participating in the SALT deliberations. Moreover, by 1967 it had established a permanent military presence in the Mediterranean and a high degree of political influence in several littoral countries. This remarkable recovery in Moscow's overseas strategy was due to substantial allocations of critical national resources, the exigencies of the Arab-Israeli conflict, American acquiesence, and European passivity.[1] Equally important, the Soviets mastered the technical essentials of a viable overseas strategy, such as at-sea replenishment techniques. The acceptance of strategic fundamentals was a significant departure from both the Stalinist era, when the primary national concern was defense of the continental fronts and ventures abroad had been avoided, and the Khrushchev era, when Soviet strategy was aimed at eroding foreign stature and keeping the West off balance throughout the world. The establishment of a permanent Soviet military force south of the Dardanelles was truly a historic turning point of a similar magnitude to the establishment of Soviet garrisons in Central Europe. But to what extent has the Soviet Union achieved its broader objective of securing regional parity with the United States and thereby solidifying its claims to be a major, if not dominant, Middle Eastern power through assertions of its military and political equality? If only a degree of parity has been achieved or is achievable in the foreseeable future, how can the Soviets be expected to exploit this new advantage against its chief adversary and against smaller regional powers?

The Soviet Mediterranean Threat Revisited

Since 1964 the Soviet Union has been developing a capacity to support its ambitions of global power through a steady quantitative and qualitative improvement of its military forces in the Mediterranean. The Soviet navy expanded operations in the Mediterranean from 650 ship-days in 1964 to 20,000 in 1970. The number of vessels varies at any time from 40 to 70, including a balanced force composed of nuclear-missile-equipped surface combatants, submarines, intelligence-collection vessels, and auxiliary ships.[2] (See figure 1.)

The Mediterranean Fleet, identified in Russian as *Escadra,* is

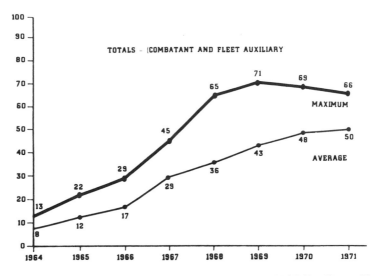

Figure 1. The Soviet Mediterranean Fleet. Source: *NATO's Fifteen Nations,* April–May 1972, p. 51.

composed of elements of the Northern, Baltic, and Black Seas Fleets that conduct out-of-area training in the Mediterranean before returning to home waters or steaming to alternative naval facilities for specialized maintenance or refitting. This provides valuable training in new waters and command and control exercise in interfleet coordination—former weaknesses in Soviet naval proficiency. Flagship duties for the squadron are usually performed by cruisers of the Kirov, Sverdlov, or Kresta class. The bulk of the force is composed of Kynda guided-missile frigates, (equipped with two quad SSMs and one twin SAM), Kryppny guided-missile destroyers (with two twin SSMs), and Kashin, Kildin, and Kotlin SAM-equipped destroyers. Varying combinations of these classes provide the squadron's firepower and air protection.[3]

When the squadron was augmented to an average of 35 vessels following the June War (it had numbered as high as 45 before the war), the composition included a 15,000-ton guided-missile cruiser with twelve 6-inch guns, three other heavy cruisers, five to seven missile-equipped destroyers of the 4,300-ton Kynda and smaller Kotlin class, ten conventional and two nuclear submarines, and twelve to fifteen modern supply ships and amphibious craft.[4] (In 1970 the number of medium-size, Alligator-class amphibious craft was doubled to 12. It is now estimated that the squadron could land several battalions against only light resistance.) In September 1970 there were more Soviet combatants in the Mediterranean than American.

These forces have not always operated alone. Since September 1969 the Soviets have periodically conducted limited naval exercises with the Egyptian and Syrian navies, which have been supplied by a small number of landing craft and coastal defense vessels. These maneuvers have provided potentially valuable experience for other types of naval undertakings. (See table 1.) It can now be expected that Egyptian and Syrian units in these classes will commence exercises with Soviet vessels in antisubmarine-warfare (ASW) operations, defensive screenings, and routine patrols, as occurred in the Red Sea during the October War. But proficiency among Arab navies is not high and, until it improves, the Soviets are not likely to rely on client navies in actual military engagements. However, combined exercises will convey the powerful impression that, in conjunction with local forces, the Soviet navy could attempt in the future to deny limited sea space for limited periods to Western fleets.

Finally, an occasional Rumanian and Bulgarian warship has exercised with the Soviet *Escadra,* giving the impression of Warsaw Pact solidarity for Soviet Mediterranean ventures. These periodic visits by Pact warships, however, are purely symbolic, designed mainly to bolster confidence among sponsored Arab states rather than to increase Pact deterrence against NATO.

Nonetheless, this was a significant buildup for a five-year interval. The Soviet press has put it this way: "Our navy grew up in a historically short period of time, a navy that is completely new in composition and armament and new from the point of view of its strategic and operational-tactical possibilities. It became a

Table 1 Naval Forces of Selected Mediterranean Countries

	Destroyers, frigates	Coastal escorts, subchasers, patrol craft, escort minesweepers	Minesweepers	Submarines with torpedoes	Landing craft	MTB/MGB	Missile patrol boats
Syria		2	2			12	6
Egypt	5	14	11	12	12	20	12
Israel	1	12		2	10	4	12
Morocco	1	3			1	11	
Algeria		6	3			12	9
Tunisia		3				4	2
Libya	1	1	2			9	3
Lebanon		8			1		
Yugoslavia	1	19	30	5	30	65	10

Source: *The Military Balance: 1972–1973,* IISS, London.

long-range navy capable of exerting substantial influence upon the course and outcome of vast theaters of military actions." [5] It must be remembered, however, that the Soviet squadron has no strategic strike role—it is strictly theater-oriented. But despite its exclusive theater mission, the Soviet defense minister, Marshal Andrei A. Grechko, and the commander-in-chief of the Soviet navy, Admiral Sergei G. Gorshkov, visited the Mediterranean Fleet on 13 June 1971. This was the first such high-ranking Soviet visit to an operational unit abroad and implied that the squadron had been raised to the status of a permanent Soviet fleet, as it is now referred to by many Western authorities.

Soviet naval shore activities in the Mediterranean have established a trend. Soviet naval units replenish and provide running repairs primarily at sea. However, selected shore facilities are now in regular use because of their convenience, not necessity, and because of the political and psychological profit this regular presence provides. The Soviet Union has extended technical aid in the form of harbor improvements and repair facilities to Egypt, Syria, Iraq, Somalia, Yemen, and Algeria. These commercial facilities are occasionally leased and are sometimes augmented by the positioning of Soviet repair shops nearby. [6] This affords a compatibility between repair facilities and Soviet vessels which can be used without the formal establishment of legal basing rights.

President Sadat has acknowledged that, as part of the terms for Soviet resupply efforts after June 1967, Cairo granted the use of naval storage and repair facilities. The use of facilities at Mersa Matruh, Alexandria, and Port Said (as well as at Latakia and Tartus in Syria) allowed for more extensive servicing than running repairs while avoiding the political stigma involved in manning military bases on foreign soil. While not essential for sustained naval operations when access to the Black Sea is assured, these facilities increased the flexibility of the fleet by allowing greater utilization of assigned units and more efficient logistics and repair operations. Such facilities also provided somewhat more staying power in the event the Dardanelles should be closed and the host country is not at war. When the Suez Canal is re-opened, the Soviets can be expected to seek similar facilities at Hudagdah, Berbera, and Aden on the Red Sea. The extensive Egyptian bunkering privileges, however, were severely curtailed after the expulsion of the Soviet Advisory Mission in July 1972. The Soviet fleet retains only limited facilities at Alexandria and has shifted a portion of its former logistic requirements to Latakia; the remainder are being routinely accomplished at sea, imposing a minor curtailment of operations.

Moscow has also advanced the psychological and political value of its naval presence through an active campaign to "show the flag." Soviet warships made port calls to 28 nations in 1969 and to 47 in 1970, including all the Arab countries—even Libya and Morocco. "Visits by Soviet sailors helped to raise the international standing of the U.S.S.R. Last year [1970] the red-star flag of our [naval] ships proudly flew in 62 ports of 47 countries." [7] Thus, Soviet vessels are now an accepted feature of the sea space in Syrian, Egyptian, and Algerian ports, while Sixth Fleet warships have been barred from these harbors and are reluctant to call even at Lebanese, Tunisian, and Turkish ports.

Prior to the expulsion, Soviet offensive naval capabilities were significantly improved by the maritime reconnaissance of Western naval units conducted by Egyptian-based, medium-range TU-16 Badger aircraft and BE-6 Madge amphibious aircraft. These aircraft provided target-location data to surface combatants from extended ranges. Captain Alexander Grozny, an occasional commander of the Mediterranean Fleet, stated that "no Western ship could move undetected by the Soviet navy. . . . Our submarines, ships, and naval air force follow their movements with a watchful eye." [8] Operating from Cairo west, these aircraft ranged as far as Malta. When they occasionally recovered in Algeria, they extended surveillance to the entire Western Mediterranean. TU-16 aircraft also can be configured to carry air-to-surface missiles, as well as 20,000 pounds of bombs, and they have a low-altitude-penetration capability. [9] Thus, NATO warships were subject to low-level attack throughout the Eastern Mediterranean from a

southerly direction. This was the first instance of Soviet operational elements being based in a Middle Eastern country.[10]
In 1970 the Soviets deployed 150 MIG-21J interceptor aircraft to six main operating bases in Egypt as a partial compensation for their lack of fleet air cover, and a year later they assigned four MIG-25 Foxbats. The MIG-21Js were primarily engaged in air defense missions over the Nile Valley and the west bank of the Canal, but could have been redeployed north for fleet protection. The MIG-25s were based at Mersa Matruh and were assigned reconnaissance as a primary mission.[11]
After July 1972 Soviet naval reconnaissance was terminated. Moscow responded by augmenting the number of trailing vessels surveilling American warships. Surface surveillance is much more expensive, however, and the Soviets have reportedly pressed for a return to the status quo of July 1972 for both bunkering facilities and aircraft-basing rights. To date, however, Sadat has shown no indication that he will grant this request.

The Soviet Union's Long-Range Lift Capability
One of the important factors in the Soviet Union's military buildup has been the development of a long-range massive-lift capability that can sustain Soviet or proxy forces over extended periods. Moscow has sought an appropriate surface-air mix to meet this logistic requirement. Soviet airlift capability has reached impressive proportions. The Soviet commercial carrier Aeroflot is the largest and fastest-growing airline in the world. In 1968 it carried 62 million passengers. It opened 80 new services and carried six million more passengers in 1969—the equivalent of the combined operations of the Royal Dutch Airlines (KLM), the British Overseas Airways Corporation (BOAC), and Iberia Airlines. Aeroflot and six other communist commercial carriers have landing rights in 24 Middle Eastern and African countries —Saudi Arabia being the only Arab state that does not receive communist carriers. An additional four or five new lines are planned per year with other Afro-Asian countries. Ultimately, the Middle Eastern schedules will be linked with around-the-world

services via South America and Asia. By the mid-1970s communist commercial airlines expect to be able to land in any potentially troubled Afro-Asian nation or an adjacent neighbor.[12]

Communist commercial carriers are operated as an adjunct of the Soviet air force. Commercial aircraft and support facilities are generally identical to their military counterparts, permitting the transfer of resources from one type of mission to the other without additional training or administrative logjams. This high degree of compatibility between military and civilian airlift capabilities facilitates overseas operations. No information is available as to the existence of agreements about overflights and landing privileges by Mediterranean countries for Soviet military aircraft. To date, however, both Soviet military and civilian aircraft have been allowed to use normal ground installations and to make repairs using stocks of spare parts designated for the support of the Soviet-supplied commercial airlines in these countries. The Soviet air elements have thus enlarged their sphere of operations without having to build up a major logistical system.

The professionalism of the Soviet airlift capability was demonstrated during the June War. Moscow launched a massive airlift operation before the war ended and sustained it until surface transportation could begin replenishing Arab losses. Within several weeks after the airlift commenced, Israeli sources claimed that 200 crated fighters had been delivered to Arab armed forces.[13] This performance was surpassed in the October War.

If overflight rights can be assured from Yugoslavia, Turkey, or Iran, the Soviet air force has the capability of transporting seven of its existing airborne divisions simultaneously.[14] Moreover, its military lift capability can be augmented by the employment of up to one-fourth of the civil fleet without seriously jeopardizing commercial schedules. (This concept was exercised by the Pact in Shield '72.) The ranges of lift operations have been extended as the AN-22 Cock, with its capacity to carry 88 tons 3,100 miles or 50 tons 6,800 miles, has come into general use. This does not compare with American lift capabilities, but it is significant when viewed in the perspective that single battalions of British marines and French paratroops have successfully preserved existing regimes in Kenya, Tanzania, Uganda, and Gabon. Soviet sealift capability is growing as fast as its airlift forces. The Soviet Union has the world's second largest number of merchant ships and in November 1972 replaced the United States with the fifth largest tonnage. It is presently one of the youngest fleets afloat, having grown from 735 vessels of 3.3 million tons in 1958 to over 1,442 ships of nearly 12 million tons in 1969. The fleet expanded by roughly one million tons per year and reached nearly 2,000 ships of 14.3 million tons by the end of 1970 and 16.2 million by 1972. In the 1970s it is programmed to grow by nearly 100 percent to 27 million.

The commercial fleet can and does augment naval needs afloat. Between 1958 and 1968 the Soviet global fishing fleet doubled in size and is now by far the world's largest and most modern. It includes just under two-fifths of the world's trawler tonnage and over four-fifths of fish-carrier and fish-factory ships. The reason for this preponderance in high-seas fishing capabilities is that, while fish is an important ingredient in Soviet economy, the world's best fishing grounds are thousands of miles from Soviet coasts. The Soviet Union has now become the world's third largest fishing nation. (The United States has dropped in 20 years from second to fifth.)

Similarly, between 1963 and 1967 the Soviet oceanographic service trebled in tonnage and now has greater resources than the rest of the world combined. Thus, Soviet vessels now ply all major shipping lanes and fishing waters, providing valuable maritime experience and services for naval needs and allowing the most economical utilization of all existing bottoms.[15] In analyzing this trend, David Fairhall has recently observed that, of all facets of Soviet maritime policy, fishing has proven the most aggressive. Fishing and commercial shipping have served as disciplined, reliable government services that are rapidly becoming competitive with the individualist, anarchistic Western maritime industries. Nonetheless, the recent Soviet penetration of international shipping conferences has not yet produced the general threat once predicted. The Soviets have behaved with prudence and circumspection in international maritime matters. Their performance to date demonstrates remarkable parallels with the British admiralty experience of the eighteenth and nineteenth centuries, when naval expansion was motivated by both political desires to protect state interests and commercial demands that the flag follow trade.[16]

After the June War the Soviet Union demonstrated a high degree of maritime proficiency in its readjustment of programmed commercial schedules to meet its resupply commitments in the Middle East. Three to five ships per week arrived in Egypt alone, and by October 1967 80 percent of the Egyptian losses had been replaced. Once again this performance was replicated after the October War. Those efforts confirmed Moscow's ability to replenish rapidly proxy or Soviet forces abroad. In conjunction with its airlift capability, the Soviet Union now, for the first time, has the sealift capability to support its political ambitions in the Mediterranean Basin.

Trends in Fleet Modernization
The Soviet Mediterranean Fleet is highly transitory, and its size and capabilities at any time are difficult to predict. A brief review of the 1973 inventories and ship capabilities of the Soviet navy will indicate the degree of modernization that has been achieved, the force mix that is now possible, and the weapons selection and flexibility that can now be expected in its Mediterranean Fleet. First, in terms of force modernization, the Soviet navy has been reduced in size during the tenure of the present commander-in-chief, Admiral Gorshkov. Personnel strength has declined from 800,000 in 1955 to 475,000 today. This includes a cut in the naval infantry force from 100,000 to 14,000, leaving a sufficient capacity to land against only light resistance at battalion strengths to accomplish such largely political missions as humanitarian evacuations or security for client leaders, as well as minor flanking attacks during land operations.[17] Naval aircraft strength has decreased from 4,000 to about 1,000, including helicopters. Major

surface combatants have dropped from over 300 to 231, and the
submarine force has declined from a high of 475 to around 350.[18]
During the past several years there has been a similar decline in
the American navy from 932 active fleet ships in 1968 to a
planned 523 in 1974, with only 311 classed as warships. In 1973
the United States had only 243 major surface combatants, the
lowest level since 1950.[19] Over the past decade the heaviest cuts
have been 91 conventional attack submarines, 186 destroyers, and
76 mine warfare vessels. There was also a sizeable turnover of
light coastal and river craft to the South Vietnamese navy.

Until recently, the American navy seemed trapped in the downward spiral of aging ships, while the Soviet navy had the youngest fleet afloat. For example, the average age of the Sixth Fleet
vessels in April 1971 was 18.5 years, while the average age of the
ships assigned to the Soviet Mediterranean Fleet was only 8.5
years.[20] This discrepancy is being slowly reversed. The ships de-
commissioned by the United States were usually the oldest in each
class, thus decreasing the average age of the remaining active
list. Furthermore, in 1971 the American navy commissioned 35
new vessels and recommissioned 10 modernized ships. At the same
time, the Soviet Union has been falling behind the United States
in construction of most classes of warships. Michael McGwire
has convincingly shown from procurement lists that, except for
diesel submarines, the West in general, and often the United
States, has procured more new ships than the Soviet navy of com-
parable classes over the past decade.[21] These trends will gradually redress the age differential between the American and Soviet navies and will reduce total American operational costs. On
both sides, reductions of the older classes and ships have increased
the general readiness and effectiveness of the remaining warships.
On the Soviet side, for example, over one-half of all combatants
will be missile-equipped by 1977. Table 2 shows a rough comparison of the inventories of the two navies.

In offensive capabilities, the Soviets introduced in 1962 the
Kynda-class frigate, carrying two quad SSN-3 Shaddock surface-to-
surface missiles with a range of 400nm (nautical miles) and a full

Table 2 Total Strengths of the Soviet and American Navies, 1972

Category of Vessel	Soviet Union	United States
Attack carriers		14
Helicopter carriers	2	2[a]
Missile cruisers	12	8[b]
Cruisers	10	1
Missile destroyers and frigates	38	65
Destroyers	57	97
Missile patrol boats	153	
Oceangoing escorts	112	
Coastal escorts	250	56
Fast patrol boats	250	
Minesweepers	305	20
Landing ships	105	72
Landing craft		100
Logistics and support		155
	1,294[c]	580
Missile submarines		
SLBM nuclear	39	20
SLBM diesel	22	41
SSCM nuclear	26	
SSCM diesel	25	
Attack submarines		
Nuclear	34	56
Diesel	210	35

[a] U.S. helo carriers are Essex-class and are nearly twice as heavy and carry over twice as many aircraft, including fixed wing S-2Es and A-4s.
[b] Missile category includes only SAM; the United States has no SSM capability.
[c] Soviet total roughly doubling the U.S. figure is due to heavy historic emphasis on coastal-defense vessels.

Source: *The Military Balance: 1972–1973*, IISS, London.

load of 16 missiles, plus the Goa SAN-3 surface-to-air missile and two twin 76-mm AAA guns. This warship was followed by the Kresta-class cruiser carrying two twin SSN-3 launchers, a helicopter for limited-range aerial target acquisition for its missiles and for ASW operations, two twin Goa SAN launchers, plus 57-mm AAA gun mounts and impressive air-surveillance and electronic-warfare equipment.

In 1968 the Soviet Union introduced a new class of cruiser, the helicopter cruiser Moskva. It is the largest warship in the Soviet inventory (18,000 tons) and is armed with twin SAN launchers and the latest fire control system. The vessel's primary mission is antisubmarine warfare (ASW), and it carries a complement of about 20 helicopters and ASW rocket launchers for sustained area surveillance and defense. This vessel represents the first serious Soviet attempt to undertake realistic air antisubmarine warfare, though the equipment aboard and observed techniques indicate that the Soviets remain about five years behind the West in such operations.[22]

In June 1970 a new offensive warship was first reported, the 7,500-ton Kresta II, armed with eight SSN-3 launchers, two twin SAN-3 launchers, ASW torpedoes, two helicopters, 3-D radar, and the missile-fire control system that had been first observed on the Moskva.[23] This vessel was regarded then as the Soviets' most lethal threat on the high seas and a clear demonstration of their intention to introduce greater staying power to their high seas capability, an essential requirement in fulfilling the goal of asserting their claims to maritime authority.

In 1971 a new class of Soviet destroyer was observed. The Krivak class displaces 3,800 tons and is armed with a quadruple launcher for an SSN-9 surface-skimming missile. It also carries four 76-mm guns in twin mounts, two retractable SAN-4 antiaircraft-missile launchers, eight torpedo tubes, and two 12-barrelled antisubmarine-rocket launchers. The vessel is equipped with an impressive array of semihardened sensors and gas turbines that generate a top speed of 35+ knots. It is regarded as the most versatile, self-defensible vessel in the Soviet inventory.

The 1972–1973 edition of *Jane's Fighting Ships of the World* reported a new 10,000-ton Nikolayev-class cruiser "with every available type of missile, gun, radar, and electronic-warfare device," except for long-range strategic missiles. The ship is "very fast" and has a worldwide capability. The editor predicted construction of a considerable number of this class, along with the Krivak and as many as six carriers. The Soviets clearly outclass the American navy in this category.

On 14 August 1973 Admiral Zumwalt, chief of staff of the

American navy, confirmed reports circulating in the press since January 1972 that two aircraft carriers are under construction at the Nikolayev Nosenka shipyard on the Black Sea. The ships will apparently have a 30,000-ton displacement, similar to that of the Essex class. It is widely believed in the West that with this size limitation the ships will employ VSTOL (vertical short takeoff and landing) aircraft for air defense and attack missions and helicopters for ASW tasks. VSTOL aircraft are far less effective than conventional fixed-wing aircraft, but under favorable conditions the Soviets will be able to control a limited airspace. The advent of the Soviet carriers only partially ends a long debate both in the Soviet Union and the West about the relative vulnerability of Soviet warships to air attack and the necessity for air cover. It does add, however, a new dimension that deserves closer analysis (see below). (It may be worth noting in passing that the reported acceleration in the carrier construction program indicated by the laying of the second keel in late 1972 was almost certainly spurred in part by the Soviet expulsion from Egypt, which denied Moscow a base for aerial reconnaissance in the Mediterranean.)

At present Soviet naval air remains land-based. It is composed of 300 ASM-equipped TU-16 Badger and 60 TU-22 Blinder medium-range bombers, 200 TU-16 and TU-95 surveillance aircraft, 80 BE-2 Mail and 40 IL-38 May ASW amphibious aircraft, 40 IL-28 Beagle light attack bombers, 240 ASW helicopters, and the MIG family of interceptors. The MIG-25 was originally designed to oppose the American B-1 bomber, which has yet to be built, and it has now been assigned as a long-range interceptor for fleet protection. Authoritative reports indicate that the MIG-25 is also capable of employment as a fighter-bomber. A Mach-3 aircraft equipped with ECM and forward-looking radar for low-level penetrations, and fire control for its AS-6 Mach-3 300-mile-range missiles from altitudes of over 80,000 feet, it is a serious threat indeed.[24]

The bomber aircraft have likewise been assigned a defensive role, that of protecting the seaward approaches further from the homeland. They are equipped with 1,500 air-to-surface antiship

missiles with ranges of from 63 to 350 nautical miles, speeds from
Mach 0.5 to Mach 3, and some form of organic guidance. Thus,
these missiles can in most cases be launched beyond the range of
the American navy's 3-T ship-borne SAMs. To date, however, the
air arm has remained largely defensive, despite modernization,
while submarine and combatant units have been designed increasingly for offensive operations. The improved ranges of the advanced aircraft extend the protective cover of the surface units
and landing operations but do not significantly alter the air defense problem on the high seas, where the Soviets rely exclusively
on ship-borne defenses.

This forward look is best illustrated by the latest nuclear cruise-
missile submarine, the C class. It is reportedly the quietest boat
the Soviets have yet produced, and its nuclear propulsion gives it
unlimited range. It is armed with the SSN-7 supersonic cruise
missile, with a range of 30 nm and an organic target-acquisition
capability. The missile is fired from a submerged position and has
a surface-skimming capability.[25] These characteristics make it
suitable for employment in almost any waters and will present
formidable problems for the air defense envelope of the most
modern carrier task forces.

The Mission of the Soviet Navy
Thus, the Soviets have steadily sought increased flexibility and
mobility for their naval forces. As construction programs have
changed to accommodate these aims and other national priorities,
the overall mission of the navy has also been modified and expanded. It is no longer charged merely with the defense of home
waters and support for the army as it was in the wake of the two
world wars and the subsequent periods of national reconstruction.
Officially, the Soviet navy now has two missions: a deterrent role
in peacetime and a combat role in wartime. In peacetime it has
been assigned:
1. to defend the territory of the Soviet Union against any preemptive attack;

2. to counter the threat posed by the nuclear missiles of the submarines and carriers of the Western navies; and

3. to launch missiles against targets in Western countries which are far removed from the sea, as well as against naval targets.

In wartime the tasks of the Soviet navy are:

1. to insure the fulfillment of the three peacetime missions;

2. to cooperate with the Soviet land forces, especially in mounting seaborne landing operations;

3. to harass the enemy's sea communications;

4. to destroy the enemy's surface ships, submarines, and aircraft; and

5. to help in the defense of the coastal air defenses.[26]

There are several notable features about these priorities. First, defense of the homeland remains the highest consideration for the navy, as it does with any other maritime nation. Second, the emphasis placed on participation in and coordination with the broad air defense system reflects earlier Soviet apprehensions about vulnerability to low-level penetrating aircraft over its seaward approaches. It can now be assumed that SAN destroyers and escorts will be stationed in screening positions, adjacent to land-based air defenses, to counter low-level penetrations by NATO tactical aircraft over the Baltic and Black Seas and by SAC aircraft over the White Sea. Third, no mention is made of providing protection for its own sealanes. A unique feature of the Soviet Union as a maritime power is that in wartime it will rely mainly on its existing continental resources and, therefore, does not have the heavy escort requirements that burden NATO. Accordingly, its primary offensive goals are not to secure control of the high seas or even to deny the enemy portions of his own vital sealanes. The chief aim is to destroy his warships, making his sealanes and airways progressively more vulnerable to interdiction. The Soviet navy's peacetime mission is of course deterrent, but its wartime mission has now been augmented by an offensive role reminiscent of the force allocations between other smaller and larger navies. (For example, during both world wars the mere presence of German light-battleship task forces in friendly ports succeeded in tying the

vastly superior British Home Fleet to the North and Norwegian
Seas, denying these resources for the protection of vital North
Atlantic and Mediterranean sealanes.) The Soviet offensive threat,
then, is designed to force the Western navies to commit far greater
resources to the protection of vital sealanes than would be necessitated by the actual Soviet danger, and thereby to reduce the
overall potential challenge to the homeland. Therefore, the Soviets need not seek a numerical parity with the West. Merely a
credible offensive threat consisting of reliable weapons, survivable
warships, and maritime proficiency will create sufficient military
parity. In a relatively short time, then, the Soviet navy has been
expanded from a primarily defensive to a powerfully offensive
naval force. It is no longer the passive arm of the ground forces;
it may now even be the favored son of the Kremlin, as the Strategic Rocket Forces were under Khrushchev. As Admiral S. N.
Lobov, commander-in-chief of the Northern Fleet, has said, "The
Soviet navy, together with the Strategic Rocket Forces and our
long-range aviation, forms the nuclear-missile shield of Russia and
all socialist systems." [27]

The Aircraft-versus-Missiles Debate: The Aircraft Side
In assessing the posture of the Soviet Mediterranean Fleet, analyses are required of the relative capabilities of the rival navies'
main weapons systems and concepts of operation and their appropriateness for various contingencies in widely diversified regions.
    Despite the growing strength of the Soviet Union's strategic
capabilities, Western naval experts hold differing opinions about
their actual effectiveness and applicability, since Soviet armaments have not been fully combat-tested and Soviet concepts of
weapons deployment are regarded as unorthodox. (In meeting
their particular requirements and following their separate naval
background, the Soviets have been less concerned with endurance
and have emphasized armament and, recently, survivability,
while the Americans have stressed longer cruising time and
out-of-home-water replenishment to offset their reduced firepower.)

In 1953–1954 the Soviets elected to construct relatively light vessels heavily equipped with SSMs and SAMs, rather than rely on large-caliber guns and the development of aircraft carriers. Since then the Soviets have demonstrated a high degree of confidence in this new concept and have sought, not alternative systems, but rather a rapid conversion from conventional armaments to missiles. Thus the three latest Soviet-designed cruisers have no large-bore conventional guns. The largest-caliber guns aboard are AAA mounts designed to combat low-level attacking aircraft. Countership and shore bombardment is conducted exclusively by cruise missiles. (Shore bombardment is a relatively minor requirement in Soviet naval policy since opposed landings have not been envisioned.)[28]

Such heavy reliance on missiles is a sharp departure from accepted Western concepts governing naval bombardment and fleet air protection. Western analysts argue that missiles alone cannot deliver sufficient firepower to translate naval power effectively to land or to assure control of the high seas. Moreover, the principal defense against the Soviets' cruise missiles is the availability of carrier-borne tactical aircraft and the presumed vulnerability of Soviet ship-borne air defenses. This has led to the general conclusion that the Soviet naval buildup is still primarily for deterrence, without sufficient versatility to contest the Western navies' dominance of the high seas. Accordingly, former British Defense Minister Healey has assured the world that because of the West's preponderant strength it could sink the entire Soviet Mediterranean Fleet within the first few minutes of a war.[29] But Soviet Fleet Admiral S. G. Gorshkov refuted Healey's assertion in a 1969 Navy Day speech: "In a word, a navy's strength is determined not by the tonnage or displacement of its ships, or by the caliber of its guns, but first of all by the presence and quality of missiles, electronic-warfare equipment, and level of training. . . . We can be proud of the ships and armament provided by our country." [30]

Soviet confidence in its seaborne air defenses has undoubtedly been strengthened by the limitations on high-performance aircraft that have been demonstrated in Southeast Asia. Against heavily defended fixed targets in Southeast Asia, average circular bombing errors exceeded the breadth of Soviet warships by five to six times.[31] Even the use of ripple-release techniques and massive ECM barrages did not bring bombing accuracy to acceptable standards.[32] Attacks by tactical jet aircraft against highly mobile, heavily defended, relatively small naval targets with conventional bombs will thus have a very low probability of kill. Conversely, in situations where these optimum conditions do not exist and where little or no surprise can be achieved, Soviet ship-borne defenses—the SAN low-level missiles, twin AAA guns, 3-D radar, electronic-warfare equipment, and advanced fire-control systems—will probably inflict heavy losses. Thus, in a conventional conflict the attrition rates against attacking aircraft equipped to sink Soviet warships will probably be high. In other words, the standard mode for sinking hostile warships with armor-piercing bombs has not yet been made readily compatible with the high-performance characteristics of jet aircraft.

Early-1960s-vintage aircraft were designed for nuclear warfare, in which delivery accuracy was given lower priority than assured penetration of hostile land defenses. F-4, A-4, and A-7 aircraft of the mid-1960s were designed to accommodate more conventional requirements and are equipped with advanced computer-based bombsights. But torpedo bombing was unfortunately discarded years ago and these advanced aircraft must still use antiquated techniques. The advent of "smart bombs" and standoff weapons has been the first significant conceptual departure in dive-bombing techniques since World War I. Before the standoff weapons, the pilot had to locate and identify the target visually (sometimes aided by radar) and then align the aircraft on the appropriate trajectory (often aided by computer corrections) before releasing his weapons. The standoff weapons allow the pilot to release the bomb independently of the trajectory and then either guide the missile to target or rely on organic guidance systems.

The standard standoff weapon in the 1960s was the Bullpup series, with a range of six to twelve miles and warheads weighing 250–1,000 pounds. The bomb was aimed at the target and guided optically until impact. The system has several disadvantages. Optical tracking is subject to almost as many human error factors as conventional dive-bombing: the command guidance system is susceptible to jamming; the aircraft must loiter in the vicinity of the target until impact and is therefore exposed to hostile actions; and, finally, it is dependent upon good weather conditions. The system proved only marginally effective in Vietnam.

Air defenses in Vietnam were sufficiently effective and bombing accuracy so marginal that the United States developed or improved a variety of "smart bombs" on a crash basis. After years of delay the American navy will soon have the TV-guided Condor in service. It has a standoff release distance of 30+ miles, a 1,000-pound warhead and a fire-then-aim sequence. At release, the missile is switched to autopilot and the TV camera scans roughly a 60° arc for the target, relaying the terrain picture back to the operator's screen. The missile remains completely operator-controlled, and he can attack targets of opportunity or prescribed targets, or can abort the missile if the target proves friendly. After releasing the missile, the pilot can take limited evasive action.

The Condor also has several weaknesses. First, the video and command radio links are partially susceptible to jamming. Second, such systems are expensive and cannot be wasted. Third, because of the size and weight of the pilot's guidance package, only one missile can be carried per sortie. Most serious, the missile is limited by visibility: the camera cannot penetrate haze, mist, or night darkness. This is a severe limitation in a highly mobile, tactical naval confrontation.

The Paveway laser systems were also developed for use in Southeast Asia. The guidance kit can be installed in either gravity bombs or missiles. It has proven the most accurate system yet developed and, because of its expense, is usually confined to larger ordnance. Upon release, the bomb homes on a laser beam illuminating the target. The laser is interference-proof, that is, it cannot be jammed or deflected; but it also has several weaknesses. First, the aircraft must continuously illuminate the target and loiter until impact. Second, although the laser can be locked onto the navigational radar during poor visibility if the target is positively identified, generally clear visibility is required.

The Standard Arm antiradiation missile is an improved version of the smaller Shrike missile. A Mach-2 missile with a 20-mile range and a 250-pound warhead, it can home on a wide spectrum of radar emissions. When the aircraft's passive detection equipment picks up radar emissions, the missile can be locked onto the most threatening source. Unlike the Shrike, which can be confused by shutting down the emitting gear, the operator can either input geographic coordinates of the target or guide the missile until impact.

This system does not have sufficient payload to inflict serious hull damage against heavy vessels, since it will impact in the electronic gear aloft; but in the missile age, equipment exposed above deck—missile launchers, surveillance radar, fire-control systems, ECM gear, and communications equipment—is as important as the superstructure that supports it. Modern warships can be neutralized without damaging the hull or superstructure if the exposed launchers and antennas can be destroyed. When fully operational, the Standard Arm is expected to be highly effective in this role, especially if the warhead is configured to accommodate cluster munitions or multiple bomblets. The problem with incapacitating rather than sinking hostile ships is that it is often difficult to differentiate between reparable damage and the destruction of vital equipment. Until reconnaissance drones become readily available, bomb-damage assessment after each strike will require the exposure and possible expenditure of another aircraft.

The United States presently has no all-weather, hull-damaging, standoff missile. The Harpoon is its first effort toward an all-weather capability. It has a 50-mile range, a radar terminal-guidance system, and a 1,000-pound payload, and it can be launched from aircraft or ships. Flight testing began in 1973 and full production is expected by 1975. In comparison, the United States is clearly behind the Soviet Union in antiship, air-to-surface missiles, despite its development of "smart bombs." Desperate efforts to compensate technologically for a traditional preference for manned delivery vehicles have not yet offset the advantages the Soviets gained by stressing in the 1950s reliable, all-weather, unmanned systems.[33]

For ship attack, the Soviets have built approximately 11,000 (see table 3) surface-to-surface and air-to-surface missiles, and over 5,000 are currently deployed. The U.S.S.R. did important pioneering work in the 1950s on ASMs, and this has paid impressive dividends. The Naval High Command apparently has firm confidence in the present generation of missiles since little research and development on possible follow-on systems has been noted by Western observers. The Soviets' tapered ASM development effort is probably due in part to the nature of the delivery vehicles. The TU-16 is nearly obsolete, and a decision on a possible follow-on aircraft to augment the small TU-22 force has apparently not yet been made. Perhaps carriers are to take over this mission.

Cruise Missiles
Because of their wider deployments, the chief Soviet tactical threat is the seaborne cruise missile. Antiship missiles are carried by over 50 major combatants, 65 submarines, and 160 fast coastal patrol boats. These are relatively inexpensive weapons with organic guidance systems. Only one, the most plentiful SSN-3, has a long-range (400 nm) capability. It requires target-location data from horizon-limited surveillance systems (submarines, aircraft, or trailing surface vessels), accurate to within 10 nm terminal distances, to deliver a 1,000-pound warhead. A command-guidance and autopilot system is augmented by infrared or semiactive radar terminal homing. All other missiles, by virtue of their aerodynamic properties, cruise 50–60 feet above the water and are usually horizon-limited. Surface-skimming capabilities generally favor the attacker since:
1. the small cross-section of a missile is difficult to detect by radar at such low altitudes;
2. conventional gun firing is complicated by such extreme deflection angles;

Table 3 Soviet Antiship Missiles

The Soviets have initiated a new antiship cruise missile program at a rate of once every three–four years since 1950. Over the same period they have launched a new program for air-to-surface antiship missiles about every five years, for new patrol boat and land-launched cruise missile systems once every ten years, with major modifications to existing hardware once every five. Current surface-to-surface cruise missile inventory includes:

SSN-1, with a minimum range of 12 nm (nautical miles), a maximum of 130 nm, a speed of Mach 0.9, and an autopilot guidance system. Based on the available technology of the late 1940s, it currently is being phased out of the Soviet inventory.

SSN-2A, with a minimum range of 5 nm, a maximum of 23, a speed of Mach 0.9, and an autopilot guidance. It is deployed aboard the Komar, Osa-1, and Osa-2 patrol boats.

SSN-2B Styx, with a minimum range of 4.5 nm, a maximum of 22, a speed of Mach 0.9, and autopilot guidance. It also is deployed on the Komar, Osa-1, and Osa-2 platforms.

SSN-3A Shaddock, with a minimum range of 12 nm, a maximum of 450, a speed range of from Mach 0.9 to above Mach 1.5, and an autopilot/command guidance system. It is carried by the E-11 nuclear-powered and J-class diesel-powered submarines.

SSN-3D, with a minimum range of 12 nm, a maximum of 450, and autopilot guidance. It is used aboard the Kynda and Kresta-1 guided missile warships.

SSN-7, with a maximum range of 30 nm and autopilot guidance. It is carried by the C-class nuclear-powered submarine and has submerged launch capability.

SSN-9, with a minimum range of 40 nm, a maximum of 150, a supersonic speed, and autopilot guidance. It is deployed on the Nanuchka-class guided missile gunboat and also possibly deployed on the J- and P-class submarines.

SSN-10, with a minimum range of 15 nm, a maximum of 25, a speed of Mach 1.2, and autopilot guidance. It is carried by the Kresta-2 guided missile warship.

SSN-11, with a maximum range of 25 nm, a speed of Mach 0.9, and autopilot guidance. The SSN-11 is used aboard the Osa-3 patrolboat.

Total current Soviet seaborne cruise missile inventory stands at about 2,500, including approximately 900 SSN-2s and 600 SSN-3s. These are further augmented by two land-based systems—the SSC-2B Samlet and a version of the Shaddock. There are over 600 of these. Range of the beam-rider Samlet can be varied from 3 to 45 nm. Its speed is Mach 0.9.

The Soviets currently have about 1,500 air-to-surface antiship missiles in their operational inventory, including:

AS-1 Kennel, with a range of 55 nm and a speed of Mach 0.9. Kennel is a beam rider with a semiactive terminal guidance system. It is being phased out of the Russian inventory but has been supplied to Egypt and Indonesia.

Table 3 (Continued)

AS-2 Kipper, with a maximum range of 100 nm and a speed of Mach 1.2. Guidance is by autopilot with a command override capability. It is carried by the Tupolev TU-16 Badger C long-range bomber.

AS-3 Kangaroo, with a maximum range of 350 nm and a speed of Mach 2. It has an active guidance system. The Kangaroo is used on the TU-95 Bear heavy bomber.

AS-4 Kitchen, with a maximum range of 160 nm and an inertial guidance system. It is carried by the TU-22 Blinder medium-range jet bomber.

AS-5 Kelt, with a maximum range of 180 nm and an autopilot guidance system with a command override. It is replacing the AS-1 on the TU-16 Badger bomber.

AS-6, with a maximum range of 300 nm and a speed of about Mach 3. It is inertially guided with a command override capability and carried by modified versions of the Badger.

Source: *Aviation Week*, 21 February 1972.

3. ships are hot against a cool sea background for infrared homing devices;

4. ships are large, easily distinguished reflectors for radar terminal-guidance devices; and

5. for radiometric seekers, ships are massive metal structures.

As a result of these advantages, if a ship fails to take any defensive countermeasures, the probability of a cruise missile hitting its target is greater by a factor of three than the likelihood of a surface-to-air missile hitting an undefended, nonmaneuvering aircraft.[34] Six Soviet SSN-2 missiles have been fired in anger. Four were fired against and hit the Israeli destroyer *Eilat,* indicating the missile's capability to strike a maneuvering target, and two struck and sank an Israeli merchant vessel in the Red Sea. The Soviets' improvised policy of opting for a navy with smaller, missile-equipped warships, augmented by long-range submarines, as the most plausible means of opposing American naval supremacy now appears vindicated.

The United States produced the first operational cruise missiles, but it is now many generations behind. In 1947 the navy began work on Regulus I, which became operational in 1955, and later developed Regulus II, which was deployed in 1960. (The Soviets' SSN-1 came into operation in 1958, the SSN-2 in 1959, and the SSN-3 in 1961.) During this period the navy began development of an advanced, Mach-3.5, long-range penetration missile, the Triton. In the American budgetary crises of the early 1960s that stressed the urgency of strategic strike systems, tactical SSN missiles were abandoned, and the navy has had to restart work on its Harpoon cruise missile and the proposed submarine-launched antiship missile from almost ground zero. (The Norwegians, French, British, Italians, and Israelis have developed highly effective SSN missiles, underscoring American complacency about entering the field.)

American Seaborne Air Defense Capability

Against this combined ASM and SSN threat, the relevance of American naval air defenses becomes critical. Western air defense concepts have traditionally stressed the employment of SAMs and carrier-borne aircraft against bombers, and the use of ECM against missiles. The Standard-T and the follow-on Aegis SAM systems are reputed to be the best in the world. The Standard-T has an extended range and may be able to engage Badger aircraft before ASM release, depending upon weapon type and altitude. It has not been tested against Soviet ECM and would be less effective against low-altitude penetrations, but it has a reasonably reliable all-weather capability.

The Soviet cruise missile threat has finally alarmed American naval circles. In 1968 a Ships' Antimissile Integrated Defense (SAMID) program was launched to provide rapid incremental improvement in antimissile defenses. Due to lack of funding, however, the program has not yet become operational. Ideally, the system will be based on a high-speed, computer-based defense that fully integrates surveillance, weapons, ECM, and command and control. The system would accelerate warning and weapons-response time by designating appropriate weapons and ECM measures. Even so, ship survivability would not be assured, especially against multiple attacks. Current thinking in some naval circles points toward an integrated system of supportive functions by several ships acting in concert. One feature of this latter concept is the destroyer-based LAMPS helicopter program.[35] LAMPS is designed to provide over-the-horizon early warning for antisubmarine warfare and anti-SSN missile defenses. Improved radars and the not-yet-operational Close-In Weapon System, or Phalanx, are to provide more reliable warning and a wall of fire (6,000 rounds per second at a range of one mile) against low-level missiles. These systems appear to be the most promising, but the navy's increasing concern about the missile threat is indicated by the number and variety of other countermeasures that are being studied, including chaff, rocket-fired infrared and radar decoys, tethered floating decoys, tethered drone helicopters, expendable jammers, deceptive ECMs, flame-throwers, and high-pressure water jets. Though somewhat exotic, such endeavors underscore the current naval anxiety, which is compounded by the prospect that the Soviets might develop a new ramjet-powered missile which would permit a low-level penetration, a steep climb, and then a high, short-range ballistic descent on target, a concept for which the navy is completely unprepared. (For example, the Soviets reportedly completed in 1971 preliminary testing of an air-breathing, ramjet, Mach-4 SSM with a range of 300–500 miles, surface-skimming and 15-g-load capabilities for low detection, high-speed penetration, and extremely light maneuvering.[36]

Role of the Carrier

Historically, naval aviation has been oriented more toward land than sea; and the chief air threat has been thought to be nuclear-armed bombers. Both circumstances have now changed. The key argument for the continued use of carrier aircraft is the need for heavy bombardment to support opposed landings beyond the range of naval guns and to carry out interdiction operations beyond the range of land-based tactical aircraft. But the argument for their continued priority in the future hinges on whether landings will be required and on the degree of opposition likely to be encountered.[37] The present tone of American policy suggests that the United States need not plan on unilateral intervention in the future. It seems safe to assume that the United States will intervene only upon invitation and in conjunction with like-minded states, conditions that mitigate the opposed-landing concept. Furthermore, the most likely areas for intervention will be against tertiary Third World powers, where determined opposition requiring carrier aircraft is improbable. Thus, the ground-attack role for carrier aviation is waning and is likely to decline even more in the future, leaving advocates of carrier airpower searching for new roles and missions to preserve the carrier's stature.

Submarines equipped with both ballistic and cruise missiles are the most lethal strategic and tactical threats in the Soviet navy. The sheer numbers are a formidable problem; and, given the complexities of detection, ASW is thus the West's gravest naval task. The scale of the challenge is such that all available resources are likely to be diverted to this increasingly urgent problem. On the other hand, the employment of the Blinder and possibly the follow-on Backfin medium bomber, equipped with Mach-2 and 3 ASMs, indicates the continuing potency of the air threat within a range of approximately 1,000 miles from the Soviet Union.[38]

Thus, given the growing number and sophistication of opposing combatant systems, the priority for the carrier aircraft should be air, surface, and subsurface surveillance and fleet air protection, rather than land operations. In fluid situations a carrier's reconnaissance capability is the most effective means of maintaining tactical surveillance of Soviet SSN-equipped combatants and submarines at extended ranges. True, patrolling interceptor aircraft play a very limited role against the SSN missiles, but they are effective against low-level attack aircraft, especially with the advent of the Phoenix-equipped F-14. Carrier aviation, then, is likely to be allocated a growing proportion of the area-defense mission, supporting convoys and friendly screening forces.

Acceptance of the changing role of the attack carrier (CVA)

has been a cathartic experience for the American navy. "Shall we risk a *Nimitz* to chase a submarine?" [39] But the increasing limitations on carrier operations forced the air admirals to adopt new concepts in order to preserve the carrier force. The most recent concept is the "sea control ship," in which the carrier's aerial resources are divided more or less equally between ASW, intercept, attack, and support roles. With this flexibility the carrier is expected to combine operational durability, a high sortie generation rate, and multiple missions. In 1973 the *USS Saratoga* successfully completed sea trials of this concept.

But the application of the concept may not be radical enough to insure control of the sea. For example, when a carrier force is committed to a high-threat area (e.g., the Eastern Mediterranean), its air components should be shifted to two squadron ASW, one squadron intercept, and two squadron attack aircraft. As the surface-vessel or air threat is neutralized, an attack squadron can be replaced by an ASW squadron. The major argument against implementing such a versatile operation is that aircraft maintenance precludes altering the assigned aircraft mix. But this limitation could be overcome by containerizing spare parts to facilitate replacement. Alternative concepts, such as carrier specialization, have not yet received adequate study. In this scheme each carrier is equipped for a single mission (nuclear strike, air defense, attack, or ASW) instead of proportionally weakening the capabilities of each sector by incorporating all missions into a single carrier. The major argument against such a radical departure is, of course, that versatility in meeting unexpected contingencies has been the carrier's strongest attribute. But overseas contingencies are likely to become less critical and less time-sensitive, allowing for more deliberate preparations. More serious study by analysts outside the navy concerning the future of the carrier is urgently needed.

How does the belated Soviet acceptance of aircraft carriers relate to these postures and concepts. It should not vindicate those who have argued in the past that, lacking air cover, Soviet warships were confined to a defensive role within the protective zone of shore-based aircraft. The Soviets have designed a ship-borne air defense system in which they retain a high degree of confidence, and they have based unit survivability on self-sufficiency —a trend now adopted and pursued by the United States as well. The Soviets have developed a high-seas capability based on SAM defenses without carrier aircraft protection.[40]

After years of justifying missiles over carriers, the authoritative Soviet journal *Morskoi Sbornik* (Naval Almanac) carried a series of lengthy articles throughout 1972 under the imprint of Admiral Gorshkov.[41] The author stressed the strategic significance of naval operations, their relevance in theaters of secondary importance, and their value in the economic and political aspects of war. Referring to World War II, he repeatedly emphasized the necessity of developing balanced naval forces that are equipped to perform a wide variety of specialized tasks. Gorshkov gave the strong impression that the Soviets are seeking flexibility and adaptability in applying naval power in its global dimensions. They see the carrier as a means for exploiting their arrival on the high seas, not as a means for achieving access to deep waters; and they now have greater endurance and wider options for intervention or contingency operations in critical areas such as the Indian Ocean.

Carriers are not likely to be used to contest the high seas with the American or NATO navies. There is no need for another Battle of Midway Island between rival carrier forces. John Erickson has observed, "It is late in the day for the Soviet naval command to place its faith in the mobile power of the aircraft carrier when the improved ship-to-ship missile offers growing tactical advantages, and, even more, when such missiles do not have to be launched from surface ships. In what seems to be the present standoff between carrier and the missile weapons systems, the Soviet command does not appear to have relinquished even a particle of its faith in the missile." [42] Indeed, the new Krivak-class ships that look like "pocket battleships" are the most lethal general-purpose ships afloat and are likely to receive higher priority over the long term than the carriers with their more restricted utility.

On balance, then, both navies are developing capabilities to achieve their respective missions: the American objective of controlling the high seas by neutralizing all targets, and the less ambitious Soviet aim of containing a superior opponent by destroying key targets. With different tasks and capabilities, comparisons are dangerous. But it appears likely that during the next decade there will be more radical changes in American and Western naval air defenses and concepts of operation than in Soviet (despite the new carriers), which seem destined for continued modernization rather than basic modification. In the offensive mode, the United States will have no option for some time but to continue reliance on tactical aircraft. In the view of one experienced American naval officer, "the U.S. surface navy is no match for the Soviets," [43] who have opted for high quality missiles that give assurance they would survive and win any confrontation not involving the maximum use of tactical aircraft from optimally equipped carriers.

Other Comparative Assets and Deficiencies
The United States and the Soviet Union have asymmetrical strengths and weaknesses in aspects of naval operations other than main armaments that must also be considered in any appraisal of their relative effectiveness in various contingencies.

The announcement in 1971 of funding for the development of a new superquiet nuclear submarine and a new underwater-launched, long-range ballistic missile was a clear indication of Washington's determination to preserve its lead in submarine warfare. As Paul Cohen has observed, "Overall antisubmarine capability is losing ground to submarine capability because, on balance, the latter is benefitting to a greater degree from a variety of expanding technologies. Among these, specifically, are navigation, long-range communications, satellite and undersea surveillance techniques, underwater propulsion systems, life-support systems, and homing weapons." [44] In other words, satellite and submerged sensors, global communications, and air-flight missiles launched from submerged positions beyond the limits of hostile sensors give submarines greater advantages than ever before. These advantages are becoming increasingly ominous as merchant vessels become larger and as modern industry becomes more dependent upon foreign trade. Evidence supporting these views became so convincing that the 1971 Pugwash Conference concluded that the area of most intense great-power rivalry in the 1970s will probably be in antisubmarine warfare. In both strategic submarine technology and antisubmarine warfare the United States is still believed to be five years ahead of the Soviet Union.

In conventional armament, however, the Soviets have made substantial headway over the Americans. Their heavy conventional cruisers have guns with 30 percent longer range and a 5-knot speed advantage over their American counterparts. With the decommissioning of the battleship USS New Jersey, the Soviets now have the fastest-firing, longest-ranged, and most maneuverable naval guns afloat in the world. These developments were due to the increased Soviet naval presence in the relatively restricted waters of the Baltic and Mediterranean Seas, which reintroduced the possibility of sudden, close surface-to-surface engagements, which had long been thought to be a practical impossibility. Accordingly, the United States has done little about the improvement of guns since World War II. The latest five-inch gun, the Mk 45 5"/54, fires only twenty rounds per minute, less than one-half the rate of the modern guns of several NATO navies.[45]

The June 1970 contract awarded Litton Industries for thirty 7,100-ton destroyers will be an important step in restoring American ship-design supremacy. This class will be the first to incorporate gas-turbine propulsion (pioneered by the Soviets in 1962 with the Kashin-class frigate), Independent Variable Depth Sonar, two manned helicopters, Sea Sparrow point air defense system, combined Mk 26 launchers for ASROC, Standard-T, and possibly Harpoon missiles, two 5″/54 gun mounts, the Tartar D air defense fire-control system, and the follow-on Aegis guidance system. The first ship is to be completed in 1974 and will be the most self-sufficient, self-defensible American unit afloat.[46]

For its part the Soviet navy suffers from a major policy omission: Moscow has not converted any portion of its surface fleet to nuclear propulsion. The staying power and the amount of on-station time for any of its units will continue to depend upon the length of its logistics train and the availability of shore supply points and repair facilities abroad. This deficiency will be a severe restraint in wartime or in contingencies where the Soviet Union seeks to apply limited naval force. Meanwhile, the United States plans to have four nuclear carriers and fourteen nuclear escorts by the late 1970s. Even if only ten escorts are constructed because of budgetary cutbacks, the United States will still have an impressive endurance capability that the Soviet Union will not be able to match.

The Impact of Intercontinental Nuclear Parity
While the military buildup in the Mediterranean outlined at the outset and the general naval expansion are significant, they are more impressive when related to the Soviets' attainment of intercontinental nuclear parity. Secretary of the U.S. Air Force Robert C. Seamans pointed out several years ago the significance of the Soviet buildup in intercontinental offensive and defensive strategic weapons:

The Soviets have surpassed us in number of ICBMs and are still building both land-based missiles and ballistic missile submarines. Counting the ICBM sites that we know to be under construction, they have about twice as much missile payload as our own ICBM and Polaris force—payloads that can be very threatening to us if an expanding force is converted to multiple warheads. . . . They have now tested an improved ABM which can coast or "loiter" above the atmosphere. We don't know the Soviet intentions, but their ABM sites as well as several of their other weapons raise certain questions.[47]

This new intercontinental posture has had a profound impact on theater force structures and concepts of employment. As more ICBMs become operational, Moscow will be able to release a corresponding number of medium-range delivery vehicles for operations in adjacent theaters, such as the Mediterranean Basin. Precedents for such deployments have been established by the visits of Soviet medium-range bomber aircraft to Damascus and Cairo and the routine training missions over the North Sea. Likewise, a greater number of medium-range ballistic and cruise-missile submarines can now be transferred to Mediterranean duty. Indeed, the number of Soviet U-boats in these waters in 1972 reached an unprecedented peak, regarded by Vice Admiral Kidd as the most dangerous threat to the Sixth Fleet because the Mediterranean has the poorest sonar and ASW conditions in the world. Thus, intercontinental parity has increased the potential Soviet nuclear and conventional firepower in the Mediterranean Basin above what is indicated by the mere numerical strength deployed at any given time.

Intercontinental parity has also afforded Moscow for the first time the possibility of exploiting more fully the natural advantages inherent in its strategic Mediterranean posture. For example, intercontinental parity limits the use of America's vast nuclear strategic resources exclusively to provocations endangering vital American interests. Yet the introduction of Soviet tactical nuclear weapons into the Mediterranean injects a lower nuclear threshold that must be calculated in any great-power confrontation. The introduction of a second, lower-intensity theater threshold increases uncertainty but also affords Moscow flexibility in capitalizing on the conventional portion of its force mix, while minimizing the impact of its persistent weaknesses. With this combination of thresholds, Moscow can raise tensions to a high but not critical level. Moreover, if Moscow should miscalculate and regional tensions should reach a critical point, they would carry little risk to the vital national interests of the Soviet Union or of its principal allies—yet any destabilizing situation in this region could endanger the vital interests of many NATO members. Furthermore, regional stability is not as important to Soviet economic interests as it is to the West: the Soviet Union can sustain a reprisal in kind for attacks on Western communication lines without fear that interdiction would seriously impair its economic or security interests.

Finally, at a time when ultimate weapons are becoming progressively less appropriate as military instruments, regional political instability remains high, providing opportunities for the application of a minimum amount of conventional power for the extraction of significant political profits. Thus, the combination of intercontinental parity and powerful, applicable theater forces places Russia in the strongest military position outside its immediate continental confines that it has ever enjoyed—the Soviets have complicated NATO naval defenses in the Mediterranean and have largely bypassed the American strategic deterrent at a minimum cost.

NATO Capabilities and Advantages
Nonetheless, the Soviets' Mediterranean Fleet is confronted with several weaknesses and handicaps that still inhibit Moscow's attempts to demonstrate convincingly its military strength in the Mediterranean. Most important, it is faced with the awesome naval and tactical air power of NATO. (See tables 4 and 5.) The mission of these forces, according to their commander-in-chief, Admiral Horacio Rivero, is "to conduct defense of NATO territory as far forward as possible; to restore territorial integrity, if necessary, by controlled escalation; to maintain and protect nuclear capability; and, if and when directed by SACEUR, to retaliate with a general nuclear response." [48] Admiral Rivero holds that the Southern Flank in effect has been turned and has become the Southern Front. The net effect of the Soviet submarine, missile-warship, and air threats has been to dilute the NATO forces, which have not been augmented proportionally to the Soviet buildup.

Despite this pessimism, if the NATO machinery is activated as planned under general war, naval forces assigned to Allied Forces South (AFSOUTH) will retain a predominance in conventional

Table 4 Naval Forces in the Mediterranean

	U.S.S.R.		Atlantic Alliance					
	Min	Max	United States	Italy	Greece	Turkey	Great Britain	France
Attack and ASW carriers			3					1
Helicopter carriers		2						
Missile cruisers			2	3				
Missile escorts	2	3	4	2			1	3
Escorts	5	9	16	19	12	10	1	22
Coastal escorts	4	5	16	11	6			7
Patrol boats	6	10		14	12	21		
Mine warfare			4	61	22	25		18
Landing ships	2	4	3	1	14			4
Missile submarines	1	2	4					
Attack submarines	6	10	2	9	2	12		12

Notes: 1. Soviet figures relate to the period 1967–1971. They do not include auxiliaries.
2. These are average fleet strengths for the Mediterranean; each of these countries deploy naval forces elsewhere.

Source: *The Military Balance 1972–1973*, IISS, London.

surface firepower, amphibious-landing capabilities, naval air support, reconnaissance, fleet-escort assets, and submarine resources. Greek and Turkish destroyers and mine layers can block the Dardanelles, quadrant the Aegean Sea, and provide protection to their important maritime centers, while shore-based aircraft would provide cover and reinforce the blockade. Then, even if the Straits were seized, the numerous Aegean Islands would serve as additional choke points: Thrace and the Aegean Islands would

Table 5 Tactical Air Power of Selected Mediterranean States

	Combat aircraft	Specialized aircraft available for use in the Middle East
Great Britain	750 (air force) 250 (?) (naval air)	20 Vulcan bombers Shackton and Canberra Recce Buccaneer bombers Phantom and Sea Vixen fighter-bombers
France	475 (air force) 275 (naval air)	1 sqd A-1D (Madagascar) 1 sqd A-1D (Somaliland) 53 fighter-bombers 38 interceptors Recce ASW
Greece	215 (air force) 7 sqd fighter-bombers	
Italy	450 (air force) 7 sqd fighter-bombers 1 sqd ASW	
Portugal	100 (air force) 3 sqd fighter-bombers 1 sqd ASW	
Turkey	500 (air force) 16 (?) sqd fighter-bombers	
Spain	186 (air force) 5 sqd fighter-bombers 1 sqd ASW	
Yugoslavia	315 (air force)	

Source: *The Military Balance 1972–1973*, IISS, London.

have to be taken before access to the Mediterranean could be assured. The Portuguese navy, with assistance from other NATO members in IBERLANT, can effectively block the Strait of Gibraltar. Italian warships and aircraft can conduct screening operations in the 45-nm-wide Otranto Straits and participate in a barrier of the 75-nm-wide Sicilian Straits, which are shallow enough for mining. Italy could also contribute cruisers for offensive operations. The French Mediterranean squadron, though not firmly committed to NATO, would probably provide token forces, if not its total resources, which alone surpass those of the

Soviet fleet. If Spain should participate, its navy also equals the Soviet fleet in size and could contribute to the defense of Gibraltar. This superiority would allow NATO sufficient forces to seal and quadrant the Mediterranean and leave the Sixth Fleet, the British naval commando assault group, plus other NATO contingents free for offensive operations.

It should be noted that the Greek, Turkish, and Portuguese navies are equipped largely with old or obsolete vessels that are adequate for their assigned missions but are not capable of repelling missile attacks and are vulnerable to determined air assaults. Because of these persisting weaknesses, Sixth Fleet aircraft may have to be diverted from their primary missions for the protection of friendly forces exposed to air attacks from Bulgaria.

The bulk of NATO's nuclear and conventional striking power in the Mediterranean consists of the U.S. Sixth Fleet and one wing of Phantom fighter-bomber aircraft assigned to the 16th U.S. Air Force. The Sixth Fleet consists of approximately 40–50 warships and support vessels, normally divided into two carrier task groups and a marine assault task group. The carriers have a complement of 80–100 aircraft. Escort and screening duties are performed by destroyers and frigates, and fire support is provided by cruisers and frigates accompanying the assault group. Possibly the most potent threat to Soviet vessels is the large number of attack submarines assigned to these waters. Moreover, these in-place forces can be rapidly reinforced from NATO's Atlantic assets or the U.S. Second Fleet.

NATO capabilities are regularly exercised and their effectiveness publicized. The annual spring maneuvers, Dawn Patrol, usually involve 60–70 warships and 300 aircraft from five nations. Deep Furrow, the annual fall exercise, includes over 100,000 men from eight nations and incorporates all aspects of combined service maneuvers under a "total force" concept of integrated task assignments, including British clandestine reconnaissance missions, Greek paratroop drops, Turkish air defenses, American airlift operations, and all types of joint naval maneuvers. A review of these activities confirms that NATO still has the most balanced force posture in the Mediterranean and important advantages in providing the widest possible variety of options for limited intervention or general conflict.[49] (Nonetheless, these advantages may gradually diminish, not because of an increase in Soviet capabilities, but because of a decline in the variety of contingencies in which they would be appropriate.)

Despite this seeming advantage, confidence declined between the United States and the Soviet Union in the fall of 1970, and political developments in the Middle East led to a substantial escalation in force postures by both sides that has altered former estimates and prompted the introduction of new concepts. On 18 September 1970 the United States announced the movement of Sixth Fleet elements into the Eastern Mediterranean to aid American hijack victims in Jordan. TASS responded by issuing a mild warning that foreign intervention would complicate the international situation, but the Soviet squadron moved into trailing but nonprovocative positions. The United States then dispatched four additional destroyers for permanent duty with the Sixth Fleet, bringing the total number of ships to fifty-five. The Soviets also added five surface vessels and five submarines, raising their total to fifty-one. Next, as a show of flexibility, the United States advanced the departure schedule for the relieving carrier and marine task-group forces for the Sixth Fleet by one month, giving the fleet three carriers and two marine task groups at the time of President Nixon's visit to the Mediterranean in September.

In response to questions on this escalation Deputy Secretary for Defense David Packard stated that the buildup of the Soviet navy in the Mediterranean was much more of a factor than ever before in American planning during the Jordanian crisis. He estimated that in several years the United States might be unable to have a meaningful military presence in the Eastern Mediterranean, but that it would continue to have a peacetime presence of some value in the Mediterranean.[50] (As a matter of practice the Sixth Fleet since 1968 has remained outside the Eastern Mediterranean.)

In December 1970 the chief of naval operations, Admiral Elmo Zumwalt, announced the assignment to the Sixth Fleet of two fast escort ships armed with missiles. They have been given a task parallel to that of their Soviet counterparts, namely trailing the principal SSM combatants. "If the Soviets are going to fire at an aircraft carrier, we get a free shot at them. If they fire at one of our trailers, our carriers receive warning and get the aircraft off." [51] (The thinking behind this new American concept of operations is that an attack will require the unsheathing of the missile launchers above deck, which will provide adequate warning for the surveillance vessel. Should the Soviet ship maneuver into a position where it could unsheath a single launcher undetected, the trailer could attempt to destroy the ship's fire-control system after the missile had been launched, thereby rendering the missile ineffective. Thus, given enough trailers, the probability of the Soviets coordinating a saturation attack against several key targets simultaneously will be extremely low.)

U.S. Defense Secretary Laird again raised an alarm at the December 1971 NATO Defense Planning Committee meeting when he charged that the alliance's position in the Eastern Mediterranean was in danger of being lost by default and that, unless steps were taken to maintain a NATO presence, the area would soon be regarded as a Soviet preserve. (Southern Flank navies spend an average of only 30 days per year at sea; Sixth Fleet units average 200 days per year, with amphibious landings every two months.) Laird proposed establishing an integrated NATO naval force in the Mediterranean similar to the Five-Nation Standing Force in the Atlantic.[52] The suggestion was not accepted, and the momentum for force modernization has lagged since the expulsion of the Soviet forces from Egypt.

Constraints Against Both Sides

Laird's pessimistic estimate must be qualified by the constraints that govern possible military undertakings for both sides. From the American viewpoint the NATO alliance remains brittle and somewhat inflexible. It was designed for the principal contingency of general war with the Soviet Union, and its political cohesion below that level of conflict is questionable. It is highly improbable that the northern partners will supply more than moral support for their southern allies involved in a regional dispute not clearly threatening the entire alliance; it is questionable whether even the southern partners can act in unison (at present they are reluctant even to train together). Malta is a case in point. It was denied full NATO membership by the northern allies and in the summer of 1971 formally reexamined its limited relationship with the alliance. The threat of Maltese neutrality and the denial of its strategic basing facilities became almost as serious to NATO as the Soviet challenge itself.

On the other hand, it is apparent that the United States will be increasingly reluctant to undertake unilateral military operations in the Mediterranean. The most likely mode of Western military alignment in situations less serious than outright conflicts, then, will be some form of ad hoc coalition of several allies and friendly states, with the remaining alliance partners maintaining varying degrees of neutrality and vigilance. Such an arrangement is sufficiently reminiscent of the recent coalition in Southeast Asia to be distrusted by many American leaders. Accordingly, the very format of American involvement is likely to be a serious constraint on any less-than-total military undertaking.

The present American basing structure is another serious constraint. In 1954 the United States had 126 major, tactical air-base installations in foreign countries. Today only 59 are still available.[53] All of the air facilities in Arab and North African countries have been closed. Even more serious, friendly states and allies have denied air access or operational rights on their territory during past crises. France, Spain, Greece, and Turkey have, on separate occasions, either refused to allow American aircraft to conduct missions from bases formally leased by the United States or have denied overflight rights; and, in the most recent test of access rights, all the Southern Flank allies except Portugal denied landing and overflight rights to American aircraft engaged in airlift operations during the October War. Denial of overflight rights by France adds over 1,200 miles to flights from Germany to Italy; denial of overflight rights by Spain adds 1,000 miles to flights to the Middle East. Without landing rights in Spain, strategic airlift operations from the United States are confined largely to C-5 and C-141 aircraft carrying substantially smaller cargoes. Without operational rights in Greece or Turkey, tactical air operations in the Eastern Mediterranean are confined to carriers, which might necessitate undue risks in view of the present naval threat. Furthermore, in areas beyond the littoral (e.g., the Persian Gulf, Arabian Peninsula, or Ethiopia), tactical aircraft operating from carriers, even with permissive overflight rights and aerial refueling, can accomplish little more than a show of force. In the past these denials have seriously impeded air operations, and they indicate both the fragility and the necessity of American cooperation with friendly states to support military operations. Thus, the nature and scope of American military undertakings in the Middle East may in large part be dependent upon the basing structure that can be cultivated before the contingency arises and the ability to make do with ad hoc arrangements when prior consent is not gained.

The Soviets are also operating under important constraints, not the least of which are budgetary limitations. At the expense of its Warsaw Pact allies Moscow has diverted major funds to the buildup of its forces along the Chinese border (now representing 40 percent of the Soviet ground and air forces)[54] and in the Middle East (Egypt alone has received over $5 billion in military aid since 1967).[55] These allocations do not include funds for Soviet forces operating in the Middle East, which are mounting annually. These heavy expenditures have occurred at a time of overall national monetary restrictions. The Soviet economy slowed down substantially in 1970, with a planned growth rate for 1971 of only 4.7 percent, the lowest since the mid-1950s. The defense budget for 1971 of 17.9 billion roubles was a reduction in "real" terms and represented only 11.14 percent of the total national budget, the smallest proportion allocated for defense since the early 1950s.[56] This reduction in available funds may impose serious constraints on future construction and on operational costs for navy programs. Other constraints relate directly to the Mediterranean confrontation. Protracted naval hostilities in such confined waters as the Mediterranean would require assured control over one of three possible access routes. However, at present there is little likelihood that Moscow will secure benevolent neutrality or direct control from any of the sovereign states involved. Soviet lines of communication into the Mediterranean are thus always vulnerable to blockade by powerful NATO forces and to the whims of the controlling authorities, seriously complicating the logistics problems. (Indeed, Soviet submarines can normally enter submerged only at Gibraltar.) The use of Arab ports or leased harbor facilities during a protracted conflict would be questionable, since the West would have to disregard international law governing neutral ports and attack SSM-equipped warships wherever they were located. (Target data can easily be transmitted to a SSM vessel, which can launch its missiles even at anchor, and this would obviously jeopardize the possible neutrality of a host government.) Moreover, Soviet airlift operations during hostilities would be readily vulnerable to interdiction by carrier and land-based aircraft, unless they were conducted over Eastern Iran and Iraq en route to Syria, and over Saudi Arabia en route to Egypt. (In contrast, the NATO navies have distinct resupply advantages. They will be operating in the vicinity of home ports or reliable shore supply points, with much broader maintenance and logistic support available than the Soviets can expect from their jointly operated Arab facilities.)

A further constraint on Soviet initiatives is that as many as 1,000 merchant vessels flying socialist flags ply the Mediterranean and European waters or are in NATO ports on any given day. They would become important hostages during crises involving the NATO alliance. In a high-tension situation Moscow would be faced with a choice between curtailing its published maritime schedules and confining its merchant fleet to sanctuaries, knowing the West would regard this as a major precautionary step, and risking the sacrifice of much of its commercial carrying capacity in the hope of preserving an element of surprise. Such sobering options should induce prudence rather than recklessness.

An additional diminution of Soviet military potential centers on the political stability of the Balkans. Hostile operations in the Mediterranean will require dominance of the Black Sea and Turkish neutrality, both of which are contingent upon the formal support or neutrality of the Balkans. Resistance to Soviet efforts by Yugoslavia or Rumania would compromise the moral support needed to justify an aggressive thrust into the Mediterranean, and this could reduce the possibility of Moscow drawing on Warsaw Pact support and resources for operations in a noncontiguous area. Moscow has apparently succeeded in alleviating its allies' most serious reservations about its Middle Eastern policy that were raised in the wake of the June War. At present the Pact nations are displaying a measured disinterest in the Soviet involvement (see appendix 1). Yet its allies' abstention and the greater cohesion of NATO is a good symbol of the marked contrast between fragile Western unity and Moscow's utter isolation in the Middle East from its traditional allies.

Probably the weakest facet of the Soviet strategic posture in the Middle East is the reliability of its new "allies," its sponsored Arab states. In comparison with NATO countries, the military proficiency of Arab armed forces is marginal, and the political vagaries of the Arab world are so uncertain that no single personality or regime can be regarded as a reliable asset for Soviet contingency plans.

Theoretical Projections about Soviet Maritime Intentions
In light of these new maritime capabilities and interests, coupled with the noted deficiencies and constraints, is it possible to forecast Soviet intentions, or the purpose for which these unprecedented resources will be used? Michael McGwire has skillfully analyzed the growing tendency in the West to assess Soviet naval

developments by means of two conflicting schools of thought that emphasize offensive and defensive capabilities, respectively:

The one approach is concerned with the theater-tactical level of threat, and concentrates primarily on Western vulnerability to possible Soviet maritime aggression. Since it reflects the imperatives of contingency planning, its purpose is to identify the most dangerous, rather than the most likely, course of Soviet action. The other approach is concerned with the politicostrategic level of threat, and tries to unravel the main strands of Soviet naval policy since the war, and to assess the Soviet navy's evolving and varying capacity to meet the threat to Russia that the West's maritime superiority has posed. It therefore concentrates on Russia's naval requirements in the face of this threat and tends to highlight the extent of Soviet rather than Western vulnerabilities, as it seeks to identify the nature of their intentions and the most likely course of Soviet action at sea.[57]

While insisting that both approaches are valid and equally necessary, since they represent the distinction between contingency planning and long-range policy formation, McGwire argues that the offensive school makes the logical fallacy of asserting that possible courses of action are categorical statements of Soviet intentions. The theater-oriented interpretation tends to favor "worst-case" assumptions, and therefore generally reflects more alarmist estimates of one's opponent's intentions.

On the other hand, it is too simplistic to accept McGwire's equally categorical assertion that Soviet naval developments have been merely a conditioned-reflex response to Western superiority in aircraft carriers and nuclear submarines. The logical deduction derived from this assumption is that Soviet intentions are purely defensive and that a naval stalemate could be possible if the American carriers and Polaris submarines would only withdraw from the high seas. It is true that, when its maritime resources were literally at a minimal level, Moscow was compelled to adapt as much of its total strength as was feasible to counter principal threats. But, as John Erickson has pointed out, the Soviet Naval Command has been surprisingly tenacious in its attempt to establish an independent naval mission, divorced from army requirements, that could project and protect Soviet interests on the high seas.[58]

As its naval strength began to increase and diversify, a growing proportion of its total inventory could be allocated to fostering and protecting legitimate Soviet national interests that may or may not have been a product of Western maritime activities. But it is fallacious to argue that the Soviet navy entered the Indian Ocean in 1968, for example, primarily to oppose American Polaris submarines. An effective hunter-killer operation in the vast reaches of the Indian Ocean would require far more intensive efforts than the Soviets have so far mounted. Even if such an operation were conducted, its costs would immeasurably exceed its prospects of success against the one or two Polaris submarines that might be in these waters.[59] (Robert Weinland of the Center for Naval Analysis claims that American strategic strike forces have never been assigned to the Indian Ocean, because of exigencies of geography. Therefore, deployment in these waters must have had nothing to do with any strategic threat.)[60] It is more accurate to suggest that Soviet nuclear submarines have been assigned to the Indian Ocean because of their greater endurance, Soviet political interests, and the protection requirements of Moscow's new commercial activities in the Southern hemisphere.

Various Options for the Use of Naval Force
It thus seems accurate to conclude that Moscow is trying to achieve a desirable mix between offensive and defensive naval capabilities and that its overall planning for any given contingency has been guided by the objective of forcing the West to commit a far greater percentage of its offensive resources to the protection of vital maritime objectives than the Soviet Union will have to expend to threaten them.[61] From this point of departure, it is appropriate to examine the possible types of conflict the U.S.S.R. has envisioned in its naval policy and the compara-

tive suitability of the Soviet and American naval units to each situation. Several military contingencies can be itemized for convenience of analysis:

General War Involving Both Great-Power Alliances

In the past both Soviet and Western military writers have usually considered that any great-power conflict would inevitably become nuclear in a short period. The Soviets' classical scenario for Warsaw Pact war games involves either massive retaliation or rapid escalation; that is, NATO attacks the Pact conventionally, the Pact counterattacks conventionally, NATO responds with tactical nuclear weapons, and the Pact retaliates in kind. In general war there are four sets of circumstances that bear on the outcome of this scenario, namely, tactical and strategic warning and no-warning situations:

1. It is conceivable that a defender can be attacked without any prior warning of impending hostilities. In this case the strategic and tactical forces will be struck by a preemptive attack without warning, as apparently occurred at Pearl Harbor.

2. A defender may have confirmed indications that an adversary is mobilizing with hostile intentions. The extent of his preparation and tactical deployments may not be known, but it is evident that his national resources are being readied. In this situation the attacker may achieve complete tactical surprise since the defender will have strategic but not tactical warning, as occurred in the 1968 invasion of Czechoslovakia.

3. A defender may gain both strategic and tactical warning of an impending attack, or may be fully alerted upon receipt of strategic warning so that no tactical surprise is gained. This is then a case of adequate strategic and tactical warning, as seen in the 1943 Battle of Kursk.

4. Upon receipt of strategic warning, a state may attempt to preempt the opponent's attack, as is conceived in the strategic concept of launch-on-warning.

In each of these warning situations, the conflict may be either conventional or nuclear and may involve any combination of allies or friendly states.

Limited Wars Involving Great Powers
American policy makers have sought to reduce the possibility of
a nuclear holocaust by advocating a strategy of flexible response
and minimal use of force. On the other hand, the Soviets have
never formally adopted a strategy of flexible response and are
equipped and trained for a maximal use of force to achieve any
given objective. But as their weapons systems become more sophisticated and their political interests more refined, and as the
risks of a strategic nuclear exchange magnify, the Soviets have
demonstrated a keener interest in containing any conflict with
the West or the United States to a less-than-total engagement.
Thus, each great power may now envision limited conflict as the
most probable means of applying military pressure against its
adversary. It is, then, conceivable to foresee a limited great-power
conflict, either conventional or nuclear, either tactical or strategic, with either warning or no warning.
Conflicts Between Local Contestants
This is the most likely mode of great-power involvement in military operations in the near future. In view of the full spectrum of
local conflict in the twentieth century and the prospects of local
disputes in the 1970s, the opportunities for great-power intervention are already enormous and are likely to increase.[62] Both
great powers now have the physical capability to intervene in
selected local conflicts, and the Soviets' appetite for intervention
may be cautiously increasing while the United States is becoming progressively disinterested in foreign involvements,
especially in unilateral operations. Thus, it is conceivable that
either or both great powers could become involved in a local conflict, unilaterally or in conjunction with a variety of allies or
friendly states. Such an involvement would almost certainly remain conventional.
**Great-Power Peacetime Rivalry with the Threat of Limited
Naval Action**
The threat of limited naval action has been used at least once in
every one of the last 50 years, except 1944. It has been used by 24
states against 52 separate countries, some without even a coast-

line. During the 1960s there were at least two and usually more instances per year. It is important to note that the threat of naval action is a highly refined instrument of policy, applicable to only a small minority of disputes. It has not been employed, for example, in European waters for the past thirty years; yet the Soviets effectively deterred Israel from further attacks against Egyptian ports by permanently stationing warships at Port Said and Alexandria in October 1967.[63] The optimal use of the threat of naval action requires a balanced naval force that can provide maximum mobility and flexibility. The ability of either great power to employ naval threats will remain a function more of the refinement of its fleet composition and the dexterity with which the fleet is applied, than of raw numbers or firepower indices. Nonetheless, it is likely to become an increasingly useful tool, especially for the Soviets.

Has Parity Been Achieved?
The successful establishment of a Soviet presence in the Mediterranean is a genuine historic turning point. Whether this physical asset can be converted to political profit will depend in part upon the extent to which the Soviet Union has reached military parity with other regional powers and upon the susceptibility of local governments to alien pressures. There is no such thing as military equality or absolute parity. The influence of one nation on the policies of others depends largely upon their calculations of the power that can be applied against them and their estimate of how it will be used. Official pronouncements, threats, and promises will not compensate for power that either is dissipated elsewhere or cannot be utilized.[64] Strategic parity in a given region, then, is a function of the degree of symmetrical deterrence and the calculus of risks and uncertainties inherent in any policy or action that may alter the status quo to the detriment of an adversary.

While strategic parity is a relative factor, it can be measured by several criteria: To what extent can each great power protect its interests in any given crisis, unilaterally if necessary? To what extent can one power exploit the weaknesses of the other? To what extent is either prepared or able to protect the interests of clients or allies? By these standards, both great powers suffer important constraints, yet both enjoy limited maneuverability.

In terms of military force, the Soviets have achieved powerful deterrence against the United States by their operations in the Mediterranean. If the Soviets could achieve complete tactical surprise and launch a preemptive nuclear strike against only American capital ships and key bases in this region, it could inflict severe damage, and it would be a long time before sufficient replacements could be deployed to restore the balance. On the other hand, if both sides had adequate warning of an impending nuclear engagement to initiate appropriate defensive precautions, the Soviets would probably sustain such losses that surviving units would no longer constitute a viable fighting force, while the United States would likely forfeit its key warships and numerous aircraft. In a protracted, bilateral, conventional engagement, the United States would have sufficient advantages from the outset that in-being Soviet forces and reinforcements could be effectively neutralized with minimal American losses. If only the Southern Flank of NATO were involved in a conventional conflict with the Soviets and their regional clients, it would likely end in a "superb live-fire exercise" for the West. The number of forces alone ensures that the West can sustain significant attrition rates and still protect its interests. Thus, the degree of military parity exists in proportion to the level of conflict: at the lower end of the spectrum, the West retains sufficient advantages to impose asymmetrical deterrence when important interests are threatened, but the advantages diminish as the scale progresses toward a no-warning nuclear war. On the other hand, the United States has been forced to recognize the Soviet Union's naval stature, since under low-risk circumstances Moscow can also intervene militarily by invitation, in combination with local forces, or unilaterally, with sufficient force and staying power to present NATO with a fait accompli when its important interests are threatened. In other words, the Kremlin now has the strength to alter the status quo in its favor when propitious conditions occur. Thus, it is Moscow's advantages at both ends of the conflict spectrum that have afforded it general recognition as a major Mediterranean power. Sufficient military deterrence has been achieved that Moscow must now be regarded as a political equal with the most powerful regional state or coalition. The United States and NATO must now add anticipated Soviet reactions into all decisions that might be regarded as provocative or might afford opportunities for adverse exploitation. Furthermore, even after accepting calculated risks, American decisions are circumscribed now by the nature of the crisis, the reactions of its individual allies to Soviet responses, and the specific military requirements. Thus, the Soviets' minimum conditions for regional stability can no longer be ignored by other interested powers.

Conclusions: The Implications of Parity

The debate over whether the Soviet navy is basically an offensive or defensive instrument of policy is likely to terminate at last. There is increasing evidence that, during the two periods of national reconstruction, Soviet naval allocations were secondary to those of the ground forces, and the fleets' missions were confined to local defense. In both periods the U.S.S.R. sought to return to the high seas as soon as possible, and it has now achieved a favorable offensive/defensive force mix. While still inferior to the American or NATO navies in terms of balance, Moscow has altered its maritime ambitions to fit its capabilities: to compel its adversary to operate or fight more on its terms than ever before and to commit substantially greater forces than the Soviet Union deploys.

Moscow has succeeded in its aims by employing a wide variety of conceptual improvisations. As a result the United States, long regarded as the oracle of maritime wisdom, has had to modify its concepts of operation and ship design to accommodate the new challenges from the Soviet navy (e.g., Sea Control Carrier trailer vessels and gas-turbine propulsion). Moreover, Moscow apparently has now concluded that in selected contingencies it could inflict sufficient damage against Western or American forces and interests to deter its opponents from risky undertakings, affording it a degree of military parity adequate to allow a significant expansion of its political maneuverability.[65]

In assessing the implications of parity and how this new posture is likely to be applied, it is necessary to emphasize that even limited parity could not have been achieved in response to the purely defensive demands of the Soviet Union. The U.S.S.R. remains a continental power with no strategic naval positions adjacent to oceans whose control is vital to its national security. Accordingly, its naval policies and doctrines have been shaped as much by geography as by the technological developments of its opponents. Its motivation is that of a superpower with global political ambitions that require unprecedented measures to compensate for historic constraints.

Now that the Soviet Union has achieved a strategic/defensive balance that projects a degree of parity and latitude for political maneuver, it is dedicating an increasing portion of its naval operations to the political mission of "advancing Soviet state interests," as announced by Admiral Gorshkov as early as 1967. Politically motivated missions are now conducted in the Mediterranean, the Indian Ocean, and in West African and Latin American waters. Moscow's growing emphasis on the classical facet of seapower as an instrument in influence competition introduces mounting reservations about the long-standing notion that the only value of seapower is to convey nuclear strike forces.[66] The Soviet Union has clearly grasped the importance of the political function of gunboat diplomacy and can be expected to place increased emphasis on this option. (This does not mean that the priority mission of the Soviet forces in the Mediterranean is political; the chief task remains military.)

The utility of this new naval parity in the Mediterranean has already been demonstrated. The Soviet Union is dealing with the United States on the Arab-Israeli settlement from a position of greater military and political equality than at any time in the history of the two countries. It has demonstrated repeatedly that it has sufficient regional power and authority that its clients will not be forced to deal with their local adversaries from a position of inferiority, despite strong adverse American reactions. This new freedom of action has allowed Moscow to exercise a somewhat greater control over local tensions than before and to use them as a means of legitimizing its continued presence in the region. The Soviets are likely to continue this trend in the future even though they have been unable to satisfy all of their sponsored states' demands—in fact, the continuing requests perpetuate the vital legitimizing process.

The U.S.S.R. has also used the demonstration of its new prowess as evidence that its policy of parity is more judicious than that of local radicals or Maoists who demand immediate confrontations with the "imperialists." Moscow argues it can contribute more to a sound basis for the ultimate achievement of its sponsored states' foreign policy aims by first deterring the West, then constraining its freedom of action and policy options, and finally undermining its influence. Such argumentation has had a forceful impact on many local leaders and more than any other instrument of Soviet policy has contributed to the aim of polarizing the region and cultivating political inroads. Thus, the broad aim of Moscow's new overseas strategy in the Mediterranean is to deter the United States, reduce Western influence, and provide staying power for its own political influence among local clients (which is becoming increasingly independent of the East-West challenge-and-response syndrome). The success of this policy to date suggests that it will be pursued with appropriate modifications for the foreseeable future.

Finally, the question must be asked whether appropriate modifications include the objective of gaining naval superiority in the Mediterranean. The answer lies in the linkage between theater and strategic naval policies. The Soviet Union remains a geographically restricted naval power, and it cannot easily compensate for this disadvantage through technology. Nowhere is the Soviet navy more vulnerable to geographic handicaps and its forces more susceptible to hostage practices than in the Mediterranean. In-being forces cannot be reliably reinforced by strategic forces. They cannot even be employed in a classical raider role, as the Northern Fleet might, without jeopardizing the entire theater naval posture. Militarily, these forces can be used only at the extreme ends of the violence spectrum, only preemptively, and only when and where risks permit.[67]

Thus, there appear to be two discernible upper limits to Soviet naval expansion in the Mediterranean. Militarily, its present limited parity cannot be enhanced beyond its ability to maintain a credible integration between its strategic and theater naval forces. There appears to be no assured means of overcoming its geographic disparities in the future, and this will force Moscow to exploit the political utility of its naval power.

The second ceiling on Soviet naval expansion is harder to pin down. It is the degree of political opportunism the Soviets can exercise. Political maneuvering in the Mediterranean is a function of manipulating a wide variety of competing, and often hostile, pressures and interests. The recent experience of the Soviet Union in the Canal War should therefore be examined with several questions in mind: To what extent did the war provide an opportunity for the extension of Soviet political influence? To what extent has this influence been contained? And, finally, can the political function of Moscow's naval posture be more effectively isolated from its purely military presence?

Appendix 3
U.N. Security Council Resolution 242 and Document S/10070

Resolution 242 (1967)

The Security Council,

Expressing its continuing concern with the grave situation in the Middle East,

Emphasizing the inadmissibility of the acquisition of territory by war and the need to work for a just and lasting peace in which every state in the area can live in security,

Emphasizing further that all member states in their acceptance of the Charter of the United Nations have undertaken a commitment to act in accordance with Article 2 of the Charter,

1. *Affirms* that the fulfillment of Charter principles requires the establishment of a just and lasting peace in the Middle East which should include the application of both the following principles:

(i) Withdrawal of Israeli armed forces from territories occupied in the recent conflict;

(ii) Termination of all claims or states of belligerency and respect for and acknowledgment of the sovereignty, territorial integrity, and political independence of every state in the area and their right to live in peace within secure and recognized boundaries free from threats or acts of force;

2. *Affirms further* the necessity

(*a*) for guaranteeing freedom of navigation through international waterways in the area;

(*b*) for achieving a just settlement of the refugee problem;

(*c*) for guaranteeing the territorial inviolability and political independence of every state in the area, through measures including the establishment of demilitarized zones;

3. *Requests* the secretary-general to designate a special repre-

sentative to proceed to the Middle East to establish and maintain contacts with the states concerned in order to promote agreement and assist efforts to achieve a peaceful and accepted settlement in accordance with the provisions and principles in this resolution;

4. *Requests* the secretary-general to report to the Security Council on the progress of the efforts of the special representative as soon as possible.

Adopted unanimously at the
1382nd meeting, 22 November 1967

Document S/10070 [4 January 1971]: Report of the Secretary-General on the Activities of the Special Representative to the Middle East

Introduction

1. On 22 November 1967 the Security Council adopted Resolution 242 (1967). . . .

2. On 23 November 1967 I reported to the Council [*S/8259*] that I had invited Ambassador Gunnar V. Jarring of Sweden to accept the designation as the special representative mentioned in paragraph 3 of the Council's above-mentioned resolution. Ambassador Jarring accepted this designation and arrived at United Nations Headquarters on 26 November, where he entered into consultation with the representatives of Israel, Jordan, Lebanon, and the United Arab Republic (Syria, the other state concerned, did not at that stage or later accept the Security Council resolution). After those consultations with the parties, Ambassador Jarring established the headquarters of the United Nations Middle East Mission in Cyprus.

3. In reports dated 22 December 1967, 17 January 1968, 29 March 1968, 29 July 1968, and 3 December 1968 [*S/8309 and Add.1 to 4, respectively*], I reported to the Security Council on the progress of the efforts of Ambassador Jarring. On 7 August 1970 I was able to inform the Security Council [*S/9902*] that

Israel, Jordan, and the United Arab Republic had agreed to take part in discussions under Ambassador Jarring's auspices for the purpose of reaching agreement on a just and lasting peace between them. Unfortunately and for well known reasons those discussions were interrupted immediately after they began. The members of the Security Council will have been able to observe that in the last few days it has become possible to arrange for the resumption of the discussions. I hope that these resumed discussions will be fruitful. However, it seems appropriate at this time to provide the Security Council with a somewhat fuller account of the activities of the Special Representative than heretofore.

I. Activities of the Special Representative During the Period 9 December 1967 to 26 November 1968

4. When the special representative first met with the parties in December 1967, he found that the Israeli government was of the firm view that a settlement of the Middle East question could be reached only through direct negotiations between the parties culminating in a peace treaty and that there could be no question of withdrawal of their forces prior to such a settlement. On 27 December, the minister for foreign affairs of Israel, Mr. Abba Eban, communicated to the special representative a proposal that Israel and the United Arab Republic representatives should, as a first step, discuss an agenda for peace. The Israeli proposals for such an agenda were:

"1. *Political and juridical problems:* The replacement of cease-fire arrangements by peace treaties ending the state of belligerency, ending all hostile acts and threats, and embodying a permanent undertaking of mutual nonaggression.

"2. *Territorial and security problems:* The determination of agreed territorial boundaries and security arrangements. Agreement on this measure would determine the deployment of armed forces after the cease-fire.

"3. *Navigation problems:* Practical methods should be discussed for ensuring free navigation for all states including Israel in the Suez Canal and the Gulf of Aqaba when the cease-fire is replaced by peace. In the light of tragic experience, it is evident that international declarations cannot by themselves solve this problem. Concrete measures and guarantees are required.

"4. *Economic problems:* Proposals for terminating boycott practices and instituting normal economic relations."

5. The United Arab Republic and Jordan, for their part, insisted that there could be no question of discussions between the parties until the Israeli forces had been withdrawn to the positions occupied by them prior to 5 June 1967. Reacting specifically to the Israeli proposals for discussing an agenda for peace, the minister for foreign affairs of the United Arab Republic, Mr. Mahmoud Riad, stated that the withdrawal of Israel's forces to the positions held prior to June 1967 was a basic and preliminary step to a peaceful settlement in the Middle East.

6. An Israeli proposal for discussions on an agenda for peace with Jordan was submitted to the special representative on 7 January 1968. It followed the same general lines as the proposal for the United Arab Republic but contained more detailed suggestions for economic cooperation, as well as the following new topics:

"*Humanitarian problems:* In the proposed negotiation, high priority should be given to a solution of the refugee problem with international and regional cooperation.

"*Religious and historical sites:* Access to sites of special religious significance should be discussed. The government of Israel clarified its views on this subject in several verbal and written communications to the United Nations."

It was also stated:

"In the meantime, it is urgent that breaches of the cease-fire and activities by El-Fatah and other such organizations should be suppressed and every effort made on both sides to avoid exchanges of fire."

7. The proposals, when communicated to the Jordanian authorities by the special representative, were objected to in the same way as the proposals to the United Arab Republic had been.

8. Faced with these conflicting positions, the special representative sought to obtain from the parties an assurance that they would implement Security Council Resolution 242 (1967), in the

hope that such a declaration would be regarded as a basis for subsequent discussions between the parties. The special representative received from Mr. Eban a number of formulations of Israel's
position on the Security Council resolution, of which the last,
dated 19 February 1968, read as follows:

"1. The government of Israel, out of respect for the Security
Council's resolution of 22 November 1967 and responding affirmatively thereto, assures you of its full cooperation in your efforts
with the states concerned to promote agreement and to achieve
an accepted settlement for the establishment of a just and lasting
peace, in accordance with your mandate under the resolution.

"2. Israel's position has throughout been that the best way to
achieve the objective of the Security Council resolution is through
direct negotiations. However, as a further indication of Israel's
cooperation, we are willing that this be done in a meeting convened by the special representative of the secretary-general.

"3. On 12 February 1968 I informed you of Israel's acceptance
of the Security Council's call in its resolution of 22 November
1967 for the promotion of agreement on the establishment of
peace. The United Arab Republic is also aware of Israel's willingness as explained on 1 February to negotiate on all matters
included in the Security Council's resolution. We accept the
sponsor's view that the principles recommended for inclusion in
the peace settlement are integrally linked and interdependent.

"4. We have noted the United Arab Republic's willingness to
'implement' the Security Council's resolution and fulfill its obligations thereunder. It is a matter of concern that the United Arab
Republic statements, unlike those of Israel, do not specifically
use the precise terms of the resolution in such crucial matters as
'agreement' and the 'establishment of a just and lasting peace',
and that the United Arab Republic has not yet agreed to a process
of negotiation without which, of course, a declaration of willingness to fulfill the resolution is of no substantive effect. The resolution is a framework for *agreement*. It cannot be fulfilled without
a direct exchange of views and proposals leading to bilateral contractual commitments. The United Arab Republic position is,
therefore, still deficient in important respects. We are, however,
conscious of the importance of the fact that the United Arab Republic and Israel have both responded affirmatively to the call
for cooperating with you in the mission laid upon you by the Security Council. At the same time, it would be unrealistic to ignore
that there have been sharp differences of interpretation of what

the resolution entails. To subscribe to similar declarations does not of itself solve practical issues at stake.

"5. It is accordingly urgent to move forward to a more substantive stage and to embark on a meaningful negotiation for achieving the just and lasting peace called for by the Security Council."

In discussions with the special representative, Mr. Eban stated that Israel would not object to an indirect approach to negotiations provided that it was designed to lead to a later stage of direct negotiations and agreement.

9. The United Arab Republic foreign minister gave repeated assurances that the United Arab Republic was ready to implement the Security Council resolution as a whole and to fulfill its obligations under it, but stated that it would not accept direct negotiations. The United Arab Republic accepted indirect negotiations; however, the first step must be an Israeli declaration "in clear language" that it would implement the Security Council resolution.

10. The Jordanian authorities expressed a similar point of view to the special representative.

11. The special representative then proceeded to United Nations Headquarters for consultations with the secretary-general. Returning to the area at the beginning of March, he informally presented to the parties, to ascertain their reactions, a draft letter from himself to the secretary-general, which would be worded as follows:

"The governments of Israel and the United Arab Republic [Jordan] have both indicated to me that they accept Security Council Resolution 242 (1967) of 22 November 1967 for achieving a peaceful and accepted settlement of the Middle East question and intend to devise arrangements, under my auspices, for the implementation of the provisions of the resolution.

"The two governments have expressed their willingness to cooperate with me in my capacity as special representative of the secretary-general in the discharge of my tasks of promoting agreement and achieving such a settlement.

"In view of the urgency of the situation and with a view to expediting efforts to reach settlement, I have invited the two governments to meet with me, for conferences within the framework of the Security Council resolution, in Nicosia. I have pleasure in informing you that the two governments have responded favourably to this invitation."

12. When Ambassador Jarring presented this text to the United Arab Republic foreign minister on 7 March 1968, the latter stated that recent statements by Israeli leaders showed that they were following an expansionist line. It was no longer sufficient to have Israel give an assurance of intent to implement the resolution; the Arabs had to be satisfied that the Israelis were going to "implement it for action." If the Israelis withdrew completely from the occupied territories, peace could be arrived at by the implementation of the other provisions of the Security Council resolution under the Council's guidance.

13. In a meeting on 10 March, the special representative informed the Israeli foreign minister of the United Arab Republic attitude. He then informally showed his draft letter to the foreign minister, who expressed the personal view that it would be fully acceptable to the Israeli authorities if it was also accepted by the other side and led to contacts between them. Subsequently the special representative was informed of Israel's official acceptance, without conditions, of the text.

14. In a meeting on 14 March, the Jordanian authorities stated that they were ready to accept the proposed meeting in principle provided that the text was modified to read that the parties had "declared their readiness to implement the resolution."

15. During the following weeks, Ambassador Jarring paid repeated visits to the countries concerned in an endeavor to obtain from the Israelis a more precise formulation of their acceptance of the resolution and from the two Arab states acceptance of the idea of meetings between the parties under his auspices.

16. At a meeting in Amman on 16 April 1968, the Jordanian authorities stated that they were prepared to accept the text of the special representative's draft letter provided that the third paragraph was amended to read as follows:

"In view of the urgency of the situation and with a view to expediting efforts to reach settlements, I will meet with representatives of Israel and Jordan for conferences within the framework of the Security Council resolution, in New York. I have pleasure in informing you that the two governments have responded favourably hereto."

The acceptance was based on the assumption that the United Arab Republic would accept an identical text.

17. The Israeli authorities found difficulties in the Jordanian amended text. They had accepted meetings at Nicosia, on the understanding that the special representative's invitation would lead to joint meetings. The new text appeared to give the impression that only meetings between the parties and the special representative were intended. The change of venue, while not objectionable in principle, tended to create the impression that only discussions with the permanent missions in the scope of normal United Nations activities would take place; a change from Nicosia to a European city would be acceptable.

18. The United Arab Republic foreign minister at first continued to insist on a prior declaration by Israel of its intention to implement the Security Council resolution. Finally, however, on 9 May, on the eve of the special representative's departure from the area [*see following paragraph*], he replied to the special representative's proposed invitation in the form amended by Jordan in the following written statement:

"With reference to your indication to me today of your desire to meet with a representative of the United Arab Republic in New York, I wish to reaffirm the readiness of our permanent representative to the United Nations in New York to meet with you to continue the contacts which you have been conducting with the parties concerned in accordance with Security Council Resolution 242 (1967) of 22 November 1967 for the implementation of that resolution.

"I have referred in the course of our previous meetings to the importance of the setting of a timetable for the implementation of the resolution of the Security Council, and offered you several alternatives towards that end, one of which was that you present a timetable prepared by yourself for the implementation of the resolution. These suggestions emanate from the United Arab Republic's indication to you of its acceptance and readiness to implement the above-mentioned resolution.

"I wish to express anew our willingness to cooperate with you in your capacity as special representative of the secretary-general in the discharge of your tasks as defined in the Council's resolution of 22 November 1967."

The United Arab Republic foreign minister repeated that the United Arab Republic was ready to implement the resolution as a whole and as a "package deal." It insisted, however, that Israel should do likewise, including complete withdrawal.

19. Ambassador Jarring was faced with a position where there was now agreement, though clearly with considerable differences of interpretation, on the first two paragraphs of his proposed invitation, but where there was disagreement on the third paragraph containing the actual invitation. Further journeying backwards and forwards between the various countries was unlikely to be productive. In consultations with me, he considered issuing a formal invitation along the lines of his proposal, but with the venue at New York, but it was felt that a forced acceptance obtained by such an invitation would not be helpful. Instead it was decided that the talks in New York should begin without a formal invitation by the special representative or a letter from the special representative to the secretary-general but on the basis of a short statement to the press in which it would be announced that the special representative was arriving in New York for consultations in continuation of his mission.

20. During his stay in the area, the special representative visited Beirut on three occasions. The Lebanese government expressed its full support for a solution according to Security Council Resolution 242 (1967). Lebanon, however, had no territory under occupation and therefore did not have the same detailed involvement in the settlement as the United Arab Republic and Jordan. The special representative did not visit Syria, whose government, as noted above, had not accepted the Security Council resolution.

21. Ambassador Jarring left the area on 10 May 1968 and arrived at headquarters on 15 May 1968.

22. In the five weeks following his arrival in New York, Ambassador Jarring pursued actively his contacts with the permanent representatives of the parties at both a formal and informal level. Unfortunately these contacts did not serve in any way to break the deadlock between the parties concerning the interpretation of the Security Council resolution and the manner in which it should be implemented. In that regard, the representative of Israel had stated in the Security Council on 1 May 1968:

"In declarations and statements made publicly and to Mr. Jarring, my government has indicated its acceptance of the Security Council resolution [242 (1967)] for the promotion of agreement on the establishment of a just and durable peace. I am also authorized to reaffirm that we are willing to seek agreement with each Arab state on all the matters included in that resolution." [1418th meeting, para. 111.]

This statement was not regarded as acceptable by the Arab representatives.

23. Returning to New York on 22 July after a short stay in Europe during which he had met in various capitals the foreign ministers of the United Arab Republic, Israel, and Jordan, Ambassador Jarring decided, with my approval, to return to the Middle East and resume his direct contacts with the parties. This second round of discussions, which began on 16 August 1968, took the form of an exchange of questions and of comments between the parties through the special representative. Some progress in the clarification of the respective positions of the parties had been made when the opening of the twenty-third session of the General Assembly caused the venue of the discussions to be transferred to New York, where they could be carried out with greater convenience. With the arrival of the foreign ministers of the parties for the session towards the end of September, Ambassador Jarring began a series of frequent meetings with them individually, which were at first mainly of an informal nature but which, following the delivery by the foreign ministers of their

speeches in the general debate, assumed a more formal character and concluded with written communications from the foreign ministers of Israel and of the United Arab Republic restating the positions of their respective governments. Those written statements were in amplification of the positions of the parties as publicly stated in the General Assembly and made clear the essential differences between them. On the one hand, Israel regarded the Security Council resolution as a statement of principles in the light of which the parties should negotiate peace and, on the other hand, the United Arab Republic considered that the resolution provided a plan for settlement of the Middle East dispute to be implemented by the parties according to modalities to be established by the special representative. It was also abundantly clear that there was a crucial difference of opinion over the meaning to be attached to the withdrawal provisions of the Security Council resolution, which according to the Arab states applied to all territories occupied since 5 June 1967 and according to Israel applied only to the extent required when agreement had been reached between the parties on secure and recognized borders between them.

24. Discouraging though the prospects seemed, Ambassador Jarring decided to carry out another brief round of discussions in the Middle East. As he explained in a letter to me dated 26 November 1968, he had in mind inviting the parties to a new round of discussions in the middle of January 1969 in order to give them time for reflection and for careful consideration of their respective positions.

II. Activities of the Special Representative from 27 November 1968 to June 1970

25. Ambassador Jarring departed from headquarters on 27 November 1968 and met representatives of Israel in Nicosia on 2 and 3 December, of the United Arab Republic in Cairo on 4 December, and of Jordan in Amman on 7 December. Unfortunately, these meetings did not reveal a change of position in the attitude of the parties that would have made it expedient for Ambassador Jarring to convene a meeting of the parties in the

middle of January 1969, as envisaged in his letter of 26 November 1968.

26. After resuming for a time his duties as ambassador of Sweden to the Union of Soviet Socialist Republics, Ambassador Jarring returned to headquarters on 29 January 1969. He there undertook a series of personal contacts with the representatives of the parties and the representatives of other member states.

27. At that stage Ambassador Jarring concluded, with my concurrence, that the best contribution which he could make to breaking the existing deadlock was to make a further tour of the Middle East in which he would formally submit to the parties a series of questions designed to elicit their attitude towards Security Council Resolution 242 (1967). He accordingly left New York on 21 February 1969 for the Middle East. At meetings with the foreign ministers of the United Arab Republic on 5 March, of Jordan on 8 March, of Israel on 9 March, and of Lebanon on 14 March, he submitted the questions which he had previously prepared. The replies of the parties were received by Ambassador Jarring as follows:

Israel: handed to Ambassador Jarring in Jerusalem by the minister for foreign affairs on 2 April 1969.

Jordan: received by Ambassador Jarring in Nicosia on 24 March 1969.

Lebanon: received by Ambassador Jarring in Moscow on 21 April 1969.

United Arab Republic: handed to Ambassador Jarring in Cairo by the minister for foreign affairs of the United Arab Republic on 27 March 1969.

The questions and replies are reproduced in annex I.

28. It had been the hope of Ambassador Jarring, in submitting his questions, that the replies might show certain encouraging features which might make it possible to invite the parties for a series of meetings between them and him at some mutually convenient place. Unfortunately, the replies were in general a repetition of attitudes already expressed to Ambassador Jarring on numerous occasions from the beginning of his mission. They

showed continued serious divergencies between the Arab states and Israel both as regards the interpretation to be given to the Security Council resolution and as to the procedures for putting its provisions into effect.

29. Ambassador Jarring was regretfully forced to conclude, with my agreement, that the conditions for convening a useful series of meetings at that time did not exist and that there was no further move which he could usefully make at that stage. He therefore returned on 5 April 1969 to Moscow, where he resumed his duties as ambassador of Sweden to the Union of Soviet Socialist Republics.

30. Ambassador Jarring continued to keep in close touch with me and with representatives of the parties and of other interested states.

31. Ambassador Jarring returned to headquarters from 12 September to 8 October 1969 and from 10 to 26 March 1970, but found no new elements which would permit him to organize active discussions with the parties. On each occasion he returned to his post in Moscow.

32. On 3 April 1969 the representatives of France, the Union of Soviet Socialist Republics, the United Kingdom of Great Britain and Northern Ireland, and the United States of America began a series of meetings on the Middle East question, which have continued at various intervals up to the present time. After each such meeting, the chairman reported to me on the substance of the discussions and I kept Ambassador Jarring informed.

III. The Attempt to Hold Discussions Under the Special Representative's Auspices (June 1970 to 4 January 1971)

33. In June 1970 the government of the United States of America proposed to the governments of Israel, Jordan, and the United Arab Republic that they should each advise Ambassador Jarring as follows:

(a) that having accepted and indicated their willingness to carry out Resolution 242 (1967) in all its parts, they would designate representatives to discussions to be held under his auspices, according to such procedure and at such places and times as he might recommend, taking into account as appropriate each side's preference as to method of procedure and previous experience between the parties;

(*b*) that the purpose of the aforementioned discussions was to reach agreement on the establishment of a just and lasting peace between them based on (1) mutual acknowledgment by the United Arab Republic, Jordan, and Israel of each other's sovereignty, territorial integrity, and political independence, and (2) Israeli withdrawal from territories occupied in the 1967 conflict, both in accordance with Resolution 242 (1967);

(*c*) that, to facilitate his task of promoting agreement as set forth in Resolution 242 (1967), the parties would strictly observe, effective 1 July at least until 1 October, the cease-fire resolutions of the Security Council.

34. Having been informed by the United States government that the states concerned had accepted its peace initiative, I invited Ambassador Jarring to return immediately to headquarters, where he arrived on 2 August. I informed the Security Council in a note dated 7 August 1970 [*S/9902*] that Ambassador Jarring had received confirmation from the representatives of those states of their acceptance and that he had addressed to me a letter as described above. I was informed by the United States representative that his government had received the acceptance of the governments of the United Arab Republic and Israel to a standstill cease-fire for a period of ninety days from 2200 GMT on the same day. Ambassador Jarring and I had previously been informed by the secretary of state, Mr. Rogers, that his government would take responsibility for organizing the standstill cease-fire.

35. Ambassador Jarring at once entered into contact with the parties and, after considering their views on the time and place of the discussions, on 21 August 1970 addressed to them invitations to take part in discussions opening in New York on 25 August 1970. On the appointed day he met representatives of each of the parties. However, Ambassador Tekoah, who had been designated by Israel as its representative for the initial phase of the talks, then stated that he had been instructed by his government to re-

turn to Israel for consultations. On his return on 8 September, he communicated to Ambassador Jarring the following decision of his government:

"Israel's acceptance of the United States peace initiative according to its decision of 4 August 1970, and the appointment of a representative to the talks under the auspices of Ambassador Jarring are still in effect.

"The government of Egypt has gravely violated the cease-fire-standstill agreement, and this violation is continuing without let-up.

"The strictest observance of the cease-fire-standstill agreement is one of the central elements of the American peace initiative and of the talks under the auspices of Ambassador Jarring. Therefore, so long as the cease-fire-standstill agreement is not observed in its entirety, and the original situation restored, Israel will not be able to participate in these talks.

"Ambassador Tekoah, who is returning to his post as head of the permanent delegation of Israel at the United Nations, has been authorized to bring this decision of the government of Israel to the attention of Ambassador Jarring."

The special representative thus found himself precluded for the time being from holding formal meetings with the Israeli representatives, and his talks with the representatives of the Arab states, though they continued, could not be productive because of the lack of contact with the Israeli representative. After a brief visit to Moscow from 6 to 14 October to attend to his affairs as ambassador of Sweden there, the special representative returned to New York and had a wide range of contacts with representatives of the parties and of other member states during the commemorative session of the General Assembly and the debate on the Middle East, which followed that session.

36. Immediately following the adoption of General Assembly Resolution 2628 (XXV), Ambassador Jarring entered into contact with the representatives of the parties in order to invite them to reenter into talks under his auspices for the purpose of reaching agreement on the establishment of a just and lasting peace. The representatives of Jordan and the United Arab Republic informed him that their governments continued to be willing to

do so; the representative of Israel stated that the matter was under consideration in the Israeli cabinet.

37. On 19 November and pending a decision by the Israeli cabinet, Ambassador Jarring returned to Moscow. On the eve of his departure, he addressed a letter to the Israeli minister for foreign affairs, in which he formally invited the Israeli government to resume its participation in the discussions, as well as letters to the representatives of Jordan and the United Arab Republic, in which he took note of the position of their governments.

38. On 30 December, Ambassador Jarring received in Moscow a message from the foreign minister of Israel in which the latter informed him of the readiness of the government of Israel to resume its participation in the talks.

Annex I to Document S/10070: Questions Submitted in March 1969 by the Special Representative to the Governments Concerned and Their Replies*
A. Questions Submitted by the Special Representative
Security Council Resolution 242 (1967) sets out provisions and principles in accordance with which a peaceful and accepted settlement of the Middle East question should be achieved. Some of these provisions would impose obligations on both sides, some on one side, and some on the other. It has generally been accepted that they should be regarded as a whole. The following questions designed to elicit the attitude of the parties towards the provisions of the Security Council resolution are based on this

---

* Ambassador Jarring submitted his questions to the states concerned in the form of separate lists specifically addressed to each government. Those lists were, however, prepared from a general list applicable to all the parties and that list is, to save repetition, reproduced here. As some questions related to provisions of Security Council Resolution 242 (1967) which applied to only one or some of the parties, the numbers of questions in the specific lists were not always the same as those in the general list. Where the number of the answer differs from that of the question in the general list, the latter number is added in square brackets.

Specific lists of questions based on the following general list were submitted by Ambassador Jarring to the governments of the United Arab Republic on 5 March, of Jordan on 8 March, of Israel on 9 March, and of Lebanon on 14 March 1969.

assumption and are to be understood in the context that each provision is regarded as part of a "package deal."

1. Does Israel (Jordan, Lebanon, United Arab Republic) accept Security Council Resolution 242 (1967) for implementation for achieving a peaceful and accepted settlement of the Middle East question in accordance with the provisions and principles contained in the resolution?

2. Does Israel (Jordan, Lebanon, United Arab Republic) agree to pledge termination of all claims or states of belligerency with Jordan, Lebanon, and the United Arab Republic (Israel)?

3. Does Israel (Jordan, Lebanon, United Arab Republic) agree to pledge respect for and acknowledgment of the sovereignty, territorial integrity, and political independence of Jordan, Lebanon, and the United Arab Republic (Israel)?

4. Does Israel (Jordan, Lebanon, United Arab Republic) accept the right of Jordan, Lebanon, and the United Arab Republic (Israel) to live in peace within secure and recognized boundaries free from threats or acts of force?

5. If so, what is the conception of secure and recognized boundaries held by Israel (Jordan, Lebanon, United Arab Republic)?

6. Does Israel agree to withdraw its armed forces from territories occupied by it in the recent conflict?

7. Does the United Arab Republic agree to guarantee freedom of navigation for Israel through international waterways in the area, in particular:

(a) through the Straits of Tiran, and

(b) through the Suez Canal?

8. Does Israel (Jordan, Lebanon, United Arab Republic) agree that, if a plan for the just settlement of the refugee problem is worked out and presented to the parties for their consideration, the acceptance in principle of such a plan by the parties and the declaration of their intention to implement it in good faith constitute sufficient implementation of this provision of the Security Council resolution to justify the implementation of the other provisions?

9. Does Israel (Jordan, Lebanon, United Arab Republic) agree

that the territorial inviolability and political independence of
the states in the area should be guaranteed:

(a) by the establishment of demilitarized zones;

(b) through additional measures?

10. Does Israel agree that such demilitarized zones should include areas on its side of its boundaries?

11. Does Jordan agree that a demilitarized zone should be established in Jordanian territory from which Israeli armed forces
have been withdrawn?

12. Does the United Arab Republic agree that a demilitarized
zone should be established:

(a) at Sharm el Sheikh;

(b) in other parts of the Sinai peninsula?

13. Does Israel (Jordan, Lebanon, United Arab Republic)
agree that demilitarization of such zones should be supervised
and maintained by the United Nations?

14. Would Israel (Jordan, Lebanon, United Arab Republic)
accept as a final act of agreement on all provisions a mutually
signed multilateral document which would incorporate the
agreed conditions for a just and lasting peace?

**B. Reply of the Government of Israel (Handed to
Ambassador Jarring in Jerusalem by the Minister
for Foreign Affairs on 2 April 1969)**

[2 April 1969]

Israel's position on all the subjects raised in your eleven questions has been stated in detail in my address to the General Assembly of 8 October 1968, and in the memoranda presented to
you on 15 October 1968 and 4 November 1968.

I now enclose specific replies in an affirmative spirit to the
questions as formulated. It is my understanding that on the basis
of the answers received from the three governments you propose
to pursue further mutual clarifications in an effort to promote
agreement on all the matters at issue in accordance with your
mandate. We are ready to join in this process at any appropriate
place.

Israel's statements of attitude, including her replies to these questions, has taken into account recent developments in Arab policy including the speeches recently delivered by President Nasser and other Arab leaders. We have noted the specific and emphatic reiteration of their refusal to make peace with Israel, to recognize Israel, to negotiate with Israel, to cease terrorist attacks on Israel, or to admit the possibility of sovereign coexistence in any field. It would appear at this time that the effective negation by the United Arab Republic of the principles of the Charter and of the Security Council's resolution is obvious and vehement. We hope that this policy, to which effect is given every day, will change; but these authoritative statements have caused deep concern and have intensified the tension which we would have wished to see relieved.

It is also our view that highly publicized encounters by four member states have weakened the attention which should have been concentrated on the efforts of the parties themselves to move towards agreement. They are causing a duplication and dispersal of effort. They have also encouraged a wrong impression in some quarters that a solution can be sought outside the region and without its governments. Israel recognizes your mission as the authoritative international framework within which peace between the states in the Middle East should be promoted.

I recall the idea which we discussed some weeks ago that the foreign ministers of the three governments should meet with you soon at a suitable place to pursue the promotion of agreement. As you will remember, I reacted positively to this idea. I wish to reaffirm that Israel will continue to cooperate with you in the fulfillment of your mission.

(Signed) Abba EBAN
Minister for Foreign Affairs
of Israel

Answer to question 1

Israel accepts the Security Council Resolution 242 (1967) for the promotion of agreement on the establishment of a just and

lasting peace, to be reached by negotiation and agreements be
tween the governments concerned. Implementation of agreements should begin when agreement has been concluded on all
their provisions.

Answer to question 2

It is the Arab states, not Israel, which claimed and originated
states of belligerency. They declared themselves for two decades
to be in a state of unilateral war with Israel. It is therefore primarily incumbent upon them to terminate the state of war with
Israel.

On the establishment of peace with its Arab neighbours, Israel
agrees to the termination, on a reciprocal basis, of all claims or
states of belligerency with each state with which peace is established. A declaration specifying each state by name would be
made by Israel in each case.

The corresponding statement by any Arab state must specifically renounce belligerency "with Israel" and not "with any state
in the area." Legal obligations must be specific in regard to those
by whom they are bound.

Renunciation of belligerency includes the cessation of all maritime interference; the cessation of boycott measures involving
third parties; the annulment of reservations made by Arab states
on the applicability to Israel of their obligations under international conventions to which they have adhered; nonadherence to
political and military alliances and pacts directed against Israel
or including states unwilling to renounce claims or states of belligerency with Israel and maintain peaceful relations with it; the
nonstationing of armed forces of such other states on the territory
of the contracting states and the prohibition and prevention in
the territory of Arab states of all preparations, actions, or expeditions by irregular or paramilitary groups or by individuals directed against the lives, security, or property of Israel in any part
of the world.

The last stipulation is without prejudice to the fact that the
responsibility of Arab governments for preventing such activities

is legally binding under the cease-fire established by the parties in June 1967.

Answer to question 3

Israel agrees to respect and acknowledge the sovereignty, territorial integrity, and political independence of neighbouring Arab states; this principle would be embodied in peace treaties establishing agreed boundaries.

Answer to question 4

Israel accepts the right of Jordan, Lebanon, the United Arab Republic, and other neighbouring states to live in peace within secure and recognized boundaries, free from threats or acts of force. Explicit and unequivocal reciprocity is Israel's only condition for this acceptance. "Acts of force" include all preparations, actions, or expeditions by irregular or paramilitary groups or by individuals directed against the life, security, or property of Israel in any part of the world.

Answer to question 5

Secure and recognized boundaries have never yet existed between Israel and the Arab states; accordingly, they should now be established as part of the peacemaking process. The cease-fire should be replaced by peace treaties establishing permanent, secure, and recognized boundaries as agreed upon through negotiation between the governments concerned.

Answer to question 6

When permanent, secure, and recognized boundaries are agreed upon and established between Israel and each of the neighbouring Arab states, the disposition of forces will be carried out in full accordance with the boundaries determined in the peace treaties.

Answer to question 7 [General question 8]

The refugee problem was caused by the wars launched against Israel by Arab states, and has been perpetuated through the refusal of Arab states to establish peaceful relations with Israel. In view of the human problems involved in this issue Israel has expressed its willingness to give priority to the attainment of an agreement for the solution of this problem through regional and international cooperation. We believe that agreement could be sought even in advance of peace negotiations. We suggest that a conference of Middle Eastern states should be convened, together with the governments contributing to refugee relief and the specialized agencies of the United Nations, in order to chart a five-year plan for the solution of the refugee problem in the framework of a lasting peace and the integration of refugees into productive life. This conference can be called in advance of peace negotiations.

Joint refugee integration and rehabilitation commissions should be established by the governments concerned in order to work out agreed projects for refugee integration on a regional basis with international assistance.

In view of the special humanitarian nature of this issue we do not make agreement on plans for a solution to the refugee problem contingent on agreement on any other aspect of the Middle Eastern problem. For the same reason it should not be invoked by Arab states to obstruct agreement on other problems.

Answer to question 8 [General question 9]

The effective guarantee for the territorial inviolability and political independence of states lies in the strict observance by the governments of their treaty obligations. In the context of peace providing for full respect for the sovereignty of states and the establishment of agreed boundaries, other security measures may be discussed by the contracting governments.

Answer to questions 9 and 10 [General questions 10 and 13]

Without prejudice to what is stated in answer to question 8, it is pointed out that experience has shown that the measures mentioned in questions 9 and 10 have not prevented the preparation and carrying out of aggression against Israel.

Answer to question 11 [General question 14]

Peace must be juridically expressed, contractually defined, and reciprocally binding in accordance with established norms of international law and practice. Accordingly, Israel's position is that the peace should be embodied in bilateral peace treaties between Israel and each Arab state incorporating all the agreed conditions for a just and lasting peace. The treaties, once signed and ratified, should be registered with the Secretariat of the United Nations in accordance with Article 102 of the United Nations Charter.

C. Reply of the Government of Jordan (Received by Ambassador Jarring in Nicosia on 24 March 1969)
[23 March 1969]

Following are the answers of my government to the questions which you presented to us in Amman, on Saturday, 8 March 1969. The answers as numbered, hereunder, correspond to your questions.

These answers explain my government's position, which position has repeatedly been stated to you throughout our past meetings.

May I take this opportunity to express to you my continued sincere wishes for your success in the important mission with which you are entrusted.

(Signed) Abdul Monem RIFA'I
Minister for Foreign Affairs
of Jordan

Answer to question 1

Jordan, as it has declared before, accepts Security Council Resolution 242 (1967) and is ready to implement it in order to achieve a peaceful and accepted settlement in accordance with the provisions and principles contained in the resolution.

Answer to question 2

Jordan agrees to pledge termination of all claims or states of belligerency. Such a pledge becomes effective upon withdrawal of Israeli forces from all Arab territories which Israel has occupied as a result of its aggression of 5 June 1967.

A pledge by Israel to terminate the state of belligerency would be meaningful only when Israel withdraws its forces from all Arab territories it has occupied since 5 June 1967.

Answer to question 3

On 5 June 1967 Israel launched its aggression against three Arab states, violating their sovereignty and territorial integrity. Agreement to pledge respect for and acknowledgment of the sovereignty, territorial integrity, and political independence of every state in the area requires the termination by Israel of its occupation and the withdrawal of its forces from all the Arab territories it occupied as a result of its aggression of 5 June.

Answer to question 4

Jordan accepts the right of every state in the area to live in peace within secure and recognized boundaries free from threats or acts of force, provided that Israel withdraws its forces from all Arab territories it occupied since 5 June 1967, and implements the Security Council resolution of 22 November 1967.

Answer to question 5

When the question of Palestine was brought before the United Nations in 1947, the General Assembly adopted its Resolution

181 (II) of 29 November 1947 for the partition of Palestine and defined Israel's boundaries.

Answer to question 6 [General question 8]

It has always been our position that the just settlement of the refugee problem is embodied in paragraph 11 of General Assembly Resolution 194 (III) of 11 December 1948 which has been repeatedly reaffirmed by each and every General Assembly session ever since its adoption.

If a plan on the basis of that paragraph is presented for consideration to the parties concerned, its acceptance by the parties and the declaration of their intention to implement it in good faith, with adequate guarantees for its full implementation, would justify the implementation of the other provisions of the resolution.

Answer to questions 7 and 8 [General questions 9 and 11]

We do not believe that the establishment of demilitarized zones is a necessity. However, Jordan shall not oppose the establishment of such zones if they are astride the boundaries.

Answer to question 9 [General question 13]

If demilitarized zones are established, Jordan accepts that such zones be supervised and maintained by the United Nations.

Answer to question 10 [General question 14]

In view of our past experience with Israel and her denunciation of four agreements signed by her with Arab states, we consider that the instrument to be signed by Jordan engaging her to carry out her obligations would be addressed to the Security Council. Israel would likewise sign and address to the Security Council an instrument engaging her to carry out her obligations emanating from the Security Council resolution of 22 November 1967. The endorsement by the Security Council of these documents would constitute the final multilateral act of agreement.

D. Reply of the Government of Lebanon (Received by Ambassador Jarring in Moscow on 21 April 1969)

In reply to the questionnaire which you addressed to me on 14 March 1969, I have the honour, on behalf of the Lebanese government, to inform you of the following:

Lebanon is essentially involved in the general context of the Israeli-Arab conflict—and, therefore, in the consequences of the war launched by Israel on 5 June 1967—because of its brotherly solidarity with the Arab states and of the threats which are constantly directed at it by Israel.

Lebanon is justified in considering, however, that the armistice agreement which it concluded with Israel on 23 March 1949 remains valid, as indicated in its message of 10 June 1967 to the chairman of the Mixed Armistice Commission and as confirmed by U Thant, secretary-general of the United Nations, in his report to the General Assembly of 19 September 1967. In that report, Mr. Thant, referring to the actual text of the agreement, said that it could be revised or suspended only by mutual consent. In view of Lebanon's circumstances, now and in the past, the armistice lines have, of course, never been changed. These lines, it should be noted, correspond to the frontiers of Lebanon which have always been internationally recognized in bilateral and multilateral diplomatic instruments as well as by the League of Nations and the United Nations. Lebanon participated actively in the drafting of the United Nations Charter and was admitted in its present form and structure to membership in the organization. Its frontiers have not undergone any de facto or de jure alteration as a result of the cease-fire decisions taken by the Security Council after 5 June 1967.

It may be appropriate to state the above-mentioned facts, more particularly with a view to explaining the nature and character of the only reply which we are in a position to give to the questionnaire you sent to us on 14 March 1969.

In this reply, which reflects the position taken by Lebanon at inter-Arab conferences, we proclaim Lebanon's support of the position of the Arab states whose territory has been occupied by

Israel and which have accepted the Security Council's decision of 22 November 1967.

The present note is consistent with the spirit of the talks which you have already held with various Lebanese officials.

(Signed) Yousset SALEM
Minister for Foreign Affairs
of Lebanon

E. Reply of the Government of the United Arab Republic (Handed to Ambassador Jarring in Cairo by the Minister for Foreign Affairs of the United Arab Republic on 27 March 1969)

[27 March 1969]

The memorandum handed to you on 5 March 1969 during your recent visit to Cairo clearly expresses the realities of the present situation. In its items 1 to 7, the memorandum gives a clear restatement of the position of the United Arab Republic which is based on the acceptance of Security Council Resolution 242 (1967) of 22 November 1967, and its readiness to carry out the obligations emanating therefrom.

The memorandum also clearly expounds Israel's persistence in rejecting the Security Council resolution and its refusal to carry out its obligations emanating from it as well as Israel's plans for annexation of Arab lands through war; a policy which is not only prohibited by the Charter of the United Nations but which also violates the Security Council resolution which specifically emphasizes the inadmissibility of the acquisition of territory by war. It has become obvious that Israel, in its endeavour to realize its expansionist aims, is no longer satisfied with the actual rejection of the Security Council resolution but actively works against it.

The same memorandum also states Israel's expansion plan as revealed by the quoted statements of Israeli leaders. This plan aims at:

1. annexation of Jerusalem;
2. keeping the Syrian Heights under its occupation;

3. occupation of the West Bank in Jordan and its complete domination, practically terminating Jordan's sovereignty in that
   part;
4. economic and administrative integration of the Gaza Strip
   into Israel and the systematic eviction of its inhabitants;
5. occupation of Sharm el Sheikh and the Gulf of Aqaba area as
   well as the continued military presence in eastern part of
   Sinai;
6. the establishment of Israeli settlements in occupied territories.

This Israeli position constitutes a flagrant violation and clear
rejection of the Security Council resolution of 22 November 1967
and of the peaceful settlement for which it provides.

In the light of these undeniable facts, I find it incumbent
upon me to state categorically, at the outset of the replies to the
specific questions you addressed to the United Arab Republic on
5 March 1969, that all the answers of the United Arab Republic,
which reaffirm its acceptance of the Security Council resolution
and its readiness to carry out the obligations emanating from
it require, likewise, that Israel accept the resolution and carry
out all its obligations emanating from it and in particular withdrawal from all Arab territories it occupied as a result of its
aggression of 5 June 1967.

Answer to question 1

The United Arab Republic, as it has declared before, accepts
Security Council Resolution 242 (1967) and is ready to implement
it in order to achieve a peaceful and accepted settlement in accordance with the provisions and principles contained therein.

Answer to question 2

The United Arab Republic agrees to pledge termination of all
claims or state of belligerency. Such a pledge becomes effective
upon withdrawal of Israel's forces from all Arab territories occupied as a result of Israel's aggression of 5 June 1967.

A declaration by Israel terminating the state of belligerency would be meaningful only when Israel withdraws her forces from all Arab territories it has occupied since 5 June 1967.

Answer to question 3

On 5 June 1967 Israel launched its aggression against three Arab states violating their sovereignty and territorial integrity. Acceptance by the United Arab Republic to pledge respect for and acknowledgment of the sovereignty, territorial integrity, and political independence of every state in the area requires the termination by Israel of its occupation and the withdrawal of its forces from all the Arab territories it has occupied as a result of its aggression of 5 June, and the full implementation of the Security Council resolution of 22 November 1967.

Answer to question 4

The United Arab Republic accepts the right of every state in the area to live in peace within secure and recognized boundaries free from threats or acts of force, provided that Israel withdraws its forces from all Arab territories occupied as a result of its aggression of 5 June 1967, and implements the Security Council resolution of 22 November 1967.

Answer to question 5

When the question of Palestine was brought before the United Nations in 1947, the General Assembly adopted its Resolution 181 of 29 November 1947 for the partition of Palestine and defined Israel's boundaries.

Answer to question 6 [General question 7]

We have declared our readiness to implement all the provisions of the Security Council resolution covering, inter alia, the freedom of navigation of international waterways in the area; provided that Israel, likewise, implements all the provisions of the Security Council resolution.

Answer to question 7 [General question 8]

It has always been our position that the just settlement of the refugee problem is embodied in paragraph 11 of the General Assembly Resolution 194 of December 1948, which has been unfailingly reaffirmed by each and every General Assembly session ever since its adoption.

If a plan on the basis of that paragraph is presented for consideration to the parties concerned, its acceptance by the parties and the declaration of their intention to implement it in good faith, with adequate guarantees for its full implementation, would justify the implementation of the other provisions of the Security Council resolution.

Answer to questions 8 and 9 [General questions 9 and 12]

We do not believe the establishment of demilitarized zones is a necessity. However, the United Arab Republic will not oppose the establishment of such zones if they are astride the boundaries.

Answer to question 10 [General question 13]

In case demilitarized zones are established, the United Arab Republic accepts that such zones be supervised and maintained by the United Nations.

Answer to question 11 [General question 14]

In view of our past experience with Israel and her denunciation of four agreements signed by her with Arab states, we consider the instrument to be signed by the United Arab Republic engaging her to carry out her obligations should be addressed to the Security Council. Israel should, likewise, sign and address to the Security Council an instrument engaging her to carry out her obligations emanating from the Security Council resolution of 22 November 1967. The endorsement by the Security Council of these documents would constitute the final multilateral document.

Notes

Preface

1. David Morison, "Soviet Dilemma in the Middle East," *New Middle East,* January 1970, p. 42.

Chapter 1

1. I. F. Stone, "Holy War," in *The Arab-Israeli Reader,* edited by Walter Laqueur, Bantam Books, 1969, p. 324.

2. David Ben Gurion, *Ben Gurion Looks Back,* Simon and Schuster, 1966, p. 33.

3. Dan Avni-Segre, "Israel: A Society in Transition," *World Politics,* April 1969; see also Amos Perlmutter, *Military and Politics in Israel,* Frank Cass (London), 1969.

4. Amnon Rubinstein, "The Struggle Between Founders and Sons," *Encounter,* November 1968, pp. 64–69; and S. C. Leslie, "The Rift in Israel," *International Affairs,* July 1969, pp. 437–451.

5. Herbert Pundik, "Israel's Arabs Establish Their Identity," *New Middle East,* August 1969, p. 563; see also Don Peretz, "The Arab Refugees: A Changing Problem," *Foreign Affairs,* April 1969, pp. 31–32.

6. *New York Times,* 31 January 1969; see also Y. Harkabi, "Fedayeen Action and Arab Strategy," Adelphi Papers No. 53, International Institute for Strategic Studies (IISS), 1968.

7. Moshe Dayan, interviews in *Der Stern,* 28 September 1969, and the *Jerusalem Post,* 16 September 1969; and Amos Perlmutter, "The Real Power of Moshe Dayan," *New Middle East,* May 1969, pp. 26–27.

8. *New Middle East,* May 1969, p. 49.

9. The "four powers" referred to here and in the remainder of the book are the Soviet Union, the United States, Egypt, and Israel. The term "four big

powers" will be used to refer to the United States, the Soviet Union, Great Britain, and France.

Chapter 2

1. Quoted in Ivo J. Lederer, "Russia and the Balkans," in *Russian Foreign Policy: Essays in Historical Perspective,* edited by Ivo J. Lederer, Yale University Press, 1962, p. 420.

2. Firuz Kazemzadeh, "Russia in the Middle East," ibid., p. 520; Max Beloff, *The Foreign Policy of Soviet Russia, 1936–41,* Oxford University Press, 1949, pp. 39–42; Walter Z. Laqueur, *The Soviet Union and the Middle East,* Routledge and Kegan Paul, 1959, passim; and H. N. Howard, *The Problem of the Turkish Straits,* United States Department of State, 1947, pp. 1–68.

3. Kazemzadeh, "Russia in the Middle East," pp. 507–515.

4. R. Ainsztein, "Soviet Policy of the Trail of the Golden Horde," *New Middle East,* July 1970, pp. 31–35.

5. Rene Mertens, "The Soviet Fleet in Arab Politics," *New Middle East,* November 1969, p. 22.

6. Quoted in Serquis Yakobson, "Russia and Africa," in Lederer, *Russian Foreign Policy,* p. 456.

7. Jan Pennar, "The Arabs, Marxism and Moscow," *Middle East Journal,* Autumn 1968, pp. 443–447; Jane Degras, *The Communist International 1919–1943, Documents,* Oxford University Press, 1956, pp. 143–148; and Walter Z. Laqueur, *The Struggle for the Middle East,* Macmillan, 1969.

8. Stalin's indifference toward the Middle East, and toward the Arabs in particular, was registered by one of his frequent sarcastic comments made to the former head of the Near Eastern Department of the Comintern during the 1930s: "There will be revolutionary developments in the Hawaiian Islands before anything will move in the Arab East." Quoted in Oded Eran and Jerome E. Singer, "Soviet Policy Towards the Arab World 1955–71," *Survey,* Autumn 1971, p. 10.

9. *Pravda,* 15 February 1956 and 17 April 1956.

10. Uri Ra'anan, "Moscow and the Third World," *Problems of Communism,* January–February 1965, pp. 22–31.

11. Walter Z. Laqueur, "An Independent Radical Movement for the Middle East," *New Middle East,* August 1969, p. 20; and Fritz Ermath, *The Soviet Union in the Third World: Purpose in Search of Power,* RAND, 1969, p. 7.

12. Karen Brutents, *Kommunist*, no. 17 (1964).

13. Soviet writers by no means concur on the merits of "revolutionary democracy." See John Leep, "The Soviet Union and the Third World," *Survey*, Summer 1969, pp. 19–38; and Pennar, "The Arabs, Marxism and Moscow," for summaries of the divergent Soviet viewpoints.

14. It seems logical now that the Soviet Union would have chosen to challenge the West at what was probably its most vulnerable spot, arms limitation, especially since Nasser had sought a private arms accord as early as 1953. See David J. Dallin, *Soviet Foreign Policy After Stalin*, J. P. Lippincott Co., 1961, p. 389. Dallin also points out that an important Soviet motive behind the arms deal was apparently to use it as a bargaining counter for higher political stakes: in April 1956 Khrushchev and Bulganin told Eden that the U.S.S.R. would support a general Middle Eastern arms embargo, which would have meant at that time the disintegration of the Baghdad Pact (p. 403). See also Uri Ra'anan, *The U.S.S.R., Arms, and the Third World*, MIT Press, 1969, pp. 100–130. For a synopsis of the position of the United States during the period, see the entire series "America and the Middle East," *Annals*, May 1972.

15. Amos Perlmutter, "The Fiasco of Anglo-American Middle East Policy," in *People and Politics in the Middle East*, edited by Michael Curtis, Dutton, 1971.

16. *Pravda*, 11 and 13 September 1957; TASS, 15 and 18 October 1957; *New York Times*, 11 October 1957. See also Nadav Safran, *From War to War*, Pegasus, 1969, pp. 115–120.

17. There is strong circumstantial evidence that Chinese communists, adopting a more militant line, were behind the Kirkuk uprising and that this reversal became an important polemical counter against Chinese "putschism" in Arab politics. It also signalled the decline of Chinese influence among radical Arab movements. See Eran and Singer, "Soviet Policy," p. 19.

18. See L. L. Whetten, "Soviet Policy Toward Radical Arab Movements," *New Middle East*, March 1970.

19. For an examination of the systematic character of Soviet efforts at rapprochement, see "Joint Communiqué," TASS, 6 November 1964, 22 May 1965, 16 August 1965, and 27 December 1966; also Nicolai V. Podgorny, "The Soviet and Turkish Peoples Want to Live in Peace and Friendship," *New Times*, 17 February 1965, pp. 3–6; and A. Millar, "Renewal of Soviet-Turkish Friendship," *New Times*, 27 January 1965, pp. 6–7.

20. Moscow's skillful maneuvering during the crisis is reflected in the official press releases. See *Pravda*, 31 January 1964, 8 February 1964, 9 July 1964, 10 and 19 August 1964; *Izvestia*, 14 March 1964; and *Red Star*, 27 June 1964.

21. *Red Star*, 6 January 1966.

22. Wynfred Joshua and Stephen P. Gibert, *Soviet Military Aid as a Reflection of Soviet Objectives*, Georgetown Research Project, 1968, pp. 36–37.

23. Jean-Jacques Berreby, "Growing Oil Needs Influence Soviet Policy," *New Middle East*, December 1969, p. 44.

24. Aggregate figures for Soviet economic aid for Middle Eastern and North African countries up to September 1970 include: Iran, $290 million; South Yemen, $10 million; Yemen, $65 million; the Sudan, $60 million; Libya, $25 million; Iraq, $690 million; Syria, $490 million; a total of $1.6 billion; see Bernard Lewis, "Conflict in the Middle East," Hearings Before the U.S. Senate Subcommittee on National Security and International Operations of the Committee of Government Operations (Part 4), 1971. According to Melvin Laird, communist countries have supplied almost $10 billion in military aid to Third World states, mainly in the Middle East; see *National Security Strategy of Realistic Deterrence*, Secretary of Defense Melvin R. Laird's Annual Defense Department Report FY 1973, 8 February 1972, pp. 50–55; see also chapter 10, note 11, of this book.

25. Walter Z. Laqueur, "Russia Enters the Middle East," *Foreign Affairs*, January 1969, pp. 301–302.

26. Kosygin's Speech to the Egyptian National Assembly, TASS, 18 May 1966.

27. See, for example, Andre Fontaine, *History of the Cold War*, vol. II, Random House, 1969, p. 171.

28. For the opposite viewpoint see, among others, Eugene V. Rostow, "The Middle East Crisis in the Perspective of World Politics," *International Affairs*, April 1971, pp. 275–288. For a more balanced appraisal see Arnold L. Horelick, "Soviet Involvement in the Middle East and the Western Response," Joint Hearing Before the Subcommittee on Europe and the Subcommittee on the Near East of the Committee of Foreign Affairs, House of Representatives, 92nd Congress, First Session, 19–21 October and 2–3 November 1971, pp. 189–198.

Chapter 3

1. John C. Campbell, *Military Forces and Political Conflicts in the Mediterranean*, Atlantic Institute, 1970, p. 17.

2. Nasser acknowledged in his public confessional on 11 June 1967 that the fabricated Soviet reports were responsible for triggering the June War. By the end of May, however, events began to outstrip consultations; the Soviets were apparently unaware of Cairo's intention to close the Straits.

3. For an authoritative Israeli estimate of the Sinai threat see Yigal Allon, *The Making of Israel's Army*, Universe Books, 1970.

4. For further comments by Bar Lev on cease-fire see the radio interview transcribed in *New Middle East*, March 1971, p. 37.

5. The strength of the U.S. commitment was partially diluted by a specific question on the matter put to Secretary of State Rusk by Chairman of the Senate Foreign Relations Committee William Fulbright: "Does the United States . . . have a national commitment in the event of attack from an external source or from internal subversion to come either to the military or economic aid of Israel or any of the Arab states?" The State Department issued a formal reply: "President Johnson and his three predecessors have stated the United States' interest and concern in supporting the political independence and territorial integrity of the Near East. This is a statement of policy and not a commitment to take particular actions in particular circumstances." *Washington Post*, 18 August 1967. This amplification made clear that the State Department felt there was no firm obligation toward either Israel or the Arab states in all circumstances and would continue to keep its options open for any contingencies.

6. Gideon Rafael, "U.N. Resolution 242: A Common Denominator," *New Middle East*, June 1973.

7. Ralph H. Magnus, ed., *Documents on the Middle East*, American Enterprise Institute for Public Policy Research, 1969, pp. 201–202; and *U.N. Documents*, General Assembly Fifth Emergency Special Session, especially 1525th–1540th Plenary Meetings, 17–29 June 1967. The Soviet letter requesting the Emergency Session is reference A/6717, 13 June 1967. For the speeches of Goldberg, Gromyko, and Eban at the regular 22 September session of the General Assembly, see Official Records for the 1562nd, 1563rd, and 1566th Plenary Meetings, on 21, 22, and 25 September 1967.

8. The United States was the first to publicize a detailed proposal for a solution to the crisis in the five-point Johnson Plan—later expanded to the seven-point Rusk Plan. Both proposals were the basis of the U.S. bargaining position beginning with the U.N. Security Council and the Special Session of the General Assembly, and both included the fractioning out of individual package settlements from a larger peace accord. The Israeli-Egyptian agreement would provide for:
1. Israeli withdrawal from Egyptian territory;
2. an official end to the state of war;
3. freedom of navigation in the Canal;
4. a solution to the refugee problem based on personal choice;
5. an international presence at Sharm el Sheikh to be terminated only with approval of the U.N. Security Council or the General Assembly;
6. formal accord on these provisions by both states; and
7. a general understanding on an arms ceiling.

For this period see U.S. Senate, Foreign Relations Committee, *A Select Chronology and Background Documents Relating to the Middle East,* May 1969.

9. Rafael, "U.N. Resolution 242."

10. *New York Times,* 25 June 1967; and Lyndon B. Johnson, *The Vantage Point,* Holt, Rinehart and Winston, 1971.

11. *Le Monde,* 16 August 1967; *New York Times,* 2 and 19 September 1967; and *The Observer,* 3 September 1967.

12. *Washington Post,* 27 August 1967.

13. Ibid., 4 October 1967.

14. *New York Times,* 1 November 1967.

15. *The Observer,* 14 October 1967.

16. For the legal arguments of the respective parties on the two waterways see L. L. Whetten, "Legal Aspects of the Aqaba Dispute," *Revue de droit international* (Geneva), April–June 1968. The central issue is whether the Straits and the Gulf of Aqaba are international waterways or a closed inland Arab sea.

17. See the analysis in the *Economist,* 18 November and 2 December 1967; and an interview with Lebanese Foreign Minister Georges Hakim in the *Washington Post,* 4 November 1967.

18. Rafael, "U.N. Resolution 242."

19. U.N. Security Council Proceedings, 15 November 1967.

20. U.N. Document S/10070, 4 January 1971. See appendix 3.

21. Ibid.

22. Ibid.

23. U.N.G.A., 1686th Plenary Meeting, 8 October 1968.

24. U.N.G.A., 1689th Plenary Meeting, 10 October 1968; see also Gromyko's statement, 1679th Plenary Meeting, 3 October 1968.

25. President Nasser's 1 May 1970 address, Foreign Broadcast Information Service (FBIS), 2 May 1970.

26. Given these dismissals and pending trials for negligence in the June War, a group of officers, incensed over the seeming injustice and possibly fearing a similar fate, unsuccessfully plotted in August 1970 to overthrow Nasser—in their view the true perpetrator of the debacle. The plot was discovered, and this undoubtedly convinced both Nasser and the Soviets of the necessity of dealing harshly with the entire officer corps. The result was an extensive purge, including prison terms, forced retirements, and demotions for hundreds of officers. Nonetheless, Egyptian students shook the regime by staging massive protests in February and November 1968 to condemn the sentences as too light and to demand a more thorough purging of the military.

27. James Cable, in *The Soviet Union in Europe and the Near East: Her Capabilities and Intentions,* Royal United Services Institute, 1970, p. 57.

28. "The Ups and Downs in Dayan's Defense Strategy," *New Middle East,* March 1970, pp. 17–19.

Chapter 4

1. TASS, 10 July 1968.

2. *Al Ahram,* 12 July 1968.

3. Ibid., 23 December 1968.

4. TASS, 24 December 1968.

5. *Al Anwar,* 10 January 1969.

6. *Al Ahram,* 19 January 1969. A U.S. State Department official later confirmed that *Al Ahram* had published an accurate version of the U.S. note; see *New York Times,* 21 January 1969.

7. *New York Times,* 11 January 1969; *Al Ahram,* 18 and 20 January 1969; *Washington Post,* 27 January 1969. For an amplification of Nasser's position see his interviews in *Newsweek,* 3 February 1969, and *New York Times,* 2 March 1969.

8. "Secretary Rogers's 1969 Galaxy Conference Speech, 9 December 1969," *Department of State Bulletin,* 5 January 1970, p. 7.

9. Ibid.; also *Department of State Bulletin,* 12 January 1970, pp. 21–28, and 19 January 1970, pp. 53–58.

10. *New York Times,* 13 June 1969.

11. Ibid., 26 June 1969.

12. *Al Ahram,* 27 June 1969.

13. *New York Times,* 18 July 1969.

14. *Al Ahram,* 24 July 1969.

15. U.N.G.A., 1756th Plenary Meeting, 19 September 1969; also 1757th Plenary Meeting, 19 September 1969.

16. For the first instances of Egypt's public agreement to negotiate under this formula see *Al Akhbar,* 4 October 1969, and *Al Ahram,* 6 October 1969.

17. *New York Times,* 22 December 1969.

18. Ibid.

19. *Le Monde,* 11 November 1969.

20. *New York Times,* 13 January 1970; Associated Press, 12 January 1970.

21. Mrs. Meir's Knesset Statement, *New Middle East,* February 1970, p. 49; see also *Le Monde Weekly,* 24 December 1969.

22. Irving Heymont, "Israeli Defense of the Suez Canal," *Military Review,* January 1971, pp. 3–11.

23. Moshe Dayan, *Diary of the Sinai Campaign,* Harper & Row, 1966, pp. 54–57.

24. Interview with General Dayan, *Der Stern,* 28 September 1969.

25. Prime Minister Meir's address to the Knesset, 1 July 1969, FBIS, 3 July 1970.

26. *Department of State Bulletin,* 5 January 1970, pp. 8–11.

27. *Le Monde Weekly,* 24 December 1969.

Chapter 5

1. Jon Kimche, "Whose Shackles," *New Middle East,* February 1970, p. 4.

2. *New York Times,* 25 January 1970; *Washington Post,* 28 January 1970.

3. Ibid., 8 February 1970.

4. Ibid., 15 February 1970; also Nasser's Speech to the A.S.U. Congress on 23 July 1970, FBIS, 24 July 1970.

5. *New York Times,* 23 January 1970.

6. *Pravda*, 13 February 1970.

7. *New York Times*, 15 February 1970.

8. Ibid., 4 February 1970.

9. *Pravda*, 17 February 1970.

10. *Department of State Bulletin*, 2 March 1970, p. 222.

11. Ibid., 1 June 1970, p. 693.

12. *Strategic Survey, 1971*, IISS, p. 46.

13. *Christian Science Monitor*, 23 May 1970.

14. *Jerusalem Post*, 5 May 1970.

15. President Nasser's 1 May 1970 speech, FBIS, 2 May 1970.

16. In December 1969 the I.D.F. captured an Egyptian radar site, and on 22 January 1970 they captured the Egyptian island of Shadaw in the Red Sea, transporting captured equipment back to Israel.

17. General Chaim Herzog, commentary on *Radio Israel*, 28 March 1970, FBIS, 29 March 1970.

18. Dayan commented in mid-April that "the Russians have become our central problem. There is a danger that we may find ourselves in a situation against our will, in which we may have to attack the Russians and they our planes. And this would mean war with the Russians." *Bamahane* (I.D.F. magazine), 14 April 1970.

19. *Die Welt*, 20 May 1970.

20. *New York Times*, 15 February 1970.

21. President Nasser's 1 May 1970 speech. It should be noted that the Israeli Mirage III had established a 20 to 1 kill ratio over the MIG-21 before the F-4 sale.

22. *New York Times*, 16 May 1970.

23. TASS, 20 May 1970.

24. *USIS Bulletin*, no. 122, 26 June 1970.

25. Israeli Domestic Broadcasting Service, 27 May 1970, FBIS, 28 May 1970.

26. The texts of Rogers's note to Egypt on 19 June 1970 and Rogers's letter to the Egyptian foreign minister on 19 June 1970 are reprinted in *New Middle East*, August 1970. See also "Rogers's Press Conference," *New York Times*, 26 June 1970.

27. Yet Riad made a secret visit to Washington on 25 June to discuss the Rogers Plan. See *Washington Post*, 29 June 1970.

28. TASS, 30 June 1970.

29. *New York Times*, 25 June 1970.

30. I. Belyaev, "How the Soviet Union Visualizes a Middle East Settlement," reprinted in *New Middle East*, June 1970, pp. 30–33.

31. *Soviet News*, 21 July 1970.

32. Nasser's speech is reprinted in *New Middle East*, August 1970.

33. Reprinted in *New Middle East*, September 1970, pp. 27–29.

34. *Krasnaya Zvezda* (Red star) 21 June 1970, claimed that between 1 January and 30 April 1970 the I.A.F. completed 3,300 sorties and 900 reconnaissance missions in Egypt. "A sharp increase . . . took place in May. In the single night of 31 May, the I.A.F. carried out 400 sorties within a ten-hour period and dropped over 2,000 tons of bombs."

35. *New York Times*, 6 July 1970; *Aviation Week*, 13 July 1970, p. 15; and *Strategic Survey, 1971*, IISS, p. 48.

36. Quoted in *New Middle East*, September 1970, p. 16.

37. *New York Times*, 24 July 1970.

38. Ibid., 2 and 4 July 1970.

39. *USIS Bulletin*, no. 349, 14 July 1970.

40. *New York Times*, 21 July 1970.

41. Following Nasser's acceptance of the American peace bid, the Iraqi Baath party's National Command in Baghdad issued a confidential circular to party members on 26 July. It stated, "Comrades, Abd-al-Nasser's acceptance of the liquidationist and capitulationist solutions has provided our party with a golden opportunity to lead the Arab masses in cooperation with all forces which still consider Nasser their enemy No. 1. . . . If our party is able to grasp the new circumstances, it will have eliminated its strongest foe,

Nasser and the Nasserist masses behind him." Published in *Al Ahram*, 11 December 1970.

42. *Washington Post*, 27 July 1970 and 9 August 1970. The U.S. Sixth Fleet was augmented shortly thereafter to support possible contingency operations related to the Jordanian crisis. The rapidity and size of the augmentation was also intended to improve the credibility in Israeli eyes of the U.S. military commitment in the Middle East.

43. *USIS Bulletin*, 31 July 1970.

44. *Pravda*, 30 July 1970; TASS, 5 August 1970.

45. Text reprinted in *New Middle East*, September 1970, pp. 22–24.

46. Ibid.

47. *Radio Cairo*, 26 March 1970.

Chapter 6

1. *New Middle East*, September 1970, p. 16.

2. *New York Times*, 18 July 1970.

3. *London Times*, 31 July 1970; and *Strategic Survey, 1970*, IISS, p. 48.

4. *International Herald Tribune*, 27 October 1970.

5. *New York Times*, 29 March 1970.

6. TASS, 29 August 1970.

7. Israel's chief of military intelligence, Major General Aharon Yariv, claimed that the new Egyptian air defense was "one of the world's most advanced"; see *New York Times*, 26 October 1970.

8. *Aviation Week*, 31 August 1970; and Neville Brown, "Reconnaissance from Space," *World Today*, February 1971, pp. 68–76.

9. *USIS Bulletin*, 14 September 1970.

10. Ibid., 17 September 1970.

11. Riad later read a letter at a November news conference purportedly guaranteeing that the United States would not send arms to Israel while the peace talks were underway; see the *International Herald Tribune*, 14 December 1970. The United States apparently did refrain from making arms de-

liveries through mid-September, when new electronic-warfare equipment was reportedly sent to Israel.

12. General Dayan's interview on *Radio Jerusalem*, 5 September 1970, FBIS, 6 September 1970.

13. Ibid.

14. TASS, 29 August 1970.

15. See U.N.G.A., 1851st–1896th Plenary Meetings, 28 September–4 November 1970.

16. *New York Times*, 18 November 1970; *Washington Post*, 20 October 1970; and *International Herald Tribune*, 21, 25, and 26 October 1970.

17. *International Herald Tribune*, 20 November 1970.

18. Ibid., 20 and 28 November 1970.

19. It was revealed on 17 November that Palestinean charges of Hussein's collaboration with the enemy were accurate; Deputy Prime Minister Allon had met secretly with Hussein on six occasions to discuss differences; see the *Washington Post*, 17 November 1970.

20. *International Herald Tribune*, 18 November 1970; *New York Times*, 23 November 1970; and *Ma'ariv* (Jerusalem), 17 December 1970. Israeli hesitation to resume the talks received a jolt on 1 November when the British government announced a policy shift strongly endorsing the "no territorial acquisition" feature of 242. At the end of a visit to England, Mrs. Meir stated, "To my sorrow there was no meeting of minds on basic issues." London's change significantly hampered Israeli options among the four big powers since France had been consistently pro-Arab since 1967. See *Ma'ariv*, 2 November 1970; and the *New York Times*, 5 November 1970.

21. Text reprinted in *New Middle East*, February 1971, pp. 4–6.

22. *New York Times*, 23 December 1970.

23. TASS, 26 December 1970.

24. *International Herald Tribune*, 11 January 1971.

25. Ibid., 20 January 1970.

26. Ibid., 14 January 1970.

27. A signed article in the *International Herald Tribune*, 14 January 1971; Egyptian ambassador's letter to *The Guardian*, 20 March 1971; and the Egyptian chargé d'affaires' letter to *The Times*, 15 May 1971.

28. U.N. Document S/10070, 4 January 1971. See appendix 3.

29. *USIS Bulletin*, no. 46, 9 March 1971, and no. 56, 23 March 1971.

30. *Ma'ariv* and *Jerusalem Post*, 14 February 1970. Sisco responded in a television interview to Israeli complaints, "In my judgment, both parties are committed to abide by whatever procedures Ambassador Jarring decides to pursue, and no procedure is barred"; see *USIS Bulletin*, no. 32, 17 February 1971.

31. *Al Ahram*, 26 February 1970.

32. U.N. Document S/10070.

33. Ibid.

34. Interview with Borchgrave, *Newsweek*, 1 March 1971. Each of these actions was strongly opposed by the United States; see *USIS Bulletin*, no. 109, 11 June 1971. On the other hand, in its first effort around this obstacle Tel Aviv announced on 29 June that it was prepared to compensate Arab residents of East Jerusalem for property held before the state was established. This went beyond the former offer that dealt largely with residents of West Jerusalem and Haifa, and it could amount to $100 million over 20 years for 10,000 claimants. When completed, this program will solidify Israel's authority over united Jerusalem.

35. *Ma'ariv* and *Ha'aretz*, 23 February 1971.

36. The text of Mrs. Meir's statement is reprinted in *New Middle East*, April 1971, p. 46.

37. "The Party's New 'Heroes' Promise New Ideas and Policies," *New Middle East*, May 1971, p. 10.

38. *New York Times*, 11 March 1971.

39. "Rogers's 16 March Press Conference," *USIS Bulletin*, no. 52, 17 March 1971.

40. *USIS Bulletin*, no. 60, 29 March 1971.

41. Moscow first officially announced its endorsement of four-big-power guarantees at the 24th Soviet Party Congress in March when Brezhnev said that the U.S.S.R. was ready to take part, together with the other permanent

members of the Security Council, in the creation of international guarantees for a political settlement in the Middle East.

42. *International Herald Tribune*, 18 March 1971.

43. Ibid., 8 June 1971.

44. *USIS Bulletin*, no 50, 15 March 1971; no. 52, 17 March 1971; no. 55, 22 March 1971; no. 78, 26 April 1971.

45. For example, when the Congress of Meir's Labor party adopted a policy on 7 April calling for the retention of "substantial" Arab territories without being seriously challenged by opposition parties, many American observers concluded that the government's hard line resulted only from conviction and not domestic pressures—stubbornness rather than political prudence. See, for example, former U.S. Ambassador Charles Yost's bluntly critical charges in *Life*, 11 April 1971.

Chapter 7

1. Dan Gillon, "The Prospects for the Jarring Talks," *The World Today*, February 1971, p. 51; *Strategic Survey, 1971*, IISS, pp. 42–50; *New York Times*, 11 and 25 April 1971; *Washington Post*, 14 March and 16 April 1971; and *Bamahane*, 12 May 1971.

2. *International Herald Tribune*, 3 and 4 June 1971. In a 22 June 1971 speech at the Alexandria Naval College, Sadat calculated that Egypt was spending one million pounds per day on missile defense systems alone; see *New Middle East*, June 1971, p. 5.

3. Martin J. Miller, Jr., "Israel's Quest for Military Self-Sufficiency," *Military Review*, March 1971, pp. 67–73.

4. *New York Times*, 26 April 1971.

5. E. Romano, "General Okunev on Mission to Egypt," *Radio Liberty Research*, CRD 171/71, 14 May 1971.

6. See Sisco's testimony to this effect before the Senate Foreign Relations Committee, 9 March 1972.

7. "On the Washington Brink," *New Middle East*, January 1971, pp. 6–7.

8. It later became apparent that the Meir government had tolerated Dayan's unauthorized venture into foreign policy for a variety of reasons: Meir couldn't block his initiative without creating yet another cabinet split; she did not think it was saleable; and if it did succeed as a trial balloon it could

be reclaimed as a government-endorsed proposal with only minimum loss to Meir's prestige.

9. Sadat's 4 February speech, in *New Middle East,* March 1971, pp. 32–35.

10. Meir's 9 February speech, ibid., pp. 35–39.

11. Ulrich Harms, Inc., a salvage firm in Hamburg, was awarded a contract for removing sixteen sunken ships, barges, and dredges, plus military equipment and steel bridge girders. It was estimated the operation would take four months. On 19 February it was announced that the Canal Authority had ordered three dredges from the Dutch De Liesbosch Shipyard. The fourteen trapped ships could be freed when the Canal was opened to small-class vessels but it could not be dredged to the 1966 level of 38 feet draught for at least six months. It would also take time to restore vital communications and reemploy the scattered pilots.

12. "Whose Blunder?" *New Middle East,* April 1971, pp. 4–6.

13. *USIS Bulletin,* no. 33, 18 February 1971.

14. Ibid., no. 58, 26 February 1971, and no. 65, 5 April 1971.

15. Ibid., no. 47, 10 March 1971. The cease-fire was not extended formally beyond 7 March, but Egypt declared its intentions not to resume fighting at that time.

16. Published originally in *Ma'ariv* and *Yediot Aharanot* (Jerusalem), 25 March 1971.

17. *Jerusalem Post,* 29 March 1971.

18. Middle East News Agency (MENA), 1 April 1971.

19. *Jerusalem Post,* 15 April 1971. At the same time a public opinion poll indicated that 85 percent of Israeli Jews believed that their government was doing all it should to negotiate a peace treaty. Seven percent thought the government should be more flexible, but virtually all Jews supported the annexation of East Jerusalem. Eighty-six percent favored annexing the Golan Heights and 72 percent advocated retaining Sharm el Sheikh; yet 75 percent wanted some Arab territories returned.

20. *International Herald Tribune,* 28 May 1971.

21. *New York Times,* 21 April 1971.

22. *USIS Bulletin,* no. 75, 21 April 1971.

23. *Ha'aretz,* 28 April 1971.

24. *USIS Bulletin,* no. 81, 29 April 1971.

25. Speech by Sadat, 9 June 1971, FBIS, 10 June 1971; see also his speeches of 10 and 22 June 1971.

26. Ibid.

27. From personal interviews with observers closely connected with the talks.

28. *USIS Bulletin,* no. 89, 11 May, and no. 96, 18 May 1971.

29. P. J. Vatikiotis, "Egypt's Politics of Conspiracy," *Survey,* Spring 1972; and Per Gahrton, "President Sadat's New Brand of Nationalism," *New Middle East,* January 1972.

30. Statement of policy made by Prime Minister Golda Meir in the Knesset, 9 June 1971, FBIS, 10 June 1971.

31. *USIS Bulletin,* no. 102, 2 June 1971, and no. 105, 5 June 1971.

32. TASS, 27 May 1971.

33. *USIS Bulletin,* no. 107, 8 June 1971; no. 108, 9 June 1971; and no. 122, 1 July 1971.

34. Ibid., no. 120, 29 June 1971.

35. Ibid., no. 114, 21 June 1971.

36. See General Bar Lev's statement on the resumption of fighting in *New Middle East,* March 1971, p. 37.

37. For U.S. denial of further arms agreement with Israel in the immediate future, see *USIS Bulletin,* no. 77, 23 April 1971, and no. 79, 27 April 1971.

38. *Radio Tel Aviv,* Home Service, 10 July 1971.

39. *USIS Bulletin,* no. 70, 14 April 1971.

40. Ibid., no. 75, 21 April 1971.

41. Ibid., no. 78, 26 April 1971.

Chapter 8

1. State Department spokesman Robert McCloskey acknowledged that Joseph Sisco would be going to Israel not to present another package deal but to explore "specific ideas"; *USIS Bulletin*, no. 145, 4 August 1971.

2. *United States Foreign Policy, 1969–1970*, U.S. Department of State, publication no. 8575, 1971, p. 75.

3. *Ma'ariv*, 11 August 1971.

4. "Interview with Joseph Sisco," *New Middle East*, July 1972, p. 5.

5. *Al Ahram*, 12 and 27 August 1971; *New York Times*, 25 August 1971.

6. MENA, 17 September 1971.

7. *Jerusalem Post*, 26 October 1971. Deputy Prime Minister Yigal Allon said over *Radio Israel*, 30 October 1971, that forward movement in the negotiations was contingent upon U.S. guarantees of uninterrupted sale of arms. "But even with more F-4s, Israel would not accept the Rogers Plan; the U.A.R. must agree to direct talks."

8. *New York Times*, 28 January 1972.

9. In November 1971 heads of state from Senegal, Cameroon, Nigeria, and Zaire also conducted futile talks in Cairo and Tel Aviv.

10. *New York Times*, 14 January 1972.

11. Ibid., 28 January 1972.

12. For a detailed description of contemporary U.S. and Soviet electronic capabilities see *Aviation Week*, 21 February 1972. The effectiveness of U.S. ECM equipment was demonstrated in the April 1972 raid on Haiphong when 242 SAMs were launched "blind."

13. Yet total sales in 1971 were $150 million, with $9.2 million in export profits coming from the sale of its Commodore executive jet and a modified Boeing 707; *New York Times*, 15 September 1971. See also *Aviation Week*, 27 March 1972.

14. *USIS Bulletin*, no. 146, 5 August 1971. Israel's fallback position was a request for Lance 70-mile-range SSMs with cluster munitions as the best anti-SAM weapon available. While militarily sound, the request was denied.

15. The new U.S. aircraft were to be replacements for 150 French Mirages, but this would depend upon when precisely the older aircraft were phased

out. Even so, the new additive significantly upgraded the quality of the I.A.F., as Sadat charged, by as much as one-third. Why such a quantum leap, he complained, when they already have air superiority?

16. See Sadat's interviews in the *New York Times*, December 1971, and *Newsweek*, 6 March 1972.

17. *Al Ahram*, 31 March 1972; see also Raymond Hutchings, "Soviet Defense Spending and Soviet External Relations," *International Affairs*, July 1971, pp. 518–531.

18. The compromise solution of ten additional TU-16s was neither a conceptual breakthrough nor a significant incremental increase in Egypt's deterrent and strategic power.

19. *Newsweek*, 31 July 1972.

20. Sadat's visit to Moscow and the Arab capitals produced "gigantic results; an important turning point"; *Al Ahram*, 8 February 1972.

21. *Newsweek*, 31 July 1972.

22. TASS, 9 February 1972.

23. Radio Free Europe Research Memo, 13 April 1972; and *al-Rayah* (Beirut), 28 June 1972.

24. MENA, 30 March 1972; and *International Herald Tribune*, 25 April 1972.

25. See also "Interview with Joseph Sisco."

26. *Al Ahram*, 25 April 1972.

27. On 12 April 1972 MENA announced Soviet aid for a nuclear power plant in Egypt, indicating that Moscow was still willing to extend its commitments to Cairo.

28. *Aviation Week*, 22 May 1972.

29. It is likely that the Soviets used their shipment of more sophisticated weapons to Egypt than to North Vietnam for double advantages. In Hanoi they could argue that such exotic weaponry required more Soviet advisory personnel and therefore more influence to insure proper use commensurate to the risk to Soviet prestige involved; and in Cairo they could point out that Egypt could not legitimately expect what it called "decisive" weapons when it was already receiving higher priority systems than any socialist state, including North Vietnam which was under heavy attack.

30. One major weakness persisted: Egyptian strategic delivery systems. Without an SSM capability, Egypt would be forced to rely upon its 28 ASM-equipped Badgers for strategic deterrence. After the confirmed delivery of 10 additional TU-16s, Israel's chief of staff, General Bar Lev, commented about Egypt's long-range ASM threat by warning that any attempt to bomb civilian centers would result in retaliation in kind. He implied that Israel would employ its Jericho force when he said that the I.D.F. had an answer to Egypt's ASMs. But Soviet ASMs are designed for nuclear warheads or conventional warheads for isolated targets such as ships. They are too inaccurate and the conventional explosives are too small for effective use against military land targets. This resulted in the Egyptians' quest for an SSM force.

31. On 27 June 1972 Lebanese Prime Minister Saeb Salam and guerrilla leader Yasser Arafat signed an agreement reducing guerrilla operations from Lebanese soil and evacuating refugees from southern towns and villages. Only one of many accords and understandings with the guerrillas, this one will probably hold. It was the end product of the Lod Airport massacre, in which 26 people were killed, and eight days of Israeli retaliation against Lebanon, in which 191 casualties were inflicted. Israel's time-honored strategy of reprisals still works in prescribed situations and the guerrillas have probably been eliminated for the foreseeable future as a military force in the area.

32. *The Guardian*, 3 and 8 April 1972. When queried about the maps, officials did not deny that their general outline was consistent with government thinking. Indeed, Allon told an interviewer that Hussein's plan was compatible with his own, with the compromise that an I.D.F. garrison remain on the hills along the West Bank; *Ma'ariv*, 24 March 1972. Mrs. Meir stated to the *New York Times* on 28 January 1972 the now-trite contention that Israel was not laying down preconditions for talks and then recited several prerequisites: "We must have full control of Sharm el Sheikh. There must be a territorial connection between Sharm el Sheikh and Israel proper. . . . The Sinai cannot again be filled with the Egyptian army. . . . to allow Egyptian troops to cross [the Canal] is an insult to intelligence." See also Yosef Goell, "The Hussein Plan, Expectations and Realities," *Bulletin of the American Academic Association for Peace in the Middle East*, April 1972.

33. By July 1972 the Western press reported that Israel was nearing completion on a de facto agreement for one portion of the Hussein Plan, Jordanian use of the port of Gaza. Israel has reportedly invested $200,000 in construction of a 300-foot pier, cargo cranes, and storage facilities. It is interested in increasing the port's activities to relieve pressure on Israeli harbors and to provide employment for 400 Arab stevedores. Jordan is seeking an accord to provide sea access for the West Bank and Jordan proper; *Washington Post*, 25 July 1972.

34. *Al Ahram*, 24 March 1972.

35. *Pravda*, 2 June 1972. For Soviet interests in Arab oil see, among other sources, John A. Berry, "Oil and Soviet Policy in the Middle East," *The Middle East Journal*, Spring 1972, pp. 149–160; and Thomas C. Barger, "Middle Eastern Oil Since the Second World War," *Annals*, May 1972, pp. 31–44. By the end of the decade the U.S.S.R. plans to import 100 million tons of oil annually at a cost of over two billion dollars. It is expected that these deliveries will come mainly from the Middle East, increasing substantially Soviet interests in regional stability.

36. Paradoxes that have frequently characterized Libyan politics were revealed in a vehement attack by Qaddafi on 5 June 1972: "I say with great conviction that the Soviet Union is responsible for this fluid situation of no-peace and no-war in the Middle East. . . . We must fight, even if we have to fight with stones" (MENA).

37. *Al Ahram*, 16 June 1972; *An-Nahar* (Beirut), 9 July 1972; and MENA, 19 July 1972.

38. MENA, 16 July 1972. The authoritative Beirut daily *An-Nahar* asserted on 9 August that Soviet-Egyptian relations had entered a Cold War stage. Both countries recalled ambassadors, according to Mohammed H. el-Zayyat, minister for information, for consultation on a Brezhnev note in early August dealing with the future talks on arms aid; *Al Ahram*, 7 August 1972.

39. *New York Times*, 27 July 1972.

40. MENA, 23 July 1972.

41. Acknowledged by Heikal in *Al Ahram*, 21 July 1972.

42. *International Herald Tribune*, 21 July 1972.

43. *Al Ahram*, 27 July 1972.

44. *International Herald Tribune*, 28 July 1972.

45. *Pravda*, 23 July 1972. The first TASS statement on the subject, 20 July, conveyed the impression that the decision was a mutual agreement. *Pravda* carried a subdued statement on page four, and the army publication *Red Star* gave it front-page coverage.

46. Richard Pipes, Hearings Before the Subcommittee on National Security and International Operations of the Committee on Government Operations, U.S. Senate, 92nd Congress, 10 January 1972.

47. For other versions of this idea see Richard Pipes, "Prospects for Peace in the Middle East," *Bulletin of the American Academic Association for Peace*

in the Middle East, April 1972; Alfred Cattani, "The Exodus of Soviet Jews," *Swiss Review of World Affairs,* March 1972, pp. 12–13; and David G. Nes, "The Soviets in the Middle East," *Military Review,* June 1972, p. 85.

48. U.S. Senate, Committee on Foreign Relations, *A Select Chronology and Background Documents Relating to the Middle East,* May 1969, p. 242.

49. Hearings Before the Subcommittee on National Security and International Operations of the Committee on Government Operations, U.S. Senate (Part 4), 92nd Congress, 1971.

Chapter 9

1. *The Sunday Times,* 14 October 1973.

2. The SAM-6 is technologically superior to any SAM in the U.S. inventory. It has an integral rocket/ramjet system, which means that its range is limited by the radar employed with it. To overcome this limitation, at least three separate radars are used for tracking/detection at various altitudes, operating in the G-band, H-band, and I-band frequency ranges. It has a command guidance system and probably a semiactive and infrared terminal guidance capability. See *Aviation Week and Space Technology,* 22 October 1973, p. 21.

3. *Military Balance 1973–1974,* IISS, London, plus I.A.F. F-4 deliveries announced in 1973.

4. *The Sunday Times,* 14 October 1973.

5. The SAM-7 was employed with an infrared screen that eliminated spurious wavelengths. Accordingly, the 7 effectively avoided decoy flares and pursued the exhaust heat of the aircraft. *Aviation Week and Space Technology,* 5 November 1973, p. 17.

6. The SAM systems employed operated radars in the C-, E-, F-, G-, H-, and I-band wavelengths and the gun employed radars in the J-band. A pilot must respond to I.F.F. queries simultaneously in all these bands, a task that is apparently beyond the technical capability of present Soviet equipment.

7. The Arabs seldom fought well at night. The original war plan sought to capitalize on the surprise offensive at 1800 hours by conducting a night offensive.

8. *International Herald Tribune,* 23 October 1973.

9. Ibid., 22 October 1973.

10. FBIS-SOV-73-208-40, p. 6.

11. *International Herald Tribune,* 10–11 November 1973.

Chapter 10

1. Israel's military potential is awesome even in relative terms. Abba Eban claims it is the strongest small power in the world and that in all history "there has never been a case of so much firepower per citizen of a small state" (interview in *The Guardian*, 5 May 1973); see also Moshe Dayan, "Israel's Military Strength and Political Confidence," *Survival*, November–December 1972.

2. Nahum Goldmann, "The Future of Israel," *Foreign Affairs*, April 1970, pp. 443–459, and "Israel and the Arabs," *Le Monde*, 27 May 1970.

3. R. Waring Herrick, "Soviet SALT Strategy and Tactics," Radio Liberty Research, CRD/363/69.

4. Malcolm H. Kerr, *Regional Arab Politics and the Conflict with Israel*, Rand Corporation, RM-5966-FF, October 1969, pp. 33–35.

5. Ibid., p. 31.

6. Leo Mates, "Nonalignment and the Great Powers," *Foreign Affairs*, April 1970, pp. 525–536.

7. For details of recent communist activity in the Sudan see Tia Gilta Tutu, "Black Power in the Sudan—New Divisions in Africa," *New Middle East*, July 1971, pp. 21–25; and Anthony Sylvester, "Mohammed versus Lenin in Revolutionary Sudan," ibid., pp. 26–28.

8. *Pravda*, 19 August 1970.

9. See *An-Nahar*, 1 June 1969; *An-Anwar* (Beirut), 11 October 1969; *Radio Omduran*, 28 October 1969; and *Pravda*, 5 November 1969.

10. *Pravda*, 5 November 1969.

11. The Soviet aid program has been plagued with chronic shortfalls. During the 1950s deliveries for development projects were only 15–20 percent fulfilled. To date the accumulative expenditure of Soviet credits has amounted to little more than one-third of its total aid commitments. Table A lists the accumulative credits extended and the actual amounts drawn by the recipient countries. These shortfalls have been due primarily to outmoded planning principles and the low absorption abilities of the recipient countries; this latter factor has become the object of extensive debate among economists. To overcome these deficiencies, Soviet planners have accepted the economic necessity for adopting some of the aid principles that govern Western assistance programs. More strings are likely to be attached in the future, and the total size of Soviet endeavors will probably remain at its present level. Consequently, the political profit from Soviet aid programs will probably not become sig-

Table A Soviet Aid, 1954–1968 (millions of U.S. dollars)

	Total credits extended	Total amount drawn through the end of 1968
Algeria	300	31
Morocco	90	6.2
Iraq	210	137
South Yemen	?	?
The Sudan	70	15
Syria	400	100
Tunisia	110	20
Egypt	1600	790
Yemen	110	55
Iran	850	90
Total	3740	1244.2

nificant. This trend will likely accompany a general recognition that material aid is a poor substitute for political influence gained by the establishment and defense of national interests through traditional political means.

In contrast, economic aid from the West remains by far the most important contribution to the economies of the Arab countries, amounting to $4.854 billion between 1960 and 1965. Between 1946 and 1967 the United States alone contributed over $1 billion. Western capital remains the largest source of

Table B Trade with the Middle East,* 1966
(millions of U.S. dollars)

	Exports	Imports
France	228.5	525.5
West Germany	408.6	432.8
EEC	1113.0	2234.5
Italy	251.3	784.5
Japan	288.2	870.3
The United States	859.0	258.5
Sino-Soviet Area	426.5	556.2
The Soviet Union	144.7	186.6

* Countries included are Cyprus, Israel, Egypt, The Arabian Peninsula, Syria, Jordan, and Iraq. Iran and North Africa are not included.

Source: International Monetary Fund, International Bank for Reconstruction and Redevelopment, *Direction of Trade*, 1962–1966.

development funds available to the Arab world, and the Soviet Union will not be able to supplant the West in this vital function in the foreseeable future. The West also ranks far above the communist bloc in overall commercial relations. The trade figures in table B reveal the continuing preference among Middle Eastern states for Western markets and sources of supply.

See: *Communist Governments and Developing Nations: Trade and Aid in 1966,* U.S. Department of State Research Memorandum, RSB-80, 21 July 1967, p. iv; *Communist Governments and Developing Countries: Trade and Aid,* U.S. Department of State Research Memorandum, RSE-120, 14 August 1968; Wynfred Joshua and Stephen P. Gibert, *Soviet Military Aid as a Reflection of Soviet Objectives,* Georgetown Research Project, Atlantic Research Corporation, October 1968, pp. 256–285; Phillip Mosely, "The Kremlin and the Third World," *Foreign Affairs,* October 1969, pp. 69–73; Robert S. Jasper, "Foreign Aid and Economic Development: The Shifting Soviet View," *International Affairs,* July 1969, pp. 452–464; and Elizabeth Dridd Valkenier, "New Trends in Soviet Economic Relations with the Third World," *World Politics,* April 1970.

12. Curt Gasteyger, "Conflicts and Tensions in the Middle East," Adelphi Papers, no. 51, IISS, September 1970.

13. Arguments that the effectiveness of gunboat diplomacy have now reached an alltime peak because of the abilities of both great powers to deploy and sustain large military forces ashore seem unsound. See T. B. Millar, "The Indian and Pacific Oceans: Some Strategic Considerations," Adelphi Papers, no. 57, IISS, May 1969, p. 7.

14. The concept of compellance was first developed by Thomas Schelling in *Arms and Influence,* Yale University Press, 1966.

15. See Eban's news conference on the second anniversary of the 1970 cease-fire, *New York Times,* 8 August 1972.

16. *Aviation Week and Space Technology,* 29 October 1973, p. 7.

17. Ibid., 22 October 1973, p. 14, and 5 November 1973, p. 12.

18. Ibid., 12 November 1973, p. 11.

19. Richard Lowenthal, "Soviet-American Relations and World Order: The Two and the Many," Adelphi Papers, no. 66, IISS, March 1970, p. 11; Zbigniew Brzezinski, "The Soviet Past and Present," *Encounter,* March 1969; and Tibor Szamuely, "Five Years after Khrushchev," *Survey,* Summer 1969.

20. Gasteyger, "Conflict and Tensions."

21. Dan Avni-Segre, "Pre-Risorgimento and Post-Risorgimento," *New Middle East,* December 1969, pp. 24–27.

22. Alan Dowty, "Israeli Dilemma," *New Middle East,* June 1971, pp. 36–37.

23. On 22 November 1970 Great Britain blocked the sale of 200 Chieftain tanks following a decision to halt all sales of tanks to Israel; the United States subsequently fulfilled this order. London then announced the suspension of all offensive arms deliveries to the Middle East until movement was made toward a peace treaty.

24. For the legal aspects of the Tiran Straits question see L. L. Whetten, "Legal Aspects of the Aqaba Dispute," *Revue de droit international* (Geneva), April–June 1968. For the most detailed proposal yet advanced see Ammon E. Rafael, "A Proposal for Peace in the Middle East," *Orbis,* Spring 1972.

25. Pierre Hassner, "Pragmatic Conservatism in the White House," *Foreign Policy,* Summer 1971, p. 42; and Richard Nixon, *U.S. Foreign Policy for the 1970's (II): Building for Peace,* Government Printing Office, 1971.

Appendix 1

1. TASS, 21 June and 11 July 1967; *Pravda,* 28 June 1967.

2. For summary of even sharper condemnation by West European Communist parties, see "The Communist Parties of West Europe and the Crisis in the Middle East," RFE Research Memo, 19 June 1967, and "Debate—An Assertion of Emancipation but No Political Sensations," RFE Research Memo, 27 July 1967.

3. Agerpres (Rumanian News Agency), 24 July 1967.

4. Ibid., 15 and 18 July 1967.

5. Ibid.

6. Reorganization of Ministry of Interior was directed by State Council Decree no. 710, 21 July 1967; also see *Scanteia,* 25 July 1967.

7. *New York Times,* 13 June 1967; *Le Monde,* 14 June 1967.

8. FBIS, 20 June 1967.

9. *Radio Warsaw,* 17 July 1967.

10. Ibid., 15 and 17 June 1967.

11. PAP (Polish News Agency), 19 and 20 July 1967; *Radio Warsaw,* 21 July 1967.

12. Wlodeinierz Brus, *Rinascita,* 25 June 1971, pp. 27–29; also RFE Research Memo, 30 June 1971.

13. Ibid.

14. For the most comprehensive statement of Prague's position see Premier Josef Lenart's speech of 20 June to the U.N. General Assembly, *Rude Pravo*, 21 June 1967.

15. For extensive excerpts from his Congress speech see *Die Weltwoche*, 21 July 1967; and RFE Research Memo, 31 July 1967.

16. *Radio Prague*, 28 July 1967.

17. *Literarni Noviny*, 8 and 29 July 1967; *Kulturny Zivot*, 28 July 1967.

18. Statement published in *Frankfurter Allgemeine Zeitung*, 11 August 1967.

19. RFE Research Memo, 6 June 1967; *Borba*, 26 and 28 June 1967.

20. "Some Yugoslav Papers Critical of Nasser's Attitude," RFE Research Memo, 22 June 1967; and "Tito's Anti-Israeli Policy, an Effort to Restore Domestic Balance," RFE Research Memo, 15 June 1967.

21. *New York Times*, 9 August 1971.

22. *Borba*, 2, 3, and 4 July 1967; see *Radio Zagreb*, 1 July 1967, for a summary of the 7th Plenum of the party's Central Committee.

23. *Radio Zagreb*, 11 July 1967.

24. *Ekonomska Politika* (Belgrade), 8 July 1967; *Politika*, 2 July 1967.

25. *Knjizevne novine* (Belgrade), 22 July 1967.

26. "Yugoslav Economic Policy Criticized in Parliament," RFE Research Memo, 26 July 1967.

27. *Review of International Affairs* (Belgrade), August 1967; also RFE Research Memos, 31 August and 14 September 1967.

28. Explained by Ignacy Kasicki, *Zycie literackie* (Cracow), 14 December 1969; see also L. L. Whetten, *Ostpolitik: West Germany's Relations with the Warsaw Pact*, Oxford University Press, 1971.

29. *Strategic Survey, 1971*, IISS, pp. 46–48.

Appendix 2

1. Mohamed Masmoudi (foreign minister of Tunisia), "The Mediterranean," *Survival*, December 1970, p. 39.

2. Melvin Laird's 28 May NATO Speech, Associated Press, 28 May 1970.

3. For Soviet order-of-battle figures see: *Military Balance, 1970–1971*, IISS, Table II; Edmonds Marten and John Skitt, "Current Soviet Maritime Strategy and NATO," *International Affairs*, January 1969, p. 30; and also note 37 to this chapter.

4. "The Changing Strategic Naval Balance—U.S.S.R. and U.S.A.," Committee on Armed Services, House of Representatives, December 1968, p. 31.

5. *Kommunist Vioruzheennyski Sil,* July 1969.

6. See Curt Gasteyger, "Conflict and Tension in the Middle East," Adelphi Papers, no. 51, IISS, September 1968, pp. 3–4; Robert S. Jasper, "Foreign Aid and Economic Development," *International Affairs*, July 1969, pp. 452–464; and J. C. Hurewitz, *Middle East Politics: The Military Dimensions*, Praeger, 1969, passim: detailed data has been provided by the *Washington Star*, 30 November 1969.

7. *Morskoy Sbornik,* June 1971.

8. *Radio Moscow,* 2 December 1968; see also: *Radio Liberty Research,* 4 August 1969; Robert E. Hunter, "Soviet Dilemma in the Middle East," Adelphi Papers, no. 59, IISS, pp. 13–14; and W. T. Wilson, "A New Vitality in Soviet Defense Posture," *Air University Review,* July–August 1969, pp. 78–86. *Red Star* commented on 16 April 1970, "Aviation, for the collection of data about the enemy, plays the decisive role at sea."

9. *Military Balance, 1972–1973,* IISS.

10. *Pravda,* 2 July 1971. On Navy Day in 1970 Admiral Gorshkov stated that missile-carrying naval aircraft and submarines are the main striking force of the Soviet navy.

11. See *Aviation Week,* 4 October 1971, for an unclassified estimate of the Soviet threat.

12. *Aviation Week and Space Digest,* 20 October 1969, p. 112; Thomas Wolfe, *Soviet Quest for a More Mobile Military Power,* RAND Memo, RM-5554, December 1967.

13. *Jerusalem Post,* 16 June 1969; *New York Times,* 10 June 1969.

14. *International Herald Tribune,* 3 May 1974.

15. *Annual Report, Ship Builders Council of America,* March 1969; TASS, 27 July 1969; TASS, 7 August 1969; "NATO Documents: The Soviet Sea Threat," *Navy,* December 1968, pp. 13–19; TASS, 8 August 1970. For contrast, the active

merchant fleet numbered, in December 1971, 563 vessels, with 1,392 under U.S. registry. The total active U.S. merchant fleet grossed 16.2 million tons. Because carrying costs are roughly 30 percent more than average world costs, however, 90 percent of U.S. foreign trade is carried by foreign shipping lines. From the military perspective it is more accurate to include in this figure vessels under flags of convenience, or virtually all of the Liberian and Panamanian fleets, which are American-owned but registered abroad for tax-evasion reasons. These combined assets give the United States an overwhelming lead over any competitor in numbers, tonnage, and modernization, i.e., 4,139 ships of over 107 million tons with the world's largest collection of supertankers, bulk carriers, and container ships. In October 1970 the United States tried to overcome the backward condition of its own fleet by passing the Merchant Marine Act, which authorized $4 billion for 300 ships over ten years. Critics claimed that this amount could only provide replacements for vessels constructed under legislation passed in the 1930s, underscoring the need for the United States to consider appropriate measures for the incorporation of its foreign assets during emergencies. See Admiral George H. Miller and Max McLean, "The U.S. Shipping Emergency in the Seventies," *U.S. Naval Institute Proceedings* (hereafter *USNIP*), May 1972, p. 144.

16. David Fairhall, *Russia Looks to the Sea: A Study of Soviet Maritime Power*, Andre Deutsch, 1971.

17. Soviet concepts of amphibious landings and the role of supporting fire were revealed in the October 1970 Warsaw Pact exercise. Tactical aircraft from nearby land bases gained air superiority over the landing zone. Then, naval gunfire and bomber aircraft destroyed enemy defenses before a regiment of naval infantry was landed. Reliance on air power indicated that the Soviets do not anticipate undertaking opposed landings beyond the range of land-based tactical aircraft, at least until their carrier force is fully operational. See E. Van Veen, "Soviet Naval Infantry," *NATO's 15 Nations*, March 1972.

18. Norman Polmar, "Alarmist versus Realist," *Atlantic Community Quarterly*, Fall 1972, p. 369.

19. *USNIP, Annual Naval Review*, May 1973, p. 363.

20. Interview with Vice Admiral Isaac N. Kidd, commander of the Sixth Fleet, United Press International, 30 April 1971.

21. Michael McGwire, "Soviet Naval Capabilities and Intentions," in *The Soviet Union in Europe and the Near East*, Royal United Service Institute (RUSI), London, 1970, pp. 48–51.

22. *Christian Science Monitor*, 30 August 1969; Siegfried Breyer, "Hubschrauber-Kreuzer Moscova, Die neueste Entwicklung der Sowjet-Marine" [Helicopter cruiser Moscova: the newest development in the Soviet Navy], *Soldat und Technik*, December 1968, pp. 660–663 (gives detailed performance

data); and Geoffrey Jukes's review of "Soviet Naval Strategy," *Survival*, September 1969, pp. 298–299.

23. Richard F. Cross III, "Destroyers 1970," *USNIP*, May 1973, p. 253.

24. *Aviation Week*, 19 April 1971.

25. McGwire, "Soviet Naval Capabilities," p. 44.

26. *A Soviet History of Naval Warfare, 1970*, reviewed by P. H. Vigor, RUSI Research Bulletin, *RUSI Journal*, June 1971, p. 40.

27. *Morskoy Sbornik*, April 1970, p. 35.

28. *Jane's Fighting Ships of the World, 1972–73*, McGraw-Hill; *Jane's Weapons Systems, 1972–73*, McGraw-Hill; Siegfried Breyer, *Guide to the Soviet Navy*, Naval Institute Press, 1970.

29. Dennis Healey, "Speech at the Association for Defense Studies, Munich, 1 February 1969," *Survival*, April 1969, pp. 110–115; R. W. Herrick has made the most definitive statement on this position in his *Soviet Naval Strategy*, Annapolis, 1968. This book ignited an intensive debate, conducted mainly in *USNIP* and beginning with Carl Amme's endorsement in the October 1968 issue.

30. *Radio Moscow*, 25 July 1969.

31. Robert Thompson, *No Exits from Vietnam*, McKay, 1969; and Oleg Hoeffding, *Bombing North Vietnam: An Appraisal of Economic and Political Effects*, RAND Research Memo, RM-5213-1-ISA, December 1966.

32. The use of the ripple-release technique, in which bombs are released at adjustable intervals from multiple-ejector bomb racks, results in a long pattern of impacts along the projected ground track of the delivery aircraft. For example, twelve bombs released at .04-second intervals from a typical delivery maneuver would give a pattern length of 330 feet, with impacts every 30 feet. On a target 50 feet wide, assuming a correct left-right alignment, at least one and probably two hits would result, and two of the bombs would be near misses with impacts close enough to cause possible hull damage. These scores could be made in an attack perpendicular to the long axis, and the probability of two hits could be increased 90 percent by attacking on an angle 60 degrees from the long axis. These are drawing-board calculations that have proven exceptionally difficult to achieve in Vietnam against fixed but defended targets.

33. *Jane's Weapons Systems 1971–72*, McGraw-Hill, 1971; and John Marriott, "TV-Guided Missiles," *NATO's 15 Nations*, April–May 1972, pp. 68–71. Other Western states have developed operational antiship missiles as advanced or superior to those of the United States: Albatros (France), Kormoran (West Germany), Martel (Great Britain), Otomat (France–Italy), Robot (Sweden).

34. *Aviation Week,* 21 February 1972; also Robert D. Colvin, "Aftermath of the Eilat," *USNIP,* October 1969, p. 63. Rear Admiral E. P. Aurand in "Blue Water Strategy for the 1970s," *Astronautics and Aeronautics,* November 1969, optimistically claimed that sea bases would have a .225 probability of survival over land bases in nuclear war.

35. Michael R. Bonsignore, "A Look at Our LAMPS," *USNIP,* December 1971, pp. 26–31.

36. *Aviation Week,* 21 February 1972 and 8 November 1972.

37. During the first bombing offensive of North Vietnam, American carriers were at sea 75–80 percent of the time. In 1965 ten carriers conducted 30,993 combat sorties over North Vietnam and 25,895 over South Vietnam in 11 months. During the monsoon season of March through June 1966, 10,349 sorties were conducted over North and 12,065 over South Vietnam; Vice Admiral Malcolm W. Cogle, "Task Force 77 in Action Off Vietnam," *USNIP,* May 1972, pp. 72, 77, and 82.

38. It is beyond the scope of this study to examine the merits of the perennial debate about vulnerability, cost-effectiveness, and versatility of land-based versus carrier aircraft. It is assumed that both modes will remain available for many years: land-based because of their greater numbers and carrier-based because of the contingencies when they are likely at times to be the only air power available. On this debate see: *Setting National Priorities: The 1972 Budget,* Brookings Institute; Vice Admiral Sir Arthur Hexlet, *Aircraft and Seapower,* Stein and Day, 1970; Captain Stephan T. De La Mater, "The Role of the Carrier in Control of the Seas," *USNIP,* May 1972, pp. 112–125; Arnold M. Kuzmach, "Where Does the Navy Go From Here?" *Military Review,* February 1972; Norman Polmar, "Rebuttal," *Military Review,* May 1972; and "The CV: Capable Vigilance of Continued Vulnerability," *USNIP,* March 1972, cites details of the *Saratoga* test.

39. It is interesting to note that both political parties in Britain have agreed that the utility of carriers has been overrated and that Britain should terminate the carrier force without restricting the navy's role. True, the Tories did extend the life of the force beyond 1971, but for the economic reason of recouping the costs of recent refittings, not for strategic reasons. The smaller French naval air arm is likely to be the next victim. See *Integral Naval Air Support Will Be a Requirement for the 1970s: How Shall It Be Provided? RUSI Journal,* February 1970; and Captain Robert H. Smith, "ASW—The Crucial Naval Challenge," *USNIP,* May 1972, pp. 128–141.

40. Polmar, "Rebuttal." If U.S. warships could not venture onto the high seas without carrier protection, the navy could not do its job.

41. See also *A Soviet History of Naval Warfare, 1970,* pp. 533–536; and the *Great Soviet Encyclopedia,* 1970–71.

42. John Erickson, "The Soviet Naval High Command," *USNIP, Annual Naval Review,* May 1973, p. 84.

43. De La Mater, "Role of the Carrier," p. 118.

44. Paul Cohen, "The Erosion of Surface Naval Power," *Foreign Affairs,* January 1971, p. 334.

45. In August 1971 the U.S. navy contracted for 54 Mk-45 gun mounts—the first naval guns developed by the United States in twenty years.

46. Cross, "Destroyers 1970," pp. 247–248.

47. *Air Force Policy Letters for Commanders,* no. 8-1969, pp. 2–3.

48. Admiral Horacio Rivero, "The Defense of NATO's Southern Flank," *RUSI Journal,* June 1972, p. 3. For estimates of the land situation along the Southern Flank see Neville Brown, *European Security 1972–1980, RUSI,* pp. 131–137; and *Strategic Survey, 1971.* NATO has a heavy naval responsibility along the Southern Flank since 90 percent of the commercial commodities required by Greece, Italy, and Turkey must be transported by sea; further, an average of 2,600 NATO ships are in the Mediterranean on any day. See also Admiral Isaac Kidd, "View from the Bridge of the Sixth Flagship," *USNIP,* February 1972, pp. 18–29; John Erickson, *Soviet Military Strategy,* RUSI.

49. Carl H. Amme, Jr., "The Need for Assault Capabilities," *Military Review,* November 1970, pp. 12–22; see also Daniel M. Korcher, "The Service Force in Action," *USNIP,* December 1970, pp. 28–37. Both Spain and France exercise bilaterally with U.S. naval, air, and marine assault forces.

50. *USNIP,* May 1971, p. 341.

51. *Washington Post,* 7 March 1971.

52. *New York Times,* 28 May 1971.

53. James D. Hittle, "The Soviet Naval Challenge," *East Europe,* April 1971, p. 22.

54. John Erickson, "The Army, the Party, and the People," in *The Soviet Union in Europe and the Near East,* p. 17.

55. *Strategic Survey, 1970,* p. 46.

56. Ibid., p. 6. For a more elaborate analysis of Soviet defense spending see Raymond Hutchings, "Soviet Defense Spending and Soviet External Relations," *International Affairs,* July 1971, pp. 518–531.

57. McGwire, "Soviet Naval Capabilities," p. 33; see also Herrick, *Soviet Naval Strategy*.

58. Erickson, "The Soviet Naval High Command."

59. James Cable, "Political Application of Limited Naval Power," in *The Soviet Union in Europe and the Near East*, p. 53. See also: Geoffrey Jukes, *The Indian Ocean in Soviet Naval Policy*, Adelphi Papers, no. 87, IISS, May 1972; P. M. Dadant, *American and Soviet Defense Systems vis-à-vis the Middle East*, RAND, p-4352, July 1970; J. C. Hurewitz, *Changing Military Perspective in the Middle East*, RAND Research Memo RM-6355, September 1970; and Robert E. Athay, "The Sea and Soviet Domestic Transportation," *USNIP*, May 1972.

60. Robert G. Weinland, *The Changing Mission Structure of the Soviet Navy*, Professional Paper No. 80, Center for Naval Analysis.

61. Admittedly, guarded use should be made of official comments by Soviet military authorities because of the military or political composition of the desired audience, but Admiral Gorshkov has commented specifically to this point when he said, "The Soviet navy has been converted, in the full sense of the word, into an offensive type of long-range force . . . which could exert a decisive influence on the course of an armed struggle in theaters of military operations of vast extent . . . and which is also able to support state interests at sea in peacetime." TASS, 8 July 1967. For related commentaries see: "Admiral Baykov's Speech," TASS, 27 July 1969; V. Kasatonov, "The Mediterranean Is Not an American Lake," *Soviet Military Review*, January 1969, pp. 53–55; and N. Smirnov, "Soviet Ships in the Mediterranean," *Red Star*, 12 November 1969.

62. David Wood, *Conflict in the Twentieth Century*, Adelphi Papers, no. 48, IISS, June 1968; see also Lincoln Bloomfield and Amelia C. Leiss, *Controlling Small Wars: A Strategy for the Seventies*, Knopf, 1969.

63. James Cable, *Gunboat Diplomacy: Political Applications of Limited Naval Force*, Chatto and Windus, 1971.

64. For example, Egypt's large military force in Yemen increased Israel's confidence that the rapid destruction of Egypt's Sinai units would paralyze the nation's total armed forces. Furthermore, smaller nonnuclear powers, e.g. North Vietnam and North Korea, have concluded that the United States will not use its tactical nuclear force against them regardless of the level of local provocation.

65. Brezhnev signalled Moscow's confidence that parity had been achieved when he called for mutual balanced naval reductions in the Mediterranean; TASS, 11 June 1971. In contrast, see Admiral Arthur W. Radford, former

chairman of the Joint Chiefs of Staff, *New York Times*, 16 February 1971, for a definition of the role of the Sixth Fleet.

66. Vice Admiral Peter Grelton, *Maritime Strategy: A Study of British Defense Problems*, Cassell, 1965; Lawrence W. Martin, *The Sea in Modern Strategy*, Chatto and Windus, 1967.

67. Rear Admiral Edward Wegener, "Theory of Naval Strategy in the Nuclear Age," *USNIP*, May 1972, pp. 192–207.

Bibliography

Abboushi, W. F. *Political Systems of the Middle East in the 20th Century.* New York: Dodd, Mead, 1970.

Abdel-Malek, Anouar. *Egypt: Military Society: The Army Regime, the Left, and Social Change Under Nasser.* New York: Random House, 1968.

Adams, Michael, ed. *The Middle East: A Handbook.* New York: Praeger, 1971.

Allon, Yigal. *The Making of Israel's Army.* New York: Universe Books, 1970.

Al-Marayati, Abid, et al. *The Middle East: Its Governments and Politics.* Belmont, Calif.: Duxbury Press, 1972.

American Friends Service Committee. *Search for Peace in the Middle East.* New York: Hill and Wang, 1971.

Antonovsky, Aaron, and Arian, Alan. *Hopes and Fears of Israelis: Consensus in a New Society.* Jerusalem: Jerusalem Academic Press, 1972.

Antoun, Richard, and Harik, Iliya, eds. *Rural Politics and Social Change in the Middle East.* Bloomington, Ind.: Indiana University Press, 1972.

Arian, Alan. *The Elections in Israel.* Jerusalem: Jerusalem Academic Press, 1972.

————. *How Israel Votes: Public Opinion and the Electoral Process.* Cleveland: Press of Case Western Reserve, 1973.

Aruri, Nasser H. *Jordan: A Study in Political Development (1921–1965).* The Hague: Nijhoff, 1972.

Avnery, Uri. *Israel Without Zionism: A Plan for Peace in the Middle East.* New York: Collier, 1971.

Backer, A. S., and Horelick, A. L. *Soviet Policy in the Middle East.* Santa Monica: RAND, 1970.

Badeau, John S. *The American Approach to the Arab World.* New York: Harper & Row (for The Council on Foreign Relations), 1968.

Barbour, K. M. *The Growth, Location and Structure of Industry in Egypt.* New York: Praeger, 1972.

Beaufre, Gen. Andre. *The Suez Expedition, 1956.* New York: Praeger, 1969.

Be'eri. Eliezer. *Army Officers in Arab Politics and Society.* New York: Praeger, 1970.

Bell, J. Bowyer. *The Long War: Israel and the Arabs since 1946.* Englewood Cliffs, N.J.: Prentice-Hall, 1969.

Ben-Gurion, David. *Israel: Years of Challenge.* New York: Holt, Rinehart and Winston, 1963.

————. *Israel: A Personal History.* New York: Funk and Wagnalls, 1971.

Bentwich, Norman D. *Israel: Two Fateful Years, 1967–1969.* New York: Drake, 1972.

Berque, Jacques. *Egypt: Imperialism and Revolution.* New York: Praeger, 1972.

Birnbaum, Ervin. *The Politics of Compromise: State and Religion in Israel.* Rutherford, N.J.: Fairleigh Dickinson University Press, 1970.

Brecher, Michael. *The Foreign Policy System of Israel: Setting, Images, Process.* New Haven: Yale, 1972.

Bruno, Michael. *Economic Development Problems of Israel, 1970–1980.* Santa Monica: RAND, 1970.

Buehrig, Edward. *The UN and the Palestinean Refugees: A Study in Nonterritorial Administration.* Bloomington, Ind.: Indiana University Press, 1971.

Burns, Lt. Gen. E. L. M. *Between Arab and Israeli.* New York: Obolensky, 1962.

Campbell, John C. *Defense of the Middle East: Problems of American Policy.* Rev. ed. New York: Praeger, 1961.

Cattan, Henri. *Palestine: The Road to Peace.* London: Longmans, 1971.

Confino, M., and Shamir, S., eds. *The U.S.S.R. and the Middle East.* New York: Wiley, 1973.

Davis, John H. *The Evasive Peace: A Study of the Zionist/Arab Problem.* Rev. ed. New York: New World Press, 1970.

Dayan, Moshe. *Diary of the Sinai Campaign.* New York: Harper & Row, 1966.

Dekmejian, R. Hrair. *Egypt Under Nasir: A Study in Political Dynamics.* Albany: State University of New York Press, 1972.

Donovan, John, ed. *U.S. and Soviet Policy in the Middle East.* New York: Facts on File, 1972.

Dotan, Uri, ed. *A Bibliography of Articles on the Middle East, 1959–1967*. Tel Aviv: Tel Aviv University Press, 1970.

Draper, Theodore. *Israel and World Politics: Roots of the Third Arab-Israeli War*. New York: Viking, 1968.

Eban, Abba. *Voice of Israel*. Rev. ed. New York: Horizon, 1968.

Ehrman, Edith, ed. *Middle East and North Africa: A Bibliography for Undergraduate Libraries*. Williamsport, Penn.: Bro-Dart Publishing Co., 1971.

Elkordy, Abdul-Hafez. *Crisis of Diplomacy: The Three Wars and After*. San Antonio: Naylor, 1971.

Ellis, Herry B. *The Dilemma of Israel*. Washington, D.C.: American Enterprise Institute, 1970.

Elon, Amos. *The Israelis: Founders and Sons*. New York: Holt, Rinehart and Winston, 1971.

Evron, Yair. *The Middle East: Nations, Superpowers and Wars*. New York: Praeger, 1973.

Fairchild, David. *Russia Looks to the Sea: A Study of Expansion of Soviet Maritime Power*. London: Deutsch, 1971.

Fisher, Roger. *Dear Israelis, Dear Arabs: A Working Approach to Peace*. New York: Harper & Row, 1972.

Forsythe, David P. *United Nations Peacemaking: The Conciliation Commission for Palestine*. Baltimore: Johns Hopkins (in cooperation with the Middle East Institute), 1972.

Gendzier, Irene. *A Middle East Reader*. New York: Pegasus, 1969.

Goldmann, Nahum. *The Autobiography of Nahum Goldmann: Sixty Years of Jewish Life*. New York: Holt, Rinehart and Winston, 1969.

Haddad, George M. *Revolutions and Military Rule in the Middle East*. Vol. 2. *The Arab States*. Vol. 3. *Egypt, The Sudan, Yemen and Libya*. New York: Robert Speller, 1971, 1973.

Halpern, Ben. *The Idea of the Jewish State*. 2nd ed. Cambridge, Mass.: Harvard, 1970.

Hammond, Paul Y., and Alexander, Sidney S. *Political Dynamics in the Middle East*. New York: American Elsevier, 1971.

Harkabi, Yehoshafat. *Arab Attitudes Toward Israel.* New York: Hart, 1972.

Hart, Parker T., ed. *America and the Middle East.* Philadelphia: American Academy of Political and Social Science, 1972.

Heikal, Mohammed H. *Nasser: The Cairo Documents.* Garden City, N.Y.: Doubleday, 1972.

————. *The Cairo Documents: The Inside Story of Nasser and His Relationship with World Leaders, Rebels and Statesmen.* Garden City, N.Y.: Doubleday, 1973.

Hertzberg, Arthur, ed. *The Zionist Idea.* New York: Atheneum, 1969.

Heyworth-Dunne, J. *An Introduction to the History of Education in Modern Egypt.* London: Frank Cass, 1968.

Hopwood, Derek, and Grimwood-Jones, Diana, eds. *The Middle East and Islam. A Bibliographical Introduction.* Zug, Switzerland: Inter-Documentation Co., 1972.

Horowitz, David. *The Enigma of Economic Growth: A Case Study of Israel.* New York: Praeger, 1972.

Howard, Harry N. *The Middle East: A Selected Bibliography of Recent Works, 1970–1972 Supplement.* Washington, D.C.: Middle East Institute.

Hurewitz, Jacob C. *Middle East Politics: The Military Dimension.* New York: Praeger (for The Council on Foreign Relations), 1969.

————. *Diplomacy in the Near and Middle East: A Documentary Record.* 2nd ed. New York: Octagon, 1972.

————, ed. *Soviet-American Rivalry in the Middle East.* New York: Praeger (for the Academy of Political Science), 1969.

Issawi, Charles. *Oil, the Middle East, and the World.* Beverly Hills, Calif.: Sage Publications, 1972.

Jansen, Michael E. *The United States and the Palestinean People.* Beirut: Institute for Palestinean Studies, 1970.

Kerr, Malcolm H. *The Arab Cold War.* 3rd ed. New York: Oxford, 1971.

Khadduri, Majid. *Political Trends in the Arab World: The Role of Ideas and Ideals in Politics.* Baltimore: Johns Hopkins, 1970.

————. *Arab Contemporaries: The Role of Personalities in Politics.* Baltimore: Johns Hopkins, 1973.

Khouri, Fred J. *The Arab-Israeli Dilemma.* Syracuse: Syracuse University Press, 1968.

Kimche, David, and Bawly, Dan. *The Sandstorm: The Arab-Israeli War of 1967: Prelude and Aftermath.* New York: Stein and Day, 1968.

Kimche, Jon. *The Second Arab Awakening.* New York: Holt, Rinehart and Winston, 1970.

Klieman, Aaron S. *Soviet Russia in the Middle East.* Baltimore: Johns Hopkins, 1970.

Krikler, Bernard, and Laqueur, Walter, eds. *A Reader's Guide to Contemporary History.* Chicago: Quadrangle, 1973.

Lacouture, Jean. *Nasser: A Biography.* New York: Knopf, 1973.

Lall, Arthur. *The U.N. and the Middle East Crisis, 1967.* Rev. ed. New York: Columbia University Press, 1970.

Landau, Jacob M. *Middle Eastern Themes: Papers in History and Politics.* London: Frank Cass, 1973.

————, ed. *Man, State, and Society in the Contemporary Middle East.* New York: Praeger, 1972.

Laqueur, Walter Z. *The Road to Jerusalem: The Origins of the Arab-Israeli Conflict, 1967.* New York: Macmillan, 1968.

————. *A History of Zionism.* New York: Holt, Rinehart and Winston, 1972.

Lenczowski, George, project director. *United States Interests in the Middle East: Special Analysis.* Washington, D.C.: American Enterprise Institute for Public Policy Research, 1968.

Lesch, Ann Mosely. *Israel's Occupation of the West Bank: The First Two Years.* Santa Monica: RAND (for the Advanced Research Projects Agency; order number 89-1), 1970.

Lewis, Bernard. *The Middle East and the West.* Bloomington, Ind.: Indiana University Press, 1964.

Lilienthal, Alfred M. *The Other Side of the Coin: An American Perspective of the Arab-Israeli Conflict.* New York: Devin-Adair, 1965.

Love, Kenneth. *Suez: The Twice-Fought War.* New York: McGraw-Hill, 1969.

Magnus, Ralph H., ed. *Documents on the Middle East: United States Interests in the Middle East.* Washington, D.C.: American Enterprise Institute, 1969.

Mansfield, Peter, ed. *The Middle East: A Political and Economic Survey.* 4th ed. New York: Oxford, 1973.

Marshall, S. L. A. *Swift Sword: The Historical Record of Israel's Victory, June 1967.* New York: American Heritage, 1967.

McNeill, William H., and Waldman, Marilyn R., eds. *The Islamic World.* New York: Oxford, 1972.

The Middle East and North Africa, 1972–1973: Survey and Directory. 18th ed. London: Europa, 1972.

Middle East Record: 1967. Tel Aviv: Tel Aviv University Press, 1971.

Mosley, Leonard. *Power Play: Oil in the Middle East.* New York: Random House, 1973.

Naamani, Israel T., Rudavsky, David, and Katsh, Abraham I, eds. *Israel Through the Eyes of Its Leaders: A Socio-Political Reader.* Tel Aviv: Meorot, 1971.

Nixon, Richard M. *U.S. Foreign Policy for the 1970's: Shaping a Durable Peace.* A Report to the Congress by Richard M. Nixon, President of the United States, May 3, 1973. Washington, D.C.: USGPO, 1973.

Nove, Alec, and Newth, J. A. *The Soviet Middle East: A Communist Model for Development.* New York: Praeger, 1967.

Nutting, Anthony. *Nasser.* New York: Dutton, 1972.

Page, Stephen. *The U.S.S.R. in Arabia: The Development of Soviet Policies and Attitudes Towards the Countries of the Arabian Peninsula.* London: Central Asian Research Centre, 1972.

Peres, Shimon. *David's Sling.* New York: Random House, 1971.

Perlmutter, Amos. *Military and Politics in Israel.* London: Frank Cass, 1969.

Petran, Tabitha. *Syria.* New York: Praeger, 1972.

Polk, William R. *The United States and the Arab World.* Cambridge, Mass.: Harvard, 1969.

Popkin, Roy. *Technology of Necessity: Scientific and Engineering Development in Israel.* New York: Praeger, 1971.

Prittie, Terence. *Eshkol: The Man and the Nation*. New York: Pitman, 1969.

Quandt, William B. *United States Policy in the Middle East: Constraints and Choices*. Santa Monica: RAND, 1970.

————, et al. *The Politics of Palestinean Nationalism*. Berkeley: University of California Press, 1973.

Reisman, Michael. *The Art of the Possible: Diplomatic Alternatives in the Middle East*. Princeton, N.J.: Princeton University Press, 1970.

Rosen, Harry M. *The Arabs and Jews in Israel: The Reality, the Dilemma, the Promise*. Jerusalem: Office of the Foreign Affairs Department, 1970.

Roumaini, Maurice M., ed. *Forces of Change in the Middle East*. Worcester, Mass.: Worcester State College Press, 1971.

Rustow, Dankwart A. *Middle Eastern Political Systems*. Englewood Cliffs, N.J.: Prentice-Hall, 1971.

Safran, Nadav. *The United States and Israel*. Cambridge, Mass.: Harvard, 1963.

————. *From War to War: The Arab-Israeli Confrontation, 1948–1967*. New York: Pegasus, 1969.

St. John, Robert. *Ben-Gurion: The Biography of an Extraordinary Man*. Rev. ed. New York: Doubleday, 1971.

St. Joseph's University, Beirut, Staff of the Center for the Study of the Modern Arab World. *Arab Culture and Society in Change*. New York: Near East Books, 1973.

Schlesinger, Arthur M., Jr. *Dynamics of World Power: A Documentary History of United States Foreign Policy, 1945–1972*. New York: McGraw-Hill, 1972.

Schoenbrun, David, Szekely, Lucy, and Szekely, Robert. *The New Israelis: A Report on the First Generation Born in Israel*. New York: Atheneum, 1973.

Stephens, Robert. *Nasser: A Political Biography*. New York: Simon and Schuster, 1972.

Teveth, Shabtai. *Moshe Dayan: The Soldier, the Man, the Legend*. Boston: Houghton Mifflin, 1973.

Thomas, Hugh. *The Suez Affair*. London: Penguin, 1970.

United Nations. *Report of the Secretary-General Under Security Council Resolution 331 (1973) of 20 April 1973*. U.N. Document S/10929, 18 May 1973.

United Nations, UNCTAD Secretariat. *The Economic Effects of the Closure of the Suez Canal.* U.N. Document TD/B/C.4/104, 26 January 1973.

U.S. Congress, House, Committee on Foreign Affairs, Subcommittee on the Near East. *Approaches to Peace in the Middle East.* Hearings held before the Subcommittee on 22 February–18 May 1972. Washington, D.C.: USGPO, 1972.

U.S. Congress, Senate, Committee on Foreign Relations. *A Select Chronolgy and Background Documents Relating to the Middle East.* 1st rev. ed. 91st Congress, 1st Session, May 1969. Washington, D.C.: USGPO, 1969.

U.S. Department of State. *United States Foreign Policy, 1969–1970.* A Report of the Secretary of State. Washington, D.C.: USGPO, 1970.

————. *United States Foreign Policy, 1972.* A Report of the Secretary of State. Washington, D.C.: Department of State (Publication 8699), 1972.

University of the State of New York, Foreign Areas Materials Centers. *Guide to Reference Sources on Africa, Asia, Latin America and the Caribbean, the Middle East and Africa, and Russia and Europe: Selected and Annotated.* Williamsport, Penn.: Bro-Dart Publishing Co., 1972.

Vatikiotis, P. J. *The Egyptian Army in Politics: Pattern for New Nations?* Bloomington, Ind.: Indiana University Press, 1961.

————. *Egypt Since the Revolution.* New York: Praeger, 1968.

————. *Conflict in the Middle East.* Totowa, N.J.: Rowman and Littlefield, 1971.

————, ed. *Revolution in the Middle East and Other Case Studies.* Totowa, N.J.: Rowman and Littlefield, 1972.

Yodfat, Aryeh. *Arab Politics in the Soviet Mirror.* New York: Halsted Press, 1973.

Zeine, Zeine N. *The Emergence of Arab Nationalism, with a Background Study of Arab-Turkish Relations in the Middle East.* 3rd ed. New York: Caravan Books, 1973.

Index

Abd-al-Meguid, Esmat, 227
Abdullah, Ismail Sabri, 213
Al Ahram, 68, 70, 191
Algeria, 271–272
Al-Hawadess, 43
Allon, Yigal, 117, 180
  West Bank plan, 5, 219–220
Al-Talla, 213
Amer, Abd-al-Hakim, 42, 61, 187
An-Nahar, 221
Arab Federation. *See* Federation of
  Arab Republics
Arab refugees. *See* Palestinians
Arab Socialist Union party, 74, 95,
  105, 185, 186, 212
Arafat, Yasser, 114, 239
Arab Vanguard Association, 221
Arms limitation, 93–94, 116, 133, 207,
  225
al-Asad, Hafez, 236, 241
al-Atassi, Nur-al-Din, 114

Badran, Shamseddin, 42
Baghdad Pact, 23, 27, 29
"Baku Congress of Toilers in the
  East," 21
Bandung Congress, 22
Bargaining positions, 1967–1970
  Arabs, 308–312
  Israel, 302–304
  United States, 304–308
Bargaining positions, 1970–1973
  Arabs, 312–313, 324–325
  Israel, 322–323, 325, 327–330
  Soviet Union, 313–322, 330–331
  United States, 323, 326–327
Bar Lev, Chaim, 109–110, 165
Bar Lev Line, 62, 82, 83, 96, 133, 180
  in October War, 259–266, 279

Beam, Jacob, 99
Belyaev, I., 104, 115
Bergus, Donald, 183, 190
Boumédienne, Houari, 228
Bourguiba, Habib, 50
Brezhnev, Leonid, 129, 222, 284, 286,
  290, 292–294
Bulganin, Nikolai, 27

Cairo Agreement, 296–297
Cease-fire of 7 August 1970
  acceptance of, 125–126
  extensions of, 140, 141, 143
  provisions of, 120
  violations of, 128–132, 136–137, 254,
    258–259
  reactions to, 130–135, 137, 138
Cease-fire of 22 October 1973
  acceptance of, 253–254, 290
  attempts to renew, 294–296
  violations of, 290–291
  reactions to, 291–293
Constantinople Agreement, 16, 20
Constantinople Convention, 80, 144,
  147

Daghidy, Abd-al-Hamid, 43
Damascus, 245, 251–253, 279, 286
Dayan, Moshe, 60, 117, 152, 188, 191,
  192, 199, 242
  on cease-fire violations, 130, 134–
    135, 141
  diplomatic initiatives of, 167–170,
    175, 182–183
  on strategic warfare, 74, 83, 90, 95–
    97
Defensible borders, 5, 60, 150–153,
  278, 346–348, 353

Dinitz, Simcha, 242
Disengagement accord of 18 January 1974, 298–299
Dobrynin, Anatoly, 47, 75–76, 91, 114, 115, 117
Dulles, John Foster, 42

Eastern European reactions to June War, 363–367
  Czechoslovakia, 375–378
  Poland, 371–375
  Rumania, 368–371
  Yugoslavia, 379–384
Eban, Abba, 42–46, 50, 88, 101, 202, 242, 285
  address to United Nations, 58–59
  on cease-fire, 130–131
  in Jarring Mission, 55–56, 201
  in negotiations, 80, 115–117, 140, 148, 152–153, 154, 179, 198
Eden, Anthony, 27
Edmundson, James V., 116
Egyptian defense forces
  losses, 89, 93, 97, 109, 123–124, 126–127
  in the October War
    arms, 260–261, 274, chart, 256–257
    along the Sinai front, 261, 263–267, 269–271, 282
    strategy of, 279
    III Corps, 266, 270, 279, 282, 295, 297
    strategic warfare, 60–62, 83–84, 89, 96–97
Egyptian-Soviet Seminar, 213–214
Eilat (city), 151
Eshkol, Levi, 46, 50–51
European reaction to United States role in Middle East, 299

Faisal, King, 237
Fawzi, Khaled, 170
Fawzi, Mahmoud, 209
Fawzi, Mohammed, 186
Federation of Arab Republics, 184–186, 199, 215, 226, 316
France, 71, 125

Gahal party, 117, 137
Gaza (city), 76–77, 79, 151–152
Gaza Strip, 42, 144, 147, 236, 354
Geneva Peace Conference, 356
Glassboro summit conference, 45–48
Golan Heights, 151, 235, 243, 250, 278, 354
Goldberg, Arthur, 54
Gomma, Mohammed Sharawy, 186
Great Bitter Lake, 267–269
Great Britain, 16–18, 27, 40, 53–55, 125
Gromyko, Andrei, 68, 73, 74–75, 136–137
Gulf of Aqaba, 69, 76, 77

Haifa, 151
Heikal, Mohammed Hassanein, 67–68, 74, 106, 145, 198, 210, 213, 221–222
Herzog, Chaim, 127, 155
Huleh valley, 151, 243
Hussein, King, 41, 53, 173
  in October War, 238–239, 241
  rule opposed, 115, 118
  West Bank settlement plan, 218–220, 236

India, 208
International Affairs, 104
Iran, 32–33, 185, 354
Iraq, 210, 216, 221
  in October War, 251–254, 271
Ismail, Ahmed, 236
Ismail, Hafez, 234–235
Israeli Air Force (I.A.F.). See Israeli Defense Force
Israeli Defense Force (I.D.F.)
  aerial combat with Soviet pilots, 126, 160
  air war over Canal, 84, 216, 218
  armaments, 124–125, 164–165, 205–206
  losses, 83, 96–97, 109–110, 123–124
  in negotiations, 182, 183, 197
  in October War
    air war, 248–254, 274–275
    armaments, 246, 248–249, 256–257

Israel Defense Force (I.D.F.) (cont.)
losses, 265, 267, 271, 282
along Sinai front, 264, 267–270, 280
along Syrian front, 275–276, 281–282. See also Bar Lev Line
reprisal attacks, 60–62, 82–83, 97
strategic warfare, 89–90, 95, 108, 121, 123
Izvestia, 91, 128, 129, 131

Jarring, Gunnar, and the Jarring Mission
diplomatic initiatives, 55–58, 63–65, 144–149
Egyptian negotiations, 179, 227
failure of mission, 175, 200–201, 203
Israeli negotiations, 120, 131, 143, 168, 173, 180
in Rogers Peace Plans, 75–77, 102
text of secretary-general's report, 445–473
See also United Nations, Security Council Resolution 242
Jerusalem, 51, 87–88, 98, 151
Jerusalem Post, 178
Johnson, Lyndon B., 42, 44, 48, 54
Jordan, 65, 72, 151, 210
in October War, 238, 253, 254, 271, 282
Jordan River, 151
Judea, 151
June War, 39–40
air power in, 306–307
background of, 40–43
diplomacy in, 45–52
great-power reactions to, 44–45
See also Military aid

Kassem, Abdul Karim, 24, 30
Kissinger, Henry, 111, 241, 284–285, 286, 289, 342
Cairo Agreement, 293, 294–296
cease-fire agreement, 290
Khartoum conference (Khartoum formula), 49–52, 60, 65, 107, 146, 173

al-Kholy, Lutfy, 213
Khouli, Hasan, 237
Khrushchev, Nikita, 23, 26, 27, 31
Kosygin, Aleksei, 34, 44, 46, 48, 54, 91, 100, 289
Knesset, 152
Krasnaya Zvezda, 129
Kusnetsov (Soviet First Deputy Foreign Minister), 52, 54
Kutakhov, Pavel S., 128
Kuwait, 185, 251–252, 271–272

Lebanon, 145
Libya, 16, 169, 210, 215, 221, 226
London Conference on the Canal, 27

Mahjub, Abd-al-Khalig, 315
Mahmoud, Mohammed Sidky, 43
Malik, Jacob, 46, 94, 100
Mandate borders, 146, 147, 171
Mayevsky, Viktor, 213
McCloskey, Robert, 80, 191, 193, 199, 285
Meir, Golda, 81, 84, 90, 117, 188, 223, 272
on border requirements, 151, 152, 155
on cease-fire violations, 133–135
and military aid, 200, 204, 206–207
on partial settlement proposals, 171–174, 179, 182, 190–191, 210, 227, 235
on Rogers Peace Plans, 103, 111, 123, 126–127
on Resolution 242, 101–102, 119–120, 142–145
Military aid, Soviet Union to Egypt
1967–1970: 59, 90–91, 94–95, 107–110, 132
1971 arms race, 162–164, 166
after 1971, 210, 218
in October War, 253, 287, 291
Military aid, United States to Israel
1967–1970: 89–90, 130, 135, 137, 140
1971 arms race, 165
after 1971, 203, 207, 235
in October War, 253, 289, 291

Mitla Pass, 183, 260, 266–267, 279
Montreux Convention (1936), 16, 353
Morocco, 251, 252, 271–272

Najjar, Abd-al-Latif, 237
Nasser, Gamal Abdul, 5, 23, 92, 139
  and Arab unity, 27–28, 29–31, 41, 49, 79, 82, 107, 239
  in the June War, 40–43
  in negotiations, 49, 51–52, 65, 70, 78, 95, 101, 105–107
  relations with Soviet Union, 30–31, 67–68, 90–91, 103–104, 115, 121–122, 310–311
  and strategic warfare, 74, 96–99, 103, 136
Nationalism, 2, 5, 338
National Coalition (Israeli), 117, 119
Negev, 179
Newsweek, 146, 172, 211
New York Times, 143, 174
Nile valley, 108–110, 123, 154, 192. See also Suez Canal
Nixon, Richard M.
  in negotiations, 137, 147, 176–177, 188, 284
  in support of Israel, 93, 99, 111, 114, 116–117, 140, 289
North Korea, 271–272
el-Numerei, Jaafar Mohammed, 315–316

October War
  disengagement accord of, 298
  European reaction to, 299
  military action in, 242–271
  military conclusions from, 272–284
  negotiations for cease-fire in, 288–298
  preparations for, 233–242
  Warsaw Pact reaction to, 300
Okunev, Vassily V., 165

Palestinians, 4, 61, 73, 76, 87, 95, 113, 151, 173, 213, 219, 239, 305, 351, 352–353
Peled, Elad, 290

"Pink Paper" (from Israeli embassy), 151–152
Podgorny, Nikolai, 103–104, 154, 167, 170, 188
Pompidou, Georges, 92
Pravda, 23, 43, 68, 117, 162

Qaddafi, Moamer, 215, 226, 239, 288, 324

Rabin, Yitzhak, 191
Red Sea, blockade of, 295, 297
Rhodes formula, 75, 76, 80, 175, 202
Riad, Mahmoud, 52–53, 56, 59, 75, 78, 136, 143–144, 170, 180, 190, 191, 201
Rifai, Abdul, 236–237
Rifai, Zaid, 237
Rogers Peace Plans, 173, 231, 273
  28 October, 75–77, 81, 91
  Second, 101–107, 111–120, 124–126, 159, 161
  Third, 225
Rogers, William
  on aid to Israel, 92, 100
  and great-power guarantees, 153, 155, 156–157, 159, 170
  Middle East trips, 175, 181–183, 190
  on priorities of State Department, 178, 204, 215
  on refugee problem, 87, 95
  on Resolution 242, 86, 113, 174
  and the two-power talks, 71, 80, 136, 138
Rusk, Dean, 47, 52, 231

Sabri, Ali, 143, 184, 185–186, 194, 211, 226
al-Sadat, Anwar, 78, 127, 144, 214, 215, 221, 239, 296
  and cease-fire, 140, 291
  in October War, 240–241, 276, 288–289, 297
  on partial settlements, 139, 143, 169, 170–173, 183, 198–201, 234, 236, 312
  and political opposition, 184, 186–187, 209–210

al-Sadat, Anwar (*continued*)
    and relations with Moscow, 154,
        188, 203, 211–212, 222–228, 317,
        324
    on Resolution 242, 146–147, 179,
        181, 196–197
    on United States aid to Israel, 204,
        313
Sadek, Mohammed Ahmed, 222
Samaria, 151
Saudi Arabia, 185, 240, 253–254,
    271–272
Settlement
    effects of, 361–362
    proposed form of, 345–360
el-Shafei, Hussein, 209
Sharm el Sheikh, 70, 73, 79, 144–148,
    151–152, 171, 172, 175, 179, 183,
    184, 192, 220, 235, 236
Sharon, Arik, 268
Sinai Peninsula, 42, 69, 70, 79, 151,
    152, 179, 181, 190, 236
    in the October War, 254–271, 276
Sisco, Joseph
    and arms aid to Israel, 207
    Middle East tour, 94–95
    in negotiations with Israel, 153,
        175, 182–183, 191–192, 197–198
    in negotiations with Soviet Union,
        74–76, 112–113, 137
Solodovnikov, Vasily, 213
Soviet-Egyptian Friendship Treaty,
    164, 167, 188–190, 222
Soviet-Turkish Treaty of Neutrality
    and Nonaggression, 16
Soviet Union diplomacy in the Mid-
    dle East
    current goals, 29–38, 331–333, 335,
        339–342, 359–360
    historical interests
    in Arab lands, 18–20
    in Persia, 17–18
    in Turkey, 14–16
    ideological approaches, 20–26
Sterner, Michael, 196–198
Straits of Tiran, 42, 51, 58, 59, 69–70,
    76, 77, 80, 98, 143, 146, 147, 172,
    353

Sudan, 223, 271–272, 314–317
Suez Canal
    October War and the, 242, 254–263,
        265–270, 275, 283
    peace proposals for, 51, 58–60, 69,
        76, 80, 98, 141, 143, 146–148, 171–
        172, 179, 180–183, 191, 197, 289,
        298, 353
    Soviet protection of, 127–128, 193
Suez War, 27–28
Syria
    in Arab Federation, 169
    and Communist Party, 213
    in October War
    military action, 245–254, 274–276,
        283, 288
    preparations, 241–242
    and Palestinians, 210, 239
    and Resolution 242, 235
    and union with Egypt, 29
Syrian defense forces
    fortifications, 278
    losses, 41
    in October War, 256–257, 280–282

TASS, 100, 316
Tekoah, Yosef, 70, 131
Tel Aviv, 277
el-Tias, Mustapha, 237
Tiran Straits. *See* Straits of Tiran
Treaty of London, 15
Tunisia, 271–272
Turkey, 14–16, 355

United Nations
    General Assembly Emergency Spe-
        cial Session 19 June 1967, 46–48
    General Assembly Resolution 181,
        149
    General Assembly Resolution 2799,
        201
    peacekeeping forces, 41, 42, 147,
        155, 157–158, 294–295, 350–351,
        353–354
    Security Council, 52, 69, 145, 149, 284
    Security Council Resolution 242, 7,
        52–55, 68–70, 86–87, 102, 106–122,
        181, 183, 197, 235, 290

United Nations (*continued*)
  See also Appendix 3 for text of
    resolution *and* Jarring, Gunnar
  Security Council Resolution 338,
    290. *See also* Cease-fire of 22 Oc-
    tober 1973
United States diplomacy in the Mid-
    dle East
  current goals, 333–335, 339–340, 355–
    359, 360
  Eisenhower Doctrine, 334
  historical interests, 17, 23, 27, 29,
    354–356
United States State Department,
    111, 137, 139, 190, 206, 215

Vinogradov, Sergei Alexandrovich,
    170, 222

West Bank, Jordan, 77, 151, 219,
    236, 238, 271, 354

Yost, Charles, 100
Yugoslavia, 355

el-Zayyat, Mohammed H., 51, 145,
    227, 237
Zhukov, Dr. Yevgeny, 213
Zionism, 2–3, 343–345